SONS OF THE CONQUERORS

SONS OF THE CONQUERORS

The Rise *of the* Turkic World

HUGH POPE

OVERLOOK DUCKWORTH
NEW YORK • WOODSTOCK • LONDON

First published in paperback in the United States in 2006 by
Overlook Duckworth

NEW YORK:
The Overlook Press
141 Wooster Street
New York, NY 10012

WOODSTOCK:
The Overlook Press
One Overlook Drive
Woodstock, NY 12498
www.overlookpress.com
[for individual orders, bulk and special sales, contact our Woodstock office]

LONDON:
Duckworth
90-93 Cowcross Street
London EC1M 6BF
inquiries@duckworth-publishers. co.uk
www.ducknet.co.uk

Library of Congress Cataloging-in-Publication Data

Pope, Hugh.
Sons of the conquerors : the rise of the Turkic world / Hugh Pope.
p. cm.
Includes bibliographical references (p.) and index.
1. Turkic peoples. I. Title.
DS26.P65 2005 909'.04943—dc22 2004066268

Book design and type formatting by Bernard Schleifer
Manufactured in the United States of America

ISBN-10 1-58567-804-X / ISBN-13 978-1-58567-804-4 (US)
ISBN-10 0-7156-3605-7 / ISBN-13 978-0-7156-3605-3 (UK)
1 3 5 7 9 10 8 6 4 2

For Jessica

CONTENTS

SONS OF THE
CONQUERORS

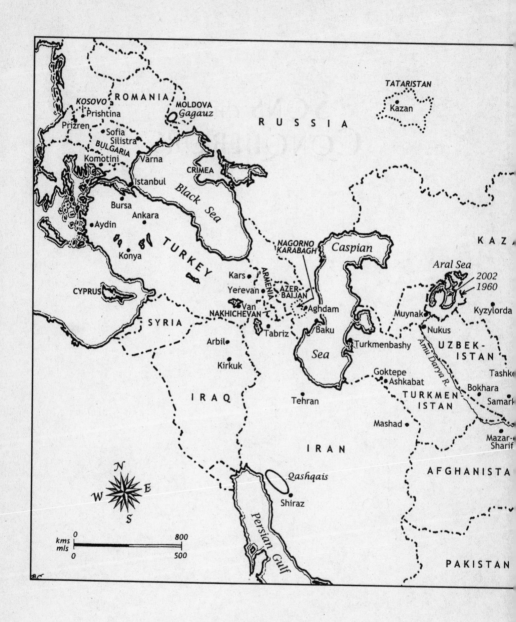

TATARISTAN
Kazan

KOSOVO ROMANIA
Prishtina MOLDOVA
Prizren Gagauz
Sofia RUSSIA
Silistra
BULGARIA
Komotini Varna
CRIMEA
Istanbul Black
Sea
Bursa
Ankara Caspian
TURKEY
Konya KAZA
Aral Sea
CYPRUS NAGORNO 2002
KARABAGH 1960
Kars
Yerevan ARMENIA Muynak Kyzylorda
SYRIA AZER- Nukus
NAKHICHEVAN BAIJAN UZBEK-
Van Aghdam ISTAN
Arbil Tabriz Baku Tashke
Turkmenbashy
Kirkuk Sea Bokhara
Goktepe Samark
IRAQ Ashkabat TURKMEN-
Tehran ISTAN Mazar-e
Sharif
Mashad
IRAN AFGHANISTA

N
W E Qashqais
S Shiraz

kms 0 800 PAKISTAN
mls
0 500 Persian Gulf

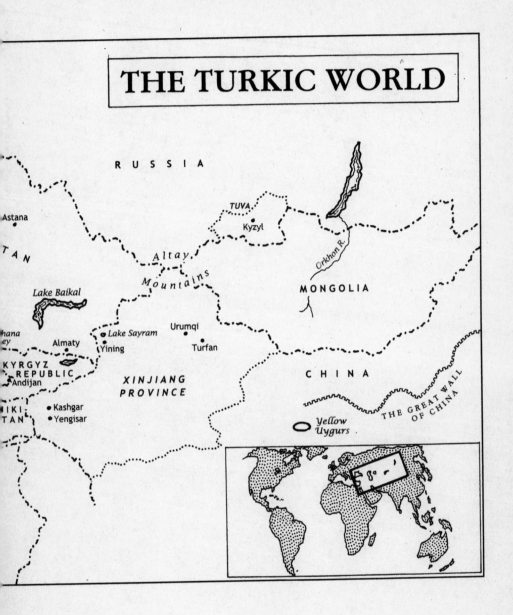

THE TURKIC WORLD

RUSSIA

Astana

TUVA

Kyzyl

Altay,

Mountains

Orkhon R.

MONGOLIA

TAN

Lake Baikal

hana
ey   Lake Sayram   Urumqi

Almaty

KYRGYZ   Yining   Turfan

REPUBLIC

Andijan   XINJIANG   CHINA

PROVINCE

IKI-   Kashgar

TAN   Yengisar   THE GREAT WALL
                                OF CHINA

Yellow
Uygurs

PROLOGUE

God Most High caused the Sun of Fortune to rise in the Zodiac of the Turks; he called them 'Turk' and made them Kings of the Age. Every man of reason must attach himself to them, or else expose himself to their falling arrows.
—MAHMUT OF KASHGAR, author of the first Turkish encyclopedia, 11th century

ONE SPRING DAY TOWARDS THE END OF THE COLD WAR, A TIME OF surprises, my teleprinter shuddered into action at the Istanbul bureau of Reuters news agency. A colleague in Beijing was sending a message: members of an ethnic group called the Uygurs, of whom I had never heard, were demonstrating in the streets of Urumqi, capital of the northwestern Chinese province of Xinjiang. The protesters were denouncing the communist leadership in Beijing and chanting the name of an exiled leader said to be living in Turkey, a man named "Isa." My colleague had a simple and urgent request: Could I track Isa down?

The strangeness of the message took a few moments to sink in: thousands of miles from Turkey, in a place I believed to be firmly within the pale of a monolithic China, demonstrators were risking their lives to honor the name of a Turk. A quick check revealed that the Uygurs are a people known as Turkic, an adjective also then unfamiliar to me. I lived in Turkey, and its inhabitants were until then the only Turks or Turkic people I knew of. It took several phone calls to lesser-known Turkish journals and exile associations to track down Isa, the Uygur activist, to an outer suburb of Istanbul by the Marmara Sea. His family name was Alptekin, and when he opened the door to his modest apartment, I took my first step into this new world. Then 87, the tall, dignified Alptekin had, forty years earlier, led an explicitly Turkic nationalist uprising against Chinese rule in Xinjiang. His Republic of Eastern Turkestan lasted just 14 months. The nearly-blind old gentleman impressed me not only with his elegant bearing and sharpness of mind, but also by the old-fashioned language he spoke. Certain turns of phrase hinted at a religious education in Arabic. Others sounded strangely familiar, a living echo of the Central Asian ancestors of the Turks of Turkey among whom I lived.

It those last 1980s days, the Soviet Union was showing its age, protests were gathering pace in Beijing's Tiananmen Square and the Berlin Wall would soon fall. Cold War-era Turkey was an isolated, lonely place, despite its loyal membership of the North Atlantic Treaty Organization. It was shunned by co-religionists in the Islamic world for its alliance with the Christian West, at daggers drawn with its neighbors Greece and Cyprus and cut off to the north by a whole third of the iron curtain between NATO and the Warsaw Pact. When the Soviet Union collapsed in 1991, all the political boundaries would be redrawn from Albania to the China Sea. What I did not realize, like many at the time, was that this broad buffer zone where Europe meets Asia was mostly straddled by Turkic populations. As a century of restrictions fell away, Turkey suddenly felt at the center of something, a more exciting and international place to be. I was hooked, fascinated by this new dimension of the country where I had chosen to live.

My conversation lasted all afternoon with Alptekin. But it was not until ten years later that I found my way to his birthplace in Yengisar, on the edge of the Taklamakan desert in northwestern China, nearly 2500 miles away from where we had talked. By then much had changed. For one thing, Alptekin himself was dead. But he would not be forgotten; in the intervening years, the Turks of Turkey became conscious of a new, wider national identity, shared with more than a dozen Turkic peoples. They rediscovered Alptekin and his history. A park was named after him in the historic heart of Istanbul, next to the old Byzantine hippodrome. When China officiously objected to this honor to a "separatist," municipalities all over the country named streets, bridges and monuments in his honor.

By the time I reached Alptekin's Uygurs in China I had spent a decade criss-crossing the Turkic states and communities that emerged from the break-up of the Soviet Union. It was my good fortune to experience at first hand the breaking down of the frontiers that had divided the Turkic peoples among the West, Russia, China and the Middle East. Numerous journeys to the booming new capitals and remoter deserts of Central Asia convinced me that from such roots a wider new Turkic consciousness is putting up shoots. I listened as Turkic dialects once relegated to second-class status became state languages, now confidently dominant on the streets of Baku, Ashgabat and Tashkent.

Unlike their fellow Muslims, the Arabs, the Turkic peoples are lucky that their interests have largely coincided with the policies of the United States. Washington made its opening move quickly in February 1992, when U.S. military flights were allowed for the first time over the airspace of the former Soviet Union. I was one of a few journalists invited to join for an inaugural American aid flight from Ankara, over the Caucasus, the Caspian Sea and then to Tajikistan in the heart of Central Asia. The U.S. had deliberately routed the flights of this "Operation Provide Hope" through the Turkish capital in order to underline its wish that the new states follow the Turkish model of secular government, pro-Americanism and a market economy. Our plane bore a 26-ton gift of medicine from Japan, raisins, sugar and cigarettes from Turkey and supplies of cookies, pasta and vanilla puddings from the U.S. This token offering was hardly likely to save the ailing and wary Central Asian republic of Tajikistan where we landed. But aboard the plane's flight deck we all knew we were entering a new era, as the enthusiastic, Russian-accented voices of air-traffic controllers crackled over the radio to welcome our plane to long-forbidden airspace over Baku, Bokhara and Samarkand.

These enlightened U.S. moves were mostly about preventing post-Cold War chaos. But the U.S. also single-mindedly led Western nations in pushing for access to the oil and gas of the Caspian basin—estimates of proven reserves start at the equivalent of the Gulf of Mexico or the North Sea—and to develop a strategic Turkic buffer zone between Russia, China and Iran through which that oil and gas could flow to Western markets. The European Union, with its own vision of opening up new markets, offered a program of loans to replace the old Moscow-centric lines of communication with east-west transit routes. Governments, companies and international organizations began to treat parts or all of the Turkic-speaking world as a coherent region of operations, if not yet a strategically important bloc. And the need to export energy resources to markets in the West may soon force more cooperation among the often rival Turkic regimes themselves.

The longer I studied the Turkic peoples, the harder it was to account for the fact that they had been overlooked for so long. Together, they constitute one of the world's ten largest linguistic families, numbering more than 140 million people scattered through more than 20 modern states in a great crescent across the Eurasian continents, starting at the Great Wall of China, through Central Asia, the Caucasus, Iran, Turkey, the Balkans, Europe and even a fledgling community in the United States. The Turkish spoken by its biggest and most developed member, Turkey, is widely spoken by significant ethnic minorities in European states like France, Britain, Austria, the Netherlands, Belgium, Russia and Romania. They are most prominent in Europe's most powerful state, Germany, where Turkish can be heard on every other street corner of the capital, Berlin. Having brushed against the language in my undergraduate days at Oxford and having spoken it for nearly two decades, I found that whether buying a carpet in a bazaar in Iraqi Kurdistan, interviewing Kosovar refugees high in the mountains of Albania, or discovering a common language at a conference in Tashkent, fluency in Turkish offered an invaluable introduction to an exclusive and unusual club. As a major in the British Army wrote to a fellow officer in 1835, while he traveled near Merv in modern-day Turkmenistan: "A knowledge of Persian will aid a traveler in these countries; but the Toorkey [Turkish] is of infinitely greater consequence."

The 19th century rise of the West now obscures the historic prowess of Turkish dynasties, which dominated the Balkans, Middle East and Central Asia for most of the past millennium. The extraordinary scope of their success in history inspired me to name this book *evlad-ı fatihan*, or sons of the conquerors, an honorific the Turks use for the colonizer descendants of the Turkic nomad armies who forged one of the greatest Turkic states, the Ottoman Empire. Turkish historians trace this military tradition back to the ancient armies of the Huns. Arab caliphs hired tough Turk fighters as mercenaries for the armies of Islam from the 7th century onwards, and soon afterwards Turkic warriors became the military backbone of the Muslim world. From the tenth through the fourteenth centuries, Turco-Mongolian horseback fighters and their families spread westwards across the Middle East under conquerors such as the Seljuks, Mamluks, Genghis Khan and Tamerlane. Then came the Ottoman dynasty, Turkic raiders who captured Constantinople in 1453 and who, within a century, had completed their conquest of the Balkans and marched on to seize the holy cities of Mecca and Medina, Egypt and most of Arabia. The Ottomans proclaimed themselves caliphs of the Sunni Muslim world and spread Turkic settlers far and wide. They ruled over this vast empire for five centuries. Few people today realize that many other conquerors who seized the thrones of Iran and India—Mahmud of Gazna, the Safavids, Nadir Shah, the Qajars, the Moguls—were also of Turkic stock.

Turkic-populated lands have not drawn intense Western interest since the time they were a chessboard for the rivalries of 19th century empires. Turkic dominance had turned to weakness and defeat. Diplomats and monarchs debated the "Eastern Question," which focused on whether the Ottoman Empire should be kept on life support as "the sick man of Europe" or carved up. Moscow and London played a "Great Game" for power and control over the Caucasus and Central Asia. In today's new Great Game, however, the major players and forces have changed. The U.S., a newcomer, is at the height of its power, and long-distracted China is now pushing forward. Formerly dominant Russia is still influential, and Great Britain, once so strong, is marginal. But another big change is that the Turkic actors, although still weak, are back in the game, and have to be taken into account. As the U.S. discovered in the Iraq war in 2003, the Turks cannot be taken for granted. And the Turkic world stretches like a long bow over what the Pentagon now describes as "arcs of instability," its new strategic worry in the post-Sept 11 world. "We will have to be out acting in the world in places that are very unfamiliar to us," a senior Pentagon planner told a colleague at my newspaper, *The Wall Street Journal*, in 2003. "We will have to make them familiar."

This book is the fruit of more than a decade of travel through the lands of the Turkic-speaking peoples, including extended expeditions along the ancient tracks that became known in the 19th century as the Silk Road. I visited communities in a belt of Turkic speakers which, if one accepts evidence of a Turkic link to the native Americans, literally girdles the globe. They took me from the edge of the Taklamakan desert in China's "Wild West" province of Xinjiang to mosques alongside Dutch canals leading to the North Sea and onward to the Appalachian Mountains in the western United States. I took many flights, of course, but I also crossed all their borders in Eurasia overland. I returned to several places repeatedly and was able to observe dramatic changes. I have steamed across the Caspian Sea both ways by ship and paid no less than four visits to the isolated Azerbaijani exclave of Nakhichevan. I have criss-crossed the Caucasus a dozen times by train, by bus and by car.

It was tempting to start my story in the east, following the great westward movement of the Turks that started more than a millennium ago and continues to this day. But having distilled my experiences from more than 20 countries, of which a dozen merit extended treatment here, I feared that a travelogue might prove confusing. Instead I have divided my impressions into six sections that I believe reflect the collective qualities of the Turkic peoples: their military vocation; their strong, quarrelling leaders; their shared history and neighbors; their pragmatic experience of the Muslim religion; their love-hate relationship with the West over issues like oil, corruption and human rights; and their conviction that the coming decades must bring better fortunes than the devastating experiences of the 19th and 20th centuries.

My argument is that Turkic peoples can no longer be treated as marginal players on the edge of Europe and the Middle East, or crushed subjects of remote parts of the Russian and Chinese domains, or distant allies taken for granted by the Europe Union and the United States. They are becoming noteworthy peoples and prosperous states in their own right, and are developing numerous new connections between each other. I hope this book will give a broader context to those who know Turkic peoples only in one guise: perhaps as minority immigrants in Europe and America, as go-getting businessmen in Istanbul, as displaced refugees in the Caucaus, as oil negotiators in Central Asia, or as dissident rebels in China. I know of few other attempts to put the Turkic peoples in the center of a narrative frame, and certainly none of this scope. I believe it reflects the Turkic peoples' attempts since the end of the Cold War to set a course to a better future—sometimes breathtaking and daring, often clumsy and controversial, but always with a passionate determination to regain control of their fate.

SECTION I

SOLDIER NATION

The military has been the backbone of most Turkic states in history

1. ORDERS CUT IRON

THE ARMY'S GRIP ON TURKEY

> *Throughout history, the Turks' political organization has developed in step with their military organization. Their hearts dedicated to soldiering, the Turks have proved to the world that their nation is an army.*
> —Turkish General Staff handbook

> *Where military service begins, logic ends.*
> —Turkish proverb

"COME ON, COME WITH ME!"

As he tugged at my sleeve, the panting young male dancer was not asking a question, but ordering. I clamped my hands under my chair. Someone else would have to play the fool between courses at a banquet in an army officers' club in eastern Turkey.

My eyes appealed for mercy from the top table, where sat the governor, the mayor, the chief of police and sundry leading citizens of the provincial capital of Kars, a Turkish garrison town high in the marches towards the Caucasus mountains. In all we were about 30 people, gathered under the patronage of our host, Brigadier General Ergin Saygun. His tank brigade barred the one mile-wide valley of the Kars Gap, an ancient invasion route through the Caucasus to the highlands of Anatolia. Right now, however, the pasha, or general, was defending the Turks' reputation for hospitality during a week-long open house to introduce the secretive Turkish armed forces to a handful of correspondents for American newspapers.

The dancer's demands on me came mid-way through our feast in a thickset gray stone building, built by the Russians when they broke into

Anatolia more than a century ago. Between each of the many courses had appeared entertainers, singers and dancers. The latest group had been the wildest. They wore tall hats of straggly white wool, tight black costumes criss-crossed with bandoliers, and long supple leather boots. They had sung an eerie song in praise of the legendary Shamil, who led north Caucasus Moslem resistance to the Russian invaders in the mid-19th century. Then they had brought out sets of knives, and, with great bravado, had hurled them at each other. There hadn't seemed to be much margin for error or concern for physical safety.

"Come on, come to the stage," the young man insisted.

I felt his grip on my upper arm tighten and pull with a pressure that brooked no refusal. Ergin *paşa* and his retinue looked on indulgently. The music stilled. A television camera focused on me.

"It's your turn," the young man said, dragging me down the long line of guests.

Joining local folk dancers is a rite of passage anywhere, and, apart from shyness at what would be my stiff imitation of these men's movements, I reckoned I had no real grounds to refuse. I steeled myself for the rite. But I had not counted on the slow drum roll, or expected that one of the young dancers would advance on me bearing the wooden board they were using for their game of darts with daggers.

"No way! I'm not doing that," I muttered to him, backing up sharply.

The young men quickly formed a dancing half circle around me, cutting me off from escape. The audience looked on with expectant glee. A young man started to prowl around me, brandishing his knives and rattling off a burst of rapid-fire tiptoeing. Another dancer coaxed me down onto my back on the floor. All eyes were on me. I wondered: should I hold the small wooden board over my guts or over my groin? Over my stomach seemed manlier. The drums rolled harder. The feet of the tiptoeing dervish disappeared in a haze of speed. He rushed forward, and, from a distance of six feet or so, hurled a dagger at me. With his teeth. Whack! It hit the board.

Smiling with triumph, I started to get up, only to feel a restraining hand on my shoulder. One of the dancers was at my head, another at my ankles. The show had not finished. Thunk! One more knife in the wood. Then another. I lost count. Finally, all of the daggers had found their home. It took a thunderous applause echoing off the heavy stone walls to lift me back on my feet. Some of the blades had landed only an inch from the edge of the board. I shakily regained my seat.

Colonel Hüsnü Dağ, the press officer who had invited me there, and who made no secret of his disapproval of what he felt was a slant that had defied the Turkish army in some of my previous articles, stood up. He walked over and put a hand on my shoulder.

"Tonight, you have proved yourself a man!" he said.

The army is just that for many ordinary Turks—a passage to manhood with the most important single institution of the state. While Persians may nurture poetry, the Armenians crafts, the Arabs language and the Jews religion, the core genius of the Turks is military organization.

It is Turkic rulers who forged most of the great empires of the Middle East and Central Asia. The strict administrative code known as the *yasak*, started by the Mongols and adopted by Central Asian Turkic khans, barely distinguished between civilian and military. The word *yasak* is used until today to mean something forbidden, or just "don't!" in modern Turkish. The Turkic gift for soldiering is even honored in neighboring Iran, where the head of the army is traditionally drawn from the one-quarter minority of the population who speak Turkic dialects. This doesn't mean Turks necessarily fight together; indeed, their history is dotted with battles in which different Turkic groups served both sides. A Turkish mercenary unit under a renegade Ottoman prince even fought alongside the Byzantines against the Ottoman conquest of Constantinople in 1453.

Not all have fared as well as Turkey, which, with 600,000 men under arms, runs the second largest army after the United States in the North Atlantic Treaty Organization. The Turks of Turkey were never colonized, and, despite many periods of weakness and grave setbacks during the First World War, have never been conquered by anyone. At the height of Ottoman power in the 16th century, Francesco Sansovino, a visitor from Venice, declared that "as far as concerns the army, I don't know which people among us can claim to be more disciplined and closer to the order of the Romans than the Turks." Their long tradition of military organization has made leadership second nature to them. The appeal of military domination is embedded deep in Turkish culture; a major brand of truck wins customers with the brand name *Fatih,* or conqueror, and, to ram the message home, many owner-drivers paint *Imparator* across the top of the cab too. As for the Turkish army, it assumes a right to rule, or to intervene in established regimes.

In the Ottoman empire, founded in the 13th Century by the warrior dynasty of Osman, elite janissary troops made or broke governments. Lady Mary Wortley Montagu, wife of the British ambassador, observed in one of her letters home in 1717: "The government here is entirely in the hands of the army. The Grand Signor, with all his absolute power, is as much a slave as any of his subjects, and trembles at a janissary's frown." During an uprising against the Ottoman sultan's government in 1908, military units rained threatening telegrams on the Sublime Porte, or prime minister's office, about how delicious it tasted to cut off the heads of traitors. The foundation of the Republic of Turkey after World War I was in large part a Turkish army rebellion against an Ottoman sultan who had fallen under the sway of foreign powers. Even today the army is no stranger to king-making and politics. It has staged coups in 1960, 1971 and 1980. Indeed, two weeks after my February 1997 tour of the Turkish east, the army launched a successful 'soft coup' to topple the government of the day. After another pro-Islamic government was elected in November 2002, the army kept signalling whenever it opposed what it considered reactionary policies. Clearly, it has no plans to relinquish its role soon.

The Turkish army views itself as the central pillar and guarantor of the Turks' independence and sovereignty, and many Turks agree. Opinion polls mostly show that the army remains the Turks' most trusted institution. Ideologically, the armed forces dominate. Conscription is universal, and the few conscientious objectors are jailed. When young Turks leave to their distant military bases, their friends send them off with dance, songs of encouragement and, in times of war, with shouted nationalist slogans. Only when their military service is over will Turkish society generally allow men to enter proper full-time employment or to get married. In later life they may joke about their experiences, but they will have learned to submit to the army's will. All believe legends that commanders mete out punishments even to inanimate objects, like putting a tank under guard if it fails to perform on exercises.

The architecture of Ankara leaves no doubt as to who holds the reins of power in the Turkish capital. The top generals and admirals live in homes dotted around the compound housing the presidential palace on the hill of Çankaya. The broad highway leading west from the parliament building in the heart of the city is flanked by vast tower blocks built for the navy, army, provincial gendarmerie and air force, until the turn of the century by far the biggest buildings in the city center. Other military complexes spread like a great encampment from a past nomad era.

The Turkish army is practiced in the art of defending its privileges. The pinkish-gray headquarters of the general staff is a heavy, intimidating structure designed by German architects in the 1930s. It looks even more awesome when the band inside the fence plays the national anthem each Friday afternoon: to show their respect, ordinary people put down their briefcases and shopping bags and stand stiffly to attention on the pavement outside. Inside the central block, a staircase curves up to the holy of holies used by the senior generals. On the walls by the steps, colorful ceramic medallions count off the Turkic empires of the past—led by merciless warriors like Tamerlane and Attila the Hun—the same states that are represented by the 16 stars around the Turkish president's seal.

Impressive Ottoman antiques line the fine reception rooms. Enlisted men, stiffly dressed in black suits and clicking their heels at every turn, serve tea in gilt-edged tulip-shaped glasses and offer plates stacked with a royal selection of miniature Turkish cakes, nuts and dried fruits. The top generals were an unpredictable mix in the 1990s. Some seemed almost aristocratic gentlemen, some were stiff martinets, and some could overflow with bonhomie—especially one who had the most intimidating reputation from the jails of the 1980-83 coup. But all glowed like the gleaming headquarters corridors with commitment to their hallowed institution. They were proud that the officer corps had its roots across the breadth of Anatolia, since the army, in an echo of the glory days of the Janissary corps, often selected, educated and promoted bright village boys. The Soviet Union used the same technique when building up the communist party cadres of the Turkic republics, who, since independence, have played a state-building role comparable to that of the Turkish army, even if in a less well-organized or legitimate way. Indeed, compared with the rest of the former Soviet Union, it is arguably in the Turkic states that the old party hierarchies have proved most disciplined and best able to retain their status as each new country's administrative backbone. Social advancement is passed on in much the same way as well. The well-educated, confident children of high-ranking members of both army and party are now disproportionately well-represented in top jobs in all the Turkic states.

When it has internal divisions or problems, the army handles them in secret. Few Turks are ready to say in public that they doubt the noble motives of their army. When journalist Nadire Mater published a book of interviews in 1998 with 42 soldiers traumatized by their experiences of war and army life, it became a sensation. She had to fight off a court case that tried and failed to ban it. In the past, the army was much tougher, as white-haired conservative politician Mehmet Dülger well remembers.

Dülger's father, a minister in the government preceding the military coup of 1960, was arrested and became a defendant in an army show trial on an island south of Istanbul. Charges against the deposed government—which had tried to sideline the army—were often merely issues of petty corruption and abuse of office. But Dülger's father was sentenced to death. Over lunch in Ankara, Mehmet Dülger told me with bitter humor how the army sent a letter demanding payment from his family for the construction of the gallows for his father's upcoming execution. The family also had to pay for the ferry tickets for the Muslim preacher to say his last rites, for the cost of his eight-month incarceration, for the coffin and finally for the nails of the coffin. Fortunately his father was reprieved—unlike the prime minister and two ministers whom the army hanged—but Dülger never forgot the humiliation.

"If we have an administration in this country, it's the army. But a big percentage of so-called public 'confidence' in the army is just fear. Civilians are not yet conscious of their power," he said. "The military consider themselves the real owners of this country because they are ready to give their lives to save us. But I would like to be governed, not saved. I want to be saved from the people who want to save me."

Dülger's dissident streak drove him to rise high in the pro-Islamic party that took power in 2002, which began to trim the army's powers. A significant element in its success was an increased Western questioning of the army's strength and position in Turkish society. So much appreciated by the West during the Cold War years, the role of the military became a major obstacle to Turkey's efforts to integrate with the European Union. The army's prickly failure to cooperate with the Iraq war in 2003 has also brought coolness with its traditional friend, the United States. The trouble for would-be reformers is that the Turkish establishment quickly presents attempts to weaken the Turkish military as another foreign attempt to weaken Turkey itself.

The Turkish army often presents itself to the West as a kind of latterday march lord, an ally defending Europe and America against refugees, Islamic fundamentalism, drugs and the violent uncertainties of the Middle East. That position was buttressed by long years at the West's side in the North Atlantic Treaty Organization and its stalwart performance in the Korean War. It has also resulted in a high dependence on U.S. armaments. Central Asian states near Afghanistan and Iran have offered themselves in this march lord role as well, with Uzbekistan favoring the United States and Kazakhstan and Tajikistan edging towards Russia. The Turkish army is certainly vigilant along its eastern borders. I was often taken to far-flung guardposts, whose narrow windows and cheap concrete construction contrast with the austerely beautiful mountains all round. One day I was helicoptered to a remote mountaintop to watch a noisy ritual shelling of the mountain just below the Iranian border. Another time, I was taken to a lonely guardroom where the duty officer showed off a small mountain of recently captured white cotton pouches of heroin.

On the rare occasions that the army felt it needed to make a stronger presentation of its case on an issue of the day, it would summon correspondents to General Staff Headquarters in Ankara for "briefings." My most formal turn came in 1997, but the message would have been much the same at almost any time in the past decade. I was ushered in with a small group of American correspondents to sit at a long curved desk on one side of an opulent lecture theater the size of a small ballroom. The number three general of the armed forces and a bevy of senior colonels faced us from a matching curved desk opposite. Watching us from the wall over the generals' heads was a ghostly white plaster death mask of Kemal Atatürk, the general and statesman who founded the Republic of Turkey in 1923. When the lights dimmed, a spooky ultraviolet light glowed behind and around Atatürk's heroically furrowed brow. As the speeches started, tense-looking soldiers went to work in a glassed-in cage to our right, operating a computerized projection system that flashed up maps and screens of bullet-pointed summaries.

After the Cold War, Turkey's importance had increased, not decreased, we were told. No longer on the front-line against the Warsaw Pact, Turkey was a buttress for Europe against "maybe the most unstable regions of world, namely the Balkans, Middle East and the Caucasus." Russia was a valuable partner, but Turkey would pursue its new role in having "historical and cultural ties" and "sharing experience" with the newly-freed Turkic states to the east.

The Turkish army felt secure of its alliance with the United States. The general staff quietly signed a military cooperation agreement with Israel in 1994, a strategic shift in which the weak coalition governments of the mid-1990s had little say. As often, when the civilian government seemed incompetent handling basic administration, the army started pulling at the reins of power. It rarely paused to consider that its own overbearing profile was one reason that civilian politicians never felt fully responsible for their actions. By 1996, foreign officials, especially from the U.S., would have their most important meetings at the General Staff headquarters. The U.S. loyally promoted their vision of a leading role for Turkey in Central Asia and the Middle East, and the generals were happy with the portrayal of themselves as the key U.S. ally in the region. It was an incestuous business. A few weeks after our unprecedented familiarization tour in 1997, I dropped by for a cup of coffee with the American officer who handled the Pentagon's relations with the Turkish army. He told me our trip had been an idea pushed for by the Americans to sell Turkey as a secular, democratic model for the Muslim world. The U.S. wasn't wrong to sponsor this relative truth, a position that seems justified by Turkey's progress. It is now the turn of the eastern Turkic states to be similarly singled out for a U.S. strategic role.

The Turkic states may be less democratic than Turkey, but they are even more secular-minded, which the U.S. appreciates as it grapples with Islamic fundamentalism. Uzbekistan, the occasional target of apparently Islamist terrorist attacks, is particularly militant in its rejection of political Islam. In Turkey, the generals were quicker than most to see the need to confront squarely the reactionary forces that were trying to drag the Turks, and by extension the Muslim world, back into a primitive and theocratic past. At our briefing in 1997, Turkish officers publicly pleaded for America to heed their warnings of trouble in store from the likes of the Taliban and Osama bin Laden's al-Qaeda. It is sobering to remember how little attention we paid to this. This was partly because of the army's awkward and occasionally racist tone against Arabs and Persians undermined their ability to convince others of the seriousness of their analysis.

"What is important for (Islamic states) is the spreading of fundamentalism," said one of the officers, Feyzi Türkeri, almost barking out his lines. "In order to survive inside Iran, they (the mullahs) need to export their ideas. Our friends the Saudis finance it too. Their regime is not compatible with the modern era, but they have activists in Turkey who are trying to impose their ideology."

While the West prevaricated, there was no doubt of the Turkish army's readiness to act against any Islamist threat in Turkey. Our host, Colonel Dağ, kept himself motivated with just one picture on the blank walls of his large, austere office: an image of turbaned Islamic zealots clipped from a newspaper report on the day in 1996 that the Taliban took control of the Afghan capital, Kabul.

"We'll never let that happen here," he said.

The armed forces rarely relax their vigilance against the threat of Islamist fundamentalism. It is one reason that Turkey, in the long run, will likely return to U.S. favor. But the methods it uses often alienate its other major partner, Europe. European pressure and a stronger government persuaded the military in 2004 to slacken its grip on the National Security Council, the country's top policy-setting body, but for decades the generals have dominated its debates.

Ilhan Kılıç, a former air force commander, was present during the long meeting on Feb. 28, 1997, when the military laid out the secularist demands that within months forced out the pro-Islamic government of the day. Two years later, I found myself sitting next to him at a dinner to promote civil society in Turkey, hosted by a well-intentioned movement of rich young business people. The Canadian-trained general's high-velocity English softened and his eyes glowed as he described how fine it felt to be part of this supreme council of Turkish affairs.

"After we sent out the briefers, it would be just us. When the 11 of us were alone, we could just be like plain citizens. I would even disagree with the chief of staff. Now, that's democracy!" he said.

The National Security Council has a staff of several hundred highly qualified people. I joked that it was probably more than the prime minister has at his disposal.

"And why are there always thick files in front of the generals, not the government ministers?" I asked.

"We prepare for the meeting. We meet the day before, and agree who should say what and when," the general explained. "The civilians don't do anything like that."

Indeed, for all the rhetoric in schoolbooks and elsewhere about Turkey being a "soldier nation," the Turkish military and civilian worlds are extraordinarily separate. Officers live in compounds everywhere in the country, and rarely socialize with their civilian counterparts. The military runs an almost distinct economy, and soldiers pay rock-bottom prices at their bases, hotels and holiday camps. The military retirement fund controls one of the biggest holding companies in the country. Their large budget—officially 10% of government spending but perhaps triple that—is traditionally voted through parliament with no debate and a unanimous show of hands. A first stab at civilian oversight was only legislated in 2004.

This status is precisely what undermines Turkey's candidate membership of the European Union, whose political culture is not just anti-militaristic but against most of the narrowly defined nation-state values the Turkish army holds dear. The Turkish army resents European demands that it subject itself to civilian control and it rejects the European vision of minority rights. The situation is changing; indeed the power of the National Security Council secretariat is now being eclipsed by that of its neighbor on the Western outskirts of Ankara, the Directorate-General for the European Union, which supervised a rapid democratization of Turkey's legal system after 1999. The grim and closed-off NSC building contrasts with the bright and open EU directorate, freshly painted and filled with colorful reproductions of contemporary Turkish art. The difference in world views persists. Before the exigencies of integration with Europe finally forced Turkey to lift the death penalty, the army even publicly declared that the death penalty was a good thing for Turks.

The irony is that it is the Turkish military that has long set Europe as an example of development for the Turks to emulate. In 1999, it even tried to legitimize the military's pre-eminent role in Turkish life by equating it to the position of the royal families of Europe. "Nearly half the countries in NATO are still run by monarchies, which, actually, could be seen as an anti-democratic arrangement," said the declaration, under the title Subjects on the Agenda. "Instead of questioning the appropriateness of [monarchies] to democracy, it is considered enough to link them to custom and tradition . . . For this reason there should be no condemnation of Turkey for having entered into certain arrangements for similar reasons according to its own needs."

Perhaps the army could have squared things with its Western critics, had it not been for a second mission that the military has imposed on itself, next to the struggle against reactionary Islam: the "civilization" and Turkification of the country in order to form a nation state. The early Turkish republic wasn't just trying to replace the explicitly Islamic identity of the Ottoman Empire and caliphate. It also wanted to create a kind of *homo turkicus*. But that goal often clashed with the aspirations of the major remaining non-Turkic ethnic group in Turkey: the Kurds. Two major insurgencies resulted, one in the 1920s and the second between 1984 and 1999. I came across such ethnic unrest in many places on the edge of the Turkic world, where tensions flared up between Azeris and Armenians, Uzbeks and Tajiks, and Uygurs and Chinese. Clashes could even break out between neighboring Turkic peoples like Uzbeks and

Kyrgyz, or Turkmens and the Ahiska Turks exiled to Turkmenistan from Georgia in the Second World War. Such violence was almost always rooted in competing claims to land. The same elemental logic underlay the strong Turkish government opposition to any strengthening of Kurdish self-rule in Iraq, which could and did fan separate aspirations among its own Kurds. Inside Turkey, Turkish-Kurdish friction remains a never-ending exercise in crisis management, pitting the Turks' atavistic desire for a decisive military solution against a growing sense of the need to compromise and to grant the Kurds more cultural rights.

Our journalistic tour of the troops in eastern Turkey in February 1997 was partly a victory tour to celebrate the suppression of the latest Kurdish rebellion. From the garrison town of Kars, the local commander, General Saygun, loaded our party into helicopters to visit Kocaköy, a remote ethnic Kurdish village whose story symbolized the army's success in that struggle. As we approached the settlement, a group of villagers rode out on horseback to greet us. One of them bore a large Turkish star-and-crescent banner that flapped in the wind as he galloped beside our minibuses. One outrider, however, took a spectacular tumble into the snow.

Young Kurds, like Turks, are obliged to serve in the army. It is part of Turkey's attempt to homogenize the people of the country, and it sometimes works. When conscripted, village men learn basic professional skills, see other parts of the country and learn working Turkish. More than half of the 10-15 million Turkish Kurds now live among Turks in the more prosperous west of Turkey. Indeed, the Kurds seem destined one day to become like the Scots in Britain, demanding respect for their own distinct identity, yet lacking a major international language and wanting the advantages of being part of an E.U.-candidate country of 70 million people. But back in 1984, Turkey's failure to do enough to make Kurds feel integrated, its brutal oppression of all Kurdish nationalism and its hostile relations with difficult eastern neighbors all helped ignite the Kurdish insurgency.

Initially, the Turkish army was slow to respond to what it saw as the mere annoyance of hit-and-run attacks. Then chaos over the mountain border with Iraq after the first Gulf War in 1991 delivered a strategic base and a windfall of weapons to the rebels.

Throughout the 1990s I had reported on the Turkey's response: an all-out campaign to re-establish control. Under the flag of a "war against terrorism" units learned to change out of their parade boots, trained to chase guerrillas high into the mountains and to fight at night. Hundreds of thousands of Kurdish villagers were mercilessly evicted from outlying hamlets where they might feed the guerrillas. Public prosecutors harassed and prosecuted intellectuals. Death squads, which human rights groups said were linked to the state, killed hundreds of Kurdish nationalists.

Around Kocaköy, the conflict raged for three years, the village elders said. Villagers didn't dare go out to sow the thin, stony soil of their highland fields. The school and health clinic closed after Kurdish militants murdered ethnically Turkish teachers and health workers nearby. Unable to work, many of Kocaköy's 5,000 Kurdish inhabitants left and drifted to the big cities of western Turkey. Luckily for Kocaköy, it was not in a remote mountain valley, and the army decided to save it, not destroy it. Soldiers had built the small village hall where we sat. They also built a new school. Within four years, eight children had even made it to university. General Saygun's wife coordinated projects for the local women. Naturally, the local Kurds were delighted at all the unusual attention.

"The one benefit of the terror is that it brought the army here. We have become a model village. If only the army had come earlier!" said the *muhtar*, or headman, in his canny welcoming speech.

Kurdish nationalists still view the Turks as oppressive interlopers from Central Asia. But others like the *muhtar* thirst for munificent, good government too. The Turks have outgrown the early republican nonsense that the Kurds are "mountain Turks," and, despite deep reservations, especially in the military, are slowly reversing bans on the public use of Kurdish and other minority languages. Most accept that the Kurds are an ancient if unruly people split between the mountains that form the border between Turkey, Syria, Iraq and Iran. The Kurds speak dialects of an Indo-European language related to Persian, but share the same religion and recent history as the Turks.

"The more we offer the villagers, the more they want. And if I can give it, I will," General Saygun said. "The terrorists had the support of the local people, but it was at gunpoint. In the past the terrorists would burn the government bulldozers. Now people see that if you don't have bulldozers, you'll get no road."

As we sipped more tea, men rose one by one to ask for more amenities and services.

"I once tried to take the army unit here back to the barracks, but the *muhtar* came and said he would resign if I did," said the general. "Soldiers here help with irrigation, painting walls, building carpet workshops, and so on. When there's an army unit here, the villagers even have a doctor and free medicine."

When our minibus pulled away from the whitewashed meeting room for the short ride to the *muhtar*'s house, an old man kissed the general's hand to beg one more favor. Others passed notes up to an equerry. A headscarved woman trotted beside the van, hanging onto the general's open window.

"You must feel like an English lord. Or maybe the old Ottoman pasha of Kars," I said to him later as we dined in the *muhtar*'s house off round brass trays piled high with mutton and rice.

"If only it was like that," the general replied. "Your English lords were very rich. And in Ottoman times, at least I would have had some tax-raising powers."

A later military flight from the airfield in nearby Van reminded me that the region has long been a fractious fault-line between Turks and their neighbors. Soon after take-off, the helicopter swooped low over a long, dragon-backed crag of rock pointing towards the phosphorescent blue waters of Lake Van. The pilot wanted to show off a touristic landmark, the tumbledown walls of Van castle on the top of the hill. My eyes, however, lingered on the ghostly field of overgrown bumps on the lakefront beside it, among which little more than a couple of ruined Ottoman mosques still stand. Here lay the ruins of the old town destroyed during and after the First World War. Its largely Armenian population was forced into exile or perished. Armenians allege it was part of a genocide that killed 1.5 million people. The claims may be exaggerated, but certainly several hundred thousand Ottoman Armenians were victims of massacres, famines, forced marches and outbreaks of disease.

The Turks, who prefer defiance to apologies, have never atoned for the awful events of that era. Government officials argue that hundreds

of thousands of Turks and Muslims also died in what was in part a struggle against Russian-backed Armenian militias. The Turkic-Armenian
struggle also continues over Nagorno Karabagh in Azerbaijan. Privately,
Turks look at payouts to Jewish victims of the World War II holocaust by
German governments and Swiss banks, and fear that if they did say sorry
or condede Armenian allegations of genocide Armenians could claim
compensation and territory. So the ruins remain, a wasteland memorial
to an unpurged sin that helped clear the way for the emergence of modern Turkey.

The pilot gesticulated to make sure we had seen enough of the castle, then gunned the engines to gain height for the mountain passes.
Nobody pointed down as we flew over Kurdish villages emptied by the
army just a few years before, their stone walls roofless and charred black
by fire.

By now, most of the military disapproved of this harsh policy. Some
of the officers that accompanied us hinted that they didn't want to be
seen as anti-Kurdish, and that they did not object to Kurdish publications. I also met Kurds among the troops who were loyal to the Turkish
order. On our flight back to Ankara, almost shyly, Colonel Dağ produced
a booklet written by himself and a group of younger officers, and distributed by the high command.

The Guide to Principles of Behavior turned out to be the most progressive sign of Turkish military modernization I had seen in our week as
his guest. It was also revealing about past practices. "Organize competitions to let the local people see that your sharpshooters shoot well. But
don't allow the bodies of dead terrorists to be robbed. Don't show damaged bodies of terrorists in the village square to try to show 'this is what
we can do.' This behavior may frighten the people but damages the
image of a caring state," it said. "Avoid the attitude that "these people
don't understand anything." Trying to base one's authority on pressure
and fear may be effective in the short term, but this is deceptive. Don't
forget that to be smiling and kind is not the same as being weak and
undisciplined."

Beneath us on the flight back to Ankara, the Kurdish mountains gave
way to the bare, rolling highlands of Central Anatolia. Then gray and
striped by snow, the valleys would be lined with green poplars in spring

and summer. The landscape looks much like the foothills of the mountains in Central Asia, and I could see why the medieval Turks felt
Anatolia was a natural extension of their domains.

Like the 17th century Turkish courtier-traveler Evliya Çelebi, who
wrote at length about Ottoman attempts to bribe, cajole, beat and control the restive Kurdish tribes, Colonel Dağ's booklet warned his fellow
officers of the Kurds' jealous conservatism towards their women. Evliya
Çelebi said he had not seen a single Kurdish woman's face. He had to
call on the services of one Kurdish khan's eunuch to send polite presents
to the leading women of the khan's harem. Colonel Dağ's booklet took a
simpler line. "Don't lecture them about the birth rate. And don't try to
shake the women's hands," it said.

Such attitudes have eased Turkish-Kurdish tensions, and hopes
rose in the late 1990s when the army began to allow a trickle of displaced Kurds back to their villages. Turkey's victory in this round of
rebellion was sealed in 1999 by the capture of the exiled rebel leader
Abdullah Ocalan. Still, there was no ideological victory, and the army
was little closer to turning the Kurds into Turks. Luckily, the moderate,
pro-Islamic government elected in 2002 successfully used a dose of
religious sensibility to move beyond ethnic labels and bind Kurds back
into a more diverse Turkish body politic. The Kurds remained focused
on winning more cultural breathing space, their burden lightened somewhat by sharing in Turkey's economic progress and by the prospect of
new freedoms as Turkey edges closer to Europe.

Turkey's relationship with Europe benefited from the fading of the
Kurdish revolt. In December 2004, the European Union promised to
start decade-long negotiations theoretically aimed to achieve full Turkish
E.U. membership in about 2015. But the promise was still hedged about
with conditions. Turkey and Europe often seemed to be locked in a kind
of unending wrestling match, each side grappling for control of the other.
Knowing European reservations about Turkey, perhaps I shouldn't have
been surprised by what I heard when I dropped by for tea with one of
the Turkey's most open-minded generals after the E.U. officially made
Turkey a candidate member in December 1999. He made one thing

clear: the Turkish armed forces had little confidence in Europe or Europeans, and would entrust the Turks' future to Brussels only on Turkey's own terms.

Having seen Western intervention split Kosovo from Serbia in the Balkans and Iraqi Kurdistan from Baghdad in the 1990s, the Turkish army was not convinced of Western commitment to the territorial integrity of states. Later it worried that the emergence of an autonomous Iraqi Kurdistan in the wake of the 2003 Iraq war could spread calls for self-rule to Turkey's Kurds. On the wall above the general's head hung a beautiful relief map. It was not of Turkey and Europe, or Turkey and the Middle East, but of Turkey, the Caucasus and all the Turkic countries of Central Asia.

"Does that mean you'll be seeking deeper ties to Turkic countries?" I asked.

"No. We just want them to be independent."

"What about the poor Uygurs? They're Turkic, they want more rights, but they're being crushed by the Chinese. Why are you sending delegation after delegation to China?"

The general paused briefly, but dismissed the subject. The previous government had even forbidden public displays of the Uygur national flag. Rumors were rife that the Turkish army was soliciting rockets and other military technology from Beijing. Messages from pro-Uygur groups kept popping up in my e-mail box, accusing the Turkish government of treachery. A dream of a greater Turkic world is all very well, but Turks everywhere are pragmatists.

"We want to keep going westward," the general said, referring to the millennial movements of the Turkic peoples from east to west in search of richer pastures, kingdoms or opportunities.

The mantra was repeated in 2003 by Hilmi Özkök, the new chief of the general staff. "I like Western values. Since the time we were in Central Asia, the momentum of the Turks has been towards the West. But this shouldn't be interpreted as worship of, or dependence on the West," he said. The Turks' dilemma is that while strongly attracted to the wealth of the West, and the achievements of Western systems, they are full of distrust of the Westerners themselves; indeed even the most pro-European Turkish officials I knew would say that even if Turkiey fulfilled all E.U. membership criteria, say by 2015, Turkey probably wouldn't want to join the E.U. unless it had evolved into a purely economic and trading organization. One historical reason for their caution towards European political union is that it was often the same European and Christian states who forced the Turks out of countries where they had been established for centuries, whether in the Balkans, south Russia, the Caucasus or the Middle East. These refugees—like republican founder Kemal Atatürk—went on to forge modern Turkey's self-sufficient and army-dominated political culture.

Such movements of Turkic peoples continued to ebb and surge through the twentieth century. One of my first trips to a Turkic community outside Turkey was to Bulgaria, where, in 1989, I witnessed one of the greatest recent waves of Turkic migrants seeking safety, solidarity and the promise of a new start just over the horizon.

2. INFIDEL PIGS

CONQUERORS TURN REFUGEES
IN THE BALKANS

Pressing close, our enemies
Bellicose, unsleeping,
Aim to make us feeble
If our name is scorned
If our fame is shamed
What defines us as a people?
—RIZA FAZIL, Crimean Tatar poet

IT WAS IN THE SPRING OF 1989 THAT I LEARNED AT FIRST HAND WHY THE Turks were unwilling to throw themselves unconditionally into the arms of the West. Crisis was once again roiling the Turkic population of the Balkans. In the wooded hills and farming valleys of eastern Bulgaria, the country's ethnic Turkish minority, sensing the impending revolutions rumbling through the old East Bloc, began to rebel against decades of oppression by the Bulgarian majority. Just as East Germans were smuggling themselves out to West Germany, a trickle of Bulgarian Turks began to leave for Turkey.

The refugees swelled to a flood that would within a few months displace more than 330,000 people. They were only the latest of millions of Muslims, mostly Turkic, who have made the same journey over the past 150 years. Most were forced out by new Christian states in the Balkans or had simply chosen a fresh start in Turkey. During the same time, of course, oppressed Christian Greeks, Armenians and others have passed in the opposite direction towards Europe. Globalization, immigrants and customs treaties are now removing many kinds of frontiers between Turkey and the West, but the 1989 emergency showed how the Thracian hills still mark a physical border of the old Europe. As a reporter for Reuters news agency in Istanbul, I was soon driving the four-hour journey from Istanbul to the Bulgarian border every day to interview new arrivals pouring over the frontier on foot, in trains, or packed into boxy Russian-made cars. Fascinated and appalled by what I heard, I persuaded my employers to let me travel to Bulgaria to report on the situation from the inside.

For me, seeing Turks as victims was an odd reversal of historic roles. Many of the Turkic peoples of the Balkans are *evlad-ı fatihan,* or sons of the conquerors, who descend from Ottoman soldiers granted land there after the great conquests several centuries ago. Also, I had been brought up with Western chroniclers who usually presented the Turks as barbarous oppressors. When I was a student of Oriental Studies at Oxford University, several courses stopped with the Ottoman Turkish conquest of Constantinople in 1453, on the grounds that Turkish hegemony ended the development of Islamic civilization.

The Turkic peoples were not necessarily ashamed of their ruthless, all-conquering reputation. As late as the 17th century, Ottoman diarist Evliya Çelebi penned tales of fantastical barbarity as the Ottomans sallied out each year with "merciless Tatars" to plunder the Balkan castles of the "infidel pigs", the Turks' principal source of revenue at the time. He wrote in tones of intrigued shock at the number of people put to the sword. Describing negotiations on one long-term truce, Evliya quotes a Christian ambassador as saying to one of the Ottoman pashas: "May this peace last 40 years." Such talk angered the pasha, who retorted: "If we make a 40-year peace with you, then who are we, the Ottomans, to make war against?"

In the past two centuries, however, the descendants of these Turkic conquerors became the victims of resurgent Christians. According to a study by American academic Justin McCarthy, Muslims at the end of the 18th century made up the majority of the population in many parts of the Balkans, southern Ukraine, southern Russia and the Caucasus. Except in the north Caucasus, most of these Muslims were Turkic. As Russian, Greek, British and other armies forced the Ottoman Empire to retreat between 1821 and 1922, McCarthy says that some five million of those Muslims were killed. Another five million were driven back into

Anatolia, where, nursing injured pride, resentment and envy of European power, they regrouped under the banner of the Republic of Turkey in 1923.

Western opinion, driven by solidarity with fellow Christians, has volubly dwelt on the atrocities committed by Turks in the last decades of this process, particularly against the Bulgarians in the west and the Armenians in the east. The Turks, all but friendless, have internalized the history of their own suffering. But, if prompted, many can tell stories of grandmothers who turned out to be kidnapped Armenian orphans, of ancestors who trekked to safety over hundreds of miles or of impoverished grandfathers who started from scratch after losing all to the advancing Christians. Nevertheless, the Balkans are still home to about one million Turkish-speakers. Some have hung on in Greece, others in former Yugoslavia. Most are in Bulgaria, where I arrived in June of 1989, at the height of the latest Turkic exodus.

Bulgaria's Orthodox Christian, Slavic majority—whose distant ancestors, ironically, were a Turkic people of Central Asia—had long harassed the 10% of the population of nine million that spoke Turkish. The cycle of oppression began again in the 1970s, when the government launched a program to assimilate these heirs of the Ottoman colonists. The campaign forced Turkish-language schools to use Bulgarian, denied jobs to Turks in the police or the army officer corps, and wiped out all references to Turkic origin in favor of an official new "unified Bulgarian socialist nation." The Bulgarians stepped up the campaign in 1984. The state outlawed the baggy Turkish *şalvar* trousers and fined people for speaking Turkish in the street. The Turks were informed that they were descendants of Bulgarians who had been forcibly converted to Islam by the Ottomans. Dissidents were locked up on a prison island on the Danube. The Turks, resistant as ever to assimilation, refused to knuckle under. Bulgarian troops were even mobilized to crush their resistance, killing at least 100 people in 1984 alone.

A second round of unrest broke out in May 1989. Encouraged by the fissuring façade of the Cold War order, the Turkic minority began to hunger strike for more rights. Clashes with the security forces killed several people. Then, extraordinarily, the Bulgarian state simply dared its Turks to go—helping things along at first by expelling nationalist and intellectual leaders of the community. Astonished by the huge numbers who soon began to leave, Bulgaria tried to stem the flow. I heard the same stories again and again from families arriving in Turkey to live in tent cities and public buildings. They lost jobs if they applied for passports. Anyone leaving had to pay water and electricity bills for months in advance. Bank accounts were confiscated. State farms appropriated treasured private livestock. Farm laborers were forced to stay to pick crops. The Bulgarian army obliged young Turks to do their national service, in unarmed, labor-oriented units, as usual. Yet still the Bulgarian Turks poured toward the Turkish border.

In Bulgaria, I started my reporting in the capital, Sofia, under the watchful eye of a lady from the Bulgarian ministry of information. After rounds of Bulgarian officials, by turn resentful and scornful of the tumultuous experiences of their compatriots, I was taken to my first Bulgarian Turk, the Grand Mufti, or religious leader. He was a smooth, round-chinned man with a trim beard, a gown and a fez bound with a flat-wound turban. Appointed by the state nine months before, he smoked the Marlboro cigarettes of the privileged and showed no sign of Turkic patriotism. But he gave me a wry smile as he obeyed the ban on calling anything Turkish and offered me a thick, sweet cup of "good Muslim coffee."

"Why haven't you spoken out for your people?" I asked.

"The mosque isn't a place to discuss politics. The most important thing is the right to work."

"What about the ban on Muslim circumcisions?"

"Sometimes they didn't observe medical rules of hygiene."

"And the destruction of mosques?"

"We have tried to clarify the privileges of Islam under socialism," continued the Grand Mufti, warming to the themes of theology taught in East Bloc seminaries in Damascus and Tashkent. "Indeed, I have found a lot of common principles between Islam and socialism. There's equality, compassion, labor, friendship, making the best of God's gifts. The Muslim community lives very well. They're quite rich. We have freedoms."

"Why is everyone leaving, then?"

The mufti's answer was to prove prescient, although only partly correct.

"Seeing is believing. Most of those going to Turkey will come back."

Leaving Sofia, I decided to follow the trail of refugees from the northeast of the country down to the Turkish frontier. Many people were traveling by train, so I started at the railhead in Silistra, a town on Bulgaria's Danube river border with Romania. In an out-of-the-way siding without even a platform, a refugee train was marked out by a rough confusion of luggage piled up by a line of big old carriages. I clambered up into one of the compartments to meet the people waiting for their train to depart.

Even though my lady minder had stayed outside, the soon-to-be refugees were silent, cold and suspicious, especially when I spoke to them in Turkish. They probably hadn't seen a reporter before, let alone one with nosy Western questions. They seemed to suspect that I was a Bulgarian agent, or some other functionary who could come between them and their long-awaited journey to the promised land of Turkey.

I headed southward. The decamping of Turkish workers had hit the Black Sea port of Varna, where my tourist hotel on the coast was filthy, the water had been cut for a week and the uncleaned bathroom stank. Out in the countryside, fields stood untended and weeds ran wild through vineyards. At a T-shirt factory, the Bulgarian boss said he was importing seamstresses from Vietnam to replace departing workers so that he could meet delivery dates. He readily summoned the last Turkish employees left for me to talk to. They looked down rebelliously and said little as we stood on a factory floor mired in decay. At a dairy farm, a manager told how his skeleton staff valiantly kept the cows milked on a huge metal turntable. A young dairy maid, allowed to speak alone with me, bubbled over with her secret hopes.

"I'd sacrifice everything to get to Turkey," she said.

I asked whether she actually agreed with the nationalists who were going from house to house, roping everyone into the exodus and making people feel like it would be treachery to stay. Under her white apron she shrugged, her eyes shining.

"We're treated like second class citizens here. It's free there, so I want to go," she said. "I have to. My fiancé already left."

Bulgarian police regulated the outflow of people by keeping lines of over-loaded cars parked at out-of-the-way intersections all over the east of the country. Milling around the vehicles were women in shapeless peasant garb, men wearing cotton tank-tops and shiny track suit trousers, and all those Turkish children whose proliferation so scared the Bulgarians. Often they were groups of relatives or neighbors. There was nothing they hadn't taken in their clan caravans—mattresses, chairs, cots, hat stands, refrigerators, beds, wooden buckets, even farm water pumps.

In village after village, fear made for reluctant informants, even when the lady from Sofia was nowhere near. No, they hadn't liked having their names changed. Yes, Bulgarians used tractors to pull Muslim gravestones out of graveyards and smashed them. A girl told me she watched her father's bones being dug up and scattered. One bearded Islamic fundamentalist said a Bulgarian official amused himself by "reconstituting" his name as "Christo." And yes, most Turks wanted to leave.

The Turkish prime minister of the day, Turgut Özal, had not made things easier with a rash invitation to all the Bulgarian Turks to come over. Turkey's prodigious powers of crisis management were quickly overwhelmed by the numbers. For the new arrivals, there was often tragic disillusionment. They discovered that their glimpses of the West through glamorous films had been no more real than the official communist propaganda they had seen about capitalist oppression. A backwash of Bulgarian Turks began to head back home.

In one village I found a man who had returned three days before to find his front door hanging on its hinges and his house stripped of valuables. Gypsies, Beyhan reckoned. Behind him, wild boar roamed in and out of the surrounding forest. He ruefully described his experience of the free market.

"For 52 days in Turkey, we went from place to place. I looked for a job. But it was very difficult. You can find a job for one day, the next day you're out again. There was nowhere to stay. We slept in the car," he said. "It was good in Turkey. But it is impossible to live there."

Round the corner, a family was stacking goods into a car before leaving.

"Aren't you going to stop them?" I asked Beyhan.

"Even if I put a rope round their necks, they wouldn't believe me."

I ended my journey at the railway station of Svilengrad, on the Bulgarian side of the border with Turkey. I was going home on board one of the refugee trains. I was about to board it when a group of young women appeared in the distance, walking up the railway tracks away from the Turkish border. When they reached the station, one girl dropped on her knees and kissed the earth of Bulgaria. They let down their heavy bags and settled on a bench, holding their heads in their hands, some sobbing. One young woman told me she had run away from relatives who had taken her to Istanbul against her will. Another complained that Turkish border guards cursed them as infidels as they left.

As we talked, the tallest of them, Ayşe, a geography graduate, went over the tracks to the train waiting to leave for Turkey. She warned some of the passengers of the difficulties they would face. But nobody would listen, and she came back shaking her head.

Ayşe had spent weeks as a refugee in a poor suburb of Istanbul. She had been repelled by how different life was there from her life in Bulgaria, where women had higher status and in the evening young people enjoyed carefree promenades between town center cafés.

"My mother practically had to tie me up to take me to Turkey. I cried all the time I was there," she said. "I'm used to wearing open clothes. I'm used to going out to restaurants and discotheques. But when I put on make-up in Turkey, I felt like I was walking through the jungle."

She had spent three days on the Turkish side of the border waiting to get back across.

"You didn't feel as though it was your motherland at all?"

"It's a totally different culture. There's no hygiene. Little children are working, it's shocking. We were really expecting to see something different in Turkey. The ignorant villagers did all this, they made us go. They're from a different world."

The train to Turkey was about to leave. The Turkish media called these "Trains of Shame," but I now felt confused about whether it was the Turks or the Bulgarians who should be feeling guilty for all this misery. On both sides, politics based purely on ethnicity had quickly reached a dead end. Meanwhile, the 655 Bulgarian Turks on board had hardened their faces into stiff, unreadable boards. They were only a short journey away from their promised land.

I put my questions one more time to a comfortably large lady in my compartment, Fatma, who wore a headscarf and a voluminous dress in a busy floral pattern. She felt prepared for her journey. She had one suitcase full of clothes, one suitcase full of food, a construction worker husband and a head full of hopes.

"They say there are good things in Turkey," she said. "I've waited for weeks for my passport. Why should I go back now? We just want simple work. *Ölüm var, dönmek yok.* Death is better than turning back. Anyway, the Bulgarians chucked me out of two jobs and haven't paid me for months."

The train pulled jerkily out of the station. The regular, European-style house-and-garden villages of Bulgaria fell away behind us. As we crossed the border into the Turkey, ragged cheers rolled through the carriage. Soon we pulled up at the Turkish border station, Kapıkule. People jammed the window. For many of them it was their first look at a foreign country. Martial music crackled out of the platform loudspeakers.

"Welcome to Turkey. May you live here happily and in peace," a male voice announced through a scratchy mechanical hiss.

We stepped out onto the platform. On the station walls, clumsy hand-written signs sought relatives, gave information where people from such-and-such a village had gone. The Turkish state offered resettlement of refugees in far-away, Kurdish-majority provinces like Erzurum, Ağri and Kars. It was an uncomfortable thought that Turkey was so callously offering the new arrivals the chance to turn from ethnic victim to potential ethnic oppressor. In the end, few stayed long in the eastern border marches, where I had already seen ethnic Kurds spit on those few Bulgarian Turks who reached there.

Bulgaria's bullying of its Turkic minority turned out to be the dying kick of the communist regime, which collapsed before the year's end in 1989. Ethnic rights were then restored, the new government apologized to its people and a Bulgarian Turkish political party at times even rose to hold the balance of parliamentary power. About half of the Bulgarian

Turks who fled to Turkey returned home, but then about half of these drifted back to Turkey again once they had sorted out their affairs. Bulgarian Turks still do not really trust the Bulgarians. But the edge is off the conflict, especially as Bulgaria overtakes Turkey in convergence with the European Union.

Many Turks in western Turkey can count at least one grandparent who fled Bulgaria or elsewhere in the Balkans. Bitterness at the past is strongest among the more recent immigrants, even though, thanks to the superior Bulgarian education system, most quickly settle into good jobs. The sense of unjust loss feeds an exaggerated sense of nationalism. Even so, it pales in comparison to the anger and frustration Azeri Turks felt about their strategic and military weakness during the wars of the Soviet succession Azerbaijan.

3. BLOODY BLACK MOUNTAIN

AZERBAIJAN'S BAPTISM OF FIRE

Nagorno Karabagh we sold, without the faintest sigh,
We auctioned off our factories until our wealth ran dry . . .
Now we are slaves or exiles, thieving strangers are our lords
For whom our prostrate backs a wide and easy road affords
—BEXTIYAR VAHABZEDE, Azeri poet, 1998

A MOULDY SMELL OF DEFEAT HUNG ABOUT THE NAFTALAN SANATORIUM, perched on an arid hill in the heart of the Caucasus republic of Azerbaijan. In its Soviet-era prime, 70,000 people flocked here each year. The sanatorium even had its own airfield, still marked, years after the last flight arrived, by a jokey, airplane-shaped metal windsock. It offered an unusual course of treatment: repeated baths in a black sludge of hot crude oil. In medieval times, the passing traveler Marco Polo praised the petroleum here as a treatment for camel sores. The Red Army put it in soldiers' packs as a balm for burns. Today's Azeri pharmacists offer it for anything from rheumatism to women's gynaecological complaints. When I arrived in 1999, the sanatorium was surrounded by a hundred nodding-donkey oil derricks—Naftalan means "oilfield" in Azeri—but the post-Soviet collapse of Azerbaijan's infrastucture meant that their electric engines no longer ran and the oil simply oozed up to the leaky surface network of pipes. For the past seven years, the sanatorium had not even had natural gas to heat the manager's office, let alone to warm up oil for the rows of chipped enamel oil-bath tubs in the basement. Just one of its six hotel blocks was still in normal use, hosting a few thousand local guests each summer. These die-hards swore to the oil's miraculous qualities, which Azerbaijani chemists say is derived from a naftene carbohydrate that acts as a steroid to rebuild skin. But there appeared to be no quick cure for the inhabitants of the other five blocks, 3,000 Azeris displaced by the Nagorno Karabagh war.

As in all the newly independent Turkic republics of Caucasus and Central Asia, Azerbaijan had little capacity to cope with independence from the Soviet Union in 1991. Its Turkic culture, Muslim identity and capacity for self-government had been crushed under two centuries of Russian and Soviet rule. The Azeris' ancestors include the great Seljuk Turk conquerors of a millennium ago. But when war broke out with neighboring Armenia over possession of the mountains of Nagorno Karabagh, they proved to have almost no military capacity. Like the Bulgarian Turks, the Azeris were ill-prepared to avoid their fate as the end of the Cold War unfroze ancient rivalries along the borders of the Turkic world.

Despite the fact that half of the staff had been fired or drifted away as salaries shriveled up, a dozen of the sanatorium's doctors had been heroic. They joined a motley Azeri militia that fought invading Armenian forces to a halt in 1993 on the mountain ridges 10 miles to the south. And when soldiers came and demanded medical help, the sanitorium museum gave up its collection of crutches and walking sticks—proud trophies once thrown away joyfully by the newly cured—to help Azerbaijan's limping war wounded.

But not much had got better since then. Where holiday makers used to congregate in the lavish reception area of one of the sanatorium's hotel blocks, homeless Azeri villagers now bought cooking oil and soap from impromptu displays spread out on a bare concrete floor. The land around the sanatorium was too salty for them to sow any crops on. Foreign aid was negligible: Turkey gave scholarships to two orphans from the community, and an American charity occasionally passed by with handouts. Sustained by remittances and tiny pensions, it was a lonely, unhappy community made up largely of women. Like perhaps one or two million other Azerbaijanis, their remaining menfolk had gone abroad to work, mainly in Russia.

Upstairs, once-proud hotel rooms had become box-sized flats in a refugee tenement. As I wandered the ill-lit corridors, everyone wanted to tell what happened to them, and wouldn't let me go until they had finished. I felt like a relay baton, passed from one tragedy to the next. A grandmother showed me the shawl she had taken from the body of her daughter, shot dead in front of her. An ex-militiaman berated me about U.S. sanctions that prevented them getting U.S. government aid. A 65-year-old complained that his pension had not arrived for three months. A woman said she was lucky to have a husband who was alive and worked in construction in Baku, and who had sent her a big television and satellite decoder. But she was still mourning three dead cousins.

One 60-year-old lady pulled me in to visit her living quarters. Nenesh Selimova's husband and three sons had been killed; one of them had been a policeman, whose two-dollar-a-month pension was her main regular income. Two of her daughters had been wounded. I sat down in her room, marveling at how she fitted her life into it. A cupboard and shelf supported a tiny kitchen in the old hotel bathroom, where she made do with one hour of water a day. A cheap carpet-style wall hanging of a tiger brightened up the wall over the bed. Plastic flowers gave some color to a little table, as did some Christmas decorations that hung all year round. A stretch of wall with photographs of men with thick 1970s hairstyles and sideburns served as a shrine for those of the family who had died. A couple of the pictures were flanked by Azeri medals. A bare electric element provided the only heat.

Nenesh had first fled from her home village deep in Nagorno Karabagh when armed conflict with the Armenians broke out in 1988. The family then moved on to the nearby town of Hodjali. I had by now realized that almost all of the refugees in the sanatorium had come from this market town, which lay over the hills a few dozen miles to the south. A bloody fate had branded Hodjali's name into my memory seven years before. In February 1992, according to the International Committee of the Red Cross, at least 600 people from Hodjali, mostly Azeri civilians, were killed as Armenian troops forced them to flee late one winter night. The Azeris say many more died. It was Azerbaijan's worst catastrophe in Nagorno Karabagh. Even the lower figure represents one twelfth of the Azeri dead in the whole six-year war.

Overall, during the war years between 1988 and 1994, one in ten of all Azeris were displaced from their original homes. Ten years later, Azerbaijan has yet to accept or adapt to its defeat. Young Azeris talk hotly of reopening the war one day, and even older people cannot forget it.

Naftalan was just one of many places to which Azerbaijan has shunted the human trauma of its defeat in Nagorno Karabagh. There, out of public view, it continues to fester.

More and more people were crowding into Nenesh's room, and I felt overwhelmed by their hopeless stories. As I left, a factory pensioner gripped my upper arm. "They always say everything will be fine," he pleaded, hanging grimly on to me, "but they never say when."

If the Azeris are clearly the losers from the still-unresolved complications of Nagorno Karabagh, there are, as in many conflicts in the post-Soviet south, no easy rights and wrongs over how the conflict began. These mountain valleys in southwestern Azerbaijan have long been mainly but not only populated by Armenians: settlers encouraged by colonial Russia, say the Azeris, or, according to the Armenians, survivors in a corner of historic Armenia who stood steadfast against marauding Turks and discriminatory Soviet Azerbaijani rule. It's a mixed-up place: its name uses the Russian *nagorno* for mountainous, the Turkic *kara* for black and the Persian word *bagh*, meaning orchard, garden or vineyard. Soviet ruler Joseph Stalin carved the territory out as an autonomous island ruled by Azerbaijan, rather than attaching it to Armenia. Such map-making allowed Moscow to divide and rule its Turkic-dominated southern borderlands. As Soviet rule weakened, Nagorno Karabagh proved to be a time bomb. It started as a cause that focused the resurgent national identity of the Armenians, a privileged minority in the Soviet Union who thought that freedom meant that Nagorno Karabagh should be placed under Armenian control. Put on the spot, Azerbaijan saw no reason to surrender the territory. As in the case of the Armenians, the conflict played a key role in strengthening the Azeris' battered sense of having a national cause and identity.

Armenian demonstrations first gathered force in 1987. After the Armenian-dominated parliament of Nagorno Karabagh voted for union with Armenia in 1988, primitive violence broke out. Neighbors drove off neighbors with knives, shotguns and arsonist's matches. In this early mutual ethnic cleansing, which fell short of war during Soviet times, the 200,000-strong Azeri community in Armenia came under pressure and departed, mostly for Azerbaijan. Similarly, the 300,000 Armenians of Baku scattered to Armenia and then the four corners of the world. The lucky ones managed to swap homes in their respective capitals; in a few cases, quiet negotiation allowed whole villages to change places. But killings were not infrequent. Families on both sides took hostages, keeping them for years as go-betweens arranged complicated exchanges. In Azerbaijan, displaced people seized apartments once lived in by Armenians and built whole shanty towns outside Baku. Later they would commandeer sidings full of railway sleeper cars, be put into refugee camps and take over public institutions like the Naftalan sanatorium. The newly homeless played leading roles in radicalizing Azerbaijani politics, fueling a struggle for independence from the Soviet Union.

On a Baku hilltop park near the Azerbaijani parliament, new lines of graves began to appear alongside the pathways of an impromptu Martyrs' Avenue overlooking the Caspian Sea. Visitors topped the carpet of carnations with a fresh layer of flowers each day. The Nagorno Karabagh conflict escalated when Armenia and Azerbaijan declared their independence in 1991. Over the years wooden markers gave way to marble stones with etched photographs. The park is now the national monument where visiting foreign dignitaries formally pay their respects to these men who suddenly found themselves soldiers, whose sacrifice despite poor leadership has become the leading symbol of Azerbaijan's bruised sense of nationhood.

Back in January 1992, a sense of unreality and amateurishness hung over the scenes I saw at the front as fighting spiraled into its bloodiest period. Porters at Baku's main train station, where I headed one afternoon to find my way to the battlefront, still sported the red-and-green uniform of the defunct Soviet railway system. Clocks still ran on Moscow time, rather than that of Azerbaijan. Destinations listed on the departure board—Moscow, Volgograd, Stavropol, Astrakhan—were all holdovers from the previous order.

Helpful Azeris guided me through the complex process of buying a ticket for the overnight journey, which cost what would have been loose change in the West, and led me to my train. Rusty plates fitted to the sides of large sleeping cars marked them for transit to Hankenti, the Azeri name for the capital of Nagorno Karabagh. In fact, the Azeris had already lost the town; our real destination was Aghdam, the last town under Azeri control. Even though most of us were civilians, my "hard class" carriage felt like a troop train, with 80 travelers fitted into bunks stacked three layers high.

The train soon reached its cruising speed, a clanking canter across the desolate, scrub-covered flatlands of central Azerbaijan. The landscape was criss-crossed with rusting oil pipelines and dotted with discarded industrial buildings. The half-Kurdish, half-Azeri conductress shoveled coal into an ancient boiler to keep us warm against the icy draughts that whistled through the cracked carriagework. She ordered me to put my shoes in the locker under my bed, since thieves were rife. She was right. I had to physically shake off cardsharps who chatted themselves into a game, asked to see the color of my money and then started plucking at my pockets.

My fellow passengers viewed all this as part of the pageant of travel. At stations, they stocked up on supplies from little kiosks and shared their booty with remarkable, if slightly surreal, joie de vivre.

"You're from England? Fantastic. This calls for champagne!" boomed an Azeri collective-farm mechanic from Nagorno Karabagh.

He returned minutes later with foamy Azerbaijani *shampanskii*, fruit juice, sausages, bread and a plastic-wrapped tube of thinly sliced pickled carrot, sold by the daughters of another of Stalin's nationality mixing games, the ethnic Koreans of the Caucasus. The conductress joined us.

"I love this job. You really see the world," she said, turning to reprimand an elderly pensioner who broke the rules by lighting up a cigarette.

There were grandmothers, chicken merchants and drunken soldiers, as well as the disappearing ethnic co-habitation of the Soviet era: Uzbeks, Dagestanis, Slavs and Jews. Upon the conductress' order, all obediently unrolled the railway-supplied bedding of clean, gray, slightly damp sheets to go to sleep. During the night, there were many long, unexplained stops. At dawn, the dark foothills of Karabagh rose on the horizon. Many of my fellow passengers had already disembarked, heading to destinations up the Kura valley towards Georgia. A weak sun had barely melted the morning frost by the time we drew into the station at Aghdam.

The city was silent, troubled, and already half abandoned. Grass

pushed up between the paving slabs in central streets. Groups of displaced people milled aimlessly around government buildings, wearing
shapeless, heavy coats against the cold. In these first months of all-out
war, many Azeri towns and villages were still holding out against the
Armenians deep in the Karabagh hills. But the Azeri forces looked beaten.
The town's mayor sent me out to view the front line on the edge of town,
where a few badly trained volunteers manned a concrete hut, chipped by
bullets that the Armenians fired every now and then from a clump of
trees half a mile down the road. A 1950s Soviet-made armored car stood
guard at the Azeri checkpoint, but it was pointing the wrong way and one
of its tires was flat.

"Why do they give us this lousy equipment?" complained one of the
soldiers, crunching over ground thickly carpeted with cartridge cases.
"The Armenian troop carriers always seem to work."

The waste of ammunition was extraordinary, and it was the sight of
an Azeri television team alongside us that stirred what military instincts
these rough-and-ready Azeri militiamen had. They volunteered to start
up a firefight then and there. There was no sign of any higher, coordi-
nating command. Azerbaijan never made up for the fact that the Red
Army had tended to assign Muslim and Turkic conscripts to non-combat
units like labor battalions, while a disproportionately high number of
Armenians became officers and generals. The one Soviet-era Azeri general I met had been in Red Army logistics, and, even though his men
were streaming down a nearby road in retreat after another catastrophic
defeat, he was preparing to sit down to a splendid feast in his red-striped
unform as an orderly polished his black Volga saloon. The lack of army
advancement for Turks or Muslims was the same in the Tsarist empire.
The Azeris I spoke to believed it was because Armenians were Christian
cousins of the Russians, a perception that encouraged them to redefine
their identity away from Soviet brotherhood towards one that was Turkic,
Muslim or simply Azeri.

Across town at Aghdam airfield, aging orange-and-blue Aeroflot helicopters shuddered down to the ground or heaved into the sky every hour
or so, flying to the Azeri villages that survived like islands in the rising
Armenian tide. Beyond the huddled groups of Azeris around the edge of
the field, one helicopter stood out of action, riddled with bullet holes.

Those still able to take off were overloaded and flown by exhausted-looking men, who often turned out to be ethnic Russians.

"Why are you doing this?" I asked one helicopter pilot, who still clung to the dignity of his grimy white-shirted Aeroflot uniform.

"I just want to help the wounded," he replied. "If we didn't do it, nobody would."

He invited me along for a ride, but a clutch of fresh bullet holes in the fuselage argued against accepting the offer. Instead, I walked over to join Alef Hajiev, the militia leader of Hodjali, then one of the major towns still controlled by the Azeris in Nagorno Karabagh. Hajiev told me he was visiting Aghdam on a re-supply run, and offered me lunch at a makeshift corrugated-iron restaurant. Holding court with a band of his men, he was a burly man whose curled hair was gray before its time. His clear blue-gray eyes shone with an unusual frankness.

"How will you win this war?" I asked as we tore off hunks of thick bread to dip into our greasy stew, "Who will help you? Turkey?"

Hajiev had no answer, and heartily cursed Turkey for its bluster and lack of action. He damned Russia, and, for good measure, his own leadership too. Afterwards I walked with him to the helicopter that was to return him to his hometown. Crowds surged forward to board it. All shouted at once, fighting to get in through the main sliding door. People squeezed through a porthole on the other side. Women yelped shrill imprecations. A boy stood in confusion next to me, clinging to a cage with his pet parakeet. Eighteen and 19-year-olds in uniform heaved wooden crates of ammunition on board, screaming at the scrum of civilians to get back.

"If the guns don't go, nobody goes!" one soldier yelled.

But even the commands of Hajiev couldn't impose order. Behind the fear, aggression or resignation I saw on the faces of the villagers around me, I sensed disbelief at how quickly their lives had descended from Soviet-prescribed order into this chaos called independence.

"Why on earth are you going back to Hodjali?" I asked one stunned-looking woman, standing on the edge of the melee with her family and some meager supplies. "It's under attack."

"It's home," she said. "There's nowhere else to go."

The pilot gunned the engines as people were still trying to climb in or push their baggage aboard. The helicopter staggered into the sky, circling higher and higher to try to avoid Armenian rifle fire before disappearing over a ridge.

The macabre scene at Aghdam airfield—from the shell-shocked apathy of the villagers to an ex-dentist militiawoman's blood-curdling lust to avenge dead relatives—haunted me the night I rode the train back to Baku, across a landscape so dark it seemed inked out. Back in the capital the next day, I sought an audience with President Ayaz Mutalibov, the Soviet placeman installed by Moscow in its last bid to keep control of Azerbaijan. The President's office seemed untouched by the events roiling the country. Soft-footed officials ushered me through marble halls into a suite with a commanding view of the Caspian seafront. As he talked from the other side of a vast desk, it became clear that the troops in Aghdam were right: they could expect nothing from their president. Far from being a leader of men, Mutalibov was a pleasant-mannered, foppish fan of Elvis Presley. Thanks to his well-tended hairstyle and his interest in weight training, he was tagged with the nickname "Tarzan." Mutalibov spoke unconvincingly of grand plans for commando strike forces to win the war. But when I switched off my tape-recorder, he leaned across the table.

"What are the men saying at the front?" he asked.

I told him they were unhappy because they didn't have enough guns and ammunition, let alone leadership. Indeed, as far as I could tell, there was no real military organization, only militias loyal to clan chiefs who were sometimes little better than gangsters. The persistence of clan allegiances, I'd learned, posed a direct challenge to the national government as it tried to extend its authority over the countryside. It also undermined efforts to bring about a sense of nationhood among the nearly 8 million Azeris.

"But we can't just give more weapons to them," Mutalibov said, thumping the table with frustration. "They're hotheads. They waste everything. We should plan. We shouldn't just attack and retreat."

It was true that Azeri forces tended to stage opportunistic hit and run raids rather than well-planned offensives. But the president's scorn for his own troops, whom he had never visited, was extraordinary. He believed that the only way to repel the Armenians was by issuing plaintive appeals to Moscow, all of which were ignored.

Such incompetence was the death sentence for the last Azeri-held towns of Karabagh. Alef Hajiev, the militia leader, helped Hodjali cling on for a few months with little food, no gas, no electricity and firefights around a contracting perimeter. Six weeks later, on the night of Feb. 25, 1992, the Armenians attacked in force. Soldiers advanced from three sides, leaving, as usual, an avenue open for the defenders to flee. Quickly overwhelmed, the people and soldiers of Hodjali struggled on foot through moonlit forest snows towards the plains and the safety of Aghdam. But halfway there they stumbled into a line of Armenian outposts that guarded an Armenian village. To cross to safety, the Azeris had to charge uphill through a gauntlet of fire.

A few months after the massacre, I tracked down one of the survivors of the retreat from Hodjali. We had coffee together in a shabby Baku seafront café. "Hajiev was a hero," the 51-year-old man told me, a carpenter who was so much in the thick of the battle that he was wounded in five places and later found a spent bullet in his sock. Seven of his close relatives were killed. "He got the fighters to make a corridor for the civilians to pass through. He was giving covering fire," the man said. "One more group was about to make the run. Hajiev was changing his magazine when he was shot in the head."

After Hodjali, the Azeris did not wait for the sound of advancing gunfire to pack their bags. Knowing the weakness of their soldiers, who sometimes fled before the civilians did, people would round up the collective farm herd and set off down the road with everything they could pack into their cars, tractors and trailers. Armenia's offensives met so little Azeri resistance that they were more akin to armed tourism. Aghdam fell soon afterwards. Armenian forces looted, burned or flattened almost every building there, as usually happened to towns they did not plan to occupy themselves. The booty of scrap metal was sold off to Iran.

By September 1993, Armenian forces were in control of almost all of Nagorno Karabagh. They also chopped off a large chunk of Azerbaijan proper by driving their front line down to the Iranian border. Their advances stopped because the Armenians ran out of troops who could hold any more territory. In May 1994, a prostrate Azerbaijan agreed to a cease-fire. Six years of fighting had killed at least 15,000, and perhaps as many as 40,000 people on both sides. Some 800,000 Azeris had lost their homes. The Azeris' military incompetence had resulted in the loss of 15 per cent of their territory in and around Karabagh, widening the geographic wedge that Stalin drove between the Turkic peoples in the 1920s.

Alef Hajiev was right in believing the Azerbaijanis were alone. No outside power publicly stepped in to help Azerbaijan, except for groups of training officers from Turkey, international mercenaries posing as oilmen and a battalion of mujahideen on hire from an Afghan warlord. These latter forces buttressed the Azeri front for over a year, but they could only postpone the inevitable rout. Bearded Pushtuns, they believed themselves to be taking part in some kind of Muslim Jihad against the infidel, but had trouble comprehending the Azeris' very Turkic take on Islam—one that saw no great sin in consuming large quantities of vodka to dull the pain of defeat.

Armenia, meanwhile, had plenty of support from outside. Armenian American lobbyists won a variety of sanctions on Azerbaijan from Washington. The most burdensome of these—a 1992 ban on direct U.S. government assistance to Azerbaijan, known as Section 907 of the Freedom Support Act—stayed in force until the U.S. dropped it in return for overflight rights in the 2001 Afghan war. More critical was support for Armenia's war effort from Russia, Armenia's long-time strategic ally against the Turks. On one occasion the Azeris showed me captured troops from the ex-Soviet unit stationed in Nagorno Karabagh, the 366th regiment, a crumpled group of silent, confused youths from Central Asia whom the Azeri government was about to send back home. In its report blaming Karabakh Armenian forces for the "slaughter" at Hodjali, Human Rights Watch/Helsinki, a New York-based group, held this Moscow-run regiment partly responsible for the killings: both it and the Armenians, the report said, "deliberately disregarded this customary law [requiring] restraint on attacks [against civilians]." A Russian investigation later revealed that Moscow supplied a billion dollars worth of arms to Armenia during the war, including warplanes and air-defense systems, in addition to maintaining army bases and providing border guards.

Russia grudgingly finalised the withdrawal of its depleted Red Army garrisons from Azerbaijan in 1993. Azerbaijan had demanded it as part of post-Soviet force reductions, but there was no coordination or good will. In the former headquarters of a tank regiment in Baku, departing soldiers ripped out every light fitting, locked the empty safes and threw away the keys. In one office hung a giant map of the Soviet Union in a Moscow-centric projection. Azerbaijan was portrayed as what it had been, a small, hard-to-find corner of a huge empire. Or a former part. Before leaving, a Russian soldier had used a bayonet blade to hack out the whole of the Caucasus.

The role Turkey played was instructive. If one excludes Turkey's umbilical relationship with the self-declared Turkish Republic of North Cyprus, Turkey and Azerbaijan are arguably the two states of the Turkic world that feel closest to each other. Given their shared national blood feud with the Armenians, it might be assumed that they would make a common Turkic cause over Nagorno Karabagh. Rhetorically, they do. In reality, as Hodjali's defender Alef Hajiev complained, the Turkish state did little more than supply some ammunition, training and technical support during the Nagorno Karabagh fighting. Most of it was done in secret. I challenged a Turkish officer once over the question, and he replied by asking me what more the Turks were supposed to do, since in the 1990s the Azeris were patently incapable of organizing anything, let alone a war. "They are the poets and singers of the Turkic world, not the soldiers," he scoffed in frustration.

For more than a decade, Turkey has officially refused to trade or open the border with landlocked Armenia until Armenians withdraw from Nagorno Karabagh. But Turkish businessmen sold goods to Armenia through Georgia, and pro-Western factions in Ankara occasionally tried to win international diplomatic credit and commercial advantage by moving to normalize the relationship with Yerevan. At such times, officials from Azerbaijan screamed blue murder. Until now, such interventions have persuaded Turkey to back off until peace talks resolve the conflict.

On the whole, Nagorno Karabagh showed the minor role of ethnic ties in the Turkic world when no strategic issue was at stake for the individual states involved. The autocrats of Turkic Central Asia abandoned Azerbaijan to its fate, and attempts to stir up rousing words of support at Turkic summits always failed. Their countries were weak, they had no

wish to offend Russia, and they disapproved of the democratic preten-
sions of Azerbaijan.

Ideally, of course, Turkey would have liked to do more for Azerbaijan,
but it was neither rich, nor powerful, nor committed enough. On one of
my trips to Baku, a Turkish diplomat tricked me into writing a prominent
story in London's Independent newspaper that the Turkish armed forces
might intervene directly against Armenia. It seemed possible. It was a
black moment in late 1993. Azerbaijani forces had collapsed, the
Armenians were advancing into Azerbaijan at will and sections of the
Turkish media were calling for something to be done. At the same time,
Turkish accusations were flying that Armenians were supporting
Turkey's Kurdish rebels. I took the diplomat at his word, and, when I was
heading back home a few days later, I flew to the isolated Azerbaijani
enclave of Nakhichevan and crossed the five-mile-long Azerbaijani-
Turkish frontier.

I crossed the bridge that is the only physical connection between the
Anatolian Turks and the Turkic world to the east. Officially, the Turks
and Azeris had blessed the 100 yard-long steel construction with the
name *Umut Köprüsü,* or Bridge of Hope, amid plentiful slaughtering of
sheep in 1992. Their hopes were not fulfilled. After a few years, local
people, went back to the name it had earned during its years of construction: the *Hasret Köprüsü,* or Bridge of Longing.

From the bridge I headed up along the Aras river to the old Turkish
border gate with Armenia at Markara, where I supposed the military
build-up the diplomat had told me about would be concentrated.
The Markara bridge was where Turkish troops crossed eastwards into
the Caucasus in 1918 after the Russian front collapsed at the end of the
First World War. Attempts by the last sultans to save the dying Ottoman
Empire with the ideology of pan-Islamic brotherhood had failed. The
flailing Istanbul government was making one last attempt to rebuild its
power around an ideology of pan-Turkism, a state to unite the Turks of
the world. It was a time when Turkish poets waxed lyrical about "Turan,"
an ancient word for lands inhabited by the Turks. One of their officers
later wrote a memoir of the expedition. "We were met by just a few men
on horseback in Caucasian dress, like fairy-tale soldiers with silver-plat-
ed sabres in their belts. Our small procession seemed to me to be the

harbinger of a great liberation, the awakening of the vast land of Turan. It was a new Ergenokon," wrote Şevket Süreyya Aydemir, referring to a myth shared by many Turkic peoples that at a decisive moment, a wolf led their ancestors to safety and new pastures. "Our duty would be to create, in the place of the outdated [Ottoman] empire, a new national entity in harmony with its historic and linguistic unity and its desires." Shortly afterwards, however, the last Ottoman government fell and ordered the Turkish units to cross back over the bridge. Turkic unity was not to be. Aydemir was among the retreating soldiers, and wrote that everyone wept.

It was still early in the morning as I drove into the army outpost guarding the bridge, but even here, few Turkish soldiers were in sight. One of them invited me to sit down and wait at a picnic table under the trees that shaded the long-closed border post. The gray outlines of the Soviet-built Armenian capital of Yerevan were discernable on the flanks of the mountains opposite. I had time to brood on the millennial nature of the Armenian-Turkic conflict. A couple of hours drive to the North lie the extraordinary stone palaces and cathedrals of the ruined old Armenian capital of Ani, captured by a Seljuk Turkish sultan 900 years ago. Like the great snow-capped cone of Mount Ararat, a 17,000-foot peak that is still a major symbol of Armenian identity, it still lies just on the Turkish side of the border. Nevertheless, the conflict was apparently not full-time. The Turkish commanding officer was asleep, and ambled out of his stone-built barracks after half an hour, wearing a crumpled track suit and scratching his hair. He gave a pleasant greeting and called on a conscript to make us some tea. There was clearly no build-up or military emergency of any kind. The diplomat had deceived me. Still, I chatted with the officer about how it felt to guard the frontier with a historic enemy which right then was shredding the army of Turkey's new-found cousins in Azerbaijan.

"For us, the Armenians are no problem, actually," he said. "We get on well with them. We even go over and meet them sometimes. The only trouble is that they've started switching on the floodlights when we open fire. That's annoying."

"You're shooting at them?!"

"No, no, not at them. We shoot on our side," he said, as if that were the most natural thing in the world. "Sometimes at night we can't see, but we think that [Kurdish] terrorists might be there. So we open fire."

I noticed that his perimeter was better defended on the Turkish than the Armenian side. Indeed, on the road past Mount Ararat to Markara, I had noted signs of Turkish-Kurdish fighting, a recently blown-up culvert and a burned-out roadworks depot. Ultimately, it was clear, the Azeris were on their own. Turkey had more immediate worries.

Eventually, the Azerbaijanis began to pull themselves together. In the early 1990s, the Azerbaijani army had been a by-word for corruption. Conscripts with no money to buy food and a proper uniform hungered, froze and routinely contracted diseases like tuberculosis. But on a visit to the last part of the Azerbaijani front line actually inside Nagorno Karabagh in 1999, I was struck by the way Azerbaijani troops, trenches and equipment had become more organized. White paint picked out the stones on the parking lot and I was received by a colonel in a neat new U.S.-style camouflage uniform. He said it wasn't surprising that the Azeris had taken so long to stir up their Turkic martial spirit. "The Turks have an army that goes back to the Ottoman Empire. Our army is very new," he said. "But there's a world of difference already between the early 1990s and now. The food and pay, it's all better." Still, the officer was a shy, young man, and I had difficulty imagining him charging the Armenian trenches up the hill. And chatting with one of his privates by one of the new-painted barriers guarding the entrance of their base, I found out that some things hadn't changed. "I've been in the army two and a half years now," he confided in me, once he was sure the officer was out of earshot. "They just won't let me go."

As borders settle down after the Cold War, military might is no longer the only force defining the future of the Turkic world. Ten years after losing Nagorno Karabagh to Armenia, Azerbaijan is winning some aspects of the peace. Commercial activity in its bustling capital, Baku, far outstrips that of Yerevan. Armenia has lost one half of its population to emigration, often permanently to Europe and America. Azerbaijan has lost at most one quarter of its population in this way, but most of it is temporary. It is also a key to Azerbaijan's survival that these emigrants are often a new kind of Turkic footsoldier: the migrant entrepreneur. Azeris have fanned out over the former Soviet Union, finding work and sending money home. Similarly, the Central Asian Kyrgyz are becoming commercial adventurers in Siberia. And in Azerbaijan itself, Turkish entrepreneurs have made their mark. I tracked some of the most successful of them down to the city of Bursa in the rich uplands of western Turkey, the same place from where an earlier generation of Turkic raiders set out with dreams of world conquest several centuries ago.

4. MERCHANT WARRIORS

THE NEW TURKISH ENTREPRENEURS
SALLY FORTH

> *trrrrum,*
> > *trrrrum,*
> > > *trrrrum!*
> *Trak tiki tak!*
> *I want*
> > *to be mechanized!*
> > > —NAZIM HIKMET, 1902-63

IN THE 1980s AND 1990s, THE LATE TURKISH LEADER TURGUT ÖZAL helped unleash a revolution in Turkish attitudes. A convert to America's zeal for free markets, Özal began to cut away at the bureaucratic red tape that suffocated private enterprise. Özal believed the state-led development of the early republic had disintegrated into dysfunction and waste. He spent his huge energy teaching his countrymen the need to cast off their passive expectation that everything would be provided for by *devlet baba*, the paternalistic state. Ironically, he used the state to achieve this. He offered fine booty for those businessmen who would follow his lead: "export incentives." Anyone who could open a foreign bank account and shift goods in and out of Turkey could manipulate invoices that made them eligible for tax rebates. At the same time, he decriminalized foreign currency holdings and freed foreign travel.

Abuses abounded and a lack of regulation meant Özal's changes fed Turkey's economic volatility. Traditional republicans viewed him as an irresponsible wrecker out to line his own and his relative's pockets. Inflation soared, persuading most Turks that real estate was their best investment. Cancerous growths of concrete grew up around Turkish cities and in "holiday villages" that blight the Turkish coastline. But, by luck or good judgement, Özal's gamble invigorated Turkey. The Turks' twin loves of risk and personal control made them natural entrepreneurs, and their desire for independent domain was channeled into everything from setting up factories at home to seeking their fortunes abroad. Turkish families often banded together as an investing unit to set family members up in business thousands of miles away. They were ready to go in the 1990s, when the collapse of the Iron Curtain reunited Turkey's industrial heartland around the Marmara Sea with its age-old commercial hinterland of the Balkans, the Black Sea countries, as well as the new horizon of the Turkic east.

About 60 miles southeast of Istanbul lies the ancient town of Bursa. The Turkic invaders from Central Asia who founded the Ottoman Empire captured the town in 1326, and made it their first capital. Led by Sultan Beyazıt the Thunderbolt, their raiders sallied forth from here to conquer the Balkans. They defeated the Byzantine Empire and challenged Europe. As the Ottoman Empire crumbled in the late 19th century, it was once again to Bursa that many descendants of the Turks who colonized the Balkans started to return. As Balkan conflicts simmered on, they were still arriving a century later, most dramatically during the 1989 exodus from Bulgaria, when factories set up tent cities for the new arrivals on their back lots.

The Balkan immigrants brought work discipline and technical education with them, helping Bursa grow into a successful center of Turkey's automotive and textile industries. They built an urban space with a more European, street-signed feel than most other Turkish towns. Bursa also led a new wave of Turkish expansion into the region, peaceful and commercial this time, but no less ambitious. Turkey's foot soldiers are now bakers, patissiers, traders and *kebab* restaurateurs. Their leaders are bankers and factory-owners. In 2006, Turkey's minister of trade likened exporters to the "broad and burly soldiers" once chosen for the front lines of Ottoman armies.

One of these latterday pashas of industry was Mustafa Barutçuoğlu. I met him by chance at a business luncheon in Istanbul, and he invited me to his Bursa headquarters. He had risen from schoolteacher to international supplier of industrial bread-baking ovens. His main factory stood in the great industrial estate that is spreading over the plain below Bursa, at the foot of the pine-forested flanks of the great mountain that rises over the city. According to family tradition, Mustafa said, his father's ancestors had arrived in Anatolia on horseback from deep in Central Asia. His mother traced her family to Turkmenistan. A fleshy ox of a man, he displayed a trace of flat Central Asian features on his face.

"My father wanted me to become a soldier or civil servant. It was the only way to earn a decent living," Mustafa said. "I got accepted by the air force college, but I failed the eye exam. So I had to take up teaching."

Like the rest of Turkey, teachers were bitterly divided between right and left in the 1970s. The rightists backed the army's choice of an alliance with the West against the Soviet Union, and saw salvation in nationalism. The leftists saw themselves as anti-fascists standing up against American hegemony, and were passionate about socialism. Both sides were authoritarian and some committed terrorist excesses, but the rightists got away with far more due to their alliance with the strongest faction in the police. Mustafa was a natural right winger, and he was sympathetic to an extension of their nationalist philosophy, a glorification of all things Turkic. He was not dogmatic, however. He had recently attended one of the right-wing National Action Party's annual summer gatherings in a highland valley near Konya, which, although it posed as a kind of celebration of pan-Turkism, was actually more of a party rally. He had left early, unnerved by all the shooting in the air.

Back in his schoolteacher days in the 1970s, Mustafa, who was born in a poor town in Central Anatolia, was able to pull political strings to get himself appointed to a school in Bursa. But when there was a change of government, he found himself "exiled" to a teaching post in a province he had no wish to go to. Then the police informed him that they had found his name on a left-wing militant death list.

"I think I was denounced by a girl I threw out of class. But already, when I got 'exiled,' I lost my taste for working for the state. I got out of teaching," he said. "First, I sold lemons in the market. Then toys. I went into real estate, selling plots of land to the refugees coming from Bulgaria. I sold building materials. But I still felt that I was being followed. There were whole areas of Bursa 'liberated' by the anarchists. I decided to go back home, to be a baker, like my grandfather was."

Turkey's military coup of 1980 intervened, changing the course of Turkey's history and Mustafa's plans. The military regime threw the leftists into jail. Mustafa decided to stay in Bursa. While trying to buy an oven in order to become a baker, he got an idea for a new line of business.

"I didn't like the way the oven-makers treated me at all. They were hard-faced people, they didn't bargain. I thought, if they can look like that and sell ovens, then I can do it better," he said. "I bought an oven from Germany and I copied it. To sell it, I criss-crossed Turkey like a politician."

Bakery ovens are a fundamental piece of equipment throughout the Turkic world, where bread is the centerpiece of any meal. Mustafa's first export opportunity came in 1986, when an ethnic Turk from Yugoslavia visited Bursa and ordered one of his ovens. Other Yugoslav sales followed. By 1989, he was in Moscow. A picture on his wall showed him proudly on one of the planeloads of businessmen that traveled with the late Prime Minister Özal, a trade-promoting habit adopted by most of Özal's successors. By the turn of the century, Mustafa reckoned his ovens were baking bread in every country in the former Soviet bloc.

His main factory could turn out 360 ovens, 150 dough-mixers and 24 flour mills a year. Great sheets of metal stood stacked up against the walls. He made some ovens big enough to feed a whole town. He had six or seven patents awarded or pending. His proudest breakthrough was an automated revolving oven fitted with stone shelves that impart the rich crustiness of a traditional Turkish loaf. In one cavernous space rose a two-story-high experiment, a 50-ton-a-day flour mill. The engineer developing it was Yiannis Papatheodoros, a 67-year-old Greek. His presence suggested that ordinary Turks and Greeks can collaborate happily despite decades of spiteful wrangling between Athens and Ankara. In fact, before the wrenching 1923 exchange of ethnic minorities between Turkey and Greece, Yiannis's family had lived nearby.

"I've made flour mills from Germany to Nigeria. Here, we're doing even better," Yiannis said, showing me a stack of steel parts for a mill about to be shipped to Moscow. "Switzerland takes at least six months to deliver a new mill and their mills produce less white flour. They sell their names; we sell our work. We can ship a month after we see the cash on the table."

Cash appeared to be flowing. Mustafa swept me up in his big

Mercedes-Benz for a tour of his other factories. His automotive company sent parts to plants making Turkish Fiats and German BMWs. A big
mill supplied Bursa with flour. To keep his father happy in his twilight
years, he had set him up with a neighborhood bakery shop where the old
man kept a hawk-like guard over the till. We ended up in what Mustafa
called his research and development department. It was a steamy room
at the back of his flour mill. Here, under the eye of his 21-year-old niece
Berna, two dozen men and women in white coats pressed out glutinous
dough with thin rollers, cooked it over a wide upside-down steel bowl
and draped the results from drying arms. Packed into plastic pouches,
this Turkish *yufka*, or phyllo pastry, was being exported to Berlin.

We repaired to his three-story villa on a slope above Bursa for dinner. Like many Turks who "turn the corner," he celebrated his wealth by
building a house with separate floors for each of his children, so they
could one day each have their own home under the same roof. The bottom floor apartment, painted in an austere white, was currently for
receiving guests. His wife had prepared us a fine meal, but, obedient to
Muslim tradition, did not join us to eat it. Mustafa served soft drinks.
Alcohol, at least in the home, would have blurred his empire-building
visions.

"I see my companies' future in processed foods. I want to be a dominant force in anything made of wheat, from grain to the table," he said.

"Aren't you looking for any foreign partners?"

His answer was like a lesson in Turkey's foreign policy—self-protec-
tive, opportunistic and viscerally independent-minded. It was directed to
achieving advantage abroad without diluting power at home. Mustafa
invested early in fast-developing service industries in the post-commu-
nist world. He was a partner in the privatization of one of the biggest
bakeries in Almaty, the commercial capital of Kazakhstan. He also
helped finance some of the Turkish schools I visited in Turkmenistan.
He and two dozen other Turkish businessmen contributed $25,000 each
to 30 Turkish-run schools in Uzbekistan before they were shut down by
President Karimov, who feared that they were indoctrinating Uzbek children with dangerous Islamist ideas.

"Doesn't Karimov have a point? Don't the people who organize those
schools have an Islamic agenda?" I asked.

"No. I call them international humanists. The survival of the world is dependent on such decent people. In Turkey, it was with faith that we helped stop the spread of communism. In Afghanistan, it was the believers who stopped the Soviets. Anyway, supporting those schools is good for business."

Mustafa himself was no Islamist warrior, for sure. Even though Russia helped bring down the Turks' Ottoman Empire in a dozen wars, and the Soviet Union had been the chief threat to the republic of Turkey, Mustafa felt just as much at home doing business with Russians as he did with the Turkic peoples in Central Asia. He put this down to the general warmth of personal relations in the East.

"You have to be able to entertain them every night for a week. And afterwards, you don't just show them how to operate a machine, you show them how to make a profit from it," he said. "Westerners don't have the patience for that. They are too cold."

Mustafa, however, did distinguish between Americans and Europeans. He said it was hard to go into partnership with the latter, despite Turkey's candidate membership of the European Union. He thought they just wanted to contain Turkey.

"We have started to compete, and the Europeans see us as rivals," he said. "It's easier to cooperate with the Americans. We're good at the small things; they're good at the big things. The Americans make great grain silos! And we need their capital, just like, in our small way, our customers need our credit."

A year after my visit to the bakery oven magnate, a massive, 45-second earthquake devastated the region between Bursa and Istanbul. Nearly 20,000 people died in the early hours of August 17, 1999. All along the western end of the north Anatolian fault, public buildings and apartment blocks collapsed due to poor design, corrupt tenders and unenforced building standards. I was lucky, only shaken awake as my century-old wooden house creaked, swayed and juddered. What surprised me more was the public sense of shock that such a thing should happen, even though, from east to west, the Turkic peoples have always lived on the tectonic edge. This denial of reality is of long standing: the

Byzantine chronicler Theophylactus of Simocatta reported 1400 years ago the boast of early Turks that earthquakes were rare in their lands. The truth is, tremors are frequent. Big quakes did great damage in Istanbul in 1894, flattened Ashgabat, the capital of Turkmenistan, in 1946, devastated Tashkent, the capital of Uzbekistan, in 1966, grazed eastern Turkey in the Armenia earthquake of 1988 and wrecked eastern Turkey's Erzincan in 1939 and 1993. The other Turkish boast, Theophylactus said, was that they had no epidemics of disease. Similarly, when HIV/AIDS swept the world in the 1990s, many Turks mistakenly believed their race was immune.

In 1999, the 100-mile wide reach of the quake along the North Anatolian Fault took a whole day to sink in. The government was paralyzed. The Turkish Red Crescent was as much use in a major emergency as the conical, rotted old tents it belatedly sent to the victims. More unusually in Turkey, where nobody needs lessons on the inefficiencies of civil servants, it brought the first public questioning of the competence of the armed forces. The army took days to take charge of security in the earthquake zone. It was seen to be selfish in its concentration on its own casualties—admittedly, over 4,000 military personnel and their families died—rather than that of the populace at large. For a while, it was non-government organizations that rode a wave of support from the public. A group of emergency volunteers from a mountaineering club achieved overnight fame. For the first time in Turkish opinion polling history, they briefly overtook the armed forces as the country's "most trusted institution."

The quake did not shake the confidence of Turkish industrialists, however. Researching a report on Turkey's booming automotive industry, I discovered that the Ford Motor Company and its local partners had decided to go ahead with a project to build a $650 million plant close to the epicenter of the earthquake, the worst-hit town of Gölcük. The company invited me over to write up their story in my newspaper.

I found the site of the planned factory down a dirt track just outside town. Ten months after the earthquake, walls still stood where they had been ripped in two like sheets of paper. The quake had sucked the whole building site six feet downward into the earth and wrenched it three feet towards Europe. Nobody had realized it before, but a 15-foot earthen ridge that defined the southern boundary of the property was the faultline itself. The earth had opened its jaws here like a mythical monster and swallowed one of Ford's night guards who had been sitting on a chair at a site entrance. The next morning all that was to be seen of the dead man were his feet sticking out of the ground, still in his shoes and socks.

Even without earthquakes, Turkey is a treacherous place for the foreign investor. Tax and company laws are based on European models, but their implementation is Byzantine and bureaucratic, pushing the country to the bottom of world lists comparing foreign investment, competitiveness and enterprise. The Turks may be frank and trustworthy, but they view any deal as permanently open for renegotiation. Personal ties are critical and contractual obligations mean little. This is true for the lifetime of a relationship—and beyond. I once bought a house in Istanbul, and, as we left the title deed office and shook hands for the last time, the former owner coolly asked me for an extra $5,000. To him, it was clearly worth a try.

Such opportunism is a common in the Turkic world. Oil majors and other big companies who arrived in Azerbaijan and Kazakhstan in the 1990s found that the most cast-iron contract didn't protect them from being treated like rich uncles who could always afford another favor. Ford, however, was typical of the kind of foreign company that had eventually succeeded in Turkey. The strategy boiled down to becoming partly Turkish. A strong manager who could understand and win the Turks' respect was the key to Ford's success in overcoming many petty obstacles towards building the Gölcük factory. They also chose a reliable partner, took a long-term, conservative view of profits, were ready to take the many complications in their stride—and proved able to walk out of situations when they were losing.

The company didn't always win. It came first to Turkey first in the days of Henry Ford himself, building an assembly plant for Model Ts on the quayside beside the Dolmabahçe Palace in Istanbul in 1929. But longshoremen threw the car kits into the sea, believing the new-fangled machines would rob them of work. Then Ford fell foul of protectionism as the republic struggled to industrialize. Customs barriers and restrictions persuaded Ford to dismantle its factory in 1934 and move it to Egypt. Before long Ford started creeping back, cautiously responding to the requests of their sales agent and future partner, Vehbi Koç, who was well on his way to becoming Turkey's most powerful businessman. After Koç set up an assembly line in 1960, Ford began supplying him with parts for Turkey's endearingly ugly first production car, the fiberglass-bodied Anadol, and bought a rising share in the venture as it prospered.

The new factory in Gölcük marked Ford's 1997 decision to take an equal stake with its Turkish partner. As it upgraded its presence in Turkey as a manufacturing hub for both Europe and elsewhere, Ford was actually closing plants in Europe. Thanks to Turkey's 1996 customs union with Europe, the country was moving into a position similar to that of Mexico and the United States. Around the same time as Ford came in, car-makers like Renault, Toyota, Fiat and Daimler Chrysler were all expanding their capacity to use Turkey as an export base. Volkswagen made electrical systems for many of its cars in Turkey, Bosch chose the country over 48 others to make a new diesel fuel-injection system, and one small Turkish family workshop turned out spares for the famous three-pointed stars for Mercedes cars. Turks simply worked harder, longer, better and cheaper than their European counterparts. In fact, while cars formerly built in some Ford plants in Europe may not have been "Made in Turkey", they had already been "made by Turks." In the 1970s, up to one quarter of Ford's assembly line in Cologne, Germany, was manned by Turkish guest workers.

The Turks are determined to do better as their influence grows; by 2005, half the television sets sold in Europe were made in Turkey. The blue-eyed chairman of Koç Holding, Mustafa Koç, grandson of Vehbi, wasn't even much impressed with the European Union's historic December 2004 decision to open formal membership negotiations with his country. Over lunch in his hilltop headquarters overlooking the Bosporus, he said he thought Turkey might be prosperous enough not to have to join the E.U. by the time the Europeans were ready to rule on Turkey's full membership in 2015. The journey towards EU membership was more important than actually getting there, he declared. For him, as for many in the Turkish élite, E.U. membership negotiations were most desirable as a stick with which to keep the country's self-serving politicians on track with long-needed reforms. He didn't see much profit growth during the next decade in the aging, hidebound markets of western Europe, even though Koç appliance makers were gaining market share there, taking over icons of European industry like Grundig and reinventing them them with Turkish technology. Instead he described his 150 companies' main potential in an almost Ottoman geography of Russia, Ukraine and the Middle East, and aimed to dominate neighboring markets in all Koç's product lines. Remarkably, one Koç supermarket executive told me, the boundary of profitability for competing trucks setting out from Istanbul and Vienna to supply Balkan supermarkets lies somewhere between Macedonia and Bosnia—the same border marches where Ottoman and Christian military forces once balanced out. Mustafa Koç took quiet satisfaction, too, in the fact that Europe was once again becoming increasingly unwieldy and fragmented through its expansion to include nearly 30 states.

"You seem to quite like that idea?" I asked.

"Divide and conquer!" he snorted with relish. With his young, almost Churchillian bulldog looks, and with a sharp, silver-haired chief executive who was the son of a Turkish air force chief, I could almost taste the hunger of his stated ambition to lead one of the largest companies in the world.

None was prouder of the new Ford factory coming to Gölcük than Nemati Erdem, the 60-year-old site manager. In his temporary hut by the construction site, panoramic photographs taken from the minaret of a local mosque showed how the plant had risen from a swamp once used as the poplar plantation for a nearby state paper mill. When the earthquake struck, the factory had been almost complete.

"We were very sad, very very sad. It was our baby, our toy," said Erdem, who had narrowly escaped with his life from a nearby apartment building. His wife was still in shock from the calamity.

Ford sent a team of geologists to determine what to do in Gölcük. Drilling deep into the fault, they discovered that the last major earthquake had struck 200-300 years before, and that another one was unlikely for a similar length of time. They gave the go-ahead to rebuild the factory, which would pay for itself in 30 years. Ominously, geologists reckon the next big quake will strike further along the North Anatolian Fault, under the Marmara Sea, directly south of the huge urban conglomeration of Istanbul.

"We're now safe here in Gölcük," Erdem said. "But my wife still insists in living in our Istanbul apartment block."

We got into his car for a factory tour. Clipped to Erdem's waist was a reel of thick metal measuring tape, which he zipped out to point to progress. Workers were reinforcing roofs with hundreds of columns and replacing thousands of bolts. The body shop was being reoriented away from the faultline. Constantly in motion and fielding calls, he broke off to reassure the local mayor that he would indeed discipline cement suppliers who were cleaning out their mixer trucks in a nearby river.

Soon afterwards, we passed a tanker truck discharging raw sewage into a miserable stream running through the site—a truck run by the same mayor who had complained about the cement-mixers. The municipal driver returned my stare with impassive haughtiness. Even when committing an outrageous act, the Turks have an indestructible, self-righteous immunity from guilt, and a miraculous number of expressions for "my conscience is clear."

"*Burası Türkiye,*" Erdem said, answering my raised eyebrows. "This is Turkey."

Actually, it was the old Turkey. For sure, much of the sophisticated machinery being installed in the plant was imported. The paint plant came from Germany, the assembly robots from Japan and handling equipment from Italy. Foreign contractors wandered between the machines. But it was all being put together and supervised by competent-looking young Turkish engineers. One of them, Yalçın Arslan, accompanied me back to Istanbul.

Arslan represented a great deal of what makes Turks confident about their future. Like many ambitious young Turks, he spoke excellent English. He was dedicated, boasting that he had shelfloads of books on the inner workings of automotives. He ran the local Ford rally team, and spent his spare time restoring a Ford Escort Mark I. Rather than have children, his wife was running what he saw as his future: a small company that imported specialty parts for the high-performance tuning of car engines. The Turks have a national obsession with the maintenance of their motor cars, even while their houses tend to be sloppily designed, half-finished, unpainted and liable to collapse in earthquakes.

"Turks won't go for a medical check-up for years, but they'll never miss a service for their car. They change the engine oil long before necessary. We know. Our service stations are flooded with people," Arslan said with an indulgent smile. "They'll suffer a toothache for two weeks without mentioning the pain, but will take a car to the garage the next day if they hear the slightest noise behind the dashboard."

This mechanization and commercialization of the Turks is nothing short of revolutionary, given their not-so-distant origins as shepherds or farmers, or their status in the Ottoman empire as men of religion, shopkeepers, landowners and above all soldiers. It is much as was planned and hoped for by the great soldier-revolutionary who founded Turkey, Kemal Atatürk. I was to discover a similar love of industrialization when I visited a Korean-funded car factory in Uzbekistan—the Turkic state arguably most similar in spirit to Turkey. But as I found on my many trips to the capital Atatürk created, Ankara, revolutions can't overthrow some traditions—especially how Turks run the machinery of government.

SECTION II

SAVE US, FATHER!

The Turkic peoples all love strong leaders.
But the leaders often come on too strong

5. *RAKI* AND THE REPUBLIC

KEMAL ATATÜRK, ICON OF THE
SECULAR TURKISH REVOLUTION

How dare you question if I fast?
Or come between my God and me?
How claim no lust for what's forbidden
Then veils wrap round the face that's free?

My vice is wine or rakı. I drink!
So what? It does no harm to you.
We'll face the hair-thin bridge together;
Blind drunk, I'll pass, if I be true.

—NEYZEN TEVFIK, 1879–1953

A JUMBLE OF PLASTIC SIGNS AND COLA ADVERTISEMENTS ON A STRIP OF box-like shops by the roadside obscured the building to which I had come to pay a pilgrimage. I stepped into the dark shadow of its large gateway arch and approached a moustachioed gatekeeper. He greeted me with a smile and, my visit being expected, dialed a number on an old black bakelite telephone. I peered into the courtyard of Ankara's first factory. Mustafa Kemal Atatürk ordered it built in 1932, nine years after he led the founding of the Republic of Turkey and moved the capital away from Istanbul deep into the wide-open highlands of Anatolia. Bundled up in this small complex of buildings was a host of symbols of the mission of Atatürk, arguably the greatest Turkish leader since the golden years of the Ottoman sultans, a beacon of independent, secular progress for the Turkic world and, in his time, a model for leaders in states like Iran, India and Afghanistan as well.

In this once minor rail-head town Atatürk took the first step in bringing a modern economy to his country, shattered by the First World War and Turkey's subsequent War of Liberation. Ethnic Turks in Ottoman times had been farmers, soldiers, bureaucrats, shopkeepers or *imams*. Trade was as much looked down on by the Turkish-Muslim ruling class as it had been by the 18th century English or indeed the Byzantine aristocracy. The Turks were fine cavalrymen, but their horses' shoes were made by Armenians. Then came the massacres, discrimination, population exchanges, punitive taxation, deportations, or simply the attractions of the more prosperous West that emptied Turkey of non-Muslims during the first half of the 20th century. A half-century later, in the 1990s, much the same happened in the east as Russian, Armenian and other minorities left the newly assertive Turkic republics.

For 1920s Turkey, this sudden Turkish-Muslim monopoly was arguably more revolutionary than their new nation-state ideology. A whole new economy had to be built from scratch. Atatürk and his republicans, taking their lead from Europe, chose the state as the locomotive of development. Atatürk's decision to make the first factory a brewery was no accident. Not long afterwards, the first industrial plant in Turkey's main Kurdish city of Diyarbakir was a distillery. Alcohol had previously been produced by religious minorities. It was forbidden by Islam and was often illegal according to the laws of the Ottoman Empire that Atatürk had overturned. The brewery would thus symbolize his uncompromising drive to lead the Turks towards a secular, European-style system.

The gatekeeper ushered me inside the brewery building. The strong sunlight flooding the courtyard only emphasized its emptiness and lack of activity. With a squat tower and thick walls, it had been designed to look like a castle by its German architects. Through a deep doorway I was led to the office of Mehmet Demirci, the white-haired bureaucrat in charge of what was left of the factory. Demirci was one of the breed of republican civil servants who had proudly pulled the country up by its bootstraps. But times were changing again. Few people now drank beer produced by Turkey's Alcohol and Tobacco Monopoly, known as Tekel, and it was no longer produced here.

"I remember the days when the country didn't even have any white sugar. For sweetness, people made and ate *pekmez* [grape syrup]. There was nothing in Anatolia, no manufacturing industry at all. This brewery was an example to the peasants, it was to start the infrastructure, it was to teach what progress could bring. When I was a boy, there was even a picture of it in my schoolbook," he said.

My visit in 1998 followed a decade dominated by the late Turkish leader Turgut Özal, an acolyte of the new Western fashion of privatization who had relentlessly attacked the now-inefficient, state-sector economy. Demirci was helping to wind up his part of Turkish history.

"The private sector is taking over everything," he said. "These institutions have completed their mission."

Demirci had resigned himself to a future where the monopoly Tekel's role would be health and quality inspections, if anything.

"They're trying to sell the Ankara brewery to foreign drinks conglomerates," he said. "The English came last week. The French are coming on Friday."

Turkish civil servants—canny heirs of the Ottoman and Byzantine Empires—knew how to fight a rearguard action. Five years later, politicians were still only talking about selling off Tekel. But by that time, the Turks had developed a bourgeoisie with a culture and financial power that rivaled the grand Christian families of a century before. Tekel's old cigarette factory on the Golden Horn became the main building of one of the universities privately endowed by the new generation of Turkish business dynasties. In the decade after the state stopped brewing beer in Ankara, the leading private Turkish brewery company had expanded so far that it owned breweries and sold beer on a territory far exceeding that of the old Ottoman Empire, from Romania to the Russian city of Rostov-on-Don.

Tekel's old Ankara brewery was built on the model farm near Ankara that Atatürk started laying out in 1925. It was one of his favorite rural retreats. Upstairs there is still a dining room where Atatürk would come with his boon companions to sit talking, dining and drinking late into the night around a long rectangular wooden table. At these dinners they would develop ideas that were to change the Turks' vocabulary, script, names, laws, habits and beliefs. In the garden near the factory, he signed the Montreux Convention in 1936. It recognized the Turks' hard-won right to guard the Turkish Straits, the international waterway and trade route between the Black Sea and the Mediterranean. Like anything touched by the memory of Atatürk, mementos are carefully preserved.

Veneered clocks and a couple of deck chairs from his yacht reflected the Art Deco taste of his era.

"This," Demirci said, picking up an outsize aluminum ladle, "was the spoon with which Atatürk used to taste the beer as it was being brewed." On his face was the reverential expression of the keeper of a shrine.

Much as Atatürk wanted to bring industry to Ankara and Anatolia, it took more than just his willpower to move Turkey's manufacturing base away from the more densely populated, sophisticated Western seaboard. His state planted enterprises all round the country—an iron foundry high in the central mountains, tea plantations on the barely suitable Black Sea coast, sugar factories far from the beetfields. Many of them withered on such stony economic ground. Still, some of the dedicated intellectual zeal for public service to the country survived, an endearing feature of the young republic. A model example of this spirit was Fügen Basmacı, whom I met in Tekel's operational headquarters in Istanbul when I asked permission to visit a distillery for *rakı*. This clear spirit is distilled from a mush of fermented raisins and aniseed, a taste that is popular round much of the Mediterranean. The Turks call it *aslan sütü*, or lion's milk, after its cloudy white complexion when mixed with water. It is such an integral part of Turkishness that it tastes wrong outside the country.

Basmaci was Tekel's *rakı* quality control chief, and, for her, serving the state was still a sacred duty. Her eyes sparkled as she told of how, when a girl at school, her heart had first filled with awe at the sight of a pencil stamped TMO, the initials of the state supply office. She struggled to pass rigorous exams to win entrance into the civil service. As we talked about the *rakı* business, Basmaci regretted that public service was no longer the honor that it was. She had been one of the last highly qualified graduates taken on by Tekel, and she felt that only second-class people were staying as state salaries lagged behind the private sector. Morale was low as the old era ended, but she was determined not to be defeated. She filled her office with old-fashioned equipment saved from the Tekel factories being dismantled. She poured her energy into preparing her beloved *rakı* for a globalized future. To ensure the same status Scotland has won for scotch whisky or the French have for cognac, she organized the drink's name to be registered as *Türk Rakısı* and patented the unique double distillation process. Unlike most Turks, who mix the national drink with water, Basmacı drank her *rakı* straight and undiluted.

"There's no cocktail recipe for *rakı*. It should be drunk pure and naked. There's nothing else like it!" she said.

Basmaci sent me up the Bosporus waterway to a distillery that was about to be closed. The waterfront property was now far too valuable to be a mere factory. The site was rumored to be due for sale to a hotel company whose shareholders were linked to one of Turkey's ruling parties. The manager, Ahmet Tugay, needed no prompting to complain of latter-day mismanagement in Turkey's state sector. He could do the same job with one tenth of his 550 workers, he said. Farmers sent truck-loads of aniseed full of earth because they knew a state-owned business wouldn't send it back. Workers fell asleep on the job, missing the exact moments when *rakı* runs from copper stills need to be diverted to different tanks, but could not be fired for their negligence. Raki was never advertised or sold on credit, and for 50 years one of three main *rakı* brand labels never changed. Managers were paid the same as workers. Even he was a misfit: his training was in the brewing of beer, not the distilling of *rakı*. Then he admitted that the most widely drunk version of the national drink, Yeni Raki, was 30% bulk French grape alcohol.

"I don't even smoke Tekel cigarettes," Tugay admitted, standing on the quayside, and taking out a box of Marlboro. A gorgeous view over a cool, choppy Bosporus contrasted with his tumbledown buildings. Strike action against the proposed closure was in progress and left-wing workers' protest banners trumpeted legends like: "The Aim is to Close the Factories and Kick Out the People" and "The Goal: to Plunder."

Plundering was in progress on all sides. Not for nothing the curious and much-used Turkish proverb: "the wealth of the state is wide as the sea, and he who does not eat of it is a pig." But, extraordinarily, Turkey can always count on the efforts of idealists like Fügen Basmacı or Mehmet Demirci. Turkey still attracts back most of the students who go to study abroad, and even high-flying graduates of U.S. universities will

accept low-paying jobs in the more powerful Ankara government agencies. It is not just to make contacts; even if they rarely serve more than
a few years, they have an ingrained sense of duty to give something back
to the mother country. This love of the national state runs deeper in the
Turkish psyche than the plundering instinct. It keeps saving the country
in times of crisis, just as disadvantaged folk still more than half believe
it when they look to the state or its leader and intone the immortal
phrase, *kurtar bizi, baba!*, or, save us, father!

To save themselves now, however, the Turks are forced to move forward, which they are slowly doing. The best Tekel factory at Tekirdağ,
west of Istanbul in Thrace, began to bottle and market its own produce
at a premium price in 2000. A private *rakı* distillery re-opened in 2003,
the first since the last private distilleries were forced out of business by
a "wealth tax" in the early 1940s, mainly because they were owned by
non-Muslims.

The competition was actually good for Tekel, according to the man
who ran the whole enterprise, Mehmet Akbay. By 2003, Tekel had been
forced to shed a dead weight of 40,000 employees. Aside from its role as
collector of tax on alcohol and tobacco, it made a 200 million dollar profit on operations in 2002. During our conversation, the director general's
telephone rang imperiously. On the other end of the line was his boss, a
Cabinet-level government minister. The general director adopted an air
of tired obeisance.

"Yes, minister. No, my effendi, we will be in Trabzon that day. Yes, I'll
attend to it, minister…"

There followed a silence of several seconds as he listened to the
politician.

"Absolutely, sir. But it cannot be done. These are not the old days,
when we could put seven people on every machine."

Putting the phone down, Akbay sighed.

"The elections are coming up. Every day I get five ministers, sometimes 15 ministers, calling me up, angling for jobs for people," he said.
"Nowadays they just want me to say 'no,' so they can tell their con-
stituents that they tried."

Such waste lay in the foundations of Tekel, set up as a foreign-run
tobacco monopoly to service the debts run up by the Ottoman Empire.

The insult to national dignity was never forgotten by Atatürk's republicans, and their one-party state was puritan in its fiscal balances. But the less idealistic politicians who took over since World War II felt free to buy popularity in return for office. They paid for it out of the state budget, a habit that has resulted in heavy foreign borrowing, repeated financial crises and 18 programs overseen by the International Monetary Fund since 1958. In the last quarter of the 20th century, the constant printing of money to fill the budgetary gaps fuelled one of the world's highest inflation rates. Even as the single biggest tax collector in the country, passing on $3 billion to the government each year, Akbay could not afford to pay Tekel employees a decent salary or to invest.

The conversation took a philosophical turn, as often happens when Turks take time out to savor the deteriorating "state of the nation." Akbay was an educated man, who read Voltaire as well as books on ancient Turkic inscriptions in Central Asia. He wondered where Turkey went wrong, compared, say, to South Korea, which was in similar condition in 1945 but has pulled economically far ahead. I put it to him that the Turkish elite had in fact decided not to be efficient, putting a greater value on enjoying its comfortable, protected lifestyle. Akbay nodded morosely.

"I get demoralized when I compare ourselves to Europe," he said. "Back in the eighth century, in the Orkhon inscriptions, the Göktürk king Bilge Kagan says 'my people were hungry, and I fed them. They were naked, and I clothed them.' That's still the problem. Even today, the Turkish concept of statehood is for a *khan* to capture the booty and distribute it to his followers. I feel the traces of these old things are still with us. Back then, of course, our rulers could invade the neighbors. Now you need to be commercial."

It was Atatürk's genius to see that his people had to make this transition. It was however hard for the Turks of the early republic, and even for Atatürk himself, to act on this. Their caution was perhaps because they were too close to the end-of-empire events that nearly extinguished their presence on the world stage. The Ottoman Turks, under German strategic command, only just beat back the British-French landings near Gallipoli in 1915. They were forced out of Iraq by Britain, a front in which Akbay's grandfather was one of thousands killed fighting the

British near Baghdad. (The Turks did, however, delay the British victory for four years and forced the British expeditionary army to lose 31,000 dead through combat and disease.) When the First World War ended in 1918, the Ottoman Empire was unconquered but in practice shared Germany's defeat. Istanbul, the Turkish straits and some territories bordering Syria were occupied by the Allies, who launched a process to carve up Anatolia between themselves, Greeks, Armenians and Kurds. A rocky northern province was theoretically assigned for the Turks.

But when Britain encouraged Greece to invade Anatolia in 1919 to stake its claim, Turkey summoned up its reserves of national spirit. This was the moment that Atatürk, one of the heroes of Gallipoli, stepped into a national role. Ranging through the fastnesses of Anatolia, he rallied nationalist ranks and turned the tide of battle against the Greeks in a three-year War of Liberation. The Allies were forced to renegotiate, and, at the Treaty of Lausanne in 1923, recognized a sovereign, independent Republic of Turkey. The Turks didn't look back. Scholars regard it as one of the only developing-world states that managed to preserve its independence from imperial powers through most of the twentieth century.

"We've never been colonized, you know," Akbay continued. "That makes us an interesting people. Imperial peoples are different. The Turks want to prove themselves. Self-esteem and ambition are in our genes."

Many Turks still love Atatürk as more than a savior of the country's independence. They also see him as a kind of secular prophet, the initiator of an Islamic reformation. Without him, they are convinced, Turkey would not have its relatively open society where Muslims are free to dress in Western fashion or indulge in tastes like their passion for *rakı*. For years, this abandonment of what Arabs considered "Islamic" made him a loathed figure in the Arab world, but he was much admired in future non-aligned countries like India and by statesmen like Winston Churchill. His impact on the wider Turkic world is mixed. He gave asylum to many Turkic intellectuals and activists who fled the advance of communism, but refused to risk his penniless young republic's future by engaging in external Turkic political adventures. His record does not diminish the respect with which subsequent Turkic leaders view his achievements. President Nazarbayev of Kazakhstan lists him first among his models of inspiration. In his austere, neo-classical mausoleum on a hill in the center of Ankara, urns with soil from all of Turkey's provinces stand beside pots of earth that presidents of Turkish north Cyprus and Azerbaijan brought to honor him.

Stern and compassionate by turn, he was indeed a Father of the Turks, the translation of the title "Atatürk" granted to him by parliament in 1934. His picture now graces the wall of every public office, and almost all private ones too. He forged an independent state for the hungry and illiterate peasants of Anatolia and the Muslim refugees from other parts of the Ottoman Empire. By force of his will, he overcame inertia and conservatism to give the country a Latin alphabet instead of its Arabic script and Western laws instead of Islamic ones. He encouraged women to come out of the *harem* and into the workplace. He gave the nation the novelty of surnames. His tough-minded people embraced this chance to call themselves Ironblood, Pure-Turk and Turk-cannot-be-defeated. Parents moved away from Islamic first names to more esoteric apellations, like Fire, Rain, War or Peace, or to the names of heroes in the proud Turkic history taught in Atatürk's unified school system, like Atilla, Cengiz (Genghis) or Timur (Tamerlane).

Atatürk himself was caught in the contradictions his Westernizing policy brought about. He employed an Ottoman-style black eunuch to look after his adopted daughters, who worked alongside a Swiss governess. He was genuinely committed to bringing women as equals into the mainstream of society, but did not countenance the same in his own private life. Like many of his people, he loved to sing the folk songs of his native region, but he forced them to learn universal "civilized" Western music. While laying the basis for his vision of a future democratic state with a progressive economy and diplomatic role in the region, he was in practice an autocrat, his one-party state was ruthless and highly centralized, and the country kept itself economically isolated from the rest of the world.

Seeking to create a pure Turkish tongue, Atatürk led a campaign in the 1930s to purge Arabic and Persian loan-words and grammatical constructions from Ottoman Turkish, which had become so artificial by the 18th century that English ambassadress Lady Mary Wortley Montagu called it another language. "The vulgar Turk is very different from what is spoke at court," she wrote home. "'Tis as ridiculous to make use of the expressions commonly used in speaking to a great man or lady, as it would be to talk broad Yorkshire or Somersetshire in the drawing room." In place of high-flown Ottoman, Atatürk, his companions and the intellectuals caught up in his revolutionary reforms forged a new language out of country Turkish and words re-discovered in the Turkic languages of the east. A blackboard for suggestions was kept by Atatürk's dining table, and many were implemented. The Turkish language lost breadth and depth, but gained modernity.

Biz bize benzeriz, Atatürk would say in answer to those who sought to classify Turks as Europeans or as Asians, "we resemble ourselves." Whereas the Ottoman Turkish aristocracy used the word "Turk" to refer to rough, peasant types, he struggled to make Turks overcome their sense of inferiority in relation to the haughty Europeans or to their imitators among the Christian minorities of the Ottoman Empire. Convincing the Europeans of Turkish respectability was hard. As historian Stéphane Yerasimos puts it, "rarely has the West in its quasi-totality taken up such a persistent and negative image" of a people; Turks were freely described in early 20th century media as torturers, murderers, pedarasts or savage beasts. Atatürk scattered his speeches with admonitions like "The Turkish Nation's character is noble," "The Turkish Nation is industrious," or "The Turkish nation is intelligent." Quite what Atatürk meant by a Turk isn't clear: he started out with the view that the new republican Turk was anyone who lived in Turkey. In his writings, however, he would also refer to the "Turkish race." And, despite his intellectual rejection of Islam, he probably meant only to include Muslims. Atatürk's republican motto "How Happy is He Who Can Say He is a Turk" is in a way just the heir of the motto of Ottoman citizenship: "Praise be to God, I am a Muslim." In practice, it even refers to the same people. Today the definition of a Turk has narrowed down further to a speaker of Turkish in Turkey.

Atatürk's revolution was not a one-day wonder. Its secularizing tenets are kept alive, not just by the Turkish military, but by civilian republicans too. Since Atatürk had no children of his own, Turkey's modest republican aristocracy is led by the descendants of his fellow Ottoman army officer, closest political ally and successor as president,

Ismet Inönü. Every year for two months, Inönü's family open up the family house granted by Atatürk to their father on the slopes of Çankaya, not
far from the presidential palace. Like the Beer Factory, the Pink Kiosk,
built in 1927, was a place where Atatürk would come and hold forth with
his companions deep into the night. The day I looked in, a certain gloom
hung over the few, suprisingly small public rooms. The biggest was the
dining room, its crockery and fine painted wooden ceiling looking much
as it must have done in the republic's early days. There was nothing
musty about the tour guide, however. Özden Inönü, the second president's 74-year-old daughter, was happily leading a group of chattering
schoolgirls round the show-cases of her family's illustrious history.

That year, in 2004, she had decided on a political theme for her display: her mother's dresses. At each model or picture she would empha-
size how even in the 1920s her mother, sisters and other republican
women showed their necks, their ankles and their hair. She pointed out
pictures of Turkey's first Miss Universe, chosen in the Belgian port of
Ostend in 1932 and congratulated with a rescript from Atatürk praising
her for making the world acknowledge the beauty of the "Turkish race".
There was a picture of Özden in a modern girl's lacy white frock, at
which moment she told the schoolgirls how well she remembered
Atatürk's visits, and how he would lecture her that she should develop
an enquiring mind, not the rote-learning of the old Ottoman schools.
There was a picture of Atatürk with the King and Queen of Afghanistan,
all dressed in the European fashions of the day. King Emanullah, like
Reza Shah of Iran, had gone home and tried to replicate Atatürk's secularization and modernizing reforms. In neither place was the effort a
great success, especially, she noted, in the question of women's freedom
to dress as they liked.

"Emanullah went back home and was deposed soon afterwards. Look
where Afghanistan is today!" Özden Inönü told the group of respectful
schoolgirls wearing pleated knee-length skirts. "If we hadn't had Atatürk,
we would have been an Afghanistan, an Iraq."

I took another message from a nearby photograph. Taken for a
French magazine in 1922, it showed the last Ottoman sultan-caliph and
his teenage daughter, who was wearing much the same knee-length
frock as Özden had worn. A year later Atatürk was to oust the sultan and

expel the Ottoman royal family as a remnant of a backward old order. But aside from his fez, the caliph looked like a kindly English country gentleman, relaxed and posing with his arm on his daughter's shoulder. The success of Turkey's modernization was clearly built on a broader base than some Islamists like to think.

Özden signed a last few autographs for the girls and graciously allowed one to kiss her hand and touch it to her forehead.

"When girls with headscarves come to visit, what do you tell them?" I asked.

"Just the same. They listen very respectfully. There's no tension," she said.

That very week, Turkey's new pro-Islamic government was pushing a bill through parliament to promote religious schools. It had also shown signs that it wanted to reverse republican bans on Islamic-style headscarves in universities and public offices.

"Isn't the headscarf just a fashion?" I asked.

I added that I reckoned that even as the battle over such public symbols raged, both sides were influencing each other. The tight clothes that Turkish girls now wear with their colorful headscarves would cause a scandal in Iran or Egypt.

"Fashion is one thing, but its wrong to think that all those girls wearing headscarves do so voluntarily," Özden pointed out. "That's what bothers me."

Despite her age, she wore an elegantly cut trouser-suit, and was a handsome woman. I complimented her on her energy as I took my leave at the french window that led into the garden.

"Reform isn't easy, and for me dress is the most important symbol of it," she said. "All revolutions must be taken as a whole. We've got to complete the mission."

We were standing in the ballroom, the first built in the new Turkish capital. It was small, with room perhaps for a dozen couples to dance. Such close public contact with someone of the opposite sex was as much of a Christian-imitating scandal as was drinking alcohol in public for most of the empire's Muslims. Özden said it was no accident that Atatürk had ordered her father to build a ballroom, just as he had chosen to make a brewery when he built Ankara's first factory.

"Everything he did, he did deliberately and in public. Everybody had to see. Our whole lifestyle had to change," she said.

Still, alcohol has never been a strong taboo for the Turks. Ottoman laws followed the Islamic ban on alcohol for Muslims, but such laws were easy to sidestep, since non-Muslims were free to produce and sell it. Clerics occasionally stirred up waves of fundamentalist indignation. Ottoman sultans sometimes tried to appease them by suppressing even the drinking of coffee as well as alcohol. "Strictures and prohibitions availed nothing. The *fetvas* [religious injunctions], the talk, made no impression on the people. One coffeehouse was opened after another, and men would gather together, with great eagerness and enthusiasm, to drink coffee . . . such things do not admit of a perpetual ban," wrote 17th century Ottoman author Katib Çelebi. A few decades later, Lady Mary Wortley Montagu was surprised to find that several of her wealthier Turkish hosts shared her taste for wine. One effendi in the Balkans explained to her that "the prohibition of wine is a very wise maxim and meant for the common people, being the source of disorders amongst them, but that the prophet never designed to confine those that knew how to use it with moderation."

Turks have a long tradition of social drinking in some form or other; some scholars date it back to the Mongol habit of offering a drinking bowl to honored guests. Back then it would have been mildly alcoholic traditional drinks like *kımız,* or fermented mare's milk, and *boza,* or fermented millet, which still have limited markets in modern Turkey. Behind closed doors, the Ottoman court may not have been much different: Turks believe that Sultan Selim the Sot conquered Cyprus because a Jewish vizier had told him of the excellence of its wine.

At his brain-storming dinners, Atatürk, who had drunk beer as a youth, preferred *rakı.* "I've got to drink: my mind keeps on working hard and fast to the point of suffering. I have to slow it down and rest it at times . . . when I don't drink, I can't sleep, and the distress stupefies me," he told a private secretary who urged him to cut back on excess. Cirrhosis of the liver, belatedly diagnosed, eventually killed him in 1938. Fundamentalist Muslims whisper darkly about it, but most Turks are proud of Atatürk's role in bringing into public acceptance the drinking that many people did privately anyway.

The Turkic world shares the same tolerance for a drink or two, but has not yet seen a leader of Atatürk's stature. Four of the five leaders of the new Turkic states were the former communist bosses of the republics in Soviet times; the fifth, the president of the Kyrgyz Republic, was a Soviet academician. All talked warmly of Ataturk's secular model for Turkic Muslim states. There was one, however, the President of Turkmenistan, who explicitly wanted the legitimacy bestowed by the legacy of the "Father of the Turks." Early on he toyed with the idea of giving himself the title Ataturkmen, or Father of the Turkmen. He was dissuaded, partly thanks to frantic diplomatic demarches by the Turkish ambassador. He settled instead on the name Turkmenbashy, or "Head of the Turkmen."

6. THE CULT OF TURKMENBASHY

THE METHOD IN TURKMENISTAN'S MAD TYRANNY

I'm an envoy from heaven on high!
Just laws, sacred spells do I bring
Giving wings to the fold who would fly
and swimsuits to those who would swim

—SAPARMURAT NIYAZOV TURKMENBASHY, July 2004

PEOPLE ARE ALREADY FORGETTING THE DYSFUNCTION AND STAGNATION OF the dying days of the Soviet Union. When I stepped off a Caspian Sea ferry onto a Turkmen quayside in the summer of 1992, the sense of a society in a dead end overwhelmed me as much as the stifling heat that welled up off the roads, the buildings, everything. I tramped the streets of sun-softened tarmac, and lost hope of finding something to see or do. Before long I was only seeking shade. The few people out and about appeared to be Slavs, pale, forlorn colonists who still dominated the Turkmen port town of Krasnovodsk, the railhead for the Tsarist conquest of Central Asia.

Life seemed to have slowed to a crawl. It had already taken me days to catch the ferry, a day to make the crossing, and I had another day to wait for a train to take me on to the capital, Ashgabat. Six months after independence was unexpectedly thrust on the desert territory of 4.5 million people, finding food, even in the port's main hotel, was a struggle. The only museum was closed all day. Taxis didn't exist, and private citizens hadn't yet learned to earn money by stopping to take fares from people on the side of the road. The thinly stocked shop shelves had little more than rough east European plastics and shiny ceramic kitsch.

Eventually, retreating to the relative cool of the town's stone-built Tsarist rail station, I was left with little more to do than trying to puzzle out the local Turkmen newspaper. The script of the language was still the Cyrillic of Russian. I persisted, and my morale rose as I found that here, as in Azerbaijan, I could slowly read the newspaper. One headline spelled out a message of national awakening that would, within a decade, gradually drive out most of the Russians who had come to live here during a century of rule by Moscow: "Let's learn Turkmen!"

Those Turkmens I saw in 1992 seemed less than thrilled at independence. Freedom had brought a new ideology and a new flag, but there was no change in their state-dominated lifestyle. The Turkmen inherited their Soviet-era leader, Saparmurat Niyazov, and they watched with a wary indifference as he reinvented himself as Turkmenbashy, or Head of the Turkmen, a vainglorious attempt to associate himself with the grand national vision of Mustafa Kemal Atatürk, Turkey's "Father of the Turks."

Turkmenbashy may have been a lesser man than Atatürk, but he certainly had an impact. He also had a wide margin of error. He benefited from the fact that the Soviet system had not done much for most Turkmen. He was little troubled by the ethnic conflict and external meddling that plagued his Turkic neighbors. The Turkmen population was already the most homogeneous of any Turkic state. Best of all, he controlled the fifth biggest gas reserves in the world.

In most ways, Turkmenbashy differed little from his fellow new Turkic leaders in Central Asia. All advanced personal fortunes at the expense of their countrymen. None could tolerate internal challenges. For sure, Turkmenbashy was unusually intent on cutting his people off from international newspapers, Russian television and later the Internet. Opposition activists were not just jailed or bought off, but sent to psychiatric institutions. But information was only slightly freer in President Karimov's Uzbekistan, and Karimov's regime threw far more people in prison.

Like Karimov or President Nazarbayev in Kazakhstan, who pursued only slightly lower-profile leaderships-for-life, the Turkmen leader's humble origin helped his Soviet career. He was born in 1940 to what his official biography describes as a workers' family, rose through

Turkmenistan's Communist Party as an electrical engineer and became the Soviet placeman at the head of the republic in 1985. As with most of his ex-Soviet counterparts, a series of well-rigged referenda kept him in place as the first overlord of independent Turkmenistan after 1991.

Like the others, Turkmenbashy ran his fiefdom by balancing tribes and regions, hiring and firing ministers. Turkmenbashy forced his subjects to study his outpourings, but Uzbekistan's Karimov published 10 volumes of speeches, and books by the presidents of Kazakhstan and the Kyrgyz Republic are compulsory subjects on their school syllabuses too. The same French company that supplied Turkmenbashy's palaces built no-less splendid ones for the Kazakh leader.

There was no question of an interview with the national leader, I discovered after the overnight train from Krasnovodsk delivered me to the Turkmen capital, Ashgabat. There were very few people to interview at all, in fact. I felt numbed from walking Ashgabat's long, hot, empty, tree-lined boulevards, none of which seemed to have any distinguishing features. Nobody had it easy: even the American ambassador worked from a small hotel bedroom with a line of his socks hanging up to dry along one wall. One day, however, a local journalist tipped me off that Turkmenbashy was to honor a glass factory with a presidential visit, and I hurried over there. A newly applied coat of silver paint on the gate dripped over the nearby greenery. Hoardings hid unsightly, half-finished machine-rooms that seemed too clean to be producing anything. As I entered the main building, a gust of wind sent a pane crashing down from a screen of freshly glazed windows.

In a meeting hall, Turkmenbashy was already addressing the workers, who sat on uncomfortable chairs as if at a school assembly. He was built as square as a provincial communist party headquarters, but seemed short and insecure under his thick shock of hair. It was still white then—later he would dye it black. His speech unfolded like that of an inadequate parent trying to buy off unruly children with treats. He offered sugar rations here, free gas there, privatization of shops, factories and collectives, and half-price everything for students.

As he spoke, the assembly of glass factory workers clapped on cue. But in those early days some Turkmens still hoped for a share of the changes sweeping the rest of the Soviet Union, and were restive.

"Why are all the state shops empty? Our salaries are not enough to buy things in private shops!" one man protested.

"I agree," the president replied. "Prices of everything will be placed under state control."

"What about the price of sugar?" called out another.

"As I said, we will be giving one kilo of sugar per month to everybody."

"What about the price of Kvass, then?" someone shouted, referring to a refreshing liquorice-flavored drink dispensed from two-wheel tanker-trailers on street corners.

"And what about bread?" cried another. "When I buy it they don't even give me change any more."

Turkmenbashy looked rattled. He talked of the need to avoid Western-style 'shock therapy' in the economy. Afterwards, a secret police agent kept both the leader and the workers safe from my attempts to approach them. Standing outside the hall, I asked one of the few Turkmen officials who would talk to me whether the economy would undergo any treatment at all.

"We are a little bit frozen in our ways. But you cannot change the Soviet mentality overnight," he said. "Our children will change this."

From my dark plywood cupboard of a hotel room, I telephoned one man who had good reason to feel thoroughly insecure in the new Turkmenistan. Akmohammed Welsapar was a writer and dissident leader from one of the nationalist groups that seized the popular imagination in most Turkic countries around the time of independence. In Turkmenistan the movement was known as *Ağzıbirlik*, or Unity of Voice. It had been founded in a flourish of small but influential daily demonstrations in 1989, around the same time as the formation of the Popular Front in Azerbaijan and Birlik, or Union, in Uzbekistan. A similarly broad movement advocating Turkic national modernization, known in Central Asia as jaditchilik, or renewal, had spread through the Turkic peoples in the last decades of the Tsarist empire. The Soviet Union wiped out such dissidents in the 1920s and 1930s. But their ideas have survived, and in some ways have been co-opted by the new Turkic regimes. The activists who kept Turkic nationalism alive have at best been sidelined.

In places like Turkmenistan and Uzbekistan, they were likely to be crushed.

Akmohammed gave me an assignation, Soviet dissident-style, in Lenin Park. A statue of the great revolutionary stood on a cubic pedestal tiled with Turkmen carpet motifs, his arm extended towards a glorious future that would always remain out of reach. It was one of the first statues in Lenin's honor in Central Asia, erected in 1927, and one of the last to survive. Akmohammed was sitting on a park bench nearby, a man in his mid-30s, with a dark-complexioned, high-cheekboned face. He had insisted that I brought no interpreter. We spoke slowly, he in Turkmen and I in Turkish, using up all our reserves of synonyms. If Turkmen was relatively easy to read for someone who spoke Turkish, it seemed to be Central Asia's roughest, least-developed language when spoken. Uzbeks joke that the Turkmens speak as if they have a hot potato in their mouths. It is a spare, hard, secretive dialect, which evoked their unforgiving deserts, autocratic rulers, sudden violence, long periods of shortages and short moments of ecstatic plenty. Still, we warmed in each other's company.

"Politically, the new republic is quite the same as the old one," Akmohammed explained. "In form it may look different, and in principle it declares itself to be liberal. But the presidential council, the departments, the ministers are all the same communists. And like a real communist, the president's only desire is to keep power."

Like many opposition activists, Akmohammed was forced to sacrifice his job for his political activity. His body seemed underfed and his eyes looked haunted. Arrest, exile to a distant desert village and labor camps were an ever-present threat. The only political party allowed was the old Communist Party, renamed the Democratic Party, with Turkmenbashy at its head. The new Turkmen newspapers differed in their mastheads, but not in their content or style.

"This is the only ex-Soviet republic where there is no free paper or magazine, no opposition whatsoever on TV," Akmohammed said bitterly. "Why is he so frightened of us, if we are just a thousand people, as he says?"

To add insult to injury, Turkmenbashy had already begun to steal *Ağzıbirlik*'s most popular ideas, beginning with its advocacy of Turkmen as the first language of the state and the building of close relations with the Turks of Turkey. Across the park stood the new embodiment of another part of *Ağzıbirlik's* policy platform, a "Palace of All the Turkmens in the World."

Aside from more than four million ethnic Turkmens in Turkmenistan, there are perhaps as many people again who think of themselves as Turkmen scattered behind modern borders in Uzbekistan, Afghanistan, Pakistan, Turkey, Iran and Iraq. Marauding nomads for many of the past centuries, their ancestors have a special place in Turkic history. It was the Turkmen who led the Turkic peoples westward a millennium ago. In about 1035, a Turkmen horde known as the Oğuz federation embarked on a campaign of Middle Eastern conquest. They rode westward under the green banner of the Seljuks, their leading clan. The same color now dominates the flag of independent Turkmenistan. They quickly overran the capital of the Arab caliphate in Baghdad, signalling the start of a millennium of Turkic dominion over the Islamic world. In 1071, the Seljuks smashed through the defenses of the Byzantine Empire at Manzikert, a battle known to the Turks as Malazgirt and one of the most important victories in Turkic history. With this, they opened the highlands of Anatolia to settlement by their tribes and flocks. They founded an empire that embraced much of today's Turkey, Iran and Central Asia. Many more Oğuz-Turkmen tribes joined them in Anatolia a century later, pushed on from the east by the 13th century advances of Mongol leader Genghis Khan. The Mongols eventually broke the power of the Seljuks, but in the Seljuks' place rose another Oğuz-Turkmen dynasty, the Ottomans. The Turkmen thus supplied much of the Turkic stock that makes Turkey Turkish today.

But Turkmenbashy's talk of Turkmen solidarity was just that: some 50,000 Turkmen refugees from Afghanistan did seek sanctuary in their new homeland, but were refused, probably for fear that they lacked the submissiveness Turkmenbashy's system required. Turkmenbashy even adopted the name of the opposition movement "*Ağzıbirlik*" as a government slogan, which he pasted up on hoardings by highways and public buildings. Now it was used to mean an obedient Unity of Voice behind him.

"The president understood that *Ağzıbirlik's* ideas were popular, so he took them as his own," Akmohammed said.

A steady procession of couples or threesomes sauntered through the park. They would often pause in front of Lenin's statue to pose for photographs taken by a man with a boxy camera on a tripod. Most were lovely, laughing Turkmen girls in fine, flowing gowns of velvet, gauze and lamé thread. A decade later—when Akmohammed would be writing bitter articles from exile in Sweden—the girls had exactly the same look of innocent happiness on their faces as they had themselves photographed outside the marble façade of one of the symbols of the new Turkmenistan, the Turkish-built Grand Turkmen Hotel. Instead of Lenin's uplifted arm, the background would be the hotel's glamorous Casino sign and the gift-wrapped cars it offered as prizes.

"Do you know what he stands for?" Akmohammed asked one girl, hand in hand with her friends in front of Lenin's statue.

"He is our grandfather," the girl replied proudly.

"They are happy, completely indifferent. They do not understand how much trouble Lenin caused," Akmohammed sighed hopelessly. "The unhappy man is the one who knows a lot."

In the early years, such dissidents were taken into protective custody when anybody like a U.S. secretary of state came by. Turkmenbashy hated the threatening American habit of wanting to meet his rivals for power. Then the United States started to demand that Turkmenistan put on a Western-style show of pluralism, otherwise their dignitaries wouldn't visit him at all. So when Turkmenbashy was invited for his first official visit to the United States in 1998, he released a token few members of the opposition from jail. When the main opposition leader in exile, Abdi Kuliev, seized this chance to return from exile in Russia, he was promptly detained, put under house arrest and escorted to a plane back to Moscow when the U.S. visit was over. Turkmenbashy knew that if some new ruler seized his throne, the Turkmen people wouldn't lift a finger. I remembered what Kuliev told me in Ashgabat in 1992, when he ran the fledgling Turkmen foreign ministry. Vividly illustrating the Turkmens' failure to rise in the Russian-dominated Soviet Union, Kuliev had found that he could call on the service of just four Turkmens who had any experience of diplomacy in Soviet times.

"People are mostly apolitical. They prefer to watch, not act. I wouldn't call it conservatism. I'd like to call it traditionalism. People did not accept Marxist-Leninist ideology, for instance. They just lived with it," he said, his thick eyelids broodily half-hooding his eyes. "The Turkmens were not happy when the Russians came, and not happy when they left."

The cult of Turkmenbashy gradually filled every corner of Turkmen life. Schoolchildren had to recite poems with texts like: "At the moment of my betrayal to my motherland, to her sacred banner, to Saparmurat Turkmenbashy, let my breath stop." A "Path of the Leader" stretched 20 miles into the mountains above Ashgabat to improve the health of young Turkmens. At New Year, children were made to dance around a Christmas tree in a central Ashgabat square chanting prayers in honor of Turkmenbashy. A 70-year-old Muslim cleric who questioned the Islamic authenticity of this was arrested and then banished to his home village. Watches bear Turkmenbashy's face, and the month of January has been named after him. Krasnovodsk, the port where I first landed, is now called Turkmenbashy. Most Lenin Boulevards are now Turkmenbashy Boulevards. Indeed, the Turkmenbashy name is borne by towns, villages, brands of perfume and yogurt, shops, factories, and even a meteor. At the Ashgabat hippodrome, four of the six horses in one race were from collective farms named in honor of the president. He has published a "Ruhname," or spiritual testament, a 500-page scattershot code of conduct for Turkmens feted by official media as the lay equivalent of the Bible or the Koran. One of his newspaper editors suggested he should be called a prophet, although the president batted that one down. Not to be outdone, the state-appointed chief of the country's Islamic religious establishment hailed Turkmenbashy as the representative of God.

The cult of Turkmenbashy has its temples, too. A 170-foot high monument thrusts up from the heart of the new city center, a cross between a marble-clad space rocket and a tripod Eiffel Tower. At its top stands a 20-foot high statue of Turkmenbashy, arms outstretched. In the morning, it greets the rising sun. The gilt ablaze with light, the statue slowly revolves, and bids the sun farewell in the evening. One Turkmen dared to joke about it to me, whispering wryly that it is not the statue that is revolving, but the sun that is orbiting around Turkmenbashy, or, as state newspapers call him, Saparmurat the Great.

Everyone is required to join in the adulation. Parliament voted him president-for-life in 1999, and then again in 2002. Foreign delegations are taken to lay wreaths at a monument Turkmenbashy erected to his late mother outside Ashgabat—her name, Gurbansultan, also graces cinemas, a perfume and a women's magazine. The Turks understand the game of sycophancy especially well. One who now dominates business in Ashgabat minted and handed round shiny golden lapel pins featuring Turkmenbashy's head in profile, similar to those the Turks themselves use for Atatürk. The loyalists of the Turkmen regime liked the image so much that they pinned a version permanently on the corner of Turkmen TV.

I felt the full force of the cult when I joined a delegation accompanying Turkey's President Suleyman Demirel for a visit to Turkmenistan in 2000. After the first day's meetings, Demirel and Turkmenbashy sat down on twin thrones in the middle of the grand new concert hall in the redesigned center of the capital—built before Turkmenbashy's 2001 decision to ban opera and ballet as alien to Turkmen culture. A poem hailed the "two states with one people, one blood, and one language." But there was no doubt about the real focus of attention: for three long hours, children, women, men, choruses, folk singers and guitarists regaled the "Father of the Turkmen." As they reached their crescendos, they would stretch out their arms in an act of loving submission to their leader. Turkmenbashy lapped up all the concocted emotion. I wondered how much his insatiable desire for love came from his childhood in an orphanage. His father was killed during the Nazi occupation of the Caucasus in 1942 and his mother, along with most of his close relatives, were wiped out by a 1948 earthquake that flattened Ashgabat. He hinted as much in an address to the youth of his country in 2004. "The most pleasant and pure feeling is to live with a sense of being part of Motherland," he said, "because exactly this feeling spares [us] from loneliness."

Demirel, a leader who himself liked to be styled *baba*, or father, as did President Nazarbayev of Kazakhstan, and whose court had its fair share of flatterers, kept looking at his watch. It was too much for him. But Turkmenbashy hadn't finished. The stage was laid out with 50 Turkmen rugs, the deep red carpets with six or eight tribal medallions sometimes known in the West as "Bokhara" rugs after the great caravan city and religious center where the Turkmen nomads used to sell them to dealers. There was to be no such putting down of the Turkmen any more. Turkmenbashy called the Turkish president and five Turkish ministers up to join him on stage and dressed them up as shaggy-hatted Turkmen elders.

"There!" he said. "Who's to say the Turks aren't Turkmen after all?"

"We are all the branches of the same plane tree," Demirel replied, swallowing his irritation.

Afterwards, Turkmenbashy invited his guests to a lavish feast. A toast of welcome was proposed by the speaker of Turkmenistan's parliament, a frog-like man who croaked out a euconium to Turkmenbashy as "a great man and a great democrat." As Demirel sipped at his glass, Turkmenbashy carried on a stilted conversation with him, often leaving the microphone in front of him switched on.

"But you're not drinking!" he said in one amplified aside, loading the Turkish president's goblet back up with cognac.

Later, Turkmenbashy took off his jacket for the part of the evening he was clearly looking forward to most. Like Tamerlane, who named the suburbs of his capital Samarkand after the great cities of his world, Turkmenbashy liked to escape from his sense of Central Asian isolation. One after the other, he called up the ambassadors to Ashgabat from many corners of the globe. Envoy after envoy went through the motions of toasting the Turkmen leader, and gamely submitted to his teasing. Midnight passed as hundreds of guests were forced onto their feet again and again to raise their glasses. At least they didn't have to drink much. At more intimate diplomatic lunches, Turkmenbashy would oblige ambassadors to drink whole tumblers of vodka poured out by his own hand.

Warily, the Chinese ambassador obeyed a call to the microphone.

"Ha! At least your human rights are all in order!" Turkmenbashy joked in his squeaky voice.

The ambassador of Uzbekistan made a speech in Russian, and Turkmenbashy ticked him off for not speaking his native Turkic tongue. At half past midnight, he treated everyone to a rambling, 20-minute speech on the need for the separation of church and state—even though he kept religious appointments tightly under his own personal control. Then he called the American ambassador to the microphone. The diplomat gave a solemn speech about Turkmenistan's development opportunities. Usually careful not to alienate the major powers, Turkmenbashy spared the American a ribbing. But he took a stab at the hapless Russian envoy.

"Ah," he gloated. "Now here's a country that needs a few billion dollars."

The lights flashed off a glittering mound of many-colored jewels on Turkmenbashy's ring finger, but all was not necessarily well with the finances of Turkmenistan. Turkmenbashy's demands for huge pre-payments held up a U.S.-backed natural gas export pipeline to Turkey for so long it fell off the oil industry's agenda; he was left dependent on half-paid-for exports to Russia, Ukraine and poverty-stricken Georgia. A plan to export gas through Afghanistan to Pakistan and India was revived after the 2001 Afghan war, but insecurity along the route kept it a long shot. ExxonMobil suspended its Turkmenistan operations in 2002. After years of trying to be Turkmenistan's best friend, Royal Dutch/Shell all but closed up shop in 2003. Turkmenbashy's palaces meanwhile sprang up all over the country, multi-million dollar affairs built by foreign contractors. But while he repeatedly promised his people incomes of $10,000-15,000 a year each, and bought himself a $50 million presidential jet with gold fittings, average wages lingered at below $20 a month. Electricity and water may have been free, but compulsory education was cut to nine years, hospitals remained primitive and medicine was hard to obtain. Foreign debt tripled in one two-year period. The closest most people came to foreign currency were the dollar, pound and yen signs that briefly represented the more obscure phonemes in the country's new Latin alphabet.

Turkmenbashy always looked as though he was trying to act a part, and would often skip regional summits, as if fearing exposure to the outside world. I watched him work a group of international oilmen at a photo-opportunity in 1998 as they all made airy new pledges of intent to build the trans-Afghan pipeline. He called them by their first names and mischievously teased them. But when I stayed behind and witnessed a private part of the meeting—I was ill and had sunk into a chair on one side of the grand chamber, and his security detail had mistaken me for a tired oil executive—he seemed to be out of his depth, as fake as the decoration of his new palace, which mixed French chateau with Oriental Disneyland. The climax of the meeting was a lavish parade of present giving from the oil company negotiators. A tall American handed over a lovely cut glass bowl figuring Mustang horses, then wrapped the diminutive Turkmenbashy in a muscular embrace. But the oilman had forgotten the president's recent quadruple heart by-pass surgery. Turkmenbashy let out an agonized groan. It was the only honest moment of the day.

Turkmenbashy may have been the weirdest Central Asian president, but he had a canny memory for names and faces. When in Central Asia, I saw Turkmenbashy in person more often than his more respected counterparts, driving himself to some occasion in an official Mercedes upholstered in Turkmen carpets, hosting visitors or surveying military parades. What he lacked in international esteem he made up for in his distance from world affairs. He managed to stay politically neutral in the great power politics swirling round him. Although a neighbor of Afghanistan, he even managed to avoid being dragged into America's war on terrorism. Meanwhile a wave of building projects transformed the once drab middle of Ashghabat into one of the more impressively designed city centers of Central Asia.

Most Turkmens pay scant attention to the cult of Turkmenbashy. They have seen little else, and have no culture of protest or conscious-ness of rights to confront Turkmenbashy's overwhelming power. It is wiser to fear the omnipresent security services. Most political dissenters leave the country; the U.S. State Department could only find one political pris-oner to list in its March 2002 Human Rights report. In the mid-1990s, I happened upon an instructive scene in the down-at-heel eastern town of Mari. It was late at night, and pollution drifted through the streets like skeins of mist. As I turned a corner, I passed a checkpoint on the other side of the road. A policeman had stopped a car and the driver was stand-ing beside it. The officer was heavily and deliberately beating him with a long, black baton. Neither man paid any attention to me, nor was there any sign of excitement. The victim just stood there, bent over his car, head down and taking it silently. The beating remained slow and regular until I turned the next corner a minute later. I did not see its beginning, nor its end.

Turkmens may be storing up their resentment for some future explosion of public anger. Dissidents decry the comic representation of Turkmenbashy in Western media, citing what they maintain is his steady takeover of Turkmens' money, their country and their minds. "It is impossible to hide any more his pure hypocrisy, the absence of elementary norms of political and diplomatic behavior, the insidiousness and cruelty in relation to the people and the spreading of an atmosphere of fear," said one of his long-serving deputies, the relatively suave, English-speaking Boris Sheikhmuradov, unfurling the banner of opposition in 2001. His supporters subsequently managed some actions like the street distribution of leaflets. But when a dramatic machine-gun ambush targeted Turkmenbashy on his morning inter-palace commute in November 2002, nobody took to the streets. A month later Turkmen police arrested Sheikhmuradov, who had left his exile in Moscow and slipped back into the country shortly before the event. He woodenly admitted being behind the plot in a neo-Stalinist trial-by-confession shown on a large screen in central Ashgabat and on TV. In the broadcasts, Turkmenbashy brushed aside demands from viewers to put Sheikhmuradov to death, and sentenced him to life in jail.

Boris Sheikhmuradov was not alone, and several former officials were implicated in the coup attempt. Turkmenbashy's autocratic, on-the-hoof style of misrule had pushed many high officials into opposition. Once the director of the state airline yawned during one of his rambling live TV meditations on the national agenda, and Turkmenbashy stopped to yell at him "why are you yawning? Is this of no interest to you?." A former central bank chief described Cabinet scenes where Turkmenbashy forced ministers to beg forgiveness for mistakes by kneeling in front of him. Even a hapless weather forecaster who failed to predict three days of rain was given a televised sacking. The Turkmen leader fired so many people that few competent top bureaucrats remained. Those who did were constantly on edge. They know that Turkmenbashy knows that the principal threat of a coup attempt against a Central Asian autocrat usually lies within the ruling class.

Ordinary Turkmens, despite their continuing poverty, the weeks of forced labor for schoolchildren in the cotton fields and the degradation of their educational system, are nevertheless visibly proud when walking

through Ashghabat's lavish new city center. I discussed the matter of out-
ward Turkmen public indifference to political events one day with a
small town businessman while on a train journey to the capital. "We
know that our president is making lots of mistakes. It's natural. We have
only been free for a few years, after 70 years in jail," the businessman
said. "We have to support the president for now and make him great so
that people will know who the Turkmens are. When we've established
ourselves, then we'll fix everything up."

What Turkmenbashy liked to fix was elections: votes cast for him
progressed from 98.3% in 1990 to 99.9% with 99.9% turnout in 1994, a
target that only ex-Iraqi President Saddam Hussein was to exceed with
a full 100% in 2002. The first "hero of Turkmenistan" (awarded five
times) and "universally acknowledged leader" happily told foreign visitors
that his omnipresent portraits were part of a transitional stage to drive
into the Turkmen people's head the idea that they were now independent. After all, Turkey's Atatürk used to say the same thing in the 1920s
and 30s, and Turkey had to wait until 1950 for its first free elections.
Early in his rule, Turkmenbashy put a French newspaperman straight.
"Don't worry," he said. "All this will pass in a few years, when the people
no longer depend on me. The Turkmens have always bowed to something; once it was fire, then Islam, then Marx . . . the people have to
believe in something."

In some ways, he was giving the people what they expected. When
I drove for a day out along the Iranian border, I passed the construction
site for a new summer palace on which a swarm of workers toiled in a
barren bowl in the Kopet Dagh mountains. Its crenellations and polished
marble would have done a medieval prince proud. Indeed, in their day,
the Seljuks built caravan stops so beautiful they were called sarays, or
palaces. They dotted cities and trade routes with sturdy, elegant stone
bridges, madrasas, or schools, and fine mosques. And while Turkmenbashy uses French, British and Turkish craftsmen, the Seljuks employed
Armenians, Georgians and others. And there was perhaps another reason for the Turkmens' acquiescence to his rule.

"Is that palace really a good use for your republic's money?" I asked
my Turkmen companion as we surveyed the new structure.

"Tsk, tsk," he tutted in reply.

I turned towards him. He was not angry. He was looking at the palace in admiration. On his face was precisely the expression that the 19th century Hungarian scholar and adventurer Arminius Vámbéry described on the faces of his Turkmen hosts when they surveyed the plunder and slaves won by a fellow tribesman during a successful raid against the outside world: a "mixed feeling of envy and pleasure."

Perhaps it was too much to expect the Central Asian heirs of Soviet absolutism and the brutality of medieval khanates to move quickly toward norms of Western governance or even competence. In the Caucasus, however, Azerbaijan had a more advanced history of national development. Leaders did compete openly there, and even in the last days of the Soviet Union there was no doubt that the communist leadership was patriotic and longed for Azeri independence as much as any of the more westerly Soviet republics. The question that remained, however, was what they wanted independence for: a proud, strong Azerbaijan, or simply complete freedom to line their own pockets.

7. GRAY WOLVES

NATIONALISTS PREVAIL IN AZERBAIJAN

For Turks, the homeland isn't Turkey, nor yet Turkistan.
Their country is a vast, eternal land: Turan!
—ZIYA GÖKALP, Ottoman pan-Turkist, 1911

THE IDEA THAT TURKIC PEOPLES SHOULD RALLY AROUND A NATIONALIST idea took a long time to develop. Until the 19th century, what little contact the western and eastern Turks had was based on a common Islamic identity. Central Asian rulers usually requested a confirmation of their positions from the Ottoman sultan, a formality based on his role as the Sunni Muslim caliph (although Ottoman rulers did keep as their main Turkish honorific the Central Asian title of khan). But this Sunni solidarity, and its 19th century offshoot, political pan-Islamism, had little impact in blunting the advance of Russia and other powers into Turkic-populated or Turkic-ruled territories in Asia. These mostly Christian successes spurred Turkic intellectuals to imitate the sense of nationalism that was overpowering them. Some even adopted an ideology of pan-Turkism, aiming for political unity between all the Turkic peoples. This reached a political apogee under Enver, the minister of war and chief of general staff who dominated the Ottoman Empire through the First World War. He embarked on the first serious attempt for centuries to reverse Russia's advances and to reconnect the western Turks with their cousins in the east. Most of Enver's men froze to death in the winter snows of the eastern Turkish mountains before they fired a shot. In the east, a nascent sense of local "Turkistani" nationalism fuelled a major Central Asian revolt in 1916, largely in reaction to the Russian Empire's effort to mobilize its Muslim population for wartime labor battalions. In the chaotic aftermath of the First World War, Turkic nationalists briefly seized power in Azerbaijan and the city-state of Bokhara in Central Asia—and later, in 1949, in the Uygur Turkish territories of western China—but the rise of the Soviet Union and communist China iced over any further independent Turkic political development.

Associations of exiles kept alive these Turkic nationalist ideals through the 20th century, and, in a way that was deliberately not provocative to the powerful Soviet Union, so did the Republic of Turkey. As Soviet power withered away and collapsed, the idea spread quickly again. Nationalist opposition groups cropped up in each Turkic republic. Nowhere was this more pronounced than in Azerbaijan, whose post-Soviet fate was dominated by two very different men. The first, disgraced Soviet grandee Haydar Aliyev, had once even thrown the other, nationalist dissident Abulfez Aliyev "Elchibey," into jail to break stones in the 1970s. But even though the two men's methods and philosophies were poles apart, they shared a common goal of an independent Azerbaijan. Both were secular nationalists in the Turkish republican mould. Both came closer than any other of the new ex-Soviet dictators to the Turkic ideals of Isa Alptekin of the Uygurs in 1949, or Osman Hodja, the nationalist president of the Bokharans in 1920, or Mehmet Emin Rasulzadeh, who, in 1918, briefly led the first independent state of Azerbaijan.

More surprisingly, even before independent Turkic states spun free of the Soviet Union in 1991, their communist elites had begun to pick up where the nationalists of the pre-Soviet period had left off. Already in 1990, when I interviewed the prime minister of Soviet Azerbaijan in Baku, he treated me to a nationalist, pro-Turkish diatribe. Hasan Hasanov had dug out a file of names of European and American companies who had been doing business in Azerbaijan before the 1917 revolution. There were the Nobels and the Rothschilds, of course, but also companies with old-fashioned names like Babcock and Wilcox and the Baku Wire and Rope Company.

"Does this company still exist?" he asked, pointing to a missive from Adam Opel cars of Russelheim, Germany. The letterhead advertised the company's prosperity with a line drawing of factory chimneys belching out smoke. With no consciousness of how much the economic landscape had changed—the prime minister had never even heard of my newspaper, *The Wall Street Journal*—he asked me how to get in touch with them so he could invite them to buy back their factories and land. While offhandedly saying everything would be "negotiated" with Moscow, what he wanted in practice was independence—free trade, an Azerbaijani army, maximum relations with Turkey and capitalism. He was unconcerned about the Soviet guide-books still on sale in Azerbaijan that plausibly portrayed pre-revolutionary Baku as a polluted place dominated by poverty, misery and exploitation. Hasanov, who re-emerged in the mid-1990s as a foreign minister of independent Azerbaijan, later lost his job in a corruption scandal—quite an achievement in a country known for tolerating an extravagant excesses of bribery.

"Do you see the off-shore oil field here, the one called the 26 Baku Commissars?" Hasanov said back in 1990, leaping up to show me a cluster of dots in the middle of the Caspian Sea. The commissars were the original Bolsheviks of Baku, all murdered after some treachery engineered by the British occupation force in 1918. They were still supposed to be Azerbaijani national heros, and few knew that the cemetery for thousands of their Azeri victims lay bulldozed into a triumphal Soviet park on the hilltop above Hasanov's palace. He lowered his voice and raised all the undead ethnic ghosts. "We're going to sell those fields to a Western company," he said. "But first we'll change the name to the Azeri Field. Most of those commissars were Armenians, you know."

On the streets outside, nationalist sentiment was already at a peak. I had reached Azerbaijan in 1990 with some difficulty. The country was still raw and bruised from its pivotal "Black January" earlier that year. That month, Azeri-Armenian ethnic unrest had boiled over into a pogrom in which Azeri thugs murdered some 50 Baku Armenians. This turned into a revolt by the nationalist Popular Front opposition, which led to a counter-attack from Moscow. The Soviets were acting pre-emptively to block the spread of separatist Turkic national revolution. On the night of January 19-20, Red Army tanks rolled into the streets of the Azerbaijani capital. Soviet troops regained control quickly, killing about 130 Azerbaijanis and wounding 700 more. Some of the dead were shot in the back, others were crushed by tank treads in their cars. For Azeris, it felt like the natural successor of the Soviet suppression of the 1956 uprising in Hungary or the Prague Spring in 1968. But Baku's "Black

January" went mostly unremarked in Western capitals. Azeris were not Europeans, and Moscow won foreign acquiescence by pretending that the nationalist rebels were about to take over nuclear weapons sites.

I had been turned back that January from crossing the remote Turkish-Azerbaijani border to report on the crisis. All I could do from the icy highland frontier was watch a liberated Azeri TV station broadcast grainy black-and-white footage of Azeri communists burning their party membership cards, and a little girl carrying a bunch of flowers to thank Turks close to the border for their marches in sympathy with the revolt. I was forced back to Istanbul to follow events. Turkish television stations were broadcasting telephone interviews with previously unheard-of Azeri leaders, who spoke quaint, lilting but comprehensible Azeri from safe houses. For me, as for most Turks, this sudden discovery of Turkish-Azeri kinship was new and compelling. The idea that a Turkic spirit had survived Russification and the ravages of Soviet ideology was an exciting surprise, and I wanted to experience it for myself.

Frustrated for months in my requests for Soviet visas, I finally talked my way onto a flight to Baku as an honorary member of a Turkish delegation to what was billed as the First International Azerbaijan Business Congress. We gathered at Istanbul airport, a little nervous as we boarded the Tupolev airliner chartered for the occasion, one of the first direct flights between the two cities. The cabin was gray and heavy with the stench of chemically treated sewage. The light fittings did not work. As the fuselage juddered during take off, a big chunk of plastic clunked out of the ceiling and remained suspended at head height in the corridor for the rest of the flight.

Flying east over Mount Ararat to Baku, I realized that, like me, not all of my fellow travellers were businessmen. In fact, we were a Noah's Ark of long-dormant Turkic ambitions, as well as hopes of a making quick buck. The man next to me barely met my eye; he was a jeweler from the Istanbul bazaar, through which privately held old carpets and antiques were soon to flow out of the Caucasus. Farther back was a secretive Turkic activist, who had signaled his presence to me with a squeeze on my elbow, thanks to an introduction I had arranged through Azeri exiles. Across the aisle was a silver-haired Azeri exile of officer's bearing, attached, I was later informed in a hushed whisper, to Hitler's armies as they advanced towards the Baku oil fields during the Second World War. But whether businesspeople, bureaucrats or Islamist agitators, all had taken the sensible and very Turkish precaution of packing a great deal of their own food.

When we landed in Baku, the Soviet system instinctively understood the subversion we represented. Border guards forced us to cool our heels for four hours before letting us out of the airport, a place split between a space-age terminal that was half built, and an old terminal that was half falling down. In a car park clogged with a jumble of box-like Zhigulis, wide Volga taxis and dirty buses, a bright-eyed, gray-bearded man sidled up to me.

"Are you one of the pan-Turkists from Turkey?" he asked.

Reading my astonishment as disbelief or fear of the authorities, he glanced over his shoulder and folded back his lapel. Behind it a pin pictured a wolf howling to the moon, the mythical animal that Turkish legends say led the Turkish tribes to safety during their great migrations to the west. For decades it has been the pre-eminent symbol of Turkish nationalism.

"I don't think you've got the right man," I said.

He was not put off so easily.

"Some people don't understand what it means to be a Turk. We will make them learn!" he said.

"I see," I said.

I looked round, assuming him to be an *agent provocateur*.

"We just want to be masters of our own resources," my new acquaintance continued. "The Russians treat us like cows, and are milking us dry."

He handed me his visiting card, which introduced him as Doctor Timur Ağridağ, PhD. His name could be translated into English as Tamerlane Mount Ararat. Dr. Ağridağ milked snakes. He was the director of a laboratory that specialized in the extraction of poison from Caucasus vipers.

"We produce four kilos a year, but they pay us a pittance. The stuff is worth thousands of dollars per gram on international markets," the doctor said.

As he spat more venom against the "Russian occupation," the secretive nationalist appeared to greet him and he joined our 'business' delegation for the drive into Baku. Turkic passion turned out to be main-stream in those difficult, heady days. From the front of the bus, an Azeri guide welcomed our delegation with an emotional speech about how our arrival ended a "70-year-long heartache," a reference to the enforced division of Turkic families and peoples by Soviet borders. Seventy years ago, the intoxicating sense of Turkic possibilities had been the same. A buoyant atmosphere in Baku was described by Ahmet Naim Nusratullahbek, a Central Asian student summoned back home from Istanbul in 1921 to help "save the nation." Russian obstacles meant Azerbaijan was just one place he was forced to break his journey to what he called "Turkistan," but that quenched nobody's high spirits. Celebratory meetings brought together Azerbaijani authors and poets, Central Asian envoys, the ambassador of Turkey's rebel Ankara parliament and the head of the pan-Turkic "Turkish Hearths" association. Nusratullahbek had been detailed to take a Turkish printing press back to Bokhara to spread the new nationalist ideals. "We had a lot to do. Banquets, and all. People giving speeches: 'Long Live Azerbaijan' . . . 'liberation' . . . [it was] wild . . . fantastic," he later told a chronicler.

Back then, history had seemed to be on the Turks' side at last. Turkey's First World War leader Enver's half-brother, Nuri Pasha, led a Turkic force that helped Azeri nationalists rule an independent Azerbaijan from 1918-20. In 1920, Turkey's national liberation movement sent an ambassador to the newly autonomous state of Bokhara, where Ottoman Turkish soldiers who escaped from Tsarist prisoner of war camps helped found the Bokharan army, and Bokhara sent gold coins and Astrakhan lamb pelts to help Atatürk's cause in Turkey. Both Baku and Bokhara's new national flags featured versions of the star-and-crescent symbol of the Turkish Muslim peoples. As Moscow moved to crush Turkistani independence movements in 1921, Enver, in disgrace in Turkey for his earlier military defeats, joined the "Basmachi" revolt against Russian rule in Turkistan. He fought bravely until cut down by a Red Army machine gunner in 1922. (In the best tradition of Turkic feuding, Enver's action was also an attempt to outflank his rival Atatürk, who wanted to accommodate Moscow and avoid foreign adventures.) In the Turkic east, the Basmachi rebellion in favor of an independent Turkistan remained a serious irritant to the Soviet Union for another decade. In the Caucasus, the Azeris did not surrender their brief independence of 1918-20 quickly or easily. As many as 20,000 died resisting what was effectively a Russian reconquest. Mehmet Emin Rasulzadeh, the republic's leader, ascribed their failure to ignorance and internecine strife. "A huge majority know nothing of the idea or ideal of the nation," he wrote later. "We remain without a compass and our society, like a group of lunatics, fights among itself."

In Baku in 1990, we all looked rich to our Azerbaijani hosts, a longed-for chink of light from the outside world. Many had the illusion that Turkey was a fountain of money, and that capitalism would bring everything they had had under socialism, plus free travel, free politics and consumer goods for everyone. They did not realize then that starting up the capitalist ladder meant losing their Soviet social safety net. The linguistic link between Turks and Azeris strengthened a dream that all things were possible, even if the languages were not as close as some initially thought. Indeed, when Azerbaijan Airlines was later founded, moments of panic could break out because the Azeri for "we are about to land" is understood by Turks as "we are about to crash." In my delegation, the outpouring of Azeri sentiment touched all my new friends, and all shared a problem. Orhan Oğuz, a Turkish shoe manufacturer with whom I was having breakfast, groaned that the 70-year heartache was turning to heartburn.

"I can't keep up. Just when I've finished one dinner, somebody insists I go to the next house and eat again. And the toasts!"

For the Turks the warm reception was all the more remarkable, since their trips into Europe are usually prefaced by humiliating visa regulations and accompanied by bruising experiences of prejudice.

"I never imagined such love," said Refik Onur, the owner of an Istanbul chemical plant.

There was no doubting the special relationship on all fronts, including womanizing excess. After one dinner Orhan the shoe-manufacturer and I wandered through the labyrinthine corridors of the Azerbaijan Hotel and stumbled into a wedding party. The florid gilt dining room was filled with laughter and noise. Orders were issued for us "Turkish brothers" to sit down at tables stacked thickly with grilled sturgeon, meatballs and caviar. Azerbaijani brandy, vodka and fizzy *shampanskii* flowed free.

Our appearance was an excuse for ringing rounds of toasts to eternal Turkish-Azeri friendship. They called for an address from Orhan, who wound himself up for a heartache speech. It was lyrical, and afterwards, because he had little sympathy with political pan-Turkism himself, he gave me a big wink. With the confusion of accents and alcohol, nobody realized that I was not Turkish. I played safe with a toast to the bride and bridegroom, barely visible at a table up the hall past the dance band. My next-door neighbor leaned forward and offered another toast to blood brotherhood.

"We Turks, we know how to deal with those Armenians, don't we?" he said, slapping me on the back and giving me a cut-throat leer.

It was above all the failure of the Soviet Azerbaijani leadership to solve or achieve any victories in the Azeri conflict with Armenians that fueled support for the nationalist opposition, known as the Popular Front. In its early days, the front represented a coalition of forces from social democrats to the pan-Turkists who came to dominate it. Day after day, demonstrators filled the main square where Lenin's statue stood overlooking the Caspian Sea. Their actions partly provoked Baku's "Black January" in 1990, but the Soviet over-reaction so outraged Azeri public opinion that it swept Azerbaijan's communist ruler out of office, along with his almost obscene offer of compensation, a grand new bathhouse for the city. The next president, the pro-Russian Ayaz Mutalibov, lasted nearly two years until new failures in the war with Armenia roused the Azeri opposition against him. A small Iran-backed rent-a-mob shouting *Allah-u Akbar* (God is Great) in his support never had a chance of keeping him in power. In true Great Game style, Turkish and American diplomats, who prefered the Popular Front, rallied the opposition with a mix of advice, sanctuary, encouragement, and star-and-crescent flags. The demonstrations soon forced Mutalibov to flee to Moscow.

Popular Front leader Abulfez Aliyev rode high in Baku with his fiery message of nationalist dissent. By now his supporters called him Elchibey, or "my lord ambassador," a flattering reference to his brief assignment as Arabic translator in the Soviet embassy in Cairo. When I first saw him outside a courtroom at a dissident's trial in 1990 he already

looked unusual, and almost east African: his long, dark, angular face was
dominated by a strong curved nose, a thick, wiry shock of hair swept
back from his forehead, and a beard that he combed into a parting in the
middle of his chin. He was working a crowd, focusing on their passionate sense of national disenfranchisement by Armenia and Russia. Around
us, supporters hung up the old and soon-to-be-restored flag of independent Azerbaijan from nearby windows. Before I could speak to him,
or Soviet police could arrest him, he had disappeared. By 1992, Elchibey
was unstoppable. He romped home as the winner of Azerbaijan's first
free elections in June. It wasn't much of a contest: one candidate promised cash gifts all round, another offered to pay women full salaries for
four-hour days and a third, a former car tout, felt free to admit he had no
program at all. Nevertheless, outside Turkey and north Cyprus, the
Azerbaijani poll brought the first Turkic nationalist government to power
since that of Isa Beg in Xinjiang in 1949. It also had the most demo-
cratic-looking result in the new Turkic states: he took a modest 55% of
the votes.

Elchibey hung a picture of Turkish republican founder Kemal
Atatürk by his desk and had a certain naïve integrity. But he failed to rise
to the occasion. I held my breath when, in loose and angry language that
made me think he had been drinking, he used the final press conference
of his campaign to call for his countrymen's reunification with the
roughly 15 million Azeris of Iran, making an even worse enemy of
Tehran. He refused to speak anything other than Azeri Turkish, antago-
nizing Russian reporters down for the weekend from Moscow. The insults
Elchibey had thrown at the two chief powers that have held historic
sway over Azerbaijan put unreasonable reliance on a third, Turkey, which
could not afford politically, militarily or financially to give Azerbaijan the
huge support it needed. Later he declared that the Azeri language was
not Azeri at all, but Turkish, thus offending a large section of his own
nationalist constituency.

I left the press conference early, uneasy with the ill-starred omens of
Elchibey's rambling performance. In the courtyard stood a lonely figure
in a padded Central Asian *khalat* coat and square embroidered skullcap,
an Uzbek nationalist who gleefully informed me that he had just become
Azerbaijan's first political refugee. His presence represented a noble

challenge to Central Asia's emerging despotism, and Elchibey's impending doom. Not content with alienating everyone else, Azerbaijan's new leader was alienating the only other friends he might conceivably make, the newly minted Turkic leaders to the east.

The problem wasn't just Elchibey's political judgement. Later, he would disappear from view in the presidency for days on end, apparently on alcoholic binges. Ahead of a big summit in Istanbul a few months after his election, one of his aides later told me, Elchibey drank until three in the morning in his hotel, fell fully clothed into the pool, had to be put to bed and woken up by his foreign minister tipping a wine cooler of ice and water over his head. His speech was certainly wooden-tongued.

Elchibey's team let him down, too. Interior minister Iskender Hamidov was sinister. As proof of his virulent strain of nationalism, he kept a stuffed gray wolf right by his desk. He stormed onto the set of a live TV show to shout insults at his opponents and pistol-whipped a newspaper editor in the street. He threatened to kill the Russian ambassador if the latter did not force the Armenians to halt an offensive. His police force stenciled a decal of the gray wolf symbol on the doors of their jeeps. I asked one gun-toting officer what it meant. "It's the symbol of freedom for all the Turks. We are all gray wolves now, and Elchibey is the leader of a greater Turkic world!" he replied.

There were some achievements to boast about. "Remember, we Azeris had barely a single general. But I was the one who got the Russian army out of our country," Elchibey told me during one interview. "Remember, I talked in Turkish through a translator to Yeltsin, not in Russian, something that was never done before. Yeltsin once hit his spoon on (Kyrgyz President) Akayev's head, but I refused to let them do such things to me."

Members of the old nomenklatura who had managed Soviet Azerbaijan were sidelined or ran for cover under Popular Front rule. City services declined, like other parts of the wheezing Azerbaijani economy already knocked to its knees by the departure of Armenian and Russian managers and technicians. Civil war loomed as Elchibey lost more ground in Nagorno Karabagh in 1993. A militia chief rebelled, probably with Russian encouragement, and began a march on the capital. It was a ragtag affair during which his men would wander off to visit relatives or eat in Baku restaurants before heading back to their lines. The Ottoman army's march on Baku in 1918 had had the same ad-hoc flavor. "The Turks had felt so certain of their victory that they did not hurry to occupy the town, nor did they trouble to shell it, but they decided to walk in casually that same afternoon," wrote one of the British officers in Baku at the time, Reginald Teague-Jones.

Partly because he had few forces, partly to avoid plunging his country into civil war and partly thanks to hurried interventions by Turks, Americans and the oil company British Petroleum, Elchibey decided not to fight the approaching rebels. To replace him—quite possibly on Elchibey's advice, as Elchibey claimed—they turned to Haidar Aliyev, the gray eminence of Azerbaijan for two decades. He had risen to become the country's KGB chief in 1967 and party secretary in 1969. He reached the lofty peak of the Soviet politburo in 1982, but he resigned on "health grounds" in 1987. When I asked him in 1990 about his fall from grace, he said it was because he had fallen out with Mikhail Gorbachev. Moscow rumors at the time said the clash was over corruption. Aliyev hinted it was because Gorbachev sympathized with Armenia. It may simply have been personality or the fact that Aliyev had been a protégé of old-school Leonid Brezhnev. Whichever, his flimsy track suit looked modest enough when I met him, as did his walk-up apartment in the remote Azerbaijani exclave of Nakhichevan, surrounded by Armenia, Turkey and Iran. Aliyev was determined to fight his way back to office. One of his protégés was now chief of Nakhichevan, he had just been re-elected to the local parliament and his hunger to return to power was as clear as his steely, pale blue eyes. When a desperate Elchibey called him to Baku to take over as prime minister and save the country, it was as if it had been stage-managed by this master of Azerbaijani politics. In October 1993, Aliyev was elected Azerbaijan's new president.

Elchibey retired to his home village, also in Nakhichevan, at the top of a high green valley hidden in the barren mountains overlooking Iran. I made a pilgrimage there to hear his version of what happened a few months after his 1993 ouster. Aliyev clearly believed him be no threat. Indeed, a treetrunk slung across the road and a rifleman mounted on horseback were all that guarded his retreat. The horseman dismounted to clear my passage over a hand-cranked telephone. I arrived at an idyllic hamlet by a burbling stream, and was told to wait. It took his aides six hours to rouse Elchibey from his drunken slumber, and even then I could get little from him. I only detected a dull bitterness that nobody was calling on his satellite telephone, manned by a Turkish secret agent. He spoke more freely in 1999, when Aliyev had allowed him back to live in a downtown apartment in Baku. As we sipped tea from outsize tulip-shaped glasses, he told me that he had allowed Aliyev to take over without making a fuss because he believed the tough, acute political operator would defend Azerbaijan's independence.

"I left the door open for Aliyev. I thought, he won't let Russia back in. Remember, Soviet Russia had crushed him and thrown him out," he said.

As I picked at Elchibey's offerings of Turkish chocolates and small saucers of jam, he went on to speak warmly of Aliyev's achievements since taking over free Azerbaijan: not handing the country back to the Russians, keeping the Iranians at arms' length and bringing in Western oil companies as a guarantee of Azerbaijan's independence. Elchibey reckoned both he and Aliyev were Azeri Turkish patriots, even though Aliyev was presiding over what Elchibey called a "mafia economy," was having Elchibey's car tailed whenever he drove about town and had jailed more than 100 of his National Front faithful.

It was true that Aliyev kept up much of Elchibey's Turkic nationalist agenda, even if haphazardly. The touchstone of this was seeing through the change in the script of the Azeri language from Soviet-era Cyrillic, the alphabet used for Russian, to Turkish-style Roman. The change had been one of the first decrees of the independent Azerbaijani parliament in 1991, but for years it got little further than shopsigns and newspaper mastheads. Today few children under the age of 10 know much Cyrillic. In 2000, Aliyev ordered a determined campaign to Latinize everything.

For Elchibey, it was all a question of time. Azeris were just backward, oppressed, poor, rural folk seeking education and justice. His voice took on a dreamy quality as he described their identity as part of more than 100 million Turkic-speaking people. He believed Azerbaijan was just one player in a Turkic world consisting of "maligned slaves" who had to work together for freedom. Aliyev, he said, had a simpler vision of an independent role for Azerbaijan that would be under nobody's heel any more.

"I respect him for that," Elchibey said.

When Elchibey died in 2000 of cancer at the age of 62, Aliyev gave him a state funeral. Some in the mourning crowds booed him, but that slid off him like water off an old crocodile's back. He buried his predecessor in Baku under a tombstone that reads: "Here Lies a Great Turkish Soldier." That is over-generous, considering that Elchibey's wartime failures and economic management alienated Azeris from his faith in a new beginning for the Turkic peoples. On the other hand, when pushed for a statement of their ultimate identity, many Azeris now agree that to some extent they are—as the Armenians had said all along—'Turks inside.'

When Aliyev himself died at the age of 80 in 2003, the barons of the old man's court managed a smooth transition to his son and heir, Ilham. In case anybody should get any ideas about real political change, his inauguration was accompanied by a showy display of police brutality against opposition rallies, electoral fraud and intimidation of journalists. Ilham, a smooth talker who had been learning the ropes as deputy head of the state oil company, went on to make the usual grand statements about Azerbaijan's "lucky future," "great projects" and his stubborn determination to uphold the authoritarian mantra, "stability." Azerbaijan then settled huffily back into its habitual harness. Ilham, it turned out, was not unpopular. And when leading Elchibey nationalists were gradually let out of jail, they, like many Azeris, went to pay their last respects at Haidar Aliyev's grave.

As the years went by an increased sense of confidence in an Azeri-Turkish identity could be felt everywhere, from the newly bustling shopping streets in central Baku to the emergence of Latin-script websites discussing the country's future. It had come a long way from the grim emptiness of Baku in 1990, or the old man in Elchibey's home village who told me of the humiliation of Soviet-era visits to Baku, where he could speak no Russian and few would speak Azeri to him. A similar, if slower, change is in progress in the Turkic states of Central Asia.

The country with the hardest task was doubtless Kazakhstan. A grueling experience of Soviet history stripped the Kazakhs of most bearers of their history, and in the period after independence a new Kazakh identity only reasserted itself slowly. More interesting, perhaps, was the way the former Soviet chief of the republic set about creating a multi-ethnic identity for his new state—and turned it into one of the most successful countries in the former Soviet Union.

8. OIL, MINERALS, DEMOCRACY!

A KAZAKH KHAN FINDS RICHES,
BUT CRAVES RESPECT

Returning from his flocks, pleased with his ride
Again in the aul appears the bai
His horse goes on with an easy stride,
He sits and smiles upon it, hat awry.

—ABAI KUNANBAIULI, poet and Kazakh bai,
or clan leader, 1845-1904

AMONG THE FIVE TURKIC STATES THAT EMERGED FROM THE BREAK-UP OF the Soviet Union in 1991, it was without doubt Kazakhstan that, a decade and a half later, had pulled farthest ahead. Broad growth lifted the country's economic output 50% in the four years to 2005, a rate close to Asia's fastest growing economies in China and India. An oil revenue windfall and major industries exporting steel, coal, wheat, copper, zinc and titanium were creating the beginnings of a regional financial center among the pleasant, leafy boulevards of Almaty, Kazakhstan's biggest city. A new middle class was taking root, able and willing to sign up for 20-year mortgages from dependable Kazakh banks that issued investment-grade bonds. Oil exports of 1.1 million barrels a day, already on a par with Libya or Algeria, were advancing through multiple export routes toward a target of three million barrels a day by 2015, a critical few percentage points of supply in a world hungry for energy.

It wasn't initially obvious that Kazakhstan would break away from the pack. Until the mid-1990s, neighboring Uzbekistan succeeded in maintaining its Soviet-era status and standard of living as the region's industrial powerhouse by hewing to state economic planning.

Kazakhstan, on the other hand, freed markets and within three years was rewarded with hyperinflation and near-economic collapse. Its leadership was inexperienced and its parliament ineffective. Visiting the country felt surreal. By 1999, the population of Kazakhstan had fallen to 15 million people, down from about 17 million a decade before; the country counts a million square miles, about the size of Western Europe, and it felt unnervingly empty. An outsider couldn't easily work out who or what was the power in the land. Diplomats muttered about a "kleptocracy" and well-justified rumors swirled of heady corruption as international oil companies snapped up oilfields. I met impoverished provincial Kazakhs who talked of a dismal life without utilities and burning floorboards to keep warm in the icy winter of the steppe. Interviews with Kazakh leaders were difficult to arrange and even harder to put into a recognizable context. Honest officers of the state who would actually see me seemed out of the loop. One of my early interviews with a governor of the central bank was interrupted by a phone call that confused him. "No!" he ended up saying into the chipped handset made of discolored Soviet plastic. "This isn't a shop. It's a bank!" What surprised me more than a random wrong number reaching a senior official was that it took a whole minute for him to work it out.

In the mid-1990s, however, Kazakhstan subtly changed course. Energy assets may have been sold off cheap, but at least they were being developed. By 2004, foreign investment reached $25 billion, only 45% directly into the oil and gas sector, substantially more than the sums foreign companies had entrusted to Russia's far bigger economy. One state-run and 12 private pension funds managed $3.1 billion in assets. A national oil fund on a Norwegian model to protect the country against price fluctuations had $3.7 billion under management. By 2005, Kazakhstan's average income per capita had risen to $2,500. There remained plenty to criticize, but one comparison was inescapable: neighboring Uzbekistan's per capita income was languishing at around $350, and, according to the U.S. State Department, was set to fall further. Ethnic Kazakhs in Uzbekistan, even those used to the formerly sophisticated delights of the Uzbek capital and Central Asia's biggest city, Tashkent, were queuing up at the embassy for permission to emigrate to their new motherland.

Undoubtedly, the rise in oil prices after 1998 helped change Kazakhstan's fortunes. So did a more stable situation in Russia—the two countries share one of the world's longest borders, and 27% of Kazakhtan's population is Russian. Although his record is flawed, one main reason for Kazakhstan's progress is the uncharismatic, possessive but steady leadership of Kazakhstan's President Nursultan Nazarbayev. Born to a peasant family in 1940, he joined a steel factory and overcame Slav dominance of industrial work to become one of Soviet Kazakhstan's first ethnic Kazakh steelworkers. He joined the communist party and rose through the ranks to become the last Soviet party chief of the country. In 1991, he was elected president of the independent republic. As was the fashion, he took 98.7% of the vote.

Ten years after I first asked for an interview with Nazarbayev, my wish was granted in 2003. He was still grandly hard to reach: my meeting was scheduled aboard his new presidential Boeing 767 on a flight from Kazakhstan to Singapore. I was shown to a seat at the back of the plane alongside Kazakh journalists and a troupe of slick bodyguards. In the Turkic world, there is often a thin dividing line between the press and the police.

After take-off, the foreign minister invited me up to the first class area for high officials, and I settled into a luxurious armchair in cream-colored leather. He told me the plane had cost $80 million. "It's amazing," he said. "Ten years ago such a sum would have seemed absurd. Now we can find it quite easily." The central bank governor called me over afterwards and drilled me with information about how Kazakhstan's oil fund would save it from the boom-and-bust cycles of other oil economies. He was a tall, trim ethnic Russian of frank and intellectual bearing and I warmed to him for his choice of entertainment for the journey: an English paperback copy of Rudyard Kipling's *Kim*, a tale of Great Game derring-do between Russians and Britons on the Central Asian frontiers of India. Few of his Kazakh colleagues were reading, a Turkic trait that is most staringly obvious on Istanbul's metropolitan railway, where, in contrast to London's shy, nose-buried-in-the-papers underground, the Turks' main pastime is looking other passengers in the eye. We all jumped to our feet when Nazarbayev appeared through a door in the bulkhead, casually dressed in a zippered cardigan and striped blue polo shirt, and invited me into his airborne conference chamber.

I complimented the president on his plane, and asked what made him feel best about the new Kazakhstan. Even he seemed to be barely able to believe the recent good fortune of his country. He had just paid off Kazakhstan's debts to the International Monetary Fund a full eight years in advance.

"I felt very good. The IMF closed their office and said: "Thank you very much, Mr. President. You don't need us here anymore.' Ten years ago, we were only dreaming of this prosperity," he said. "We didn't have a presidential plane. We even had to ask businessmen to pay for kerosene to fly anywhere. They had to pay for our officials' hotel rooms, too."

For 90 minutes we half-shouted questions and answers back and forth over the roar of the engines. When I asked whether he was grooming his daughter Dariga Nazarbayeva as a possible successor, he joked that he wasn't creating a monarchy but thought the U.S. model of President George Bush & Son would do. He only showed a hint of irritation when I edged the conversation round to corruption. Nazarbayev said he "paid no attention" to a U.S. indictment of his former American adviser on oil deals, investment banker James Giffen. U.S. prosecutors are looking into $78 million paid by oil majors through Giffen into Swiss bank accounts, including one in the president's name. "American companies should be grateful [to Giffen] because he brought them to Kazakhstan," Nazarbayev said.

But he argued that countries like his couldn't succeed without a strong-willed leader ready to make mistakes and move on.

"There was no such thing as Kazakhstan. It was just a chunk of the Soviet Union," he said. "I had to build a country, to establish an army, our own police, our internal life, everything from roads to the constitution. I had to change the minds of the people 180 degrees, from totalitarian regime to freedom, from state property to private property. Nobody wanted to understand that. My comrades from the communist party were against me. I had to train myself too . . . I wasn't raised with democracy and freedom of speech."

Once over the shock and disruption of the first years of independence, Nazarbayev made a new start. In 1995, he changed the constitution into a more firmly presidential system. In 1997, he moved the Kazakh capital from Almaty, tucked into the southeastern corner of the country, to an old central city which was renamed Astana, the Kazakh for capital. His daughter Dariga Nazarbayeva later told me that domestic opposition to the move was high, but that the president had several reasons to go ahead: to minimize the risk of damage to the capital by earthquakes, to mix up the Kazakh and Russian populations and to shift the nerve center of his country away from the border with China. Some people said it was so that the capital would not be dominated by any one of the three main Kazakh tribal groupings. I felt that he also wanted to make his mark, like the Kazakh khans of old, who had all founded a new capital upon taking power, or like Atatürk, who moved the Turkish capital from Istanbul to Ankara in 1923. Nazarbayev himself talked about Astana as if it was a beloved hobby. He dismissed the importance of a fancy Japanese design for the urban layout. Pride rose in his voice as he boasted that barely a nail was hammered or wall painted that did not fit into his personal plan for the city.

"That design is just a piece of paper. I'm the architect. Pushkin has a poem in which he says, I build myself a monument, but not by my hands. I'm saying, I build myself a monument, but with my own hands," he told me. He punched his point home by reaching over and grabbing my side of his plane's conference room table, letting me see just how strong his muscled forearm still was from 10 years of manhandling red-hot furnaces. "In Oriental countries they respect very much their leaders," he continued. "Some people approached me saying they would like to raise a monument to me like they do in Turkmenistan for Turkmenbashy. I asked, what for? Astana is my memorial."

The new capital is still under construction, and nobody will ever do away with its lack of vegetation, or the plagues of mosquitos in summer and the freezing gales that sweep in from the steppe in winter. But it has already been transformed since Soviet times. Luxury towers are rising alongside refurbished ranks of old concrete apartment blocks. Central Asia's only monument to the victims of totalitarianism, a great spike driven through a barrow-like mound of stone, is a reminder of how much the Kazakhs suffered from Soviet purges and policies, not least the "virgin lands" campaign that ploughed the land around Astana into a bread bowl for the Soviet Union and devastated the nomad lives of the original inhabitants. The centerpiece of the new city is a curved circle of tall, grandiose ministries rising up from the flat, empty plain. The most striking building already up is the marble-clad ministry of oil and gas, a cartoon fantasy castle blended with the chutzpah of the Stalinist wedding-cake towers of Moscow. As I watched steam rise from vents high in the superstructure, hanging langorously in the still, metallic cold of a beautiful midwinter dawn, I felt myself to be on another planet.

Nearby, an elegant if little-used new mosque built by a Persian Gulf state stands on a major new highway. In honor of Nazarbayev's determination to balance Kazakhstan's new Muslim identity with its remaining Russian Orthodox minority, there is also a Russian-style oriental dome to house a temple of interfaith understanding. The model of a possible 300-foot high pyramid for the same interfaith purpose stands on display in a municipal hall near ambitious models of the future city and photographs of the Great Wall of China, the Parthenon and Italy's Leaning Tower of Pisa. "The pyramid is designed by Norman Foster, but the idea is of course our president's," said chief architect Vladimir Laptev. The one internationally accepted role Nazarbayev has found for himself is indeed as the host of occasional high-profile summits between leaders of world faiths.

Nazarbayev has presided over many other changes in Kazakhstan since independence, although it is often hard to tell what is directly attributable to him. Watching him working informally with his often talented ministers after my interview in the plane, my impression was of a hard-driving and collegial ruler. The Kazakh language is now gaining power in the public domain after decades in which it was starved of any sense of being a national medium for social, political or economic advancement. In 1997 it was made the state language, the learning of which would be obligatory for Russians and Kazakhs alike. Half of television broadcasts had to be in Kazakh; at times, news items would be laboriously read out sentence by sentence by alternating Kazakh and Russian newsreaders. Laws began to be drafted in Russian, translated into Kazakh, and then rendered back into Russian again. I drove up to the snowy mountains above Almaty one day with Tanyar, a 25-year-old communications engineer, and his wife. They were tall, slender, subdued, and looked utterly Kazakh with an aloof, Eurasian universality about their full-moon faces. They spoke Russian together. "We were educated that way," Tanyar told me, steering his Russian Zhiguli past a new all-Kazakh military unit jogging between snowdrifts. "But we want our children to grow up speaking Kazakh."

Kazakhs are now being preferred for senior posts, and those ethnic Russians who stay find that they have to accept a second-class role. Over a mid-1990s lunch at one of Almaty's new Turkish restaurants, an unhappy Russian diplomat with a grimy shirt collar bitterly complained about what he thought of as exile in a far-flung province, helping dismantle the empire he had once represented. He dealt daily with queues of ethnic Russians wanting to leave. Likewise, many citizens of Kazakhstan who could prove descent from the ethnic Germans whom Stalin exiled to Kazakhstan during the Second World War took up the offer of a new life in Germany. As a result, the ethnic balance, about 42% Kazakh to 38% Russian at independence, had changed by 2004 into a 57% Kazakh majority to 27% Russian minority. Meanwhile, about 180,000 Kazakhs have migrated to Kazakhstan from elsewhere, and Kazakhs believe there are four million more in Mongolia, China, Kazakhstan, Afghanistan and elsewhere.

Unity has always been a difficult concept for Kazakhs, despite a common language. The Kazakhs avoid categorization—a Chinese Kazakh once told me he could only recognize his kin in the street by a certain cast of the eye—and do not open up easily. The outside world has responded by variously and mistakenly naming them Kyrgyz, Uzbeks or Turks. Even the spelling of the country's official name after independence was only settled after eight years of flip-flopping between Kazakstan and Kazakhstan. The volatile sense of national identity is not new. Kazakh historians speak of a "nomadic democracy" to describe the fractious politics of independent-minded tribal groups before the 19th-century Russian conquest. "From the Volga to the Irtysh, from the Urals to Afghanistan, a solid mass of us lived, Kazakhs," wrote Ahmed Baitursinuli, editor of the nationalist newspaper *Kazakh*, published from 1913 to 1918. "Now when different people penetrate into our midst, why are we not able to live as such, a Kazakh nation?"

With a vast territory to defend, few people and no real military power, Nazarbayev necessarily followed this Kazakh tendency to accommodate more powerful outside powers—and play them off against each other if possible. He swapped nuclear weapons inherited from the Soviet Union for U.S. support and guarantees from the U.N. Security Council. In 2005, he at last won treaty recognition from Moscow of the long, Russian-populated border, giving up half of two oil fields and a village in exchange. He satisfied China with oil and pipeline concessions. At the same time at home, Nazarbayev balanced the long-oppressed Kazakhs' urge to build their own nation-state with the needs of the 43% of his citizens who are non-Kazakhs. Luckily, perhaps due to their nomad origins, the Kazakhs have a light-footed talent for adapting to other cultures: in the former Tsarist Empire and Soviet Union, as in China, they have learned the languages of their rulers well. The nationalist group that founded an independent Kazakh entity after the First World War joined the emerging Soviet Bolsheviks rather than fight them. They became the most Russophile of all the Turkic peoples, and, although Kazakh authors laid the foundations of their literary language in the 19th century, even today the Russian-educated élite can often not speak Kazakh properly. The president's own website was for years only available in Russian and English. Kazakhs are nominally Muslims, but were among the last of the Turkic peoples to convert. They wear their religion so lightly that President Nazarbayev once patronized an Almaty Christmas Ball to raise money for, among other causes, the restoration of a mosque. As for Islamic bans on alcohol, the Kazakhs are the ones to be found at the bar at any Turkic gathering. But they are firm members of the club.

"We are all Turks," President Nazarbayev told me, arguing that Kazakhs were one of the purest Turkic peoples, and listing the conquerors who had set out from his part of Central Asia since the days of Atilla the Hun. "They started conquering the world, then they overstretched themselves and they collapsed. Today's Turkish people are those who left the territory of modern Kazakhstan and settled in the country where they live now. When we meet each other, we always remember this."

Nazarbayev was however dead-set against a pan-Turkish political union. He saw the Turkic world as a loose, diverse group, like the Anglo-Saxon or Slavic countries. Master of all he surveyed, he was not about to dilute his hard-won sovereignty. He told me how he had set things straight in 1992, when the late Turkish President Turgut Özal gathered the presidents of all the newly independent Turkic states in Ankara and urged them to sign a strong declaration of common Turkic purpose.

"Everybody else was keeping silent, so I took the floor. I said, 'Mr. President, we just left the Russian Empire. We don't want to enter another empire now. Let's recall our culture, our history and our common blood, let's cooperate and trade with each other. We are all leading hard lives now, so assist us with your investments. Kazakhstan will not go further than that,'" Nazarbayev said. "Everybody took a deep breath of relief. Özal started talking about other topics."

For all his imperiousness, Nazarbayev longed for the world to respect his country's bright future and his role in it, and saw the establishment of a democratic reputation as the key to that. But a real sharing of power clashed with his own authoritarian instincts and speeches in which he urged his people to unity and discipline. He prefaced one major policy statement with the Kazakh proverb, "nothing is more remote than yesterday, and nothing closer than tomorrow," but, to his dismay, he also could not escape his past. Without some kind of real democratic accountability, it was hard to wish away the fact that everybody knew about the U.S.-endorsed corruption allegations against him personally. Nazarbayev campaigned hard to be anointed president of even a secondary crisis observer group like the Organization of Security and Cooperation in Europe. But not a single election on his watch was free or fair, to which the 55-member OSCE itself repeatedly attested.

Nazarbayev's re-election as president in 1999 was typical. The only face on the campaign billboards was that of himself, meeting coal miners or chucking children's chins. Two significant challengers were disqualified, one of whom alleged that shots were fired near him and that his main adviser was manhandled. Of the three remaining candidates, one headed the rump of the unpopular communist party, the second declined to campaign for lack of funds and the third appeared to have been tapped for comic relief.

This last was Gany Kasimov, head of the Kazakh customs agency.

During one appearance on Kazakh state television, the interviewer asked him if he was brave. Kasimov seized a wine glass and crushed it in his bare hand. The cameraman zoomed up close to show Kasimov's fingers bleeding. In another show he threw a metal jug of flowers in the direction of his interviewer.

"Why did you do that?" I asked Kasimov later.

"It was the only way I could attract attention," he said.

At that moment, a campaign bus went by under the window, slogans blaring from a loudspeaker. I strained to hear the message—as did Kasimov.

"Oh!" he suddenly realized with a chumpish smile. "That's mine!"

Unsurprisingly, Nazarbayev won a new seven-year term with 79.8% of the vote. But this couldn't win him the international acceptance that he craved. His lieutenants cast about for a way to win broader acceptance of the next major poll, the 2004 parliamentary elections. The Senate, or upper house of the Kazakhstan parliament, decided to invite a multinational group of journalists to hear about several improvements made to the electoral system. I jumped at the opportunity to go. The attraction wasn't so much what they would say as the fact that Kazakh leaders would speak to me at all. It seemed like an opening up, perhaps a signal of democratization.

The Senate was trying hard. The first people they took us to see were a group of uncontrollable Kazakh democracy activists. And although they described a fairly bleak political outlook, the activists agreed when pressed that the system was theoretically improving, that the government was setting the right rhetorical tone, and that local officials were beginning to listen to non-government organizations. But they remained intensely suspicious, with reason, as it turned out, of innovations like paperless electronic voting that included a PIN code issued at workplaces. My relative ignorance of the recent historic details that are the reference points of such campaigners made it hard to grasp the real scope of the difficulties they experienced. It was only toward the end of the discussion that I realized that one of our interlocutors, Andrei Grishin, a lanky writer-editor affiliated to an International Bureau of Human Rights, had been grabbed in the street four years before by persons unknown, beaten badly, daubed in paint and warned about his criticism of the president.

"You can write anything, but there are consequences. The most dangerous topic is the president, his financial affairs, his family," Grishin said.

"But do you see any improvement?" I asked, braving Grishin's expression of disbelief at this positivist line of questioning. After all, I noted, nobody seemed to have been beaten for a few years.

"OK, the situation is radically different," he said with a trace of mockery. "Put it like this. If there are cases of beating, it's much less hard."

When Grishin's beating happened, he had been a member of a "Committee in Support of the Anti-Imperialist Struggle," which described itself as a "revolutionary youth organization." Perhaps there were reasons for distrust on both sides of the divide between the government and its critics. Now the government seemed to want to be seen taking some first steps towards a new relationship. Certainly, there was a long way to go. But I had seen how, given education, stability, prosperity and outside encouragement, ever-broader, multi-party democratic trust had replaced single-party rule in Turkey. It had also taken time: five decades and counting.

I hoped for some clarification of Kazakhstan's rights and wrongs over lunch with some of Almaty's leading newspaper editors, but I was disappointed. The journalists seemed powerless. Big television channels dominated the media, and Nazarbayev and his daughter Dariga Nazarbayeva controlled them. A bloody dog's head had been left at the doorstep of one stubbornly dissident writer, beatings were still fresh in their memory and some journalists were still in exile. For sure, no journalists were currently in jail, minor television channels were free to favor opposition parties and hundreds of small newspaper titles in the country were supposedly independent. All voiced satisfaction with Kazakhstan's culture of inter-ethnic harmony. But the editor of *Izvestia*'s Kazakhstan edition said there was no transparency about who owned the papers, let alone the information they printed. He questioned popular readiness for democracy in a country where, for the past six months, the 1,000 people living in his apartment block couldn't be bothered to show up to a meeting to elect a new building administrator.

"Nobody is sweeping the street in front of the building. People just do not care," he said, blaming the sweet dependency of the Soviet system. "We're used to thinking someone will care for us, and that we don't have to do anything for ourselves."

The editor of *Respublika*, a combatitive newspaper that suffered much official harassment for its attacks on the system, quietly said it would make no difference to Nazarbayev who actually won, since the parties likely to do best were all pro-presidential. The real question for her was where the oil money was going. I began to feel guilty about the government-bought Norwegian salmon and caviar on the plates in front of us.

"Society just wants transparency of these oil contracts," she said. "People trust neither the foreign oil companies, nor our own national oil company."

Up in the capital, Astana, I began to get a better feel for the inner workings of the Kazakh political machine. After a dinner round a table that groaned with cold sliced horsemeat sausage and other delicacies, I asked my host, three-term Senator Beksultan Tutkushev, what he thought about official corruption.

"In some countries there's a little corruption, in some places a lot. Here we have a lot. Not many of our initiatives result in anything being done about it," he replied with the disarming frankness that is part of the new Kazakhstan. "But the corruption started decreasing after 1995. It's not as easy as it was then. The people want these changes. So does the president and our foreign partners. The people who are corrupted are very disappointed by these trends. But when there's a lack of democratization, it's very hard to make changes."

I asked him about the future of all the oil contracts with international oil companies, the wellspring of Kazakhstan's flush finances. The investment climate was becoming rougher as Kazakhstan increasingly tried hardball tax tactics to win back revenue from assets that even the senator felt were sold off too cheaply at a moment of national weakness. I imagined that this counterattack was both because younger and increasingly nationalistic Kazakh officials saw the contracts as delegitimized by the reports of corrupt practices, and also because their more bribable elders were frightened of being caught out.

"I've been hearing about these contracts for eight years. I haven't seen one of them. We sell so much of our oil to little offshore islands. We request information about it, but we are always told, 'it's a commercial secret.' I feel like I'm being robbed," the senator said, echoing the tone of the editors and democracy activists.

"What do you think about the president's own involvement?" I asked, wondering whether to accept a waiter's offer of an after-dinner glass of 25-year-old malt whisky or an expensive-looking cognac. Tutkushev had barely touched his food, quoting the Kazakh proverb, "eat well before you entertain guests." He was talking freely instead.

"Presidents come and go. The people stay," he said, and listed rulers around the world who had been punished for their actions long after falling from power.

Just as I thought I was to learn about high-placed opposition to Nazarbayev, perhaps in the name of the rule of law backed by a freely elected assembly, Tutkushev pushed back his chair, crossed his legs and lit a cigarette. "Funny thing, you know, we just signed a bill forbidding smoking in public places," he quipped, laughing at my surprise to see someone breaking his own law. "You don't need to tell me. I'm a surgeon, I know how bad it is for you. I've cut up lungs completely choked with tar."

Confusion of perspective seemed to be the order of the day as the authorities rolled out their election machine for our inspection. I took tea with the head of the election commission, a fine-looking woman with a sculpted helmet of black hair, who turned out to be a close friend of Nazarbayev's politically ambitious daughter. "We divide our friendship and our working lives," Zagipa Baliyeva said. "Please don't believe [I'd be biased]. I'm good."

With that, she shrugged off the observation that she had presided over internationally criticized elections since 1995. She smoothed away with legalisms the list of complaints by opposition parties: lack of access to billboards, local administrative bodies backing pro-presidential candidates, municipal trucks blocking access to town squares before rallies, the house arrest of one main opposition leader and folk bands sent by mysterious authorities to play at top volume in city halls rented for opposition political meetings.

"Please call us anytime you need any information," she purred as I left.

Over at the parliament, all the officials seemed to have the same tailor, haircut and committed-to-noble-action expression as President Nazarbayev's official portraits. Speaker of Parliament Zharmakhan Tuyakbay gave his take on why democracy was so difficult for Kazakhstan to digest.

"It's our past. We only had one party. Political parties haven't learned to elaborate competing policies," he said. "Our president has a lot of power, it's true; but when our parliament had a lot of power before 1995, it was unable to do anything. Our task is to create a legislative base."

Over an opulent dinner served with bone china, silver cutlery and excellent French wines in a ballroom in Astana's wildly expensive best hotel, Senate chief Nurtai Abykayev, known in Kazakhstan as Nazarbayev's "gray cardinal," admitted that Kazakh democracy was "a work in progress." He insisted that there were advances. "Some people thought freedom was complete freedom and arbitrariness. In the first years it was important to keep strong power to keep stability. Now we've overtaken many countries in the region," he said. For him, the end justified the means.

It was hard to deny that things were getting more open, at least. We were even taken through a tortuous maze of corridors to see the chiefs of the Kazakhstan KGB. I tested them with a question about the truth of Andrei Grishin's observation that democratization meant the beatings were getting less hard. In the back row of our conference chamber, a line of colonels stifled guffaws. Bozhko Karpovich, the KGB's deputy head, did a policeman's best attempt to stay straight-faced. "Haven't heard of anybody beating the opposition in my two and a half years in this position," he said.

On a more sober note, his boss pointed out one real achievement of Nazarbayev's many balancing acts. "So far we are blessed with no terror attacks," said Nartay Dutbayev. "This is due to the domestic and international policy of Kazakhstan. We have no strong conflicts in the country."

I glimpsed more of Kazakhstan's democratizing soul when Nazarbayev's daughter Dariga Nazerbayeva joined us for a long dinner in an exclusive club high on the slopes of the mountain overlooking Almaty. She appeared in a svelte and attractive twin-set after another day's hard campaigning with her All Together Party, founded the year before.

Listening to her talking, it was tempting to see her as a strong-headed and rebellious daughter trying to earn her patriarch father's respect and love—and prise him out of the grip of his old communist party comrades, men who had doubtless deprived her of his company as she grew up. Just the day before, she said, gleefully raising her hand to her mouth in mock regret, Nazarbayev had telephoned her to make an angry complaint about one of her attacks on his party faithful as hollow yes-men. She was also scornful of her mother for watching television sitcoms all day, not reading newspapers and paying no attention to politics. "She's a bit naïve," Nazarbayeva said.

Nazarbayeva, 41 years old in 2004, also seemed naïve to be talking so openly to reporters, but she was was certainly readying herself for a more competitive political future. One big metal-extracting industrialist I met complained about her campaigning among his mineworkers, impressively deep in the middle of nowhere. From the coyness of her denial, there was little doubt that her eye was on the presidential election of 2013, following in the steps of the other latterday "republican monarchies" like Azerbaijan and Syria. She seemed to see the main threat to her chances from Almaty's new bourgeoisie. It was tempting to take Nazerbayeva seriously as she talked of the need for Kazakhstan to promote the social progressiveness it shares with other Turkic states to show the Muslim world an alternative to fundamentalism. But then the subject of her foreshortened career as an opera singer came up, and she damaged her credibility somewhat. "Ah, singing! I love it!" she said. "When I sing it's like I'm taking a shower."

Nazarbayeva didn't do very well in the 2004 elections, coming in third and winning just four of the 77 seats. The poll was calm and efficiently rigged in favor of Otan, Nazarbayev's party of government, which won 42 seats. The OSCE listed "serious shortcomings." But its report also noted progress toward a more open political system in the registration of opposition parties, lack of media harassment and television debates. Otan was allowed to be seen winning just 60% of the national vote. Such circumstances were unimaginable in Uzbekistan or Turkmenistan.

"The problem for us is that we don't want to be compared to Uzbekistan. We want to be compared to Turkey or Eastern Europe," said

Oraz Jandosov, one of the architects of Kazakhstan's success as a former director of the Kazakh central bank. He was now one of several young Kazakh high-flyers who set up the leading moderate opposition party Ak Zhol, with financial backing from some of Almaty's most influential bankers. Ak Zhol won just one seat, which it spurned.

Nazarbayev also wanted to leap past comparisons to Uzbekistan, and even Russia, boasting that Kazakhstan's financial rating put it in eastern Europe. But he was impatient on the political front, perhaps worrying about the slow but inexorable advance of the corruption case in New York against his former oil deal adviser. Like many an oil state before him, he tried to buy himself a better reputation. The government ordered an extraordinary message to be plastered in big type on full-page advertisements in national newspapers in Europe and America: "Today, Kazakhstan has another asset besides oil, gas and minerals. Democracy." Nazarbayev followed it up with a speech to the diplomatic corps in which he outlined yet more steps toward widening civil rights and fighting corruption.

For foreign embassies, however, the new democracy was beginning to expose cracks in the regime's façade. Speaker of parliament Tuyakbay resigned his seat, calling the election a "farce." He avoided directly attacking Nazarbayev, but was clearly positioning himself as another possible candidate in the 2006 presidential election. Perhaps he was hoping to stage a follow-up to the Rose Revolution of Georgia and the Orange Revolution of Ukraine, in which reform-minded officials who had once been close to the president toppled their ex-Soviet masters. Those regime changes certainly rattled Nazarbayev, who condemned them as foreign-financed and a sellout to the United States, which he seemed to feel was conducting an irrational blood feud against him with its corruption cases and pressure for immediate full democracy. In January 2005, Nazarbayev lost patience with the most virulent opposition party, Democratic Choice, which took the line that he was the base of all corruption in the country. The party had rejected the election outright, and called for civil disobedience. Nazarbayev closed it down.

Still, especially when one took into account the impressive bureaucrats of the Kazakh central bank and the increasingly international bankers of Almaty, it was hard to believe that Kazakhstan, at least in the medium term, was heading in the wrong direction. Turkey showed that democratic and secular governance could work in a Muslim society, however rough the edges might seem to Westerners, and the Kazakhs had a Soviet legacy of better formal education than the Turks. A tide of more open governance was rising in Azerbaijan, however chaotically, and beginning to lift Kazakhstan as well. It made me wonder if such a transformation could happen again among a Turkic people who experienced a year of true Turkic nationalist revolution in the late 1940s, but whose sense of an explicit national identity now seems the least well-developed of all: the Uygur Turks of China.

9. THE GHOST OF ISA BEG

KNIGHT-ERRANT OF TURKESTAN

*I was never carried away by the valuable Chinese gifts of gold,
silver, silk and sweet words. I did not forget how many Turks
who had been deceived by such things had died, how many
had been forced under the Chinese yoke.*

—Stone inscription by Bilge Kagan, an 8th century AD
Turkic ruler in what is now Mongolia

FROM HIS SPARSELY FURNISHED APARTMENT IN AN OUTER SUBURB OF
Istanbul, Isa Alptekin, the late leader of the Uygur Turks of China, never
imagined that he could free his people by force. The grand old man of
this large but little-known Turkic minority always spoke the language of
passive resistance, as did his much better-known comrade in the struggle with China for greater rights, the Dalai Lama of Tibet. Alptekin clearly felt vindicated by the fact I had sought him out for a news agency
interview in 1988, a rare moment of recognition after an extraordinary
series of protests in China during which his name had been chanted by
Uygur crowds. Alptekin chuckled lightly when I asked him if he had
agents at work, as China alleged.

"Let's just say I'm popular," the nearly blind old gentleman said, his
tall frame motionless on a sofa. Although happy to be noticed, he was not
sanguine about the outcome of the unrest in Xinjiang. The Uygurs might
number eight million souls, but they were a drop in the ocean of 1.2 billion Chinese. "We are few, and they are many," he said. "They have the
guns; we don't."

In Chinese, Xinjiang means "new borderland." In the hearts of the
Uygurs, who still number half of the population of this remote region

that makes up one-sixth of China's landmass, it is still old East Turkestan. They remember that two millennia ago China built the Great Wall to keep their unruly ancestors out. They also know that 1,200 years ago the Uygurs founded the first major Turkic state, and that Han Chinese only started arriving in large numbers after the communist takeover in the last half of the 20th century. The arrogance and high-handedness of the Beijing authorities have made them as resented among local people as they are in Tibet.

It wasn't just Isa Alptekin's archaic turns of phrase that told of his origin in a distant corner of the constellation of Turkic peoples. The pre-20th century links between western and eastern Turks were alive in his memory, too. The Ottoman Sultan Abdulaziz had sent advisers and arms to the Uygurs in China in the 1860s. "My grandfather was trained by the Ottoman officers and saw battle," he recalled. They raised a substantial army and won diplomatic recognition from both Russia and Britain in what for thirteen years would prove to be the Uygurs' most successful rebellion. "When I was five years old, my grandfather used to tell us about it, and when he got excited, he'd stand up and order us about in Istanbul Turkish: 'At ease! Attention! March! One, two, one, two!'"

The old man's mood darkened as he recounted how China crushed his experiment in Turkic nationalist government. This bloomed after the nationalist group of which Alptekin was a leading member won the region's first and last free local election in 1947, part of the confused interregnum as Russia began to disengage from Eastern Turkestan in the 1940s. It was snuffed out when the communist army of Mao-Tse Tung re-established full control in September 1949. Subsequent resistance, mainly from Uygurs and Kazakhs, was stamped out. Waves of Turkic refugees scattered for safety. Isa, his family and 450 others fled in mid-winter to Pakistan over the 14,000-foot passes of the Karakorum mountain range. One of Alptekin's sons, Arslan, today living in Istanbul, was five years old during the 10-week trek. The pain, cold and misery were so intense, Arslan would later tell me, that he even saw a horse weep. The frostbitten toes of one of his feet had to be amputated when they arrived in Pakistan. His younger sister died.

In the ensuing years of exile, Alptekin traveled widely to drum up international support for the Uygur cause. Like his ally, the Dalai Lama, he preached against violence, terrorism, intolerance or Islamic fundamentalism. But he died without seeing his native land again.

My first conversation with the elder Alptekin lasted all afternoon. Little did I realize that our chat would lead me, more than a decade later, to his birthplace in Yengisar, on the edge of the Taklamakan desert in northwestern China, nearly 2500 miles away from where I sat. Much had changed by then. The old man had died in 1995. The last time I saw him was on a chilly winter morning, and he was depressed. It was soon after Azerbaijan's "Black January" in 1990, and he believed the Soviet government had crushed the Azeri Popular Front in order to send a warning shot across the bow of all nationalist movements active in other Turkic republics. I asked him whether the bravery of the Azeris would inspire the Uygurs.

"There is a thrill going through the Turkic world," he said. When I asked what this meant for the Uygurs, he paused. He spoke of the need for caution, remembering his own futile attempts to enlist international help in the past. He correctly predicted that the Turkish state would do nothing for his people. In the late 1990s, in order not to offend China, it re-issued a ban on the public display of the blue-and-white star-and-crescent of East Turkestan, even as Uygur youths were being sentenced to death for hanging it on the vast statue of Mao in Kashgar.

"A little help would have meant a lot to us," Isa sighed. "It would have told us we were not alone, that we had a friend, that we could one day be happy too."

It was in Kashgar in 1999 that I boarded a crowded bus to reach Isa Alptekin's birthplace. The two-hour journey to Yengisar was a bumpy ride. Chinese workers swarmed over the highway leading out of town. They were busy knitting mats of steel reinforcing bars to turn it into a vast concrete boulevard. The new carriageway looked able to carry columns of tanks, which was probably the point. Alongside the raw swathe that Chinese roadbuilders had cut through the ancient fabric of the city, mudbrick Uygur houses and gardens lay ripped open and abandoned. By the time we reached the outskirts, dust kicked up by this and other engineering works had brought visibility down to a few dozen yards. The leveling of the ancient city had been going on for decades. Militants of Mao's Cultural Revolution had started in the 1960s by cutting down the trees that used to shade the roads. Next to go were the cooling water channels that ran beside the streets. Now, apparently, it was the turn of the streets themselves to be erased from memory.

Likewise, the wide tarmac highway that entered Yengisar bulldozed right through the heart of the mud-brick town that Alptekin would have known. It was a hot midday, and there was little traffic and few passers-by on the street. Over the road from the small, white-tiled bus-station, however, people stirred among the shaded tables of the New Silk Road Muslim Restaurant. I wandered over. It was a rough-and-ready Uygur establishment where the chef, 19-year-old Suleyman, sweated over a flaming wok on a stove made of an old oil drum.

Suleyman quickly whipped me up a standard Kashgar goulash—strips of beef, green pepper, tomato, and lashings of chilli pepper—served with steamed white bread dumplings. He and his family joined me at the table, friendly and curious. They loved a joke. When I showed off my tool-filled American knife, Suleyman pulled out his Uygur blade and laughed hugely at the fear in my eyes as he played out a lightning-quick game of dagger slashing. The point flashed within fractions of an inch from my chest and arms. Later, while I ate, I asked Suleyman tentatively if anyone in Yengisar remembered someone called Isa Alptekin. He shook his head; if he recognized the name, he didn't show it. I tried Isa Beg, the name by which he is known to generations of Turkic nationalists. Suleyman seemed genuinely ignorant of it, so we went back to discussing a topic he found of much more pressing importance: how he would get the money he needed to wed.

Fortified by the hearty repast, I set out to determine whether indeed Yengisar's most famous son had become a non-person in his hometown. Shady tree-lined paths wandered between earthen roads flanked by water channels that brought a delightful coolness. Tanned children splashed happily behind little dams. Stopping from time to time at garden gates that stood ajar, I looked into the courtyards of houses. Many sported small charcoal forges and piles of scrap car parts, where craftsmen kept up a knife-making tradition that makes the name of Yengisar famous among Uygurs. A group of brightly dressed women observed my investigations and, giggling over my Turkish-style Uygur, paused to chat.

The women, too, denied knowledge of Isa Beg. But after a few whispers, they directed one of the girls, a pretty young teacher, to take me to a man called Karim, who, they said, would be able to answer my questions. As she and I headed back to the town center, she recognized a man passing by on a moped as Karim's relative. He stopped, flashing us a big smile. We hailed a horse-drawn cart and he led the way to the other side of town, past big plots of farmland fringed by tall poplar trees. We stopped at a new, concrete house of unusually grand dimensions. The relative led me through a big door and a tunnel, like the entrance to a medieval English inn. Then we were suddenly out in the sun again. Here in a courtyard oasis of greenery, sat Karim, a man in his 60s with big, heavy spectacles, a diamond-studded gold watch and a goatee beard.

Karim spoke fluent Turkish. After the usual pleasantries about my journey, I came round to the subject of Isa Beg, delicately, I thought, by talking of living in Turkey and the new park in Istanbul that had been named in his honor.

"Ah, so you're a journalist, I suppose?"

"No, no, well, perhaps a kind of writer," I lied. I felt like an imposter. China forbids foreign writers from touring Xinjiang without lengthy arrangements for guides, interpreters and minders. I had come here on a tourist visa, and all of us could be in deep trouble if my true purpose were revealed. Human rights reports cite "political conversations" as a reason that Uygurs are sentenced to many years in jail or "re-education through labor."

Karim patted me on the knee and smiled knowingly. I met his eyes and we let the subject drop. But he gave away little about the story of his life. In his childhood he had been a next-door neighbor of the Alptekin family, and had joined the column of Uygur refugees who escaped over the mountains with Isa Beg to Pakistan as the Chinese communists took over. After exile in Pakistan and India, he moved, as did several hundred Uygurs, to Saudi Arabia. Enriched by a restaurant business, he had retired to Istanbul and taken a much younger Uygur wife, Fatima. But seven years before he had given in to her entreaties that they return home to Yengisar. He had let out his Istanbul flat, and his foreign income made him a wealthy man here.

"We manage. Everything we need is smuggled between here and Turkey," Karim said.

"Are you free to travel?" I asked as he invited me to pick a peach from one of the fruit trees in the courtyard of his two-story mansion. The fruit's flesh was white, juicy and exquisite.

"Coming back is easy. Going away again is hard. They won't give us our passports. I feel like one of my parrots," Karim said, pointing to his large collection of caged birds. One of them was in a pagoda-style cage, which, paradoxically, had actually been made in Turkey.

"Is Isa Beg's house still standing? Can I visit that?"

Relatives of Isa Beg lived in the old Alptekin family house, Karim said, but his land was now buried under the asphalt of the new crossroads in the center of town. He passed me some soft apricots and slices of a watermelon brought over by Fatima. He spoke of the former delights of wandering through old Kashgar's orchards, now entombed under Chinese urban development.

"Who remembers Isa Beg? What about *The Cause of Eastern Turkestan*?" I asked, using the title of one of Isa Beg's books.

"It's finished. Oppression has buried it," he said with conviction. "There's nothing left here. People don't have enough money to think about Eastern Turkestan. Everyone is afraid."

Fear had not crushed Uygur resentment or the dreams of Isa Beg, however. Back in Kashgar, one man dared to speak openly of the Uygurs' burning ambitions. I was in the knife market, and my Turkic chatter with the owner of a knife-sharpening stone—I was trying to get a respectable edge on my personal blade, and he required me to spin it by pulling a long strap—attracted the attention of a well-dressed Uygur gentleman. He introduced himself. In his thirties and of middling height, he spoke fluent Istanbul Turkish. After awhile, our increasingly intense conversation began to draw stares in the bustling thoroughfare, and he invited me to dinner at his house that evening.

Mahmut met me at the entrance of Kashgar's great Idgah mosque. I followed him through a maze of streets into a narrow alleyway, where he suddenly ducked into a low doorway. The entrance gave no clue to what lay inside, a fine, well-kept house. Built round a spacious courtyard, it shared the comfortable privacy and the wooden-colonnaded verandah of traditional Central Asian townhouses over the mountains in Tashkent, Samarkand and Bokhara.

When we walked in, Mahmut's family was sitting on carpets on the verandah, watching television. The womenfolk looked up and were about to scatter modestly, but Mahmut told them to stay since we were going inside. Mahmut's father and brother got up to greet me with a warmth that put me at ease. My host poured water from an old, intricately beaten copper pitcher to wash my hands, catching it afterwards in a matching wide-rimmed bowl on the ground. Then I was led through to the main reception room. Mirrors winked behind white stucco tracings and intricate woodwork. After I took my seat on a floor cushion against a wall, Mahmut pointed out brass and porcelain family treasures in little onion-domed alcoves. A feast of dried nuts, fruits and melons lay on the table waiting to be eaten. The political diet, however, would have made a Chinese secret policeman choke.

"We can't get a homeland without bloodshed," Mahmut declared matter-of-factly, when I asked him an innocuous question about the Uygurs' future. "Back in the 1980s, we might have succeeded with non-violent methods. But now it's too late."

I had stumbled onto an educated Uygur who could speak candidly for the Turkic cause. It was a far cry from the caution of Isa Alptekin. Mahmut had lived abroad for many years. His father began to send his children to Turkey in the 1960s, just in case the Uygurs were driven out of Xinjiang entirely. I supposed that it was this familiarity with another world that made him comfortable confiding some of his more incendiary thoughts with me. I revealed to him my identity as a writer and assured him I would not reveal his true name. Our shared fluency in Turkish and love of Turkey facilitated communication immeasurably.

"Our model should be a violent uprising, like that of the Chechens," he continued. I protested that the prospect of an endless, unspeakably bloody civil war against a powerhouse like China was hardly an appealing model for national liberation. He shook off my objections. "The

Chinese are frightened of us," he insisted. "That's why you can't see one of them on the streets after 9 p.m. They never come into our quarter here. There's no furniture in their houses! Just one incident, and they'll all run away. All the new building you see going on is just for show."

He paused to allow his words to sink in, and then he proclaimed gravely, "In fifteen years, either China or communism will have collapsed. There will either be a democratic China, or we'll have an independent state."

A knock on the door from Mahmut's mother signaled the arrival of hot food and gave me a moment to collect my thoughts. Mahmut stood up and brought in the tray. I savored the scent rising from the deep bowls of coriander-flavored *mantı*, a kind of ravioli, a dish served throughout the Turkic world. As we began to eat, Mahmut continued his story. It was in Turkey, he said, that his nationalist consciousness was born. While living in Istanbul, he discovered that just a few hundred words separated Uygur and Turkish. He also found that he felt completely at home when visiting with other Turkic peoples, such as the Uzbeks. "The Uzbeks are the same as us," he maintained as he reached for another spoonful of food, "The only difference is in the accent. They speak in the back of the throat, we speak with our tongues."

Mahmut's profession as an importer and exporter of goods from Turkic lands, a rare incarnation of trade along the full length of the "Silk Road," seemed to fulfill his dream of Turkish togetherness. From Turkey, he ordered clothes, which are preferred in Central Asia for their quality and stylishness over competing Chinese or Pakistani brands. These arrived by truck and plane in the neighboring Kyrgyz Republic, where an Uygur partner received them, packaged them and sent them down to Kashgar over the high mountain passes. In return, appropriately enough, Mahmut sent back scarves made of silk.

I asked if Mahmut's trade with other Turkic countries-almost all of which was conducted illegally-translated into outside support for the nationalist cause.

He shrugged his shoulders. "Once we do something," he said evasively, "I'm sure we'll get support. In the meantime, all we ask is that that other Turkic countries don't sell us out."

The portents, though, were not auspicious. Support could once be counted on from the main Uygur expatriate communities in nearby Kazakhstan and the Kyrgyz Republic. The latter was even home to what may be the world's only Institute of Uygur Studies, thanks to past Soviet indulgence of the Uygurs as a tool against China. But the Soviet Union was no more and the Central Asian states were vulnerable to pressure from China. Any Uygurs there had to cease providing aid to the rebels. Mahmut's partner had been interrogated and harassed in the Kyrgyz Republic for giving interviews to a separatist radio station.

Uygur exile groups also existed in Europe, Mahmut said, particularly Germany, to where Uygur students who joined in China's 1980s pro-democracy movement had fled after the massacre in Tianammen Square in 1989. The Eastern Turkistani Union of Europe claimed at one point to have thousands of members. But amid accusations of Uygur Islamist terrorism after Sept. 11, 2001, a crackdown by the German authorities curtailed the group's ability to raise funds and remit them home.

I mentioned my meeting in Istanbul with Isa Alptekin, who had complained bitterly at the attention the outside world lavishes on Tibet, while ignoring the Uygurs. Uygurs are cold-shouldered by Muslims because they are Turks, Alptekin had said to me, and by the West because they are Muslims.

Mahmut nodded in solemn agreement, and began to recite the litany of Uygur protest and Chinese repression. The modern protest movement was born in 1985, he said, when students demonstrated against Chinese nuclear testing at Lop Nor, deep in the Taklamakan Desert. Hardliners in Beijing blamed the "open door" policy of the late 1970s-which liberalized travel, economic enterprise and mosque-building-for awakening Uygur national sentiment. Others pointed to the erosion of Russian control over its Central Asian territories, culminating in the Soviet collapse and rise of Turkic states. Whatever the cause, the violence in Xinjiang soon escalated. Riots against discrimination broke out in the late 1980s. Some crowds chanted the name of Isa Beg, prompting my colleague in Beijing to alert me in Istanbul to this novel event. Chinese police met them with teargas, bullets and mass arrests. In 1990, riot police killed up to 50 Uygur protestors at Baran, south of Kashgar, after the entire town, angered by the sudden closure of a mosque, had risen in rebellion against Chinese rule. Uygur nationalists retaliated with attacks against government targets throughout Xinjiang. The separatists even struck in Beijing, where they carried out a series of bus bombings in the early and mid-1990s.

When China launched its 'Strike Hard' campaign to crush domestic dissent in April 1996, Mahmut told me, it only strengthened Uygur hatred of the Chinese. Ten months later, during the Muslim holy month of Ramadan, Uygurs in the industrial city of Yining staged the largest demonstrations yet. Though he opposed the murder of civilians, Mahmut said he had no reservations about attacks on Chinese police or military targets. The inevitable reprisals, he said, were justified by the greater cause.

"A lot of young men are ready to die," he added, abandoning his now cold bowl of manti and calling to his mother for a new pot of pale green tea.

I had certainly met Uygurs who seemed bitter enough to follow the old Turkic proverb of suicidal rebellion: "Better to be a wolf for a day than a mouse for a hundred." But I doubted it was the case with Mahmut. He'd had his own share of run-ins with the authorities, who accused him of helping Uygur rebels. But he seemed far too pragmatic to jeopardize his comfortable standing for an abstract cause. He couldn't even challenge his mother over her decision on a bride, while he preferred his lover in Istanbul. In many ways, Mahmut seemed more of a frustrated businessman than a revolutionary.

A distant muezzin sang out the call to prayer, and our conversation drew to a close. Mahmut and his brother joined the family for prayers in the courtyard. The father declaimed the Arabic cadences in a deep, unaffected voice. It was moving to see such natural piety, passed on from father to son for generations. I was asked to leave soon afterwards. Mahmut said his mother, who had overheard snippets of our conversation, was nervous that there might be another police raid on their home.

"We don't know whom to trust," he said glumly as he led me to the door, "There are spies on every corner."

The Uygur cause could look doomed in perpetuity. It has almost no foreign support, its diaspora is fractious and far-flung, and the best-known local Uygur nationalist leader, businesswoman Rebiya Kadeer, was jailed by China for eight years and then expelled to the United States in 2005. Even then she wasn't safe. Just after she set up an Uygur rights group in Washington DC, she was injured outside her home when a man in a dry cleaning van twice smashed into her car and escaped. At a meeting in Germany in April 2004, most mainstream exile opposition groups founded a World Uygur Congress that firmly backed the late Isa Alptekin's policy of peaceful struggle to free the people of East Turkestan. But it still tussled with a rival and more aggressive East Turkestan Government in Exile, set up a few months later in the United States. It was small wonder that Isa Alptekin used to lament that the Uygurs risk extinction, like panda bears.

Still, there was another way of looking at the Uygurs' chances. China's jailing of Kadeer propelled her into Uygur public consciousness, and the adoption of her cause by groups like Amnesty International gave her international fame. Powerful outsiders were beginning to take notice: in 2004, the Uygur Association of America received $75,000 from the U.S.-funded National Endowment for Democracy, a first such grant for an Uygur exile group.

More importantly, China was not winning the hearts and minds of the Uygurs. Their resistance was not just in the fervor of their prayers or in gestures like keeping their clocks and watches two hours behind Chinese standard time on an unofficial "Xinjiang time." It was a broad cultural rejection of China that reaches its most vivid and anarchic apogee each week in the pageant of the Kashgar Sunday Market. Streams of people begin arriving at dawn, with long queues of donkey carts from Uygur villages jostling past the usual traffic of Chinese-driven motor vehicles. Plunging through narrow, dusty alleyways into the pushing crowds, I felt as if I'd landed in a different century, and, if not a separate future country, certainly a region and people that showed no sign of becoming a homogenous part of China.

In fact, I felt that as a Briton I might be culturally closer to the tidy, westernized Chinese tourists in the market than to the Uygurs, who were resolutely Central Asian. In a clearing between donkey-cart parks and animal enclosures, a street circus re-enacted the entertainments of a medieval Turkic court. An Uygur man with a reedy horn cajoled a boy tightrope walker through faked stumbles and dramatically petulant protests. The boy was slowly making his way up a thick cord strung at a steeply ascending angle from the ground towards two long poles crossed at their tips. Then came a flatter section of cord to the other end, a tall mast hung with triangular pennants. It all looked like the rigging of a sunken galleon. I later came across exactly the same set-up in an early Ottoman Turkish miniature, portraying celebrations of the circimcision of one of the sultan's sons in Istanbul. Pushing deeper into the crowded market's amorphous maze of beaten earth streets and clearings, I passed an eatery built almost entirely of smooth mud bricks. A man fed wood-en branches and old housing beams into blackened holes under caul-drons cooking on a rough and ready range. Wielding an outsize colander on a stick as a ladle, he dipped into bubbling mess to serve his customers bowls of froth and bones. The scene could have been conjured to life from a Bronze Age archaeological site.

My sense of cultural difference was underlined by the Uygur treat-ment of animals. I visited an ill-defined forum where horses were traded, and found it to be a latterday kind of slave market. Bearded men in striped gowns and turbans inspected teeth and bargained implacably. I dodged boy jockeys as they tore round a dusty clearing, testing mounts for would-be buyers. At other times these boys poked and tormented horses that were helplessly tethered up to wooden rails. Beside a ram-shackle cart stood a man surveying the scene and chewing slices of melon. He occasionally passed the rinds on to his donkey to munch on. But as often as not he followed the gesture with an absent-minded punch on the animal's nose. It was all as if the Uygurs wanted to punish the animal world for the stress of their own lives. In return, a stallion fixed me with a vengeful stare, then whacked me with a well-aimed kick. Another horse made a dramatic bid for freedom while its owner was washing it in the turgid waterway that ran beside the market. Running, bucking and kicking, the horse valiantly fought for several minutes to evade re-capture, but to no avail. Peter Fleming, a British traveler through Xinjiang in the 1930s, was horrified by Uygur attitudes, espe-cially when he passed a donkey abandoned on the roadside to die of its hideous sores. "The Turkis are completely heartless with their animals, whose breakdown is accelerated by callous neglect," he wrote. Even today, there is so little trust between man and beast that in order for a

Uygur blacksmith to shoe a horse, he has to suspend it from a great wooden frame, bound up with slings and rope bonds under its belly.

I retired for the afternoon to a one-room museum near a Muslim shrine on the outskirts of town, and found that education did not patch over that sense of Uygur-Chinese separateness. The diminutive Uygur archaeologist in charge was determined to prove that Uygurs were a fundamentally separate people as he showed me round the findings from one of Xinjiang's many 2,000-year-old tombs. All dated back long before any putative arrival of Turkic peoples to these desert oases. The centerpiece of the exhibition was a mummified corpse, which the curator insisted proved that his homeland lay beyond the Chinese pale. With growing excitement, he pointed out the Uygur-style leather soles on the dead woman's slippers—not Chinese-style layers of fabric, he declared —and the way her chin and feet were bound with a fabric band, a tradition that persists among the Uygurs to this day. The painted wooden coffin also looked like nothing in China.

"Look at the onion-dome shapes! These ancient people were certainly our ancestors, not the Chinese," he concluded with a flourish. "We Uygurs just don't know our history well."

But informed Uygurs like him were becoming more common, and their story was getting out. The Uygur catastrophe of the past half-century was partly because information about the Uygurs was so scarce, and there was thus no check on China's actions. The days are gone when the Alptekin family's great victories would be a report handed to a U.S. president by the Dalai Lama or an invitation to discuss matters at a panel in a university in Malta. China is opening up to inspection as it integrates with the world, and, in intellectual circles at least, is becoming more sensitive to domestic grievances. Both Chinese and international travelers are visiting Xinjiang as never before. Quite a few of them, to judge by some professional-looking camera equipment in the Kashgar Sunday Market, are reporters posing as tourists.

"I used to pin up each article that was published about us and just gaze at it. Now I can't keep up. There are just hundreds," Isa Beg's eldest son and political heir, Erkin Alptekin, told me in 2002. Two years later, he was elected as the first president of the World Uygur Congress, a stronger new platform that would build on his years as the General

Secretary of the Netherlands-based Unrepresented Nations and Peoples Organisation.

I left Kashgar the next day convinced that rooting out the Turkic identity of the Uygurs would not be so easy for China as it had been to destroy the character of Xinjiang's cities. The Uygurs had preserved their culture through the worst of what China could do to them. But as I traveled more widely in Xinjiang, I found that this isolated and embattled history had left many Uygurs in a brittle, explosive mood.

SECTION III

A LONELY HISTORY

*Battered by more powerful neighbors in recent centuries,
Turkic peoples are recovering and boast a wide spread
of communities that literally girdle the world*

10. THE ANT AND THE ELEPHANT

THE UYGUR STRUGGLE
TO SURVIVE CHINA

*An elephant can crush an ant with one footstep. But an
ant inside an elephant's trunk can madden it to death.*

—Uygur proverb

ASLAN'S DAGGER BLADE GLINTED IN THE LATE AFTERNOON SUNLIGHT
streaming through the pointed archways of a bare room on the roof of
the Emin mosque. The young Uygur lovingly watched the knife turn in
his hand, and conversation came to a halt. Distant donkeys brayed as
they pulled carts back from the vineyards that carpeted the ancient oasis
town of Turfan with a luxuriant green. A tock-tock-tock of hammering
floated over from mud-brick towers in which desert winds dried grapes
into small grains of sweetness. From below came the squeak of wheel-
barrows. Chinese workers were ending a day's work laying out an immaculate, soulless socialist park right beside the 300-year-old place of prayer
where we sat.

Chinese communist ideologues had long brushed aside the Muslim
identity of the monument. The authorities have named it the "Sugong
Tower," after its imposing minaret. British traveler Francis Younghusband
was no more respectful of its intricate brickwork when he passed by in
1887, saying it looked "much like a very fat factory chimney." For me,
however, the minaret was a lighthouse that marked the easternmost
promontory of my journeys through the Turkic world. The Turfan oasis
is the last large Uygur settlement on the road eastward toward China's

heartland. It lies about 500 miles west of the Great Wall. Abandoned deep in the desert lie what are said to be the remains of the Jade Gate, through which trading caravans once passed as they left the realm of undisputed Chinese sovereignty. There are Turkic communities further to the east, but here in Turfan, the Turkic world can be said to properly begin. Wooden-collonaded architecture just like the Emin mosque can be seen in medieval structures as far west as Turkey, a fragment of a Central Asian style carried along the Silk Road during the many centuries of Turkic migrations.

Aslan proudly showed the blue hilt of his knife: "Made in Kashgar," it said in English, with the S of Kashgar the wrong way around.

"Why do so many Uygurs carry knives?" I asked.

"When you go out in the dark, you feel safe with a knife," he said. "You hold it like this." The thin 22-year-old wrapped the handle in his fist, lifted the wickedly curved tip of the blade slightly upwards, and gripped the lethal weapon close to his belly. A shadow crossed his face, and the skin tightened on his high cheekbones. "If you pull out a gun, people challenge you, 'Go on, shoot.' But a dagger, they're frightened of that."

A dagger hangs in a scabbard from the waist of many Uygur men in Xinjiang. Such knives are one reason why ethnic Han Chinese newcomers, who prefer electronic pagers on their belts, steer clear of Uygur neighborhoods at night. Most Uygurs, of course, only use the blades for cutting open the melons they share with all comers throughout the summer.

Aslan resented Chinese rule. Ten years earlier, he said, the authorities had shut down a religious school in the mosque. "Small groups of students were saying bad things about the Chinese," he recalled with pride.

But daggers and the odd terrorist bomb have proven no match for the world's most populous superpower. In the lengthening shadow of the Emin mosque's minaret, the Chinese workers had finished their civilizing mission for the day. A young architect wearing rimless glasses and cargo-pocketed shorts inspected a new brick terrace. Blank-eyed workers slaked their thirst with beer and plucked with chopsticks at their dumplings. The skimpy shirts and trousers, the alcohol, the forbidden pork meat in the mosque precinct would have horrified a devout Muslim of the Middle East. Their behavior did not faze Aslan, however, who quite liked the neat lines of the park. What bothered him was that there was not one Uygur among them.

"Most of us here in Turfan are Uygurs, but not one of us can get work in our own mosque," he said.

Aslan invited me home. Once I picked up speed on my rented bicycle, he jumped up onto the rear carrier frame. In the old Uygur quarter, the centuries had worn smooth the remaining beaten-earth streets. Across a wide new boulevard we walked through a rough, narrow passage between brick walls that led to a gate in his garden wall. His family came out to greet us in a dirt courtyard. Aslan's father took me to pick a bunch of small Turfan grapes from the tangle of vines on the trellis overhead, and then his mother invited me to sit on a square platform in a corner of their garden. Aslan cut open a melon. A conversation of sorts got cautiously under way with his father Mohammed.

"How is it in Turfan?"

"It is good."

"I see you have cotton, grapes, melons . . ."

"We have cotton, grapes and melons."

"So life here is good?"

"Life is good."

Silence fell. On one level, the common language and gestures made me feel as though the Uygurs were close to other Turkic nations. On another, they seemed to know remarkably little of the world outside their almost medieval domain, or of the broad Turkic resurgence of the past decade.

"Where are you from?" Mohammed asked.

"From Istanbul, in Turkey," I responded.

"Oh, isn't Turkey Muslim?" he asked, brightening considerably.

"Yes, Turks are Muslims," I said. "But they are also Turks, like the Uygurs. Aren't Uygurs Turks as well?"

"Turks?"

The family group perched on and around the wooden platform looked puzzled before they got my meaning. The name of Turkey had a positive ring to it, but even though two of Aslan's friends were studying there, it seemed to these Uygurs to exist in another, unattainable universe. Uygurs who heard me speaking an approximation of their language assumed it was because there were Uygurs where I lived. Exiled Uygur leader Rebiya Kadeer has said that as a girl, her parens whispered the name and mission of Turkish republican founder Kemal Atatürk in her ear, but few ordinary people seemed to have heard of him.

My courage faltered in this increasingly political terrain.

"What do you think makes the Uygurs special?" I asked the assembled company as the evening darkness softened the heat into a dry, blanketing warmth.

"Once we were great," volunteered Mohammed, flexing his forearms and clenching his fist. Then, with a meaningful, silent look and a nod, he added: "We are nothing now. I'll leave it at that."

Mohammed's sense of a modern Turkic identity might have been weak, but he was aware of the Turkic empires of the past. The Uygurs first appeared in the eighth century AD in what is now Mongolia, taking over leadership of a federation of Turkic tribes from the rulers of the first explicitly "Turk" state, the Göktürks. They ruled a wide empire for a century before themselves being forced to move southeast to the area now known as Xinjiang. New leaders arose in Kashgar in the mid-tenth century, known as the Karakhanids. The first Turkic encyclopedia, the Divan ul-Lugat al-Turk, the Compendium of the Turkic Languages, was written by a Karakhanid nobleman, Mahmut of Kashgar. Around the same time, Yusuf Hass Hajib of Kashgar wrote his Kutadgu Bilig, a book of advice for princes, whose 6,700 couplets are the first work of Turkic literature. Two centuries later, when the Mongol leader Genghis Khan conquered most of Asia, the educated, literate Uygur elite supplied the bureaucracy of his empire. Later, I would meet educated Uygurs who noted with satisfaction that the Mongol, or Yuan dynasty actually ruled the whole of China for nearly a century from 1279. But the dynasty fell in 1368, and thereafter the Uygurs and Chinese began to compete for territory and trade. The name Uygur fell into disuse for centuries and was only revived by Soviet ethnic planners in 1921.

"Where did the Uygurs go wrong?" I asked Aslan's father delicately.

That question was answered with a heartfelt sigh. No one spoke. I had touched on a subject that perplexes Turkic peoples everywhere: their weakness, disunity and failures in the past century. The Uygurs have a better excuse than most: their lands were a battlefield between the far greater powers of the Soviet Union and China for the first half of the 20th century. After being cast away by Moscow in the late 1940s, Xinjiang was subjugated by China for the second half of the century.

I tried to compliment him on his bright and hardworking son, Aslan. But Aslan complained that he could not speak or write proper Chinese, which blocked his access to good work.

"I always wanted to be a mechanic," he said bitterly. "Whenever I see a broken bike, I want to fix it. TVs, watches, radios too. I'd like to open a shop. But I can't. I couldn't get the parts. We're not allowed permits to get them. The Chinese don't let us do anything. All we're supposed to do is pick our grapes."

Even a half-century ago, there were clear signs that told travelers they were passing westward from a Chinese to a Turkic domain. The high-wheeled Turkic *arba* carts cut wider ruts into roadways than did the trucks belonging to the Chinese. Bread appeared in roadside stalls, and rice became rare. The ubiquitous children's kites were thinner and flew higher, and the flat faces of the ethnic Chinese gave way to high Turkic cheekbones. The sing-song staccato of colloquial Chinese would switch to the more guttural sounds of Turkic. Today, many of these signs have vanished; the physical geography has been blurred as the Chinese expand their settlement around roads and towns and push the Uygurs to the margins. Although the main body of China is hundreds of miles to the east of Turfan, it is largely the Chinese who benefit from new highway connections like the one I followed westward to Urumqi, the capital of Xinjiang. Uygurs are condemned to a parallel economic, social and political system, their villages bypassed by the new main roads. China clearly hopes such policies will lead their culture to dry up in a desert dead-end.

I boarded an intercity bus in Turfan's characterless new main square, and soon we were skirting the edge of the Taklamakan desert. Once the bed of a great sea, it is now a forbidding expanse of sand dunes whose Turkic name means "place-where-one-gets-stuck." Merchants used to set their course by the bleached bones of dead animals. For the Chinese, travel is far easier now. The driver of the bus careered around brand-new,

still-empty toll booths. The highway was even and smooth—and, I
learned later, partly financed by the World Bank. Gas stations built to
resemble great pyramids and cartoon fantasies whizzed past, as if in defiance to the harsh desert haze that hung over us.

After an hour, the rocky east-west range of hills that divides Xinjiang
into two vast, shallow bowls loomed ahead. The bus climbed out of the
Tarim basin and up the rocky river gorge that leads to the northern
plateau. A howling wind lashed the river beside the highway into galloping waves, whipping spray off the crests in long sheets that hung in the
air over the water for dozens of yards. As we emerged onto the plain at
the top of the gorge, a gigantic icon of China's modernity stood before
us. With memories of the Uygurs in their shady, timeless Turfan oasis villages still fresh in my mind, I was amazed to encounter among the barren hills the swooping propellers of a vast complex of Chinese windmills,
purposefully feeding electricity into a network of high-tension power-
lines. With a new railway line shooting straight into the heart of distant
Kashgar, and new highways all over the territory, there is no doubting
Chinese determination to impose control. Reasons are not hard to find.
Apart from defending China's northwestern frontier, officials believe
nearly 80 billion barrels of oil may lie under the province, nearly as much
as Iraq or Iran possesses, although so far only 2.5 billion barrels of those
reserves are proven. Gold, uranium, iron and coal are also abundant.

Showing a rare willingness to integrate, the Uygur bus conductress
wore an immaculate uniform and had adopted a no-nonsense, egalitarian
style. But a tacit apartheid otherwise divided our motley caravan. While
a cheerful group of young Chinese workers noisily joked and ate at the
front, Uygur families sat impassively toward the back. One couple jointly
studied a text on how to be good Muslims, and another man cradled a
cage with two canaries. Mildred Cable, a Christian missionary who
worked here in the 1920s, wrote that the "stream of Turki and Chinese
people in the bazaar only mingles superficially for, in fact, each keeps
separate from the other and follows his own way of life. The Chinese
buys at Chinese stalls, the Turki shops among his own people and the
food vendors serve men of their own race. The mentality and outlook of
each nation are profoundly different and neither trusts the other."

By the time we pulled into the hubbub of the Urumqi bus station, it was clear that the city had changed out of all recognition since Cable's day, when the Turki town and Chinese cantonment were wholly separate. Urumqi had participated fully in China's orgy of development in the 1990s, and a dozen tall glass-fronted buildings shimmered in the baking July heat. The city's skyline had become the most modern in the whole of Central Asia. Still, on street level, I was constantly reminded of the sharp divisions between Chinese and Uygurs. My first stop was to change money at the regional headquarters of the Bank of China, set in the shiny new city center. I pushed up the steps to the entrance. I had not expected a crowd of Uygur wheeler-dealers to accompany me, each of them waving a wad of currency. I asked them to let me through.

"Don't go in there!" one scruffy fellow said, answering my Turkish. "They give a lousy rate."

The brassy Uygur surprised me by sticking to my shoulder throughout, right up to the window inside, plastered with credit card and dollar signs.

"I'd like to change dollars," I said to the Chinese bank clerk.

The clerk typed out the numbers 80.7 on a calculator. My Uygur companion coolly picked up the calculator and typed the figure 87.0. I expected a quick-stepping troupe of Chinese police to come and drag us both away at any moment. But they didn't. I looked at the young clerk, who watched me impassively. The Uygur's devil-may-care attitude made me more confident. I began to bargain.

"Give me 89," I said.

"OK, 88," he retorted.

"What about the police?" I asked.

He laughed. "Oh, they won't do anything, those Chinese. But we should step outside."

I began to walk with him. The Chinese teller betrayed no sign of interest. Outside, the moneychanger produced a fat bunch of notes and began to count them into my hand. He didn't appear to care whether I had any money myself. My trust broadened. It seemed just a small step from this pavement in China to my home street in Turkey. Turks feel honor-bound to act as though the actual transfer of money to complete a deal is a matter of supreme indifference to them. This habit can infuriate foreign business partners. But it is a boon when I step out to the shops in Istanbul and find I have forgotten my wallet.

Still, it was odd that the Urumqi bank tellers were almost exclusively Chinese, while the black market was staffed entirely by Uygurs, hungrily waiting for Chinese men in sleek cars to pull up to them and slide down their electric windows.

"Why are the Uygurs the only ones who work the currency market?" I asked as we shook hands warmly on concluding our transaction.

"There are no jobs for us," he said.

Our exchange had probably netted him a day's factory wage, but he clearly didn't regard what he did as a 'real' job. Throughout the Turkic realm, paternalistic regimes make the local population believe that the only jobs that matter are sinecures in the state bureaucracy, which often come with lifelong access to housing, health benefits, privileges and pensions. Yet official employment was hard to come by. A hard-working Uygur teller in a bank in Kashgar told me that she was one of just four Uygurs working among 25 employees in the branch, and had no hope of becoming the boss. Xinjiang Airways in-flight magazine talked of a happy family of minorities in the province. But no Uygurs were allowed to be taxi drivers at the airports. Jazzy Central Asian silk neck-bows decorated the collars of the air hostesses, but all of them appeared to be Chinese. A kind of apartheid was in operation at Urumqi airport. The Chinese restaurant above the departure hall came complete with attentive wait-resses and excellent food. The pokey little "Muslim Restaurant" could only be reached through an ouside service door, where one might have expected to find a public toilet.

The Chinese bank building was built on the edge of the Uygur quar-ter, where it dwarfed what was left of the poor, untended, two-story Uygur houses across the street. I wandered into the old neighborhood over broken pavements and dusty roadways.

"Hey!" someone called.

I stopped in my tracks on a twisting street between the houses. A neatly dressed figure squatting by a pile of melons was waving me over. His arm's urgent "come on" gesticulations were an exact pantomime of an Istanbul traffic policeman. Choosing a melon, he flashed his dagger through the yellow flesh, and we shared slice after slice of cool, succu-lent sweetness. Erkin was his name, and he explained that he owned a clothes shop in the old quarter. Ten yards behind where we squatted, Chinese bulldozers had cut another great hole in the fabric of the Uygur town. A colony of Chinese laborers was laying out the foundations of a new mammoth structure. We exchanged looks.

"The Chinese," he said flatly.

Erkin invited me back to his shop. We strolled on together through the fragmented architectural battlefield in which modernity was visibly crushing tradition as each day went by. Chinese women, scrupulously clean and purposeful, cycled by in neat short skirts and straw hats made of plastic. By contrast, the disenfranchised Uygurs of Urumqi generally adopted a ragged, shambolic look.

Private Uygur gathering places were equally unprepossessing: at one restaurant I passed with Erkin, kebabs sizzled on outdoor metal braziers, the workhorse of Turkic restaurants from here to Europe. But the grubby plates and stringy mutton seemed poor cousins to the marinated grills that emerge from under the embossed and polished copper chimney hoods of Turkish city restaurants. Here, a layer of grime seemed to coat every surface, including chairs, tables and walls.

Erkin caught me looking disapprovingly at the street scene.

"You see?" he said. "The Chinese have done nothing for this street, just because it's Uygur."

I disagreed. "Why don't local people do anything to clear up this mess?"

"What can we do?" Erkin replied with a sigh of defeat. We reached his shop, a corner of a cooperative where he had four trestle tables. The priciest, fanciest dress cost $2.50.

"Can you get rich?" I asked. From a spot near here, Rebiya Kadeer had built her Urumqi cleaning shop into a company employing 350 women workers. By the mid-1990s she had created a trading empire doing business with Central Asia and Turkey, and was fêted by Beijing as China's most successful businesswoman—and proof of hapy interethnic coexistence. But Kadeer insisted on Uygur national rights, and China jailed her a month after my visit.

"They let you do business, as long as it's just business," Erkin replied.

To prosper under Chinese rule, Uygurs had to submit and work in the small, undeveloped space allotted to them by the regime. While the Chinese built with bulldozers, steamrollers, piledrivers and tall cranes, pairs of Uygur men still solemnly swung great five-foot lengths of tree trunk in an ancient rhythm to settle foundations and beat earth floors flat. Erkin didn't need to show me the way back to the Chinese new town. A 40-story blue and silver hotel, built by the Chinese Ministry of Communications, reared up overhead like a tidal wave about to engulf the district. As I headed for it, I walked passed dwellings that had been bulldozed that very morning. The era of separate, independent canton-ments for Uygurs and Chinese described by 19th century travelers seemed to be over. Tall Chinese buildings were converging on the Uygur quarter from all sides, gobbling it up, house by house. Grim-faced Uygurs, who said they had been allocated new apartments in soulless modern apartment blocks on the edge of town, picked their way through the rubble to retrieve roofing beams, windows, doors and bed frames.

China is taking a risk by stoking up Uygur resentment while brush-ing aside Isa Alptekin's model of peaceful Uygur national development. An old Turkish proverb has it that "you can hit a Turk a ten times, and he'll do nothing. The eleventh time, he'll kill you." I was to stumble onto many signs of rising fear, stress and anger as I began my journey home to Istanbul.

I had hoped to make my first stage through the mountains into the Kyrgyz Republic.Like many a traveler before me, and the Uygurs them-selves, I found that the great mountain ranges that rise up round much of Xinjiang are often its prison, cutting its people off from the outside world. My car toiled up the foothills towards peaks wrapped in dark, angry clouds. Wide riverbeds that lay dry for much of the year over-flowed with rushing brown waters that tossed boulders and splintered tree branches like pebbles and twigs. I reached the Chinese customs gate just as a minibus full of Chinese soldiers arrived from the passes high above. The soldiers were streaked with mud and soaked to the skin. The passport officer gleefully reported that the pass would remain closed for weeks. The road had washed away.

To by-pass the mountains, I had to use Xinjiang's far-flung border with Kazakhstan. This gave me the excuse to visit Yining, known in Uygur as Guldja, the capital of the province of Ili. It was off the tourist trail, and was the scene in February 1997 of some of the worst clashes between Uygurs and the Chinese security forces. After a crackdown on Uygur traditional public discussion groups known as *meshreps* and a bloody altercation during the detention of popular religious leaders, hundreds of Uygurs had taken to the streets, shouting Islamic slogans, demanding jobs and calling for equal treatment of Uygurs. Protests, knifings of Chinese, attacks on government buildings and burnings of cars continued for two days. Riot police sealed off the city for two weeks, during which time up to 5,000 people were arrested and hundreds of detainees were treated with extreme brutality. At least nine people were killed in the disturbances, including four policemen. Nine others were later executed, mostly Uygurs.

I felt the continued raw tensions of this frontier town during my first evening meal, at a pavement restaurant in the Chinese part of town. The meal of stewed snake, cooked in a fiery sauce in a wok on my table, was challenging enough. But as I sat gnawing on an unyielding cartilage, a scuffle started outside a nearby nightclub. After much shouting and brawling, a badly beaten Chinese man emerged from the scrum in the half-darkness. His face streaked with blood, he galloped past my table to the restaurant's open-air kitchen. Grabbing a meat cleaver, he charged back, hurling the knife past my head towards his assailants. The heavy blade missed and clattered along the concrete. The combatants melted away. I was frozen in surprise. My Chinese fellow-diners watched in rapt passivity. Within seconds, it was as if nothing had happened. A chauffeur-driven car pulled up, and a sharply made-up girl stepped out and sauntered over to the nightclub doorway. She simply ignored the shadow of at least one man beaten in the scuffle, who still lay unconscious on the ground.

Back at the hotel, I asked a Chinese woman in the lobby why nobody had intervened. Her answer exposed a Chinese weakness. "The problem for us Chinese here in Xinjiang is that if an Uygur gets into a fight, all the other Uygurs come to help him. But if a Chinese person gets into a fight, all the other Chinese look the other way," she explained. When ethnic tension rose in Yining, she said, any Chinese residents who could quickly found business in China proper. Indeed, many of the Chinese I spoke to were required by law or jobs to stay in

Xinjiang, and longed to go back to the safer, developed, go-ahead east of the country.

Most Chinese depended on the central government for work. About one third of the Han Chinese population in the province, or 2.4 million people, worked in the "Bingtuan," or Xinjiang Production and Construction Corps. This organization had its origins in settlers from Mao's disbanded Chinese army units, and since 1953 it has colonized Xinjiang's borderlands. It controls nearly half of the territory of Xinjiang and works nearly one-third of its arable land. But its budget and politics answer directly to the central government. It seems possible that if state support collapses for some reason, this subsidized Chinese presence might pour out again as fast as Chinese statistics show Han Chinese are now flowing in. Something similar happened in neighboring Kazakhstan, which was taken over by Russia at about the same time as China formally annexed Xinjiang as the 'New Borderland' in 1884. When the Soviet Union fell apart and Kazakhstan won independence in 1991, ethnic Russians quickly haemorrhaged out, even though there were more Russians than Kazakhs and they had grown much closer than Chinese and Uygurs have ever done. For sure, Chinese garrisons have frequently held sway over part or all of Xinjiang since ancient times, making one name for the region "Chinese Turkestan." Mao ordered the colonization to rebalance the paradox that he himself articulated: "We say China is a country vast in territory, rich in resources and large in population; in fact, it is the Han nationality whose population is large, and the minority nationalities whose territory is vast and whose resources are rich." Still, over the centuries, the region has spun out of Beijing's control more often than not.

The next morning in Yining, I discovered that the placid appearance of an enchanting Uygur quarter was deceptive. The houses were large and comfortable, and several owners were rebuilding their houses even more grandly. In an exception to the aggrieved Uygur mainstream, the border trade had been kind to the town's Uygur entrepreneurial class. A group of young men stood chatting at an intersection.

"How are you, well?" I asked.

"How are you, well?" one of them replied, the traditional Uygur response.

"What a lovely area this is," I went on. "How old are the houses here?"

"About 70 or 100 years old. They're real Uygur houses," the man said proudly.

"How many people live in each one?"

"Eight or nine."

"How much does a house cost?"

"Oh, $4,000, $6,000, maybe $8,000 for a big one. The Chinese, you know, they have to pay $8,000 for a much smaller house elsewhere in the country."

The Uygur houses were indeed palatial by Chinese standards. This seemed to be a lovely place to live. Except for one thing. They were Uygurs in China, and for them, threats lay everywhere.

"What's that written on the wall?" I continued, pointing out the Uygur Arabic lettering that was one of the only decorations on the smooth mud plaster.

"It says, 'Don't make children,'" the man said, laughing and ruffling his young son's hair.

Sometimes one, sometimes three slogans were printed neatly across the walls next to each doorway, spray-painted through stencils. The ones I could read exhorted inhabitants to remember that "Family Planning is Good," "Making Few Babies is a Virtue" and "Few Babies is a Top Government Policy." Even though allowed one more child than Han Chinese in China's strict one-baby population control system, Central Asian tradition pushed many to try to beat the system, registering new babies with all manner of female relatives. I remembered other Uygurs talking resentfully of Chinese officials coming into their houses to feel the bellies of women, and their fear of forced abortions, carried out even late in pregnancy.

Watching me puzzle through the anti-baby slogans, one of my interlocutor's friends whispered something in his ear. Apparently a warning not to talk to me, he brushed it aside. I kept smiling.

"What happens if you have more than two children?" I asked.

"I just wouldn't," he said.

Another chipped in: "You'd have to pay a $2,000 fine."

That was a huge amount of money.

"What job do you do?" I asked the boy's father.

"None of us here has a job. We just sell shirts and socks in the market," he said.

The suspicious man intervened again. "What sort of questions are these? You'd better be careful."

"They're normal questions," the friendly man replied.

"But he asks about everything you're doing!"

"So," I said, trying to brazen it out. "It's all very quiet here, then..."

"Quiet??" the friendly man shot back.

A liquid fear surged through his body. He looked at me with wide-open eyes, went pale, and staggered back to squat at the base of a garden wall. He took his head in his hands and started shaking it from side to side. He plucked his shirt off his chest between his thumb and forefinger, and flapped it back and forth, as if to fan himself with cooling air.

"Don't ask me any more questions. I'm afraid," he said in a small voice.

Just watching him set my heart racing. It seemed so incongruous on this delightful soft suburban morning.

"I'm sorry, I don't think I understand," I started to say, backing away to beat as dignified a retreat as possible. Only later did I learn that three Uygurs who spoke to foreign reporters in Yining after the 1997 riots disappeared into the Chinese gulag, and were rumored to have been sentenced to more than 15 years in jail. The reporters were expelled.

"You should be sorry," the man's sharp-eyed comrade shouted. After I'd put a dozen yards between us, he followed with a parting shot: "Mister B.B.C."

I walked hastily out of the Uygur quarter. Its edge was marked by a squalid restaurant where a fat, sweating chef gyrated round a flaming fire, hedged in by smoke-blackened walls. Somebody hustled up behind me. I expected a policeman to grip my elbow. Instead I turned to see a mad-eyed boy waiter rushing past. He disappeared into a gap in a wall that passed as the restaurant's doorway and popped up on the other side. "You English?" he called out at me. "You want hashish? Good hashish?"

I did not need hashish to make my head spin as I made my way onto the wide modern boulevard that marked the beginning of the "civilized" Chinese part of town. I felt doubly guilty. I had no plans to betray anyone. But I had put these Uygurs in danger simply by talking to them. Then I had sought refuge in the part of town built by their Chinese oppressors.

It was hard to predict the future for one of the Turkic world's oldest settled and urban cultures. Still, as recently as the 1980s, few would have foreseen the emergence of an independent Kazakhstan or Turkmenistan, countries dominated by Soviet methods of government and whose indigenous pre-Soviet state traditions were often as fluid as that of the Uygurs. Indeed, many of the more rural Turkic populations are often barely a generation or two away from their nomad past. President Nazarbayev of Kazakhstan herded sheep in his youth, as did Turkey's former President Demirel. Some Kazakhs still make their way by truck each summer to the high pastures of northwest China. My visit to their camp was the moment on my journeys that I came closest to the Turkic idyll, a glimpse of the pre-modern life of the Central Asian hills and steppe.

11. OF YURTS AND YOGURT

THE TURKIC NOMAD HERITAGE

Come to my great yurt, the steppe
With its blue shadows and yellow winds
And look in the eyes of a camel
Separated from its mare

There it lives

—GALSAN TSCHINAG, poet, shaman and chief of
the Tuvan Turkic people of Mongolia, b. 1944

HIGH ON A PASS THROUGH CHINA'S MOUNTAINOUS BORDERLANDS WITH
Kazakhstan, I stopped my car at the first structures I had seen for many
miles. Here on the edge of Lake Sayram, truck drivers and travelers
broke their journeys at a jumble of Uygur-run eateries, mostly rusty
shipping containers with an awning stretched out on tentpoles.
Flyblown animal carcasses did service as menus from which customers
chose a cut of meat, which was then laid out to cook on a smoking brazier. What interested me more than contemplating the vast lake's
expanse was the scene above the highway along the water's edge. Just
up the slope, past putrid latrines thinly veiled by waist-high cloths
wrapped round sticks, another world began. On the grassy meadows
that stretched up into the mountains, a group from China's million-
strong Kazakh minority came each year to their yayla, or summer camp,
to graze their flocks and herds. They still lived in the domed homes
used for millennia by Mongol and Turkic peoples, whose nomad communities can put up and take down the rolls of felt and poles in a few
hours before moving on to new pastures. In Kazakh, these habitations
are called *iuw*, the same word as *ev*, now used by the Turks of Turkey

to mean house and home. Other Turkic peoples call the round shelters a yurt, the word that has passed into English, and which in Turkey now means homeland.

The yurts stood in a curving line parallel to the shore of the lake. As the late afternoon sun lit the panorama in a pale golden glow, galloping hooves drummed on the grassy tracks before them. Boys as young as a few years old charged this way and that on horseback, playing and wheeling in a chaotic competition to tempt stray Chinese sightseers into the saddle. In a fold in the hills, by a stand of tall firs, foals tethered on ropes whinnied for their mothers. Higher on the slope, the mares whinnied back. As they grazed, their long manes brushed over a thick carpet of grass, edelweiss and delicate small yellow and blue flowers. At one picket of horses, a Kazakh woman milked a mare. As night fell, Kazakh riders led herds of horses back down the mountain, dragging bundles of firewood down from the forest behind their mounts.

On the hillside above the yurts, a gray-bearded butcher in an embroidered headcap slit the throat of a sheep for a family, who then helped cut it up. Instructed by his granny, a boy rammed a pointed stick into the back of the sheep's detached head, and pushed it nose first into a mud-brick oven to singe the woolly beard off the animal's face. Back down among the yurts, cows and calves poked around the mud-brick kitchen ranges. One urinated liberally against a wall of off-white felt. Families busied themselves for the evening meal. A woman laid out lines of walnut-sized kurut, or yogurt cheeses, to dry on long planks. In and around their summer homes, families settled down to eat dinners that seemed like small feasts.

Standing with his daughters in front of his yurt, a friendly Kazakh ağa, or lord of a clan, invited me in to meet his family and guests for the evening. All sat down on a carpet-strewn wooden platform that took up most of the space. Piles of bedding were folded up at the base of the yurt's cylindrical wooden lattice wall, on which hung mementos that made their summer quarters feel like home: a painted wooden dowry box, panels of hand-stitched Central Asian suzani floral brocade, and, looking seriously down at us, a black-and-white photograph of the ağa's father and mother. Long straps of woven wool strengthened the scores of curved sticks that reached up to the dome at the top of the yurt. Their ends slotted into a circular wheel with crossed sticks, a kind of chimney that in this fine weather was open to the sky. A brass charcoal-heated samovar steamed on the semi-circle of beaten earth by the door.

The wall of the yurt was also hung with a fox skin, a wolf skin and a curious bundle of bird feathers hanging above the ağa. They looked like the fetishes used by the holy men of the ancient Turks, known as shamans. When a Byzantine ambassador met Turks for the first time in the sixth century AD, their shamans made a fire that he had to step over, scattered incense and chanted verses until any evil spirits were dispersed. Another Byzantine, Theophylactos of Simocatta, came across the same phenomenon, writing that "the Turks venerate fire to an extraordinary point, and honor air and water. They address praises to the ground, but prostrate themselves only in front of him who created the sky and the earth, and call him God. They sacrifice horses and sheep to him."

Relics of shamanistic practice and belief can be found scattered all over the Turkic world. The poet-leader of what is possibly the most remote Turkic nomad community, Galshan Tschinag of the 4,000 Tuvans of Mongolia, combines his post with that of shaman. "My first verses were shamanic chants, praises and pleas to the spirits of the rocks and trees and water that surrounded me," he told a German audience in 1999, criticizing the over-stuffed materialism of the West. "Barrenness prevails in the nomadic world . . . Yet it seems as if the outer modesty necessarily provokes a counterbalance: inner abundance." Tschinag said his inner strength was partly forged by the harsh history of his people. In the 1960s, the Mongolian state forced them off their Altay Mountain pastures and settled them in houses. Their Tuvan language was banned in education and still has no script. But thanks to a quirk of communist-era social engineering—an education in the former East Germany—Tschinag was also the first Mongolian Tuvan to write down his poems. In his works a shamanistic animism stretches the imagination with horizons of "soul-white snow" and "cloud-trapping rocks"; as his American translator Richard Hacken puts it, "a poetic first person catches fire." Tschinag describes his work as "the swansong of a culture that has been overpowered." But he proved the mettle of his nomad roots in 1995, when he led his people on a 1,300-mile migration by truck and car to resettle their ancestral grazing grounds high in the Altay Mountains.

The ağa at Lake Sayram was a man of few words. Instead his wife offered glasses of koumiss, or fermented mare's milk. It is the most traditional of Turkic drinks, even if it has now ceded much ground to cola, tea and vodka. The Turks of Turkey accord it such mythical status that an Ankara winery names one of its wines kımız, and the Mongols distil koumiss into a foul-smelling brandy. The best koumiss has a slightly bitter, lightly sparkling taste, is mildly alcoholic and is served in great quantities at rural weddings in Central Asia.

Dairy products are central to Turkic nomad cuisine. After all, if linguistic parentage proves authorship, it is the Turkic peoples who gave yogurt to the world. Central Asian nomads curdle, boil, drain, shake, strain and mix the milk of cows, sheep, mares and camels to make dozens of types of yogurts and cheeses. Some are almost liquid, others so hard they have to be ground up with a mortar and pestle. Many are listed by the eleventh century encyclopaedist Mahmut of Kashgar, like "iprük: a mixture of curdled and fresh milk which is drunk as a laxative by one who is constipated from drinking sour or churned milk."

The ağa was a solid, unflappable fellow. His wheat-colored, Asiatic features, and his short, square frame gave him a universal Turkic look. His clan of 10 yurts was prospering. Each family of herders had to look after either 300 sheep or 100 cows for the Chinese state-run collective, but any surplus animals belonged to themselves to dispose of as they wished. The ağa seemed contented. After all, nomad life was never quite the free-for-all that romantics imagine, and is better called transhumance, a well-structured alternation between summer and winter pastures. Traditional tribes like the Qashqais of Iran and others in Turkey and Central Asia still make horseback treks that last several days, even weeks. The insurance policy of a big state like China wasn't all bad, since the nomads had plenty to fear from nature. In the old days, Kazakh nomads reckoned they would suffer a devastating "jut" every dozen years, in which excessive winter freezing or summer drought would wreck pastures, decimate flocks and trigger famines. The catastrophic "jut" of 1920-21 alone wiped out half the Kazakhs' livestock.

Still, the Kazakhs of China had grievances. One student visiting his family at Sayram, when I found him alone, complained that their winter quarters, was a bare concrete town on the plain. Others whispered about the 300,000 ethnic Kazakhs who had fled Chinese collectivization to the Soviet republic of Kazakhstan. An English teacher from Urumqi whose mother lived in another yurt said that the ethnic Kazakhs who remain in China are better off than Uygurs, but are still dissatisfied. He wanted to join his ethnic brothers over the border.

"Why do you want to go to Kazakhstan?" I asked, trying to be provocative. "Think of the buildings, the money, the economic energy in Urumqi! Here, you're part of a big, powerful state. Kazakhstan is in the middle of nowhere."

"Here, it's hard for ethnic minorities to get jobs. They appoint a Kazakh here, an Uygur there. But that's just to make it look fair. Even if you're well qualified like me, they see I'm not Chinese, and say, we don't need you," he said. "The Kazakhs in Kazakhstan may be poorer, they may be lazier. But at least when you look in the face of the policeman, it's a Kazakh policeman. It's our homeland."

I was indeed privileged to be able to migrate with such ease between the different Turkic domains, where people are relatively poor, uninformed, fenced in by their own possessive governments and kept at arms' length by richer countries with no time for real nomadism. Just traveling overland from one country to another could be highly instructive, particularly the dividing line between China and the Soviet Union. This was once open steppe free-ranging Kazakh and other nomads. After decades as an impenetrable border, its border gates have now opened once more to travelers and traders .

From the heights of Sayram Lake a wide road carved through the mountains to the plains and down to the frontier with newly independent Kazakhstan. On the Chinese side of the Khorgas border point, a rash of buildings testified to the sudden spike in China-Kazakhstan exchanges over the border in the 1980s and early 1990s. Trade may boom again once the cumbersome trickle of Kazakh oil shipments to China by rail turns into a planned multi-billion dollar pipeline. By 2015, the Kazakhs hope to triple their oil production to three million barrels of oil a day and to sell one-third of it to China. Beijing wants that too, and Chinese companies started buying a string of Kazakh and other Central Asian oilfields in 1997.

At the time of my visit in 1999, the first bloom of post-Soviet trade had come and gone. Khorgas looked like an out-of-season coastal resort. A faded sign in Russian greeted long-gone guests to a boarded-up hotel. Oversize buildings housing Chinese banks stood cracked and unfrequented. Little traders' booths lined up near the border were locked and weeds had grown up around the padlocks on their shutters. Kazakh businessmen had little left to sell to China other than animal skins, timber and scrap metal, and little money to buy much from China other than bales of cheap clothes.

The few remaining traders I met were resigned to another slow day. They seemed to cater mostly to Chinese tourists who came to photograph each other on this edge of empire. A group of students and young professors from Urumqi, all of them Chinese, looked brightly dressed and confident as they picked their way over stalls laden with the last of the kitsch and debris churned out by Soviet factories. Post-Soviet production had such a bad reputation that one Russian producer was stamping a prominent red hammer-and-sickle on his binoculars to try to give an image of quality.

"They've got nothing to offer us. We're overtaking them," a Chinese lecturer in biology told me in disparaging tones.

His fists acted out one car passing another.

"Our binoculars are better, anyway," he sniffed.

Before I could disagree, a student rushed up to show his teacher some purchases. Among them was a symbol of Turkey's extraordinary commercial expansion in the 1990s: a chocolate bar from Ülker, a fast-growing Turkish confectionary manufacturer in Istanbul. The chocolate bar had crossed six borders to get here, but Turkey was in fact relatively close. The ports of Turkey's Black Sea coast lay less than 2,000 miles away, while the last of the little white milestones on the Chinese side of the border tracked a distance of 3,825 kilometers, or 2,400 miles, from Shanghai. Ülker wasn't the only new Turkish player on this faded echo of the old Silk Road. On top of a stack of rough-and-ready Soviet enamel cookware near the border gate was a box of Duru soap, the product of another ambitious Turkish company. Turkish manufacturers' reputation had grown enough, in fact, that some Chinese clothing designers imitated higher-quality Turkish styles and brand names to compete in the Kazakh market.

The Chinese university group took its leave. I headed the other way, past a metal gate to a customs house where polite Chinese border guards stamped my passport out of the country. I boarded a rickety old bus with a sprinkling of Chinese suitcase traders. We headed past a last billboard of Chinese state heraldry and over a concrete bridge that marked the border itself, a small dry riverbed. After that came a serious iron curtain of Soviet border fencing, still in good shape a decade after the Soviet collapse. Its strong build symbolized the fear both Russia and the Turkic states still feel about the idea of 1.2 billion Chinese pressing against their under-populated, fertile and resource-rich lands. The nearby Kyrgyz worry that the Chinese are buying up too much real estate. The Kazakhs complain that too many Chinese traders find their way in. Still, a misspelled sign bid us "Wellcome" in cracked and faded paint.

The Soviet-era Kazakh border post was huge, misshapen, angular and ugly, built to impress travelers with their insignificance compared to the might of Moscow. Once it might have had such an effect, but now the aluminum door to the arrival hall hung half off its hinges and the cantilevered roof sheltered a motley camp of wooden huts, barriers and an incongruous surveillance point like an airport control tower. It was empty. After five minutes a blue-eyed Russian passport officer arrived at a booth, looked searchingly deep into my eyes in the unnerving old east-bloc manner and stamped my passport through. A small group of Kazakhs waited at the exit, and, never tired of testing the international reach of Turkish, I asked the most Turkic-looking of them if I was now in Kazakhstan. He had black hair and a gentle, round face.

"Sure," the youth replied in the fluent cadences of Istanbul. "You just take this minibus to the car park."

His name was Emre, he was 22 years old and he had never seen Turkey. He was from the ethnic Kazakh minority of Mongolia, and as we waited he told me how he had arrived in Kazakhstan from Ulan Bator three years before. He had been among the small hordes of high-cheekboned immigrants from Mongolia that had been a common sight in the 1990s at the airport in Almaty, the commercial and cultural capital of Kazakhstan. There had been a wide-sky look on their lean, brown, leathery faces, and a thick, rancid stench of nomad dairies had radiated from their greasy clothes. When Emre had arrived he didn't even speak proper Kazakh. But he had enrolled in the Turkish language and literature faculty of Almaty University, where his teacher came from Turkey.

"Don't you miss Mongolia?" I asked him.

"We're young. We forget quickly," Emre replied.

Emre chose a Kazakh driver with stamina to speed me on my way to Almaty. The man had just driven nine hours to Khorgas from Almaty, and barely blinked as he turned round to drive all the way back with me.

The transition from Chinese to Russian Turkestan was abrupt. Fields and villages in China were well-tended, new buildings were invading mud-brick villages and immaculate tarmac roads were overlaying dirt tracks. Kazakhstan, by contrast, had an air of decaying, easy-going and treacherous sloppiness. Axle-breaking potholes and foot-high waves of broken tarmac lurked on roads that were dilapidated beyond belief. The countryside looked unkempt, untilled and empty. Poplars grew lazily fat and bushy, unlike the straight-backed trees in China, where every twig seemed clipped and purposeful.

Collective farm buildings showed the difference between the two socialist philosophies towards their Turkic minorities. Up until recently in China, the Uygur and Kazakh peasantry was little disturbed in its daily life as the Chinese built a new world around, amongst and, eventually, on top of them. The Soviet Union, however, forced everyone, of whatever ethnicity, into the supposed equality of socialist citizenship. Soviet collective farms were built in the regulation Soviet-Russian pattern, and out here mud-brick only survived in occasional field walls. Families lived in drafty, square, Russian-style houses with pitched roofs, their lives centered on now-disused communal buildings with names like House of

Culture.

Still, there was much that was distinctly Kazakh and Central Asian that had survived. Although nomad goats and Soviet agricultural campaigns have damaged the botanic legacy of the country, there are still remote valleys on the Kazakh-China border with apple trees from where the direct ancestors of today's supermarket apples migrated to the world. In honor of that heritage, Almaty's name means "Father of Apples" in Kazakh. To celebrate my approach to Almaty, I stopped in a village where smiling, thickset ladies had laid out tables groaning with red, yellow and green bucketfuls of the fruit.

A Turkic nomad past, new oil wealth and Russian education were a heady inheritance for the young state of Kazakhstan to digest. Part of the construction of a new national identity was on show at Almaty's revamped national museum. Exhibits still honored the legacy of early Russian settlers. But the focus was now on rediscovering the history of the Kazakhs. Perhaps because they are the Turkic people closest to their nomad roots, outsiders still use the word "horde" to describe the three great tribes of the Kazakhs. The word derives from the Turko-Mongol word *ordu*, or army. In turn, those three tribes descend from the White and Golden Hordes, two successor states to the Mongol Empire of Genghis Khan. For Europeans, the word horde conjures up much that intellectuals since Voltaire have believed about the Turks and the Muslims as a whole: an inchoate oriental mass incapable of artistic imagination and unable to absorb the individual rationalism of the West. Naturally, Kazakhs feel differently about their social organization.

"Ah, you mean the three *dzhuz*," said my stout lady guide to the museum, Vahitkemal. In Kazakh and Turkish, the word means "a hundred."

She explained that the *ulu dzhuz*, or Great Horde, lives in the more fertile southeastern corner of the country, around Almaty and the northern flanks of the Ala-Too Mountains. It dominates the country's political class. Then there is the Middle Horde, which lives in the more Russified north and prides itself on a higher level of education and its more open and daring women. The Little Horde lives in the west of the country, where most of the oil is. Traditional Kazakhs typically knew their family tree back at least seven generations, Vahitkemal said, and were fastidious about not marrying a relative of any kind.

"Brides could once travel hundreds of miles," she said. "There has been constant intermixing. There are no Kazakh dialects, due to this tradition. Fundamentally, we're one people."

The nomad Kazakhs put their cultural energy into oral traditions of poetry and story telling, and left few monuments or physical records around which to construct a new national myth after independence. In their search for tangible symbols of their past, Kazakhs are rediscovering an interest in the curious marks that in the past delineated clan borders on the steppe and served as animal brands.

"People now want to be buried with them on their gravestones," Vahitkemal said.

Unfortunately for them, she added, the man who had been compiling a catalog of the symbols of the hordes died in a Soviet purge. A display of the 100-odd marks that he managed to collect showed the kind of freeform lines and circles that might decorate the walls of a pre-historic cave. They go far back in history: in the 11th century, Mahmut of Kashgar made a similar record of the livestock brands of each of the 22 clans in the then all-conquering confederation of the Oğuz Turks. Centuries later, far to the west, the early Ottoman Turks still used one of these Oğuz marks as a national symbol.

A main exhibition hall on the pre-Russian past featured grainy black and white photographs of Kazakh Khans and aksakals, or white-bearded elders, mostly taken by Europeans. Other pictures of early national leaders show gatherings of the "white-bone" Muslim clerical class, a kind of Kazakh aristocracy. Otherwise only a few scraps of fabric survive, and the wooden and woven paraphernalia of nomad life.

Echoes of a nomad past live on in Almaty's main food market, where belts of spiced and salted horsemeat hang stuffed into long gut sausages. In earlier times, a Kazakh family would kill a horse each year and slowly consume it during the long, cold months of winter on the steppe. What struck me was that next door to the horsemeat kiosk—advertised by a skinned horse's head—another Kazakh butcher had no inhibitions about selling great sides of pork, theoretically forbidden by their Muslim religion. Almaty's mix of cultures is so engrained that cups of cutlery on tables in market restaurants mix chopsticks with forks. "We would like the Russians to stay. We have a saying: If a stone is thrown at you, respond with bread," said one of the women dairy collectives standing side by side in the bazaar to sell Turkic koumiss and Russian smetana, or sour cream.

Nevertheless there is a wary diffidence in the Kazakhs' national character, which is not surprising given what happened to their grand-fathers' generation. It was only in the 1990s that Kazakhs began to learn the truth that the collectivization, purges and famines of the Soviet period had crushed Kazakh culture and wiped out Kazakh social, religious and intellectual leaders. In the Moscow-inflicted famine of 1931-34 alone, about 1.5 million Kazakhs died, about 40% of the population. By 1959 Russian immigration and Stalin's forced resettlements of Poles, Chechens and others made the Kazakhs a 30% minority in their homeland. They were controlled through a new Kazakh elite created according to methods seen all over the Soviet Union: bright and malleable children, preferably of rural or working-class origin, were channeled into Russian-speaking schools, and, if suitable, the communist party.

Now it is the turn for nomad and Kazakh history to be glorified. The main hall of the national museum and the flag of Kazakh independence is dominated by the circular image of the crossed wooden wheel at the top of a yurt. The great ancestors and khans of the Kazakh nation gaze from the new tenge currency, with wispy beards, turbans and long-necked lutes. A slow rehabilitation of the Kazakh language, long disused by the Russified elite, is underway. Still, sensitive to Russian taunts of backwardness, Kazakhs initially discouraged foreign companies from using photographs of yurts in their promotional literature.

According to Klara Sarabayeva, who has written a new history of Kazakhstan, her people have an uphill struggle to find their new selves. In her apartment in a leafy suburb on the flanks of the mountain that rises over Almaty, she explained that in some ways Kazakh culture was frozen in pre-modern times.

"The purges destroyed all the old Kazakh intelligentsia," said Sarabayeva, who declared herself a member of the better-educated

Middle Horde. "The people in power now come from the bottom of society. Nazarbayev was a shepherd as a boy. Over time, the communist party became our main horde, based on a managerial style of dog loyalty. They still never think about whether something is good or not, just what the boss will think."

Even though well educated in Russian schools, Sarabayeva was not grateful. This grandmotherly woman was angry with the Western cultural tradition, which she said engendered communist ideology and the Soviet Union. She blamed it for crushing Kazakh culture and robbing the Kazakhs of their history.

"According to our Soviet history books, everything began with the Bolshevik revolution. They kept silent about anything before that. Communism dumbed people down to the point they didn't even know they were Kazakhs. The communists invented Kazakh words our language never used before. And all those bright and shiny folk costumes. Those are not real. Kazakhs never wore things like that," Sarabayeva said, referring to the gaudy dresses and pointy hats that appear on dancing girls at all Kazakh entertainments. "The main carrier of our culture was the word. A single word could stop your enemy, change your fate. The loss of our language is a tragic state of affairs. But if we lost our Kazakh-ness, we didn't become Russians either. So we live in a kind of limbo."

Sarabayeva spoke in Kazakh, and the translator was having trouble translating this high-minded talk into English. The Soviet Union had insisted that foreign languages only be learned through the medium of Russian. Sarabayeva tried that language on me, but it didn't help. I joked that if only we had a common knowledge of Turkish, things would be fine. Sarabayeva's mouth dropped open—she did speak Turkish! She had never been to Turkey, but had taught herself the kindred language and had come to love Turkish literature. As often happened, this discovery of a common Turkic medium filled the atmosphere with smiles and warmth. Sarabayeva sent her daughter out to bring more tea.

"With us, speaking Russian brought artificiality. We have no spiritual knowledge, and so our society remains half-educated. We know how to read and write, but not how to think," she continued. "Call us cowardly, but we didn't resist. The Russians just beat our religion and language out of us."

Sarabayeva delivered this indictment of her society dispassionately, despite the fact that hard work had brought her the privileges of an intellectual within the Soviet system. The odds had been against her in other ways. Sarabayeva came from close to Semipalatinsk, where the Soviet Union carried out 445 nuclear tests from 1949 to 1989. Of these, 116 were above ground, exposing between 500,000 and 1.5 million people to radiation. One weapons testing area was a sacred site linked to Genghis Khan. Using it for nuclear explosions would, for Americans, be like bombing Thomas Jefferson's house at Monticello, she said. Sarabayeva was lucky that she was not among the many people from that area whose skin is blotched with red lesions from exposure to radiation in their childhood.

"In our village, a lot of military people came, and made a shelter, covered it with felt cloth and told us not to look out," said Sarabayeva. "But for us it was very exciting. Of course we looked out. I saw the mushroom cloud, although it must have been more than 100 miles away. After that we had strange earth-tremors for many years. Our windows kept breaking, everything kept falling off the shelves. The authorities wouldn't explain, and nobody would ask."

Sarabayeva's hopes for the future were focused on a new, more enterprising mentality that is emerging in post-Soviet youth. The new generation is breaking out of the unproductive cycle of blind acceptance of authority, coupled with passive resistance to anything that authority might try to achieve. Indeed, in all Turkic republics, new companies make a point of hiring the youngest staff possible. Similarly, just as Soviet and Russian influence is visible in anything old, much that is new in the republics bore some kind of Western stamp, often interpreted through the energetic medium of a Turkish contractor. In the urban focal point of Almaty's wide-open squares, the best new hotel of the 1990s was a brass-and-marble luxury spaceship that was Turkish-built, Turkish-managed, Turkish-catered and named after the Turkish capital.

The urbanized, Russified Kazakhs of Almaty are often quick to deny their nomadic, tribal roots. But despite their new cultural overlay, some traditions die hard, as I discovered one evening when a family invited me over to dinner in one of the apartment buildings next to Almaty's first and busiest hypermarket, owned and built by Turkey's Koç Holding. Just over the road from the president's gleaming French-built bunker of an office, the apartment's entranceway was ill lit, the concrete steps chipped, the disused mail boxes wrecked and the floor bare. The battered lift worked, but groaned unnervingly as it rose to the tenth floor. A mixture of socialism and poverty had brought disdain for the common urban spaces. Perhaps to compensate, people kept their interiors spotless and were hospitable, generous and caring in their private relationships.

Bahora, my hostess, was cooking the Kazakh delicacy known as beshparmak, or "five fingers," a sticky mess of horsemeat, chunks of lamb fat and flat sheets of pasta. She sat me down at a small dining table in a nook of the kitchen opposite the other guests, who included two of her young relatives: Nurlan, a salesman originally from a village near the Kyrgyz border, and Mira, a university-educated girl from Almaty. I asked the group about kidnapping brides, a Kazakh tradition I had heard of.

"Kidnapping brides? Nurlan knows all about that," Bahora said, a mischievous smile on her face.

Nurlan looked slightly sheepish. Many city Kazakhs deny that the kidnapping of brides still takes place, or consign it to the most isolated of rural communities. But it is far from rare.

"I had to kidnap her, it's traditional. Ninety percent of my friends did that. Mira knew that," the 22-year-old said. "And I did wait until after her exams."

Mira rolled her eyes, but let her husband start eating first, as Kazakh custom dictates.

"I'd known him for half a year. I liked him at the time, but had no thought of getting married," she said. "I still say he lied to me about where we were going that day. I thought he was just taking me for a drive round the streets. Then he said we were on the road to Kyrgyzstan. I was frightened. Then he just said: 'Now you are going to be my wife.'"

Mira had an even bigger surprise when Nurlan took her to his family house.

"I thought, when I get there, I'll call my brother, he'll come and take me back. But when we arrived, his family were all waiting there for the wedding ceremony. I called my family. But they just said Nurlan and I were fond of each other, so they left me there to get married."

Our hostess Bahora smiled indulgently at the memory. Formal negotiations between the two families over the marriage would not have led anywhere, she noted. Nurlan was just a yigit, a mere likely youth, while Mira was a descendant of the old "white-bone" aristocracy of Muslim clerics. Only by kidnapping her could Nurlan get this wife.

"It's a big shame on the woman if she refuses to get married after being kidnapped. There's almost always a wedding," Bahora said.

Tribal habits could be important on the national stage, too. President Nazarbayev, for instance, hailed from the Great Horde, as did his predecessor, long-serving Kazakh Communist Party leader Dinmohammed Kunayev. Nazarbayev was related both to his deputy prime minister and remotely to President Akayev of the Kyrgyz Republic. A dynastic link between the Nazarbayev and Akayev families was sealed in 1998 with the marriage of one of Nazarbayev's daughters to Akayev's son—both of them then students in the territory of the new great khan of the world, the United States. One of Nazarbayev's sons-in-law held a series of senior posts in the oil industry. The eldest of the president's three daughters ran the main state TV station. For years, her husband ran the tax department in Almaty, whose ferocious raids on foreign companies were the fiscal equivalent of a Mongol siege. Then he started working his way up the Kazakh security services, which, despite the placid, open feel of Almaty, react sharply and brutally to any threat to the president's position. As in other Turkic cultures, Kazakh politics are mostly about submission and rebellion. Above all, leaders want a loyal horde.

Kazakh journalist Danabek Bimenov put it in perspective for me as he finished another slab of beshparmak horsemeat over dinner at Bahora's.

"Geostrategically, the hordes don't play much of a role any more," he said. "But in the little things, it can make all the difference."

Lingering traces of nomad ways—from outdoor butchering to a love-hate relationship with established authorities—have both clashed with and enriched the settled cultures that the Turkic peoples have begun to mingle with around the world. In the cities built up by the Tsarist and Soviet empires in Central Asia, that cycle of conflict and attraction has in the past two centuries been with a dominant Russian culture. But in the ancient cities of Eurasia, in places from Samarkand to Shiraz, Turkic peoples have an older love and sometimes even more bitter rival: the literary and intellectual genius of the Persians.

12. IRAN AND TURAN

THE AGE-OLD ANTAGONISTS
OF EURASIA

I love that fair-faced Turk of Shiraz, and to win his hand
For his beauty spot alone I'd give Bokhara and Samarkand
— SHAMSUDDIN MOHAMMED HAFEZ, 1320-89

NOBODY KNOWS THE EXACT MEANING OF THIS OPENING COUPLET OF A famed *ghazal* of the great 14th century Persian poet Hafez. Did Hafez mean his Turkish heart-throb to be a him? Or a her? Or is it simply a metaphor for the love of God? Or all three? The Persians, like the Europeans, have long been ambivalent about the Turkic peoples. A *Turk* can mean firstly "a barbarian, robber, vagabond," according to the venerable Persian-English lexicon of Steingass; secondly and usually metaphorically, a Turk is a "a beautiful boy or girl, the beloved." Even if Persian Internet websites are filled with jokes about "Turkish donkeys," Turks are still associated with beauty by Persians, perhaps because their skin is of a lighter shade. Tradition has it that sparks flew when Tamerlane captured Shiraz, the native city of Hafez. When the ruthless Turkic raider and empire-builder imposed a citizens' indemnity, the poet pleaded penury to avoid paying it. Tamerlane summoned Hafez, saying anyone who could offer so much for a beauty spot could hardly be bankrupt. Hafez replied that it was just such extravagance that had ruined him. Tamerlane, pleased at this display of wit, excused him from payment—and spared his life.

On my visits to Tamerlane's old capital of Samarkand, now in the Central Asian state of Uzbekistan, I explored the complexities of this ancient love-hate relationship in a city where Persian and Turkic speakers have co-existed for centuries. Descended from an Iranian people of Indo-European origin once known as Sogdians, Persian speakers pre-date the arrival of Turkic peoples in western parts of Central Asia by several centuries. As in the rest of Central Asia, the Soviet Union renamed Persian speakers Tajiks. Samarkand and Bokhara remained the principal cities of Persian culture. But when Stalin finished years of mapping out Tajikistan in 1929, and he declared it a full Soviet republic, he left these two proud cities in Uzbekistan—partly to divide and rule Central Asia, and partly because the Turkic speakers, now called the Uzbeks, had finally conquered them.

The rivalry between Iran and Turan, that is, between the Persian and Turkic worlds, was already a central, mythical conflict one thousand years ago in the great Persian epic poem, the *Shahname*, or Book of Kings. Its author, the Persian landowner Firdausi, who lived in a part of northern Iran often ravaged by slave-hunting Turkmen plunderers, paints a clear picture of the Turkish threat. "I require a man cut from a mountain, for there is a horde advancing upon me from Turan," says one of his characters. Ironically, Mahmud of Ghazna, who commissioned the work, was a Turkic sultan ruling in today's Afghanistan. But, perhaps offended by its anti-Turkish overtones, he paid so little for it that legend says Firdausi gave the sum to a bath attendant.

The Turkic author Mahmut of Kashgar, writing a few decades later, insists on Turkic legitimacy in the lands they had come to dominate. "Now proof that all [Central Asia] is part of the Turkish domain are the names: *Samez kand* for Samarkand; Kand, in Turkish, means city. They [the Turks] built these cities and gave them these names; but when the Persians began to multiply in them they became like Iranian cities." He scorns the Persians' alleged claim to be the originators of words like *dag*, or cattle brand: "It should not be said that this is a word of the Persians since, compared with the Turks, they have no animals at all, let alone names for their brands."

In the centuries prior to the Russian conquest in the 1860s, Central Asia's governing class and military were as a rule Turkic, and preserved the clan structure of the steppe. Persian was usually the culture of literature and the administration in the towns. Arabic was the lingua franca of religion and science, like the Latin of Europe's medieval scholars. It was Turkic mastery of powerful recurved bows of horn, sinew and wood that allowed them to conquer so much of Asia, and their bowyers made them for distance, not accuracy; the Persian version of the bow, by contrast, sacrificed distance for defensive stopping power.

Ironically, Persian culture reached some of its greatest heights under Turkic patronage, and not just with Firdausi's epic. The Mogul dynasty of Babur, the Safavid founders of modern Iran, the khans of Bokhara and other Turkic dynasties adopted Persian as their court language. There was little follow-up to pioneering early works of Turkic literature like Mahmut of Kashgar's dictionary, Yusuf Hass Hajib's book of advice for princes, or indeed the efforts of Prince Babur and other early eastern Turkic writers like Ali-Sher Navai. This slim literary heritage is a major reason that Turkic culture, compared to that of the Persians, has so little respect in the West. Today, it is still Iranian films that regularly win international prizes. Only in recent years have the Turks begun to produce world-competitive art, marked by the jury's grand prize for a Turkish picture at the Cannes film festival in 2003, the same year that a major European award went to Turkey's best-selling novelist, Orhan Pamuk. In 2004, Turkish-German director Fatih Akın followed with the top prize at the Berlin Film Festival.

Some Turks worry about their late cultural development, blaming factors from Islam to poverty. Certainly, medieval Turkic societies remained trapped by Central Asia's unsettled and oppressive politics, its harsh climate, its unlettered population and its lack of peace and prosperity with which to escape the narrow ideology of Islamic fundamentalism. When Prince Babur moved from Central Asia to the gentler and more pluralist traditions of the fertile Indian plains, some members of his dynasty did take Muslim culture to great heights. Fine, cultured Turkic rulers did occasionally emerge even in Central Asia, like Tamerlane's grandson Ulugbeg. He calculated the length of a year to the nearest minute in the mid-15th century at an observatory whose underground runway can still be seen on a small hill in Samarkand. He spoke out against "the fog of religion" and had inscribed over one of the schools he founded in Bokhara: "It is the duty of every Muslim boy and girl to enlighten their minds." But Ulugbeg was killed in a coup partly whipped up by Muslim fanatics. Their spiritual heirs still stare at strangers with an almost physical hostility at the city's tomb complex for the minor Timurid royals.

The decision by Tamerlane to make Samarkand the capital of his domains in the late 14th century turned it into one of the most glorious cities—and centers of Persian culture—in the world. When on campaign, he spared the best craftsmen from captured cities, and brought them back to beautify his capital. Ruy González de Clarijo, a Spanish emissary to Tamerlane in 1404, wrote that "the richness and abundance of this great capital and its district is such as is indeed a wonder to behold." He also reported exhaustion from excessive banqueting and drinking led by Tamerlane and his queen, who built a grandiose mosque with an inscription so big that it could be read an hour's camel ride away. Its overblown dome quickly collapsed. Today the Bibi Khanim mosque stands in lonely contrast to the dreary concrete surroundings of Soviet urban architecture. Tamerlane was no sensitive Persian poet. His idea of greatness can still be relished in contemplating the mosque's enormous stone Koran stand. The Samarkand museum displays a medieval copy of the Muslim holy book whose huge pages would have fitted into it: they measure three foot by six.

Tamerlane used to say that the world was not big enough for two kings. In Samarkand today, I found the question more whether the city is big enough for its two peoples. A century ago, Tajik and Turkic Muslim intellectuals, united against Russian domination, used to write freely and supportively in each other's languages. Now, after Soviet gerrymandering of borders and the rise of new ethnic nationalisms, the struggle between Iran and Turan has risen again. The depth of feeling became clear soon after I made a telephone call to the house of an ethnic Tajik politician. Within an hour a little Lada car full of Tajik activists arrived and whisked me off to meet their leaders. Unprompted, a man in the back seat, Jamal, launched into an anti-Uzbek diatribe and voiced a fervent wish to root all Turkic words out of the Tajik language. For him, Genghis Khan, Tamerlane and the Uzbeks were part of the same Turkic plague. Genghis' 13th century razing of Samarkand and the massacre of three-quarters of its then population of 400,000 people seemed to have happened yesterday.

"These Uzbeks are barbarians, worse than the Mongols," Jamal said bitterly, drawing his finger across his neck.

In unguarded moments, it is not rare to hear self-criticism along such lines from ordinary Turkic people themselves. This is perhaps not surprising given the devastation wreaked on the world not just by Genghis' hordes, but those of Attila the Hun, Tamerlane, and the campaigning Ottoman armies. Even Prince Babur believed that "havoc and destruction have always emanated from the *Mogul* nation," quite an irony considering that his dynasty came to be known by the same name as sometime patrons of the arts. Similarly, a Turkish taxi driver once spent 20 minutes fervently arguing to me that the European Union would do best to stop negotiations on Turkey's membership immediately, since an innate wrecking spirit in the Turks would lay waste to European institutions.

In the case of my first destination in Samarkand, an old merchant's mansion that housed a Tajik Cultural Association, the destruction had been wrought by Soviet modernity. The house had stood abandoned for 60 years of the Soviet period, most of its old Islamic decorations had been vandalized and a road had been driven through one of its wings. It was a cousin of the grand houses I had seen in Kashgar: the same white stucco tracery, the same mirrors in the plasterwork, the same alcoves for long-gone family treasures. In a brief liberal glow at the time of its new independence, the Uzbek state had allowed the establishment there of the Tajik association's library and teahouse. The Tajiks had little faith that they would enjoy the premises much longer, according to Hayat Nemat, the chief of the association and a noted Tajik poet. He was so short that he was almost a dwarf, which surely swelled his sense of injustice. But he was also right. The association was closed down not long afterwards.

"We're free in theory, not in practice," said Nemat, who chose to call the Uzbeks 'the Turks'. "We are the owners of this land, but the Turks say if you want to be Tajiks, you go to Tajikistan. The state gave us this house, but harasses us a lot. I feel stateless in my own country."

After serving tea, he pulled out a lute, strummed a melody and sang some *ghazals* from the poet Hafez. He had a deep, resonant voice. The poignancy and melancholy of the lute echoed through the wreck of the mansion. Few Tajiks seemed to frequent the place, and he felt his mission to be a lonely one.

"My pain is worse because most of my people want to fill their stomachs, not their heads," he complained.

As evening fell, the Tajik nationalists led the way to a *tuy*, the wedding of the son of one of their community leaders. A back street gatehouse led into a courtyard, spread with long tables in the warm evening air. All round the walls hung *suzanis* with great fields of embroidered suns and flowers. Just as Turks and Persians contest the overlordship of carpet-weaving, both Uzbeks and Tajiks claim this lovely craft as their own. One of the guests said a black and white *suzani* represented the war between good and evil, a remnant of Iran's Manichaean religion prevalent before the arrival of Islam in the 7th century. I thought it seemed more like open-air wallpaper, a colorful attempt to make a dusty courtyard seem like a lush garden. The most gorgeous *suzani* of all formed a backdrop for the bride and bridegroom, sitting on a stage before the chattering throng. Many stood to propose toasts and to dedicate Persian verses to the newly weds. Late in the evening, fired up by their feasting, the hosts prevailed upon Nemat to recite a pungent poem of the pain and estrangement he felt in his native land. Jamal sat down opposite me and looked me deep in the eyes. Political rhetoric transported him far from the happy wedding proceeding round us.

"We are caught between the evil of pan-Turkism and fundamentalist Islam. Everyone here is in despair. I plead with you to save us," he said. "We are ruled by fascists. They want to eliminate us or drive us out to Tajikistan."

Perhaps because I spoke Persian, he felt I would sympathize with the Persian sense of entitlement due to their cultural achievements. I did, but not with all my heart. Irritation with this superior attitude prompted a satirical scene in *Ali and Nino,* a lovely romantic novel set in the brief bout of Turkic independence in Azerbaijan in 1918. While on a visit to Tehran, the hero, a young Azeri, is put down by a poetry-loving Persian prince for following Turkic tradition and being a soldier. "The prince preferred a poem to a machine-gun, maybe because he knew more about poems," muses the Azeri, protesting that Persia was falling under infidel British sway precisely because of its effete military weakness.

Weakness means Tajiks officially make up only 4% of the population of Uzbekistan, although they claim the real figure is closer to one-quarter. Many Tajiks can show that the state describes them as ethnically "Uzbek" on their identity papers, and certainly Tajik is now being spoken more confidently than in many decades on the streets of mixed towns like Samarkand and Bokhara. This mixed-up heritage is symbolized in the person of Uzbek President Islam Karimov. Uzbeks believe that Karimov has an Uzbek father and a Tajik mother. The U.S. State Department believes his father was a Tatar and his mother a Samarkand gypsy. Whatever the truth, in the first years of independence, the Russian-educated Karimov only spoke rusty Uzbek. Even so, ordinary Tajiks aren't so radical as the intellectuals, especially after seeing the upheaval of the civil war in Tajikistan.

Serving green tea on a wooden platform near the Registan, the central square of old religious schools with great *ivan* arches that are the pride of Samarkand, a Tajik restaurateur was offended by my questions about ethnic struggle. After all, the Registan itself was built by medieval Turkic rulers, but in a Persian style.

"We share the same religion. We give and take daughters in marriage. We wear the same [black-and-white embroidered] headcaps. The mayor is Tajik, and so is the governor. We can learn Tajik in schools. What is there to fight about?" he said.

Uzbeks and Tajiks also shared 70 years of Soviet education. The open-faced presence of the bride on the wedding stage and mixed-sex company of guests at the feast, for instance, would have been unthinkable in the pre-Soviet era. Other influences were purely Russian, like a taste for making toasts with vodka or reading the great novels of Tolstoy and the poems of Pushkin. Central Asian capitals were all built on the model of a Russian grid. Indeed, it is possible to argue that a hundred years of interaction with the Russians transformed both the Persian and the Turkic populations more than any previous conquest.

13. BEAR HUG

BREAKING RUSSIA'S LONG EMBRACE

We Turks obeyed orders, followed Timur the Lame,
Murdered Toktamish Khan without an eyeblink of shame.
The Golden Horde we plundered, left it rubble and flame.
Thus Moscow took our steppe. There's none but us to blame.
And today we find honor in Russification!
It is we, we who block the advance of our nation!
—Azerbaijani satirist MIRZA AL-EKBER SABIR, 1862-1911

RUSSIANS OCCUPY A MORE OBVIOUSLY GLORIOUS PLACE ON THE WORLD
stage than Turkic peoples. Even without their wider Slavic dimension,
Russians have nuclear weapons, a vast and united landmass, striking cultural achievements, a permanent seat in the United Nations Security
Council and prodigious production of oil, gas and other raw materials.
The Turkic peoples, meanwhile, add up to far less than the sum of their
parts. Their strongest state, Turkey, has long been propped up by the
U.S. and last enjoyed a temporary seat on the Security Council in 1961.
But it is possible that, when people look back in a century's time, the
break-up of the Soviet Union in 1991 may be seen as a way-station in a
balancing out of Russians' power compared to generally resurgent Turks.
Indeed, the Russian high-water mark arguably came a half-century
before, in the wake of the Second World War. Moscow then had extraordinary power over Turkic peoples from east to west: it dominated the
Uygur Turks of China, had a vice-like grip on the Turks of Central Asia,
occupied the Turkic-populated territories of northern Iran and backed
the Balkan socialist governments that oppressed Turkic minorities. And
in 1945, Soviet leader Joseph Stalin demanded that Turkey itself hand

over its northeastern provinces to Russia and grant Moscow new rights to the Turkish straits.

The Turkic wolf did not always fear the Russian bear. In the early 13th century, it was the Mongol khans and their Turkic-Tatar armies who conquered Moscow and the Russian princely states. The Russians spent 250 years under the Tatar yoke, forced to travel to deepest Central Asia to receive their titles, to sort out differences before the great khan's splendid court and to pay a tribute in gold and furs. The Russians only broke free in 1480, and it took them three more centuries to break the might of the Ottoman Empire to the south. As Ottoman power faded in the 18th century, great Russian rulers like Peter and Catherine began to push harder, conquering the northern Black Sea coast, the Balkans, pushing towards the Caucasus and twice camping on the outskirts of Istanbul. In 1828, Moscow won what is now Azerbaijan from Iran. In the later 19th century, it was the turn of Central Asia's long-independent khanates to fall.

The history of the Russian conquest of Central Asia has yet to be fully told from a Turkic perspective. It is sometimes forgotten that the Russians often had to fight hard, lost whole expeditionary armies and suffered many defeats during the 150 years of sporadic advances that led up to their final victory. The historic khanates of Central Asia only collapsed when Russia launched a decisive onslaught in the early 1860s. Tashkent was captured in 1865. Bokhara capitulated in 1868. Prickly Khiva fell in 1873. After a particularly violent popular uprising against the prospect of Russian rule, the Ferghana Valley khanate of Khokand was crushed in 1876. In the end, Turkistani bravery could not compete with modern Russian weapons and logistical supplies that arrived on railways that probed ever-deeper into Central Asia. Another reason was the feuding between the rival khanates. This tendency lives on with today's jealous Turkic autocrats, who cannot agree on a free trade area, water distribution, common security, or export pipeline routes for their oil and gas. As a result, they are still vulnerable to manipulation by Russia and other outside powers.

The elusive Turkmen proved the toughest for the Tsarist Empire to subjugate. Turkmen elders were some of the first to give an oath of allegiance to the Russians back in 1791, yet, as with today's evergreen

Turkmen promises to supply Russia with cheap natural gas, the agreement was easier to sign than to implement. Moving their tent camps
through forbidding deserts with names like the "Hungry Steppe," the
Turkmens had strategic depth. Their legendary horses could travel 60
miles a day through the desert, sometimes kept going with pills of
opium. Even today, sand dunes sometimes spill deep over the lonely
east-west highway through the Karakum, the "black sand" desert that
still acts as a barrier between the Turkmen and the outside world.

The Turkmens made their last stand against the armies of the Tsar
at the fortress of Göktepe, on the edge of the desert not far west of
today's capital, Ashgabat. The weatherbeaten mud-brick wall still traces
the line of ramparts behind which defenders crowded with their families
in the cold winter of January 1881. The Turkmens bravely withstood
Russian artillery and machine guns. But they failed to see the threat of
the Russian sappers mining towards their defensive perimeter. Goaded
by decades of Turkmen slaving raids on Russian outposts, determined to
complete their conquest of Central Asia, and wanting to define Russia's
southern frontier, the Russian commander later wrote that he was in no
mood for half-measures. "My system is this: to strike hard, to keep on
hitting till resistance is completely over; then at once to form ranks,
cease slaughter and be kind and humane to the prostrate enemy,"
General Mikhail Skobolev said. The result was a massacre: 6,500
Turkmen dead in the fortress and 8,000 cut down as the Russians pursued the fleeing. Still, it took the Russians another three years to subdue
all the Turkmen tribes.

The Tsarist Empire did little to change the basic Turkic characteristics of the Central Asian population. Indeed, modernization experienced
through the advance of Russia was a key factor in igniting Turkic nationalism. One of Turkistan's most determined reformists, Mustafa Chokay,
was educated in Russian at one of the new Russian colonial schools and
married a Russian woman. A Kazakh by birth, in 1917 he was chosen at
the age of 26 to lead Turkistan National Autonomous Region declared in
the Ferghana Valley town of Khokand. The Bolsheviks crushed it after
just two months of rule. "Our national movement had fundamental enemies [the Russians], but probably the more terrible enemy was our own
backwardness and inexperience. Left in the political darkness of Russian

colonialism, we couldn't open our eyes," he wrote in his memoirs. "Some of us thought we had to work with the Russian revolutionary democracy, while others, probably the majority, thought that political success could be won with prayers . . . and remained loyal to Russia. This group only cared whether the improvements and reforms by the revolutionary [Turkic] government complied with Islamic law." His conclusion in exile was to become the first Central Asian to stake out a position demanding complete independence for a united Turkistan, rather too late in the day in 1923. His Russian wife stuck by his side as he struggled through the world of Turkic exile newspapers and conspiracies. They even opened a small restaurant together in Paris—where Azeri nationalist leader Mehmet Emin Resulzade was shocked when dropping by to find Chokay scrubbing the potatoes.

The Soviets were relentless. Perhaps due to his familiarity with the Russians, Chokay was one of the few who understood the danger of accepting the cooperation offered by the Bolsheviks. By 1939, Stalin had killed all his former fellow leaders, and wiped out most of the Turkic intellectual and clerical classes. The "Turkis" were split up into two dozen new "nationalities." Chokay believed that the major Turkic groups deserved to be linguistically separate—politically, he advocated a Swiss-style union of cantons between them—and that Kazakhs, Uzbeks, Turkmens, Kyrgyz and others were taking root as nations before Soviet boundaries divided them. Then three generations were brought up in a system in which Russian was the language of power. Ambitious Turkic parents put their children into full-time Russian education, all Soviet teaching of foreign languages was done in Russian, and even students who wanted to write a doctoral thesis about Turkic literature had to write it in Russian. All of this, of course, was wrapped up in sugared propaganda about Soviet togetherness and progress.

Not surprisingly, there have been wild swings as Turkic states begin to rebalance the legacy of their Russian-dominated past. In Turkmenistan, the state stopped recognizing qualifications from Soviet institutions; in Azerbaijan, after a few years in which Russian was totally spurned, the new young business elite still like to show off status by speaking Russian in their offices. But as national television and education bring up a new generation, time is on the Turkic side. And only now do Turkic symbols get respect, like a Turkmen national holiday to remember the thousands killed at Göktepe.

As a result, the center of Göktepe's old mud fort is now dominated by a sterile new marble memorial mosque put up on Turkmenbashy's orders by his French palace-building company. When I visited, it was as empty as the Göktepe site had been in Soviet times. As we drove away, I asked my easy-going Turkmen driver if he didn't feel hostility to the Russians for all the bad blood of the past.

"Not hostility to Russians personally, no. I quite like them," he replied. He showed me a photo of himself that he kept in his sun visor, picturing him as a young man with a machine gun as he had unquestioningly fought his fellow Muslims as a member of the Soviet special forces in Afghanistan. "But on his death bed, my father had just one request," he said. "He wanted me to work all my life for an independent Turkmenistan."

Napoleon Bonaparte used to say: "scratch the skin of a Russian, and you'll find a Tatar," but the Russians have also managed to get under the skin of their former Turkic subjects. Respect for Russians was one of many contradictory elements that fought for the heart of Azer Sultanov, a talented and mercurial Azerbaijani whom I came to know well.

Top of his class at school, Azer was one of those who qualified to join an initial 10,000 Turkic students whom Turkey invited in 1992 to start rebuilding the long-broken bridge between the Turks of Anatolia and the Turkic peoples of the east. The experience left him confused about his identity. Some days he felt that as an Azeri he was part of a great Turkic nation; on others he would argue that Azeri-ness was an artificial construct. He struggled with ethnic and religious distinctions among the Azeris that he himself personified. His beloved mother was not originally Turkish speaking, but what he called *dağlı*, "from the mountains, "one of the many groups of a few thousand people who speak languages comprehensible only to themselves in the high valleys of the Caucasus. In a Shia Muslim majority country, Azer was also a Sunni. When he moved to a provincial town as a child, he remembered how after he used the local water pump, the Shia women would wash it three times before touching it themselves. After six years in Turkey, Azer sometimes felt like a Turk. Still, elements of Turkishness repelled him. He felt Azerbaijanis were better educated, and, thanks to 70 years of communist education, were more thoroughly secular. Indeed, as we headed by subway and taxi for dinner in his Baku home one evening in 1999, it became clear that Azer was simultaneously proud and resentful of the Russian element in his heritage.

"I always used to fight with the boys who lived there," Azer said as we lurched past a 10-story apartment block on a Soviet-era housing estate. "They went to the Russian-language school." The ill-lit, decaying concrete slabs of the exterior were hung with irregular patches of washing. It was as if a bomb had gone off inside.

"But Azer," I protested. "How come you're always talking about fighting Russians, but then keep telling me that you adore Russian-speaking girls?"

"Yes. The High Society Quality Personalities," he said wistfully, sighing again for two stuck-up Azeri girls speaking affected Russian whom he had admired in the subway carriage.

Azer, who believed that Russians disliked Turks more than the other way round, would have loved to meet an Azeri girl. But an Azeri girl who would kiss him, let alone sleep with him, would by definition not be good enough to marry him. So, often as not, Azer's girlfriends were Russians. But he never spoke again to one of them who teased him with the pejorative Russian term "black," used for dark-haired men from the Caucasus. He smarted at the memory of a Russian girl who put him down with the line that "Turkishness is not a national attribute. It is the diagnosis of an unfortunate condition." He couldn't count on Turkish solidarity, either. The mother of one of his girlfriends in Istanbulrailed against Azeri "cardsharp liars" and ordered her daughter home by 6 p.m. every evening.

Past the old Russian apartment blocks, we bumped down an unpaved, unlit road of individual houses. Azer leaped out as the taxi creaked to a halt in front of a high wall. His family's self-standing house was a palace compared to the Soviet projects. A suite of large guest rooms spread over the entire upper floor, built by Azer, his brother and their father. Turkic peoples everywhere are quick housebuilders. Inside, the house was spotlessly kept. Caucasus rugs woven by mountain village relatives mixed with large Soviet machine-made carpets. Knick-knacks filled the large, highly varnished, glass-fronted dresser that dominates every apartment in the former Soviet Union.

A warm welcome awaited us inside. Short and ingratiating, Azer's father, a former official of the tax inspection police, still had both feet in the Russo-Soviet past. He shaved his mustache to a pencil-thin line above his lips. He wore the short kipper tie of the Soviet militiaman, loosened well below his undone top shirt button, just as in the many pictures he soon showed me from his working life.

"Those were the days! Everything was so much better then," he said, pointing to a snap of him in uniform, eating and drinking with Russian colleagues.

Azer winced. On his brief visit home from Turkey, his father had already kept him up to the early hours reminiscing yet again about the good old days. I put in a good word for Azer's achievements in Istanbul.

"You have to keep a close watch on your children," Azer's father intoned, holding up his hands as if he was about wring someone's neck. "You have to be hard sometimes. They'll be grateful afterwards."

The women of the family shyly came into the room to set up a feast of chicken in a chestnut sauce, Iranian-style saffron rice, Russian salads and Azerbaijani *shampanskii*, or fizzy wine. Azer did not introduce his gentle-faced mother by name; he said she would never normally dine with a male visitor who wasn't family. I was flattered as an ambassador from the rich, wise and wonderful West. Bringing out a supply of Russian *Stolichnaya* vodka and raising his glass, the elder Sultanov said it was a privilege to welcome me to an Azeri household. The mutual toasting threatened to take us down the road to Russian-style oblivion. Confused by my unmanly sips, however, Sultanov senior left the bottle unfinished, an unthinkable disrespect to the gathering in the previous order.

"They've never met a Westerner before," Azer whispered in English, as if I came from Mars. "They don't know what to do."

We chatted about the post-Soviet plague of bribery. It had got so bad that the teacher of Azer's athletic brother had demanded money in return for a pass mark in a swimming exam, even though the pool was filthy and full of frogs. After the teacher insisted that if he didn't get at least something from his students, it made him ill, they bargained him down to a carton of Marlboro cigarettes. Azer showed me an article in a Baku newspaper about how children now talk hopefully of getting a good job that brings plentiful bribes. It all made Azer feel angry, trapped, disillusioned and, like his father, nostalgic for rule from Moscow, when bribes were rarer and merit counted for something.

"In Istanbul, we Azeri students sit up all night talking about the way our oil and our population numbers should make us the main power in the Caucasus," he said. "In fact, we're just corrupt nothings."

Azer's father offered to drive me back into town. His car had lain inactive for months until Azer gave him $50 earned in Istanbul to spend on a new alternator. The big Soviet Volga still hiccuped alarmingly. Along the road back home, we passed one of the new gas stations sprouting up all over Baku. The name of the service station was "EPP," spelled out in large red-and-yellow plastic lettering.

"Enver Pasha Petrol," Azer explained as we swung in to buy fuel.

I was astonished by this sudden tribute to the early 20th century Ottoman leader who had twice led armies in futile attempts to unite the Turkic world. The forecourt of Enver Petrol was a spaceship of floodlit cleanliness compared to the ragged road and Soviet-built suburbs all around. Azer's father ordered a couple of gallons from an attendant; nobody in oil-rich Azerbaijan seemed to have enough money at one time to say "fill her up," despite EPP's offer of a free car wash to anyone who did. Azer's father affected not to be impressed by this Turkish-equipped, Azeri-led symbol of Turkic progress. Indeed, a year later, the Russian company LUKoil bought the station, part of an expansion in Azerbaijan not unrelated to the Azeri parentage of the LUKoil chief executive. We drove out past the stink and flaring gas of a nearby refinery onto a wide boulevard.

"Ah! Here we are, Moscow Prospect! The biggest road in Baku," Sultanov senior said, opening up the throttle with a soul-felt sigh of satisfaction and pointing out a sign that spelled out "Moscow Restaurant" in old-fashioned Cyrillic script.

Without the Turkish-built gas station and the money his son earned in Turkey, Sultanov's aging Soviet car would not have been working. But for the former militiaman, true grandeur still lay in an idealized memory of the Soviet past.

"My father likes Russian things too much. I don't," Azer muttered.

The Turks' star is not just rising relative to the Russians in the east, but in the Balkans as well. In the 19th century, the Russian Tsars campaigned ceaselessly against the Ottoman Turks to win self-determination for Orthodox co-religionists like the Greeks and ethnic cousins like the Serbs. Russian-backed Balkan states finally evicted the Turks from all but Istanbul's Thracian hinterland in 1913. Now the Turks are back in a new and more positive incarnation. Hundreds of Turkish companies cut a high profile in Romania. Turkish naval engineers are building ports in Albania. Turkish Air Force jets campaigned with NATO in Yugoslavia. The Turkish army has formed joint brigades with Bulgaria and done U.N. duty in Bosnia. Relations have even improved with Greece, at odds with Turkey ever since Russia and Britain dealt a body blow to the Ottoman Empire by backing the early 19th century Greek war of independence. There has been an economic evening-out between Russia and Turkey as well. Outside great cities like Moscow, the Russian countryside has begun to look poorer than that of Turkey. And for one unusual year, during Russia's fiscal crisis in 1998, the dollar value of Turkish annual economic output even overtook that of Russia.

With Russian tourists flocking to Turkish Mediterranean beaches and Russian traders filling cargo planes with a wide range of Turkish products, the Turks no longer feel like the underdogs. I saw this clearly in the autumn of 1999, when I visited the Balkan territory of Kosovo. The occasion was the first trip there by a Turkish head of state since the Ottomans were forced out 86 years before. Now, following the 1999 Kosovo intervention, Serbia, despite Russian support, had lost control of Kosovo to NATO troops from 29 countries, including Turkey.

President Suleyman Demirel's tour showed the new influence of Turkey and the way it has reinvented itself. As we awaited the dawn start of our journey, a buzz of excitement filled the VIP terminal of Ankara airport. Travel with a Turkish leader is seductive, like cruising in a powerful, luxurious limousine compared to the Ottoman march of everyday life in Turkey—two steps forward and one step back. Courteous officials stamped my passport out. Cabinet ministers smiled and greeted me. The cream of Turkish Airlines hostesses handled tickets and passes before I had thought of them myself. After take-off, in the normal-rules-don't-apply-to-us manner of the Turkish élite, many quickly broke Turkish Airlines' no-smoking edict. Flutes of champagne helped us settle in.

Mehmet Ali Bayar, the president's young foreign policy advisor, glad-handed his way down the aisle with a beam of delighted anticipation. He paused to explain why: after the Ottoman defeat in the Balkan wars, his father's side of the family had fled from the main Kosovo town of Prishtina. As refugees, they had escaped from town to Balkan town until they reached safety in Turkey.

"My father still spoke Albanian. But it's the first time I see the place," he said.

His mother's family, on the other hand, had fled to the Crimea after Russia conquered the Caucasus. When Stalin expelled the Tatars from Crimea, they had then gone on to Bulgaria. From Bulgaria they had headed to Turkey because of the oppression of the Turkish minority there.

"I haven't got a drop of Anatolian blood in my veins," he concluded.

"How many people on the plane do you think are from the Balkans?" I asked.

"My family's from Skopje," piped up Türker Sanal from the seat behind me. The managing director of a private TV channel, he was referring to the capital of Macedonia, where another Turkic minority lives on among the low red-roofed houses of the old town.

Hasan Cemal, a newspaper columnist sitting across the aisle, listed grandparents from all four corners of the Ottoman realm. More neighbors chimed in with their stories. It is ironic that the Turks of Turkey are among the most nationalistic of Turkic peoples, yet they are ethnically the most mixed-up Turkic group of all. One of the few people on the presidential flight who could claim to be a real native of Anatolia was President Demirel himself, who hailed from a village in the Turkish south. Indeed, the Turkification of Anatolia is a triumph of national will, rather like the history of France, where few people originally spoke French. Assimilation, education, population growth and sometimes massacres mean that the proportion of those who now consider themselves ethnically Turks is more than seven in ten.

Republican founder Kemal Atatürk himself was a refugee from the Balkans. I told Bayar about an interview I had recently had with Salih Berisha, a former president of Albania. Berisha had proudly claimed that 30 grand viziers of the Ottoman Empire had been of Albanian origin, as had the family of Kenan Evren, who dominated 1980s Turkey as the leader of the 1980-83 military coup. Mischievously, Berisha had claimed that both Atatürk's father and mother were Albanian as well.

"You shouldn't say that in plane full of Turkish soldiers!" Bayar joked, and jubilantly retailed the story to all those sitting around us.

"Berisha told me I shouldn't tell that to the Turks," I said ruefully.

"We've been telling you, you're not talking to Turks!" shot back Türker, the TV director. Compounding the irony, his first name means "Manly-Turk."

We hushed as Demirel eased down the aisle to greet his guests. A man who scheduled official meetings with dozens, often hundreds of people a day, his eyes moved to the next person as soon as he began to shake the hand of the last. At grander receptions, the Demirel handshake included a sharp pull to move on. A short man of considerable girth, his wide, smooth, undulating face looked like the map of a country, but one that was in constant motion. He allowed himself to be caught in a wedge of reporters opposite me. A brave Turkish reporter raised the question of whether an interest in Turkic minority rights in Kosovo did not clash with Turkey's reluctance to give minority rights to its own oppressed Kurds.

With the slipperiness of a Turkish grease-wrestler, Demirel resorted to a legalism: Yugoslavia's Turks had been given constitutional rights in 1974, he said, whereas Turkey's Kurds had never won such a concession. It seemed appropriate that his tie was decorated with little hot air balloons.

"Mr. President, how does it feel to be a Turkish leader returning after all these years to visit Turkish troops in the Balkans?" I asked.

He paused briefly.

"This time, our soldiers are keeping the peace," he said. "But history does keep pulling on our coat-tails."

Our new Airbus soon banked low over war-damaged villages and touched down on the rough tarmac of the airport at Prishtina. Taxiing down the runway, we passed a small camp of troops from Russia. Their tents looked sloppy and threadbare. By contrast, the Turkish commandos who welcomed us as we trooped down the steps of our plane looked well-equipped and sharply disciplined; an American military attache later told me he considered the Turkish contingent superior to the Spanish and Italian units. They ushered us onto their crisply-painted American-made helicopters, which swept us over the farms and villages of southern Kosovo to the town of Prizren. Our one-day visit was on a Friday and Demirel's first action was to join the crowd at the weekly Muslim noon prayers in the main Ottoman-era mosque.

I stayed outside in the streets, where Turkey's regional comeback was much in evidence. A group of teenage Kosovar Turk girls lined up on a stone terrace of the mosque as happy as cheerleaders, swinging their hips in tight jeans, waving billowing red star-and-crescent flags, chanting "Our Army is the Greatest Army"—meaning the Turkish army—and singing hits from the Turkish pop charts. The nearby shops were filled with Turkish products, from clothes to chocolate bars. Local Albanians and ethnic Turks alike had their satellite antennas tuned to the panoply of Turkish satellite TV stations. My Turkish reporter colleagues were recognized with delight by the population, and, as elsewhere in the Turkic world, many people had picked up the Istanbul accent of the Turkish media. There was real celebration in the beating drums and squawking clarinets, and the partying youth in dance-costume skirts and fezzes.

Kosovo's Turkish minority had suffered much after Ottoman troops were driven out in the Balkan War of 1912-13. Christian and communist rulers had cut them off from Turkey, closed their schools and shut down their publications. Writers had to publish their works in manuscript. Parents taught their children Turkey's 1928 Latin alphabet at home. The main mosque in Prizren, a work of the famed sixteenth-century Ottoman architect Sinan, was blown up by the Serbs in 1915. Rebuilt later, Yugoslavia turned it for a while into a "Museum of Oriental Manuscripts", as a beaten metal sign still announced over the main door through which President Demirel entered to pray.

There was some liberalization and a flowering of Turkish publications and groups in the 1970s, however. Our party visited the small offices of one of these, Prizren's True Path Turkish Culture and Art Association, founded in 1951, the year that Yugoslavia officially recognized the Turkic identity of the Kosovar Turks. This identity now seemed to have two sides, to judge by a magazine and a cassette that were pressed into my hand by a Kosovar Turk. One was a folksy kind of nationalism, reflected in songs in Balkan Turkic brogue about brides, sheep, brave men doing battle and ladies tipsy on *rakı*. The other was a deep-felt obeisance to the powerful Turks of Turkey, including an editorial vaunting "a Turkey that can go to the Moon, to Mars." Local poet Altay Suroy Recepoğlu had penned defiant lines:

The same Turks beaten back from the gates of Vienna
Set down roots on the way, where they flourished forever.

We squeezed through a corridor into a modest meeting room. Everything in the Balkans seemed to be in miniature—the size of people, the height of houses, and the dimensions of the churches and mosques. Overflowing from a stuffed armchair, Demirel listened with hooded eyes and faint nods to appeals for support from a stream of local dignitaries. The 1999 Kosovo war had killed only three ethnic Turks, but the community was now losing jobs to ethnic Albanians rather than Serbs. Not a single member of the Turkish community was left in the judicial system. "We want to stay here and live as Turks," one local worthy told Demirel. Demirel picked up the microphone to address the people packed into the room, soothing and praising them. "We have a moral debt to you," he intoned, giving them the old Ottoman honorific for the Balkan Turks, "You are the *evlad-ı fatihan*," the sons of the conquerors.

It was at Kosovo's "Field of Blackbirds" in 1389 that the Ottoman Sultan Murat beat the armies of Serbia and secured the Balkans for Turkish settlement and the spread of Islam. The battlefield lies near Prishtina, the same place that Serbian President Slobodan Milosevic issued his ill-fated call to arms in 1989 that destroyed Serbian power six centuries later. This time it was President Demirel's turn to visit, briefly stopping by the mausoleum of Sultan Murat, killed in his moment of glory by a captured Serbian nobleman. He led the group in opening his hands before him and reciting the Muslim Lord's prayer. He then penned a short message in the visitors' book with the dedication "To My Padishah."

Our day in Kosovo drew to a close. Before our last hop into the helicopters, Mehmet Ali Bayar, the president's adviser, scooped a handful of rich Kosovo earth into a paper bag from a ploughed field. He was going to sprinkle it on his grandfather's grave back home. Also watching was a tall, straight-backed soldier wearing the black, yellow and red shoulder blaze of the German army. He seemed unusually dark-skinned for a German. I tried my luck and greeted him in Turkish. It worked. His name was Kemal.

"There's lots of us of Turkish origin in the German army," he said. "There are even more in the Dutch unit, and some in the French too. Any of us who could get permission came here to see the president."

As Kemal turned to his bemused lieutenant to explain our conversation in his fluent German, I thought to myself that it was in just the same way that the first Turks arrived in the Middle East from Central Asia 14 centuries ago. First they served as soldiers in Arab armies, then they became Muslims, and, over the next 800 years, they created empires and seized the Islamic caliphate itself.

Turks turning Christian and taking over Europe would be a far-fetched outcome of Turkey's westward momentum of the past century, whatever the fears of Europe's right wingers. But there are parallels: the Turks of Turkey turned from official Islam to official secularism in the 1920s, fought for the Western cause in the Korean war in the 1950s, guarded the southeastern third of NATO's front line against the Warsaw Pact during the Cold War, are pushing for membership of the European Union and are building on increasingly important military partnerships with the West elsewhere. In the early 1990s, it took Turkey six months to persuade the world it could be an acceptable partner in peace-keeping operations in Bosnia. By 2002, Turkey had become a natural choice to lead the International Security Assistance Force in Afghanistan.

Turkey's rise in no way eclipsed Russia. Indeed, in 2002, a Turkish general sent a wave of surprise through the ranks of Western military thinkers by suggesting that Turkey's place lay more with Russia and Iran than with the West. The general was reflecting a proud strain of republican isolationism that interpreted E.U. attempts to reduce the Turkish army's power as part of a conspiracy to keep the Turks down. But he struck a chord: Turks and Russians are neighbors, they do have flourishing trade, both have one foot in Europe and one foot in the east, and the broader Turkic-Russian relationship is deep and goes back a millennium. The intimacy of the Turks' relationship with western Europe is just a few decades old. When I went on to visit the growing, 3.5 million-strong Turkish community in Europe, I discovered that Turks like the soldier Kemal, while enjoying all that Europe had to offer, were ambivalent about the Europeans and remained tightly loyal to their Turkish roots.

14. THE GOLDEN APPLE

THE TURKS FOLLOW THEIR
LUCKY STAR TO GERMANY

Look, look around you, mate
Enemies, skinheads, spitting hate
We must unite. No time to wait.
It's us they want to incinerate . . .
America, Germany, who wants them?
A Turk needs a Turk, his only friend
　　　　—LE CADRO, German Turk hip-hop group

OVER THE CENTURIES, THE TURKS HAVE FOUND MANY WAYS TO EUROPE.
It has often been a promised land they gilded as the *kızıl elma,* or golden
apple, of their literary imagination. Not counting proto-Turkish raiders like
Atilla the Hun, the first of these tenacious infiltrators crossed the what was
to become known as the Turkish Straits in the 14th century. Byzantine
Emperor John VI Cantucazene had hired them as mercenaries in a civil
war. He had offered only a season's right to plunder his Balkan territories in
return for their services, but these early Ottoman Turks stayed on, telling
him it was "not Muslim custom to give up territory conquered from the infidel." Ottoman troops went on to conquer much of southeastern Europe.

A more subtle invasion of northwestern Europe started in 1961, also
by invitation, as Turkish guest workers set out to help power Germany's
post-war economic boom. In the four decades since then, the Turkish-
origin population in the European Union has risen to 3.5 million people,
giving them nearly the same number of people as E.U.-member Ireland.
European states have tried to persuade them to return, but, as the
Byzantine emperor discovered, the Turks have other ideas.

Two-thirds of these Euroturks live in Germany, although many travel back to Turkey every holiday. The Balkan wars of the 1990s cut once-busy rail and highway traffic to a trickle, shifting most journeys to Istanbul's Atatürk Airport. The German Turks in my queue for a 1998 workers' charter flight to Berlin seemed a tribe apart from other queues filled with more sophisticated-looking Istanbul businessmen and holi-day-makers. They were indeed of different origin, since Turkey had sent village folk to work in Germany, wanting to give industrial training to its rural underclass. In my line, family groups stood by luggage tied with washing line or wrapped in sacking. The men were short, stocky Anatolian types, wearing baggy trousers, clipped beards and gruff expres-sions, a pre-1980 rural style. Their wives wound their heads in scarves, wore baggy trousers of cheap flower print material or covered themselves with Islamic overcoats. The wealthier among them had adopted north European fashions or Islamist chic. One young woman looked like a medieval princess, wearing a flowing gown of sheer cream satin and an elegant matching turban of a kind I had never seen in Turkey. The man slouched next to me on the plane turned out to be a drug addict. His father had sent him to the family village near the eastern city of Erzurum, but if it was to detoxify him, it hadn't worked. An hour after takeoff he shuddered through a withdrawal crisis, and headed to the toilet "for a cigarette" somewhere over Hungary.

It was at the gates of Vienna, then the capital of the Austro-Hungarian Empire, that the Ottoman Turkish advance into Europe was definitively stopped in 1683. The defeated Turks abandoned their war materiel, including sacks of coffee beans that launched the Viennese coffee house tradition. As Austrian bakers celebrated the departure of the menacing horde and its crescent-moon standards, the Turkish retreat occasioned the birth of the European *croissant*. The Austro-Hungarian resistance prevented Turkish armies from reaching the Atlantic, the springboard for the next generation of imperial powers, and marked the beginning of Ottoman decline. But the Turks were never conquered themselves. They kept a conviction of their natural superiority to Europeans and a nomad determination to profit from the settled lands of Europe. Our plane was over Prague by the time my fellow-passenger returned, sated and talkative. He had to get back to Germany before he

exceeded an absence of six months, otherwise he would lose his resi-
dence permit and lucrative social rights.

During the Cold War, many Turks were attracted to West Berlin's
subsidized lifestyle. Now Berlin was on the front line of change in
Germany. The Turks were coming under threat as the city re-emerged as
the capital of united Germany and set about a passionate purging of its
recent past. Cranes swung all night over the huge floodlit buildings going
up around the Potsdammerplatz, and the city authorities had meticu-
lously erased almost every sign of the old Berlin Wall that divided the
city. Some Germans felt that the German Turks, too, should move on,
even though Turks naturally worked on these projects; indeed, by 2002,
they made up 1% of the German electorate. Racist attacks, house burnings and murders in several places in Germany poisoned the communal
atmosphere in the 1990s. Official repatriation programs tried to entice
the German Turks into leaving. Second- and third-generation minors
who had hardly ever seen Turkey were threatened with expulsion to their
motherland if they broke the law.

Reasons for German resentment were not hard to find. The presence of 200,000 Turks among Berlin's population of 3.5 million people
made Turkish the second language on the streets of the capital of
Europe's most powerful country. Amid the cobblestones and leafy trees
of the Wassertorplatz, red paint disfigured walls with crude Turkish-
language graffiti like "No to the Fourth Reich," "Long Live the People's
War," and, since many Turkish Kurds used Turkish too, "Kurdistan will
be Red." In Oranienstrasse, Turkish youths in souped-up cars burned
tires and shot stop lights. Turkish shops and restaurants stood on every
other street corner in some districts. Music shops displayed cassettes by
German Turk rappers like the "Hard Muslims," who flaunted songs like
"I Want My Revenge." Even the local Turkish television station militated
against integration. As I settled into my hotel room, I watched a program
presented by a man with a neatly cropped Islamist mustache. He spoke
earnestly against a studio backdrop representing the skyline of the
Muslim holy city of Mecca.

"We are living among other beliefs and peoples," he said in a voice
brimming with sacred certainties. "We must defend our identity and our
religion. Our mosque doors are open wide. If you don't bring your chil-

dren [into the Muslim community] today, you won't be able to bring them tomorrow. We have to teach our youths national feeling, how to clench together as one fist against the enemy."

Foreigners now make up nine per cent of Germany's population, and disquiet at such talk simmers among Germans. Over breakfast, I read an article in the mainstream *Berliner Zeitung* headlined: "Must We Tremble at the Advance of Islam?" The author toyed with Nazi-era hate words that stoked fears of an armageddon-like clash of civilizations. Anti-foreigner feelings were most acute in former East Germany around Berlin. After one attack injured some German Turk children, their school buses no longer went out of town to take them to country lakes for swims or even to enjoy the parks and palaces of Potsdam. As I walked round the city I could read the election signs tied to the lampposts by the overtly anti-foreigner, right-wing Republikaner Party. "Germany for all? No—for us," said the legend under a picture of a sharp-faced German woman with her hands folded across her chest. Another: "Criminal Foreigners Out." In the end, the Republikaners didn't attract many votes in the 1998 elections. In fact, the victory of Chancellor Gerhard Schroeder's left-leaning coalition with the Greens brought a more open-minded official point of view. But when I asked a rough *bratwurst* seller at a market under a bridge if my lunch sausage was pork, he replied nastily: "Yes, all pure Turkish pig."

If I had not been looking for it, I supposed, this civic tension might seem out on the margins of life in Berlin. But Hale Decdeli, a sociologist working in the Berlin Turkish community, said it was dead serious. Decdeli came to Germany in 1981 at the age of 28 and now lived in the suburb of Kreuzberg. Her apartment was in a leafy section of the district, away from the zones of condemned 19th century buildings close to the old Berlin Wall where poorer German Turks were numerous. As we chatted about the suburb, Decdeli quoted a German senator who had recently said: "We should dry Kreuzberg out. We cannot let it become a little Istanbul." She even voiced a worry that nagged in the back of her mind, that the Turks were entering the same cycle of ghetto conflict with the Germans as the Jews before them. She called me afterwards to say she had gone too far. Such a passionate, impetuous outburst is not the correct form in Germany, she said, and could be misunderstood.

"The Germans see me as emotional. And I am emotional," she said, somewhat unrepentant.

Decdeli was concerned that where German institutions once asked her to lecture about Turks, she was now being asked to talk about Islam.

"The change is part of the construction of a European self-identity. Europeans have an image of Christians as peaceful. It's a definition by exclusion, the construction of a new memory. They forget that the bombs they are still digging out of Berlin are not Islamic bombs. So I refuse to talk on subjects like 'Is Islam a Danger?' If I start speaking negatively about, say, Iran, I would be giving them ammunition to kill me too," she said. "Then there's the fact that you always have to prove you're an exotic camel before you have a right to talk [as a spokeswoman for an ethnic minority]. But if I'm a self-confident woman, I learned it from my grandmother in a Muslim headscarf, not from any of these European women. Their hatred of headscarves is in fact hatred of Turks."

Decdeli praised the many Germans who helped the Turks out, particularly church groups. In fact, she pointed out the irony that 80% of marchers in German anti-racist demonstrations were Germans, not German Turks. She herself had married an easy-going German expert in oriental manuscripts. Even one of the sons of Chancellor Helmut Kohl, the long-time leader of the Christian Democrat Party and skeptic about the Turks' European vocation, wed a London-based Turkish woman banker in 2001—after Mr. Kohl had properly visited the girl's parents, middle-class people from a provincial Turkish town, a gesture of respect to the Turkish tradition of asking for a girl's hand in marriage. But in the same year, former German Chancellor Helmut Schmidt said Turkey had no place in the E.U. because "the Enlightenment has never reached Turkey and will never reach Turkey."

The Turks of Turkey, too, were in two minds about Europeans. Their theoretical right to membership of what became the European Union was recognized as early as 1963, but they spurned a quiet invitation to apply to join alongside Greece in 1978. When they did make the formal application in 1987, they subsequently dragged their feet on the necessary reforms. It seemed they wanted recognition of Turkish equality with

Europe rather than a dilution of Turkish sovereignty in a new European partnership. In Europe, hostility to the idea of Turkey's E.U. membership was not limited to Germany. France's ex-president Valéry Giscard d'Estaing, the man then in charge of drafting a "constitution for a United Europe," spoke for many conservatives in the E.U. when he flatly declared in 2002 that membership for Turkey's 70 million people would mean the end of the union. Turkey, he said, had "a different culture, a different approach, and a different way of life. It is not a European country." E.U. officials rushed to reassure the Turks, but, in an unguarded moment in 2003, the German in charge of E.U. enlargement said he wished Turkey would accept a special relationship short of full membership.

"When someone German attacks you, it's done in terms that make sure you don't feel like you're a German," Hale Decdeli said. "There is constant insecurity about legal status. Even for the third generation, there is a sense that you are being told, 'you don't belong here, you are Turkish.'"

By 2004, new rules meant that 750,000 of approximately 2.8 million people of Turkish origin in Germany had taken out German citizenship, nine times as many as in 1999. A survey in 2001 for the Konrad Adenauer Foundation showed other progress. One in three of those who took German nationality mostly spoke German at home. Overall, nearly as many Turks felt an emotional bond to Germany as felt a bond to Turkey, 60% felt successful in Germany and 78% thought their children would have better lives there than them. While 48% of all Germans rejected German society as "unjust," only 8% of German Turks thought that. Still, the results were distorted by the fact that half of the Turks contacted for the survey refused to answer any questions. Less than half of those answering reported having social or sporting contact with Germans, 87% appeared to have all-Turkish family lives and 69% felt that they were treated as second-class citizens.

For Decdeli, the Christian Democrats' definition of integration could be summed up as "readiness to conform, but readiness to go back at any time." She pointed out how in the 1960s, they used the same official language against the Italian *gastarbeiters* that they use against the Turks today. I told her how my first wife was brought up in a Swiss town in the 1970s where girls were discouraged from going out with south

Europeans like Spaniards. Similarly, I noted, my second wife's liberal Dutch father used to tell her she could marry anyone, but not an Italian. North Europeans saw the swarthy workers as a poor, unreliable, non-European working class—just as they view the Turks today.

"Exactly! Then the Italians suddenly became Europeans!" Decdeli exclaimed. "In the 1980s there was a sense that we Turks were on the verge of becoming accepted as 'Italians.' But then the east Germans came, and then the ethnic Germans from the ex-Soviet Union. These ethnic Germans got language training, and quickly became foremen. The Turks have been by-passed."

German Turks were partly responsible for their own isolation, according to Hakan Doğnay, the top German Turk official at the Berlin branch of IG Metall, Germany's big metalworkers' union. We met at a restored bar-café in the Hackersdorf, an old Jewish quarter of east Berlin. Doğnay talked quietly, as if not to disturb the ghosts.

"Most of the (German Turk) workers still don't speak German. So all they really want me to do is to shout at the German foremen," he said. "The Germans call it the Turkish mentality—exaggeration, emotions, scattering roses as we talk. And in a way, they're right. The Germans come straight to the point. When a Turk comes to see me it takes 25 minutes to find out what he really wants, even longer if it has to do with his family honor. I have to make him feel free in my presence, disarm him with a moment of frankness. For people over 55 years old, I have to be a complete psychologist."

We sipped our cappuccinos, and talked about the "Turkish disease." Many of the older *gastarbeiters* suffered from crippling back and stomach pains. Doğnay thought it came from long years of revolving shifts, carelessness about health, sleeping in cheap, damp dormitories and scrimping money on heating. The workers thought only of the day when they would proudly drive their new Mercedes back to their home village.

Doğnay had arrived in Germany at the age of 16, found work at a Siemens' washing machine factory at the age of 18, and rose through union ranks. He was married to a German, but his German passport application had been refused three times, officially because he "kept

changing his life." He seemed to accept this as Germany's punishment
of his past participation in militant demonstrations. What brought a really
bitter tone to his voice, however, was the German edition of the hot-selling
nationalist Turkish daily newspaper *Hürriyet*.

"*Hürriyet's* idea boils down to this: we're a minority here and the
German state is trying to destroy us," Hakan said.

Hürriyet was stuck in a confrontational time warp, unable to untan-
gle the interests of the German Turks from the supposed interests of the
Turkish motherland, particularly on nationalist issues like the Kurds.
When IG Metall supported a much-oppressed Kurdish unionist back in
Turkey, a hostile *Hürriyet* campaign cost Doğnay 10,000 members.
When the then only German Turk member of parliament, Cem
Özdemir, simply spoke up for Kurdish rights, he too became the subject
of relentless attacks.

"It was as if he couldn't be a member of the German parliament
unless he was an enemy of Turkey," Doğnay said.

Both sides were victims of their own misinterpretations. A German
ambassador to Turkey told me of spending long hours trying to persuade
visiting German politicians that just because extreme corporal punishments are stipulated in the Koran, it didn't mean to say that all Muslims
automatically carried them out, least of all the Turks. Similarly, the Turks
sought out radical statements by Germans, and then took them to be
state policy.

While wandering through Kreuzberg, I stopped in a Turkish-run
store and started chatting with its owners, the Çelik family. The wood-
paneled shop had a pleasant, even jolly atmosphere. The young women
behind the sandwich counter joked with the customers in fluent
German and Turkish. When a disciplinarian German mother denied her
young son an ice cream, 28-year-old Funda Çelik leapt round to soothe
the tears of the sobbing infant. With her life story, she didn't feel like
adding to the sum of human hardship.

Funda had come to Germany at the age of six. Her father had started off on a factory floor with Siemens but had gone back to his original
calling as a butcher and grocer. Her parents were now well off, but
couldn't decide whether they should stay or return to Turkey, and so they
kept traveling in between. That day, her father was hovering in the back-

ground. Listening in, he complained that he had spent his savings on a big three-apartment building back in Turkey to house his brood, but none of them wanted to go and live there.

"People like my parents can't accept that they have impaled themselves on a stake that they sharpened for themselves," Funda cut in brightly. "There are lots of us here who say Turkey is a paradise, and that these *gavurlar* [infidels] have just burned us up. I say that if that's the case, then what are we doing here?"

She had little interest in going to Turkey, feeling that would mean sacrificing her German freedoms. I asked her if her wish to stay in Germany was because she had a family of her own.

"Actually, I got married. To a German."

"Was that difficult for your family?"

"Turks came round to my parents to say, 'how can you give your daughter to an infidel?' They started to boycott our shop, didn't even say hello. Then they tried to control our private life. They said, 'he has to get circumcised.' I refused to allow it," Funda said. "But because I was stressed and losing weight, he went off to hospital on his own and had it done anyway."

Her father was following our conversation from the fruit counter.

"When she got married, the others came round and said I should cut off my mustache, because I wasn't a man any more," he said. "Those were terrible times."

I was still thinking about Funda's husband's self-sacrifice when she matter-of-factly said that they had split up and now she lived alone.

"You fell out of love?"

"No, it wasn't love. I loved him too much. And he even took my name," she said.

She paused, and shifted on her wooden stool.

"The problem was that what he did had less to do with me than with his German sense of needing to prove his own non-racism. He had a political agenda."

If two people as committed and sensitive as these could not bridge the gap between the two cultures, few could, I thought. Even for Funda, completely integrated in Berlin life, Turkish citizenship was a safe haven from a new fascism she was convinced remained a threat in Germany.

"Even my good German friends have racist sides. What frightens me is that these people have read widely, gone round the world, and yet they still have such isolationist views. People are always saying to me, 'But you're so nice.' What they mean to say is 'we find all the Turks we see distasteful, but I'm pleasantly surprised to find that I am able to talk to you.'"

The Çeliks, like Hale Decdeli the sociologist and Hakan Doğnay the unionist, were part of the regular majority of German Turks who were trying to get on in Germany more or less on Germany's terms. A German Turk was elected Miss Germany 2005, saying she represented Germany as much as Turkey—even though her father was killed and she was badly injured in a racist attack on their home in 1994. But there was a minority who developed a Islamic ideology with which to strengthen communal feeling and to shield themselves from German hostility. The village Islam they brought with them had hardened into a more fundamentalist creed than that developed by the urbanized, self-confident populations of Istanbul or Ankara. A small minority remained stuck in militant fundamentalist rituals, exploiting youthful passions by parading up and down in Germany sports halls with model kalashnikovs and proclaiming an eternal caliphate under their leader.

After three of the four Arab pilots in the 9/11 attacks on America were found to have matured in Germany's Muslim fringes, the Germans no longer tolerated such posturing. But the Islamic movement among the Turks had already adopted European methods and freedoms, especially in organization, fund-raising and legal self-defense. The main group, known as *Milli Görüş*, or national vision, won substantial influence among Turks in Germany and elsewhere in Europe. The financial support and experience of Western methods transmitted home by European Turks was a critical contribution to the rise of the Islamists in Turkey. But the limitations of being in a diaspora made the European Turks inflexible, leading to later divergences with the homeland. The pragmatic, moderate nature of the ex-Islamist faction that took power in Turkey in 2002 was a new phenomenon. To be sure, Islam relates differently to power in every country. But the approach of the Turkic states to Islam has similarities that set them apart from the rest of the Muslim world.

My travels, however, turned up something else that I began to consider, a thread that linked the Turkic peoples. It wasn't Islam, and, in the end, nobody could prove that it was racial. It was more like a cultural spirit or genius, developed over centuries of being considered outsiders by more settled nations. I made this discovery in the most unexpected place, too: the Appalachian mountains of the United States.

15. CURSED SOULS NO MORE

A TURKIC FABLE IN THE
BACKWOODS OF VIRGINIA

> *When the world began, our ancestors say, three*
> *brothers lived in Altay. They split up, leading their*
> *peoples to populate the earth. One went west towards*
> *Turkey and Europe. One stayed in Altay. And one*
> *went east over the Bering Strait to America.*
>
> —NADYA YUGUSEVA, a shaman from Central Asia

THE TURKS WHO BEGAN TO HEAD TO THE UNITED STATES IN THE 20TH century may not have been the first Turkic people to reach north America. Genetic, artistic and perhaps linguistic similarities have led to the newly respectable belief that some native Americans may descend from Central Asians who migrated over the Bering Strait. The Moscow newspaper Izvestia, for instance, reported in 1998 that scientists had found a 72% correlation between genes of American Indians and a village in Russia's Central Asian republic of Tuva—and that the Turkic Tuvans looked exactly like American Indians too. Likewise, a University of Arizona study found a strong linkage between 19 native American groups and 15 from Siberia. The broadest study of Eurasia's genetic heritage yet, published in the U.S. in 2001, found evidence to support ancient Turkic legends of being a major source of Eurasian populations. Central Asian males were found to have the most diverse, and arguably oldest, gene pool, which then spread out to Europe, the Indian subcontinent and America. To be sure, Central Asia was Indo-European before the Turkic tribes took over. They don't seem to have been numerous, either. The 2001 U.S. study found that Turkic-speaking populations are actually genetically closer to their geographic neighbors than to their distant ethnic cousins, implying large-scale Turkification of diverse populations. Conquest doubtless played a large role: another study showed that 8% of men who inhabit the former Mongol Empire—including most of the modern Turkic peoples—can claim descent from Genghis Khan. Some native Americans, defending their aboriginal status and rights, reject the possibility that they are immigrants to America. Against the tide of current research, they suggest instead that it was their ancestors who migrated over the Bering Strait to populate Asia.

One native American, however, was intrigued by the idea of a Turkic connection. I met Frank Keel in a smoked-glass office building that houses the Bureau of Indian Affairs on the outskirts of Washington D.C. Here he ran U.S. government relations with the 26 native American tribes of the eastern seaboard. A state department diplomat by training, and speaking in 2000, before the latest rash of genetic discoveries had been published, he was cautious about the Bering Strait theory.

"It's not something that mainstream American archaeologists go along with," he said.

He told of Canadian anthropologist Ethel G. Stewart, who spent years among native peoples of Central Asia and the northwest Canadian seaboard. She published a book in 1991 noting cultural connections and claiming that a wave of Turkic peoples had arrived in North America by boat in the 13th century, fleeing Genghis Khan. Her work had been greeted with academic brickbats.

"Eskimos still visit each other across the Bering strait. But they aren't Indians. And some of the Indian tribes have strong traditions that they came from the south. There are all these possibilities out there. Some are goofy. But there is still no definitive answer to where the Indians came from," he said.

Keel was not ready to rule anything out. He himself was an American Indian of the Choctaw Chickasaw nation. He looked thoroughly Central Asian, too, which led to delegates clapping him on the back as a blood brother when by chance his U.S. diplomatic functions brought him to a conference of Turkic peoples in Turkey. On another occasion, he was assigned to meeting shamans and Turkic community leadres in Siberia as part of an American dialogue with Russia about minority rights.

"One of the guys looked just like my cousin," he said. "We were there to talk about economic development, but they kept sidling up to me to say: 'We're Turkic, that's what's very important to us.'"

Keel suggested I call up his friend Türker Özdoğan, a Turk who had moved to the United States in 1970 and described himself as an abstract expressionist sculptor. He is also an amateur anthropologist with a passion for proving the Turkic-American Indian connection. When I reached him, Özdoğan told the story of his epihany when he spent the night in a lakeside Indian reservation hotel called the Havasu Lodge. He had been astonished to find that the word Havasu meant much the same in both languages—air-water in Turkish, sky-water in the local tongue. He claimed to have found 500 Turkic words in Navaho Indian, and another 500 Turkic words shared with the Maya of Mexico.

"Native Americans and Turks worship the wolf. They value the color turquoise. Shamans exist in both worlds," he said. "There is a common legend, too. Kukulkan was a man who came by the sea and taught everything in the Manas epic of the Kyrgyz. In Mexican legend, he also appears as a white-bearded, knowledgeable man."

He listed American Indian tribal names like Koman and Yörük, exactly the same as well-known Turkic clans. Core Turkic words like *ata* for father and *anne* for mother are shared with Cherokee and other tongues. The word *yurt* means tent for the Obigwa. But many of the associations that he listed sounded utterly far-fetched—for instance, the idea that the Niagara Falls were named after the Turkish expression *ne yaygara*, or "what a noise."

Improbable as it seemed, there was another group that supported the theory of kinship links to the Turks. These were the Melungeons of Virginia, a people who inhabit a remote recess of the Appalachian Mountains southeast of Washington, D.C. They don't just claim a possible Turkic descent from the west, through intermixture with American Indians. I first heard of the Melungeons when a delegation of their leaders arrived in Turkey in 1996 and proudly announced themselves to be descendants of Ottoman Turkish galley slaves cast away on the coastline of the New World.

The Turks welcomed them as as long-lost cousins. Turkish newspapers conjured proof of the Melungeon link from the words *malun can*, which translates from Turkish to mean cursed soul. They accepted the

Melungeons' embrace of Turkishness much as their Ottoman ancestors welcomed anyone who would proclaim the one-sentence credo of Islam. The unremarkable-looking American tourists of the Melungeon delegation were astonished to be feted as prodigal sons everywhere they went, and even won an audience with the Turkish president.

The Melungeon idea was certainly romantic. Their claim made it possible to think of the Turkic peoples as a belt of ethnic cousins who did not just span Eurasia but also girdled the globe. I sent an e-mail message to their main spokesman, who invited me to visit him in the town of Wise, Virginia. It took me a while to find it on a map, but a few weeks later I was driving my way to the toe of Virginia that borders Kentucky, Tennessee and North Carolina.

Seen from my car on the Interstate highway, green forests carpeted gentle Appalachian slopes barely worthy of the name of mountain. But after I turned westward and began to drive uphill, valleys grew steeper and the vegetation thicker and more impenetrable. Compared to the Virginia foothills, the country was poor. The homes were often prefabricated, and the cars out front were mostly unwashed pick-ups. Many families had kept the wrecks of previous vehicles too. Businesses included an unusual number of pawnshops, car lots and gun dealerships.

A little short of Wise, I stopped to ask my way at Frank's Machine Tool Shop. I was at the foot of Stone Mountain, a legendary sanctuary of the Melungeons as the racist laws pushed them off the fertile land they once owned on the valley floor. A man left his lathe in the workshop and came outside with a slow and easy gait to greet me. I outlined the purpose of my visit.

"My wife's a Melungeon," Dwayne said. "We saw a program on them. Her surname was the same as the ones in the program. Let me call her. Ethel maybe will talk to you."

He dialed a number. The conversation lengthened.

"She feels she has nothing to tell you. She says that as a matter of fact she's not a Melungeon," Dwayne said sheepishly.

"What makes a Melungeon a Melungeon?" I asked.

"They're good folks, but they keep to themselves. They're very friendly once they know you," Dwayne said. "Then of course, they do have that kink in the hair . . ."

1. Conquering hordes: Until their powerful short bows were overtaken by Western military technology in the 18th and 19th centuries, mounted Turkic raiders under leaders from Atilla the Hun to the Ottomans conquered wide swathes of Eurasia—probably looking like this band of Karakalpak horsemen at a festival in Uzbekistan.

2. Metal beaters: Turkic peoples believe that one of their earliest distinctions was fine ironwork and knife making, as seen here in the Uygur city of Kashgar.

3. & 4. *Living history: the fur-hatted costume featured in a medieval drawing by Central Asian artist Siyah Kalem, or Black Pen, and now in the Ottoman palace archives in Istanbul, survives today in Kashgar where this Uygur man is studying the price of sheep.*

5. *Moving on: Turkic herdsmen of the Central Asian steppe accompany herds of animals in domed felt yurts, mostly following age-old patterns to seasonal pastures like this family near Kyzylorda in central Kazakhstan. War, droughts and poverty have also pushed the Turkic peoples to undertake longer-term migrations.*

6. *Soul Doctor: Nadya Yuguseva, a Turkic shaman from Russia's Atlay Mountains, with a ritual crown of twelve fox tails, says she can see inside people to cure their diseases and talk to their spirits. Traces of age-old shamanistic nature worshipping survive in many Turkic communities.*

7. & 8. *Bound together: The acrobatic displays at the Kashgar Sunday Market in Xinjiang today remain much the same as those portrayed in a 1582 miniature of an Ottoman celebration in distant Istanbul.*

9. *Reconnecting: Each day, painters seek solace and profit from the iconic beauty of the Islamic schools around Registan Square in the Uzbek city of Samarkand. Built by Turkic rulers in the 15th and 16th centuries, steeped in Persian architectural styles and restored in Soviet times, they symbolize the diverse influences on the Turkic world.*

10. *Bulldozed: A Chinese worker cuts another swathe of roadway through an ancient Uygur district of Kashgar, part of a process that is fast erasing the cultural heritage of the Turkic population.*

11. Old bills fall due: a Karakalpak official in the former port city of Muynak stares out over the bed of what three decades ago was the Aral Sea. Over-irrigation of cotton crops and wasteful water use has reduced the Aral to half of its former surface area and one-third of its volume.

12. The eagle has landed: Wary Kazakh police watch the first U.S. paratroopers to land in Central Asia. The Americans are the new boys in a Great Game with Russia and China for influence in an oil-rich strategic arc of Turkic territory spanning the northern edge in the Islamic world.

13. *Blowback: in the 19th and 20th centuries, the rising power of Europe, Russia and China forced Turks out of lands they had conquered in medieval times. Here the Turkic population of Bulgaria hits the road in a mass exodus to Turkey in 1989.*

14. *Post-traumatic order: the Turks are condemned for massacres of Armenians a century ago, but they have suffered too. This Azeri woman lost her relatives, home and all her belongings in the 1992 Armenian massacre of Azeris fleeing the Nagorno Karabagh town of Hodjali.*

15. *Fit for duty: A Turkish peacekeeper in former Yugoslavia in 2000. Overcoming neighbors' suspicions of its conquering Ottoman past, NATO-member Turkey's ever-powerful military has established itself as a regional partner in peace operations from Somalia to Afghanistan.*

16. *Last stand: the Azerbaijani army struggled against defeat, corruption and disease to recapture the martial spirit of their Turkic forebears. By 1999, these front line Azeri soldiers in the last Azeri-held corner of Nagorno Karabagh could at least put on a show of bravado.*

17. Holding the line: Turkish police form ranks before breaking up an Istanbul political rally in the late 1980s. Turkey has cleaned up its act, but throughout the Turkic world autocracies encourage rough police tactics to stamp on opposition and keep local regimes in power.

18. Boiling point: Uygurs in Xinjiang show rebellious stress after decades of watching their Turkic culture, Muslim identity and primitive economy pushed aside by the growing power of China.

19. *To your honor! Most Turkish Muslims see little sin and plenty of pleasure in a glass of strong aniseed-flavored rakı. This feast is a pre-battle ritual for these farmers on Turkey's Aegean coast, who stage annual wrestling matches between their Afro-Asian cross-bred camels.*

20. *Pious retreat: an Uzbek takes a moment's refuge in prayer from his country's impoverishment and dictatorship. The veranda's old wooden columns are copies from tent-poles, a medieval style found from one end of the Turkic world to the other.*

21. *Quality control: Turkish provincial police chief Tekin Akın energetically struggled to make his force more reputable, sometimes despite his own desire to annihilate radical opposition groups. Behind him, a pyramid displays all the flags of the Turkic world.*

22. *Beachhead to prosperity: the diver father of Mehmet Aksoy (right) founded a small boatyard on this Turkish beach with his savings from salvaging silver cutlery and iron from ships sunk during the allies' ill-fated World War I Gallipoli campaign. After thirty years of slow expansion under their own financial steam, the Aksoys now build three 8,000-ton ships a year and operate cargo vessels all over the globe.*

23. *Caspian boomlet: Central Asian oil was slow to make an impact on world markets, but the opening of the Caspian Sea to international oil investment transformed the Turkic states around it. Here a Kazakh oil worker welds a pipe at the central Kumkol field.*

24. *Shopkeepers to Eurasia: just as their forebears once sought opportunity in distant lands as herders and raiders, Turkic peoples now spread far and wide as family-funded entrepreneurs. These Uygur sisters set up shop in a shipping container in Kazakhstan.*

25. *Long march: When his short-lived state of East Turkestan collapsed in 1949, Uygur leader Isa Alptekin and his wife Fatima fled China through perilous mountain passes into exile. He died in 1995 without achieving his dream of regaining Uygur self-rule.*

26. *Cross purposes: The Kyrgyz said this 1995 summit of Turkic leaders in Bishkek forged a new "Turkish alliance." Seen here (l-r) are Kazakhstan's Nursultan Nazarbayev, Turkey's Suleyman Demirel, Uzbekistan's Islam Karimov, Kyrgyz author Chingiz Aitmatov, Azerbaijan's Haydar Aliyev, and the Kyrgyz Republic's Askar Akayev. Others were skeptical about Turkic cooperation, including Turkmenistan's Saparmurad Turkmenbashy (far left on carpet), who as usual didn't turn up. Famed author Aitmatov pleaded for Turkic states to unite.*

27. *Suspension of belief: Turkmenistan's Saparmurad Niyazov capped his personality cult by naming himself Turkmenbashy, or Chief of the Turkmen. Like him, most of Central Asia's new Turkic rulers were former Soviet placemen and struggled for popular legitimacy.*

28. *Showing the way: Mustafa Kemal Atatürk, or "Father of the Turks," created the Republic of Turkey in 1923 by force of arms, and secured his victory with the emancipation of women, industrialization and secularization. Here he opens his model farm near his new capital, Ankara, where soon afterwards he founded the country's first Muslim-owned brewery.*

29. *Lone wolf: Azerbaijan's Abulfez Elchibey once broke stones as a jailed Soviet dissident, and here emerged from hiding to harangue a crowd in 1990. In a 1992 election, he became the only Turkic nationalist to win top office in a post-Soviet state But he lost power a year later, suffering from weakness and lack of broad popularity that undermines pure Turkic nationalists everywhere.*

30. *Crocodile eyes: Until his fall from the Soviet politburo in 1987, Haidar Aliyev was the iron-willed gray eminence of Azerbaijan. He regained power in 1993 after reinventing himself as a local patriot and adopting elements of Turkic rhetoric, as did many ex-Soviet rulers of the Turkic republics.*

31. *On parade: Turkish American girls create a new identity for themselves at a New York Turkish Day Parade. The Turkish-American community still numbers only a few hundred thousand people, but is growing fast. More Turks come to study in the U.S. than from any western European country.*

32. *Prodigal son: Appalachian Mountains native Brent Keneddy first discovers a like to Turks through genetic illnesses in his Melungeon community; he now thinks their ancestry may include Ottoman galley slaves from the East and native Americans from Turkic regions in Siberia from the West. Keneddy holds a Turkish newspaper clipping proclaiming that the link means Elvis Presley and Abraham Lincoln were Turks as well.*

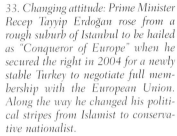

33. *Changing attitude: Prime Minister Recep Tayyip Erdoğan rose from a rough suburb of Istanbul to be hailed as "Conqueror of Europe" when he secured the right in 2004 for a newly stable Turkey to negotiate full membership with the European Union. Along the way he changed his political stripes from Islamist to conservative nationalist.*

34. *Pushing into the picture: Turkey's President Turgut Özal broke with many traditions as he opened up once-isolated Turkey to the outside world. President George Bush Sr.'s visit in 1991 was an early blessing of Turkey's rising star.*

Dwayne pointed to my onward road "up yonder," reminding me of early travelers to the region who related that the Melungeons spoke a broken Elizabethan English. Such survivals are unsurprising. Insecurity and prejudice have long persuaded the Melungeons to stay private. Dwayne's wife's reaction indicated that just the name can still be an insult in itself, a snide reference to a people at the bottom of the pile, white trash that was not quite white. But in the 1990s, circumstances conspired to break open the diffidence of this community of 75,000 people.

The catalyst for change was a brush with death by a charismatic local man called Brent Kennedy. All kinds of treatments failed to cure his painful, puffed up limbs and difficult breathing. But when doctors eventually said he was suffering from sarcoidosis and Mediterranean fever, the diagnosis raised more questions than answers. Both diseases are genetically transmitted through people of east Mediterranean origin, thereby challenging the family claim of Scots-Irish descent. He gave up a big city public relations job and started digging into his family history. Ultimately, his research and his fight against his sickness transformed him into the chief historian and then undeclared leader of the Melungeons. It was controversial in the Appalachians, where many feared that he might prove links to African-Americans and provoke new discrimination. One cousin burnt photographs rather than let him have them. But gradually his revelations fostered Melungeon community pride.

Kennedy's vision of 16th century history shoulders aside some of the Anglo-centric view of the settlement of the New World. He found that British captain Francis Drake, unable to sell a group of captives or to take them back to England, left 500 Turks and North African Moors at Roanoke. The group disappeared within a month, possibly into the near-by hills now lived in by Melungeons. Records also show that the legendarily "Anglo" Jamestown Colony included characters like "Mehmet the Turk," gypsies and Armenian craftsmen from the Ottoman Empire. He found a decree from the governor of the Commonwealth of Virginia that in 1690 prohibited the importation of any more "Turks' or 'infidels."

Parts of Kennedy's theory seem compelling, parts look dubious, and all are still unproven. Outside specialists say it is the construction of a myth, not the uncovering of history.

Whatever the science of it, the modern Melungeon-Turkish relationship is blossoming. "Welcome to our guests from Dumlupınar," said a banner hanging from one building at the University of Virginia's campus at Wise, referring to an exchange program between Wise and a small Turkish college. When I entered the rector's building and met him, Kennedy was quick to tease me about some other Turkic connections.

"Right here I'm sitting on a Mongolian blue spot," he said, referring to a discoloration he said he had at the base of his spine.

There was other evidence that he said linked him genetically to Central Asia. He clicked a nail under his front teeth and tilted his head back to show his shovel teeth, a Turkic trait.

"Here, feel the back of my head! I've got half a golf ball there," he said, putting my hand on a lump by which today's right-wing Turkish nationalists also purport to be able to tell if someone is Turkic. "I believe that Turkic ancestors came here from both directions, from east and west, and that I'm the genetic proof of it."

Originally and most frequently, the people who came to be known as the Melungeons called themselves a word that sounded like Portuguese. Given the fact that the Spanish and Portuguese roamed the coasts of America as well, ancestors from that quarter could be expected. But local slang includes many Middle Eastern leftovers, like the old Melungeon word for a watch, *saat*.

"When I started looking into our origins, I didn't go for the Turks initially. We first contacted the Spanish and Portuguese embassies. They weren't particularly interested. But there was immediately a warm response from the Turks. They invited me to Turkey, and it grew from there. I felt like an orphan who rediscovers his family, goes to visit all his grandparents, and finds that only one of them shows any interest," Kennedy said.

"Why do you think that was?" I asked.

The book Kennedy wrote about his trail of discovery gushes with comparisons between Melungeon and Turkish hospitality, his feelings on discovering that the inhabitants of the Turkish coastal town of Çeşme share his blue eyed, dark complexion—the town is now twinned with Wise—and even that he did not suffer from allergies while in Anatolia. But his answer was more interesting.

"You know how the Turks are viewed by the world. If you understand that, you understand our relationship," he explained.

Like the Turks, he said, Melungeons felt that they were isolated, surrounded and oppressed, that they had had their history written by outsiders, and that their experience taught them not show weakness, or else
they would be destroyed. He sympathized with the Turkish struggle to
counteract their negative image from films like *Midnight Express*. The
Melungeons suffer similarly from the film *Deliverance*, in which a group
of men out on a camping trip tangle with Appalachian backwoodsmen,
portrayed as retarded, sadistic, inbred anal rapists.

"I mean, we're not that inbred. We don't have six fingers, like they
keep saying!" Kennedy remonstrated.

A mischievous look came into his eye.

"Actually, it's four thumbs. I was born with them too. Here's where
they were cut off, have a look," he said, laughing and showing the two
scars.

We were having a drink with his fellow Melungeons at Mosby's, a
mall-corner restaurant dedicated to a dashing Captain Mosby and the
southerners' cause in the American civil war. The repartee was witty, self-
deprecating and good-hearted.

"For me, all the genetic evidence I'm collecting is irrelevant compared to the spiritual growth of my people," Kennedy maintained.

Harnessed to the cause, I found I could conjure Turkic links out of
almost anything. One of the confederate flags hanging over our heads
featured a red field with stars and moons, similar to many Turkic flags. I
suggested that it was copied from the star-and-crescent of the Ottoman
Empire. Nobody could prove me wrong.

"I'll tell you something else nobody can explain," said Kennedy, his
blue eyes sky-bright. "Why is it that the Seminole Indians, who were
practically naked before the arrival of people from Europe, are pictured
soon afterwards wearing Ottoman-style turbans?"

The students at Wise had an exchange program with Turkey, but
none had actually gone there. "We like it here too much, I guess," said
Kevin, a student of accountancy serving behind Mosby's bar. But Turks
are keen on coming to see Melungeons, and not just because of
America's relative wealth and many well-known attractions.

The less expected reason is a sense of racial solidarity, which bruised
Kennedy's non-Melungeon colleagues when rudely ignored by Turkish

visitors. In response, Kennedy developed an anti-racist ideology that reflects the Melungeon's mixed ancestry. He plays on this mixed origin when lecturing Turkish audiences, hoping to trump such racist thinking.

"I tell them I have Kurdish and Armenian blood too. At a speech in Dumlupınar, I told them it's all about breaking out of our shells, that we are all interconnected," he said. "Every Turk in the auditorium stood up and applauded."

Kennedy was getting 20-30 letters a week from Turkey, expressing solidarity, or looking for medical treatment, jobs or scholarships. A few were successful in their search for a new opening, like Alihan Kartal, a well-built 22-year-old from Istanbul. He'd been bitten by the American bug during a spell at school when his father was posted in New York, despite being teased about being a barbarian, about *Midnight Express*, and, the perennial complaint of Turkish-American schoolchildren, being taunted in the playground about being a "turkey." (Once discovered by Turkish-American parents, this phenomenon was the origin of a still-influential movement to change Turkey's official English name to the Turkish *Türkiye*). Alihan's family had contacted Kennedy after seeing him talk about the Melungeons on a Turkish television show. Alihan found his way to university at Wise, and, when his money ran out, Kennedy arranged for him to be supported in his business studies by local well-wishers.

"I thought I would be bored, but I loved it here! I felt something unique about this place. Deep inside, this reminds me so much of home," Alihan said.

Alihan couldn't tell if his empathy with Wise was because Melungeons looked a little like Turks, whether it was the southern hospitality, the olive oil in the food, or the Turkic echoes he heard in bluegrass music. Like many of his countrymen, migration was in his blood: half of his family came from central Anatolia, the other reached Turkey a century ago from Romania and Albania. He didn't know where he'd end up in life. But he was sure he wouldn't forget his Turkishness.

"The Turks are always represented with a negative image, so I always felt bad deep inside my heart. Now I've got a collection of 20 Atatürk pictures in my room, and a big Turkish flag. I want to raise the voice of the Turks," he said. "Here in the U.S. you have a chance to be success-

ful. But I want to end up in Istanbul, with a business trading with everyone from Americans to the Japanese. Turks are hard workers, you know.
The Central Asian Turks were nomadic. I'd like to be both, to have a
suitcase in my hand and to travel the world."

SECTION IV

ISLAM ALLATURCA

*Islam may be one, but the Islamic peoples are many,
and Turkic interpretations of Muslim duties often differ*

16. IN THE LAND OF BABUR

ISLAM AND CENTRAL ASIA'S
STRUGGLE FOR IDENTITY

> *People follow the religion of their kings*
> —PRINCE BABUR, 1483-1530

THE MOGUL DYNASTY OF INDIA AND THEIR GREAT WORKS, LIKE THE sublime white dome and minarets of Agra's Taj Mahal, are normally associated only with the Indian subcontinent. Yet the first Mogul emperor, Zahiruddin Muhammad Babur, was a Turkic ruler born in 1483 in Central Asia's Ferghana Valley. He descended from Tamerlane and Genghis Khan, and conquered India with the battle skills he honed in his youth, feuding and warring with rival princes of the blood in Central Asia. Although of distant Mongol descent—Mogul is a Persian or Arabic version of Mongol—Prince Babur spoke eastern Turkish, as did his dynastic heirs, a language still spoken at home by one or two princely families in Pakistan. Prince Babur used it to write a vivid account of the late 15th century royal life of the heirs of Tamerlane. Some of his essential strategems live on in the art of Central Asian rulership today, being a constant juggling with corruption, betrayal, risk of outside attack and the dictates of Islam.

Prince Babur's family originally ruled Andizhan, at the eastern end of the Ferghana Valley, a place famed for its pears and its great fortress. His father struggled ceaselessly to expand his domains, breaking truces, friendships and family ties along the way. Still imbued with a nomad abhorrence of settled life, princes of the era engaged in what now seems more like gang warfare than nation-building; Babur said one of his uncle's tents looked like a robber's den. They were indefatigable. As

Babur later admonished his son: "Conquest tolerates not inaction. The world is his who hastens most." When Babur's father died—he slipped while tending to a dovecot on a high castle parapet—both his brother and his brother-in-law were simultaneously marching against him. Babur was nine years old at the time, but remembered his father in typically frank style. He was short, "had a round beard, a fleshy face and was fat. He wore his tunic so tight that to fasten the ties, he had to hold in his stomach; if he let himself go, it often happened that the ties broke . . . He packed quite a punch, though, and no one was ever hit by him who did not bite the dust."

Babur had no doubt about the ethnic identity of the people among whom he was born. "The people are Turks," he wrote. "Among the city folk and merchants, there is no one who does not know Turkish." Many of his townsfolk and peasantry must actually have been Persian-speakers, and Babur was deeply influenced by Persian poetry. But his main interest was in warfare and matters of unquestionably Turkic grandeur, such as an army send-off from Tashkent. The royals stood on white cloths, threw libations of mare's milk koumiss behind those departing and saluted standards topped with yak tails. Two such tall, tufted wooden lances still flank the mausoleum of Tamerlane in Samarkand today.

Like today's Turkic elites, Babur and his fellow princes wore their Islam lightly. Babur approvingly quotes a line of poetry by one of his contemporaries: "I'm drunk, officer. Punish me when I'm sober." They imbibed wine copiously, fell in love with bazaar boys and could be violent and tyrannical. Babur related that one of his uncles "was addicted to vice and debauchery. He kept a lot of catamites. In his realm, wherever there was a comely, beardless youth, he did everything he could to turn him into one. During his time this vice was so widespread, that to keep catamites was considered a virtue." But without missing a beat, Babur added that the prince never missed his five prayers a day, knew accounting and led an excellent administration.

Islam had a central place in Babur's life, even if few of the characters he described were notable for their piety. He prayed like everyone else, and was an orthodox Sunni Muslim. He occasionally voiced distaste at the "deviations" of Shia Muslims. As for the common people, Babur barely mentioned them, let alone worry about their religious concerns. Military prowess was all: his fate depended on his personal courage and skill with the curved saber. The rare times Babur himself spontaneously got down to pray was when he was alone and fearing death, or when he needed to rouse an army under his command into battle. He did become noticeably more "Islamic" once in India, taking the title of "gazi," a title Muslims take for feats of arms against non-Muslim infidels. He ostentatiously gave up drinking alcohol two years before his death, and demanded that his court do the same. But he didn't stop chewing narcotic preparations, and didn't lose his sense of irony. "Everyone regrets drinking and swears an oath [of abstinence]; I swore the oath and regret that," he wrote.

Prince Babur's Ferghana Valley still focuses much of Central Asia's abundance and occasional beauty, as well as its moments of extremism, tyranny and turmoil. It runs for 200 miles from east to west between two mountain ranges, which protect it from the harsh winds that sweep over the steppes. It is broad, fertile and thickly populated, a source not just of food and wealth, but also of religious and ethnic conflicts. Its riches have attracted conquerors from the time of Alexander the Great. Chinese emperors sought access to its "heavenly horses" that were once the strongest in Asia. During the decades of Soviet rule, people had kept their Islamic traditions alive but undeveloped, handed down orally from father to son or in secret religious schools. After the collapse of the Soviet Union, traditional-minded study groups grew into Islamist organizations in the collective farms in the Ferghana Valley and rural Tajikistan. In Uzbekistan, where one third of the population lives in the Ferghana Valley, Islamic sentiment channeled anger with the dictatorial style of its leader. In a way that Prince Babur would have understood, Uzbek President Islam Karimov brooked no rivals. He first used the communist party machine to consolidate his rule and—while publicly brandishing his first name as proof of his piety—gradually built up an Uzbek nationalist ideology to justify it.

A secular Uzbek opposition leader, Abdurahim Pulatov, warned me of the potential countervailing power of Islam as early as 1992. Pulatov was a former professor of cybernetics and a leading light of *Birlik*, or Unity, the Turkic nationalist opposition to Karimov shortly before and after independence. In the small Russian-style bungalow where he was

hiding at the end of a Tashkent subway line, he told how *Birlik* had first
been harassed and outlawed, and then how its leaders were physically
attacked and driven into exile.

"Karimov only talks about human rights, democracy and the 'Turkish
way' to a liberal economy. But his real aim is a stronger communist-style
regime," Polatov predicted, correctly. "Our supporters remembered what
happened to dissidents under the Stalinist system, so they began to run
away from us. People depend on money from the state. They say: 'You're
right, but I have sons and daughters to look after.'"

He pointed to a scar on his head where security police had beaten
him with an iron pipe for his dissident views. Uzbek hospitals had
refused him blood transfusions after party high-ups ordered doctors to
stop his treatment, he told me. He left for exile soon afterwards, ending
up in the United States.

"The trouble for Karimov is that Islam is a very broad movement.
Karimov can't stop it like he can stop us. They have no newspapers, but they
have mosques. So radical anti-Communists go to fundamentalism," he said.

Islam was left as the only surviving platform to stand against tyranny
and injustice, whether it was from the local traffic police, the collective
farm chief, or plain bad economic management. Its adherents were amorphous and hard to target. Karimov quickly entered into a vicious cycle of
oppression and reaction with the Islamists, unwilling to distinguish
between ordinary folk and armed insurrectionists, and sometimes creating
the problem that he was trying to solve. Foreign human rights groups in
the country, observing that many of those he arrested were far from being
Islamic fundamentalists, let alone terrorists, invented a new category of
person to describe them: "pious," "observant," or "independent" Muslims.

Karimov had some cause for worry. His Islamist opponents were well
organized, divided into two main groups, both of which sought to sweep
aside the artificial borders of Central Asia under the umbrella of an
Islamic Turkestan or a revived universal Islamic caliphate. The first, the
Hizb al-Tahrir, founded in the 1950s in Saudi Arabia and generally non-
violent, grew to claim thousands of adherents in five-man cells in the
Ferghana Valley and throughout Central Asia. Its members met in each
other's houses to pray together, and were more concerned with raising
moral standards and refraining from alcohol than Islamic revolution. The

second, the late Juma Namangani's Islamic Movement of Uzbekistan, grew from modest origins—including a legendary shouting match between Karimov and Namangani before a Ferghana Valley mosque congregation around the time of the Soviet collapse—to become an organization of 2,000-3,000 militants. Most lived in exile and for a while staged showy military actions from bases in Afghanistan and Tajikistan. Karimov then used the ogre of Islamist terrorism to crack down mercilessly on real and imagined opponents, especially after he blamed them for a bomb in central Tashkent that nearly killed him in 1999. Karimov had an even freer hand to act after early American criticism of his indiscriminate anti-Islamist policies evaporated after Sept. 11, 2001. The U.S. bombing of Afghanistan killed Namangani and the ousting of the Taliban deprived Uzbek Islamist extremists of logistical support.

Tension between Karimov's vision of a Turkish-style, industry-led national rebirth and the resistance of the population to his Soviet-style enforcers colored all my visits to the Ferghana Valley. One trip followed an invitation by the Uzbek government to see the site of a new car factory near Andizhan. My sense of the state's insensitivity to religious norms was delightfully rekindled as I arrived at the place of Babur's birth. The airport policeman noted my arrival in a leather-bound register as "Pope Christ."

Every aspect of life was tightly controlled. Neat orchards and fields flanked our road to the car plant, while a hot haze swallowed up the mountains that rose to each side of the wide expanse of the Ferghana valley floor. Cotton seedlings stretched into the distance under orderly rows of plastic sheeting. A convoy of trucks and buses careened past, full of laborers heading out to the fields to mend seedbeds damaged in a recent hailstorm. The convoy had police escorts front and back, their lights flashing. Uzbek newspapers kept up the Soviet tradition of photographs of peasants cheerily working in the fields, but the state was clearly taking no chances.

We soon reached the automobile factory, built under contract with the Korean company Daewoo. Compared to shoddy old Soviet workplaces, it looked unbelievably rich, with immaculate lawns and workers in spotless new uniforms. Like Turkey not long ago, Uzbekistan was starting with simplistic assembly, manufacturing three models of car from parts shipped across China on the new Silk Road railway. The faces, work ethic and the ambitious atmosphere reminded me of Turkish factories I had toured. One of the production line managers, Hassanjan, brimmed with a nationalist confidence bordering on religious faith. "We haven't changed the cars' Korean specifications for our roads," he said, nodding proudly at the highly automated machinery. "'We are of the opinion that we have to change the roads to the specification of our new cars."

The Ferghana Valley had to live with its Islamic past, however. Two years before my visit, as the Taliban were building up to power in neighboring Afghanistan, the government crackdown on the Islamists had started with the "disappearance" of the imam of the great mosque in Andizhan, Abduvali Mirzayev. I escaped for a while from my attentive Uzbek hosts to wander through the grounds of a nearby old *madrasa* religious school. There I found a cheery, bearded youth touching up the stucco tracery in one of the domes.

"Is this, um, private work?" I asked.

"Oh no, the state's taken everything over."

"Even your mosque?"

"Yes."

"What are you doing about it?"

"Oh, people just changed their methods," he said, the untouchable smile of the fundamentalist playing on his lips. "They're organizing for the Islamic revolution in secret now."

Such fundamentalists were rare before President Karimov started his brutal campaign of arrests, harassment and show trials. Now nobody knows the strength of the Islamic movement, since it has gone underground; the government possibly does, and behaves as if it faces a growing threat. The Karimov enforcers, knowing in their hearts how well-justified it would be to oppose such a rough dictatorship, were allergic to anybody who dressed and behaved differently from the line dictated by the regime. The tragedy was that most of the people whom Karimov's policemen arrested as "Wahhabis," or ultra-fundamentalist Islamists, were pious and private Muslims rather than dangerous threats to public order. Despite Karimov's secularist zeal, most Uzbeks would not have wanted an Islamic state. Indeed, a real fundamentalist Turkish Muslim missionary next to me on one flight out of Tashkent complained bitterly that few would listen to him in the "godless" newly independent states of Central Asia, and that he was going to seek more receptive Muslims in the Russian Federation.

Although Karimov clearly feared that a well-organized coup could easily topple his regime, the Islamist threat seemed controllable in Uzbekistan, and remote elsewhere in Central Asia. There was no established, independent priesthood as in Shia Muslim Iran. There was none of the chaos and weariness with war that allowed the Taliban to come to power in Afghanistan. Unlike the Arabs, the Turkic peoples are not tightly bound to Islam by geography and language. With Turkic states usually paying for and regulating mosques and prayer leaders—in Turkey, for instance, weekly sermons are often distributed centrally to more than 80,000 places of worship—ordinary people have prefered to have their deeper religious needs catered for by sects, orders, individuals or thinkers. Most Turkic peoples are too open to outside influences, and have moved too far from ignorant poverty, than to succumb easily to the religious fascism seen in Iran, Afghanistan or Saudi Arabia.

Karimov did have reason to be scared that well-organized, armed Islamists from Tajikistan or Afghanistan could cross the porous borders of his country. Frontier controls were theoretically tight, but oppressive rules in Central Asia were undermined by an astonishing level of corruption. Just $10 once bought my way past the young conscripts on the Uzbek-Tajik border. Still, Karimov constantly meddled in Tajikistan, the only Central Asian country with a legal Islamist opposition, to the point of backing armed insurrections. Karimov was following the same logic as Prince Babur, who stated centuries ago that Central Asian rulers must fear what they don't control, for it may soon try to control them. But Babur also had an even wiser piece of advice: "Beware of inner wounds that fester. They will surface in the end."

It was in Xinjiang that I found the strongest Turkic attachment to Islam. I attributed this to the undeveloped nature of Uygur Turk society and their struggle to survive as a small minority in China. I longed to debate with ordinary Uygurs their view of Islam's role in defending themselves from the Chinese onslaught. Such talk was usually impossible, however. I feared that Chinese police would discover and expel me for unauthorized reporting. But I got my chance when the bus I was traveling in outside Kashgar suddenly ground to a halt. Ahead of us, a traffic

jam of cars, trucks and donkey carts blocked the road. The aisle of the
bus filled with cheerful curses, both secular and blasphemous. I joined
my fellow passengers in clambering over the bundles of luggage stacked
about the seats to see what had happened. We couldn't get beyond an
impenetrable crowd of onlookers, gathered round what seemed to be a
bus lying on its side. We returned to squat by the side of our vehicle on
the roadway built up off the desert floor. No Chinese were in sight. The
excitement and the desert air brought a moment never repeated during
my time in Xinjiang, a casual public political discussion.

A half-circle of young men was already engaged in an ardent debate
about the varying merits of the new Turkic-language radio stations
broadcasting to Central Asia from London and Washington. A medium-
built man in a striped shirt, in his 20s, caught my eye as if wanting to
talk. We introduced ourselves. His name was Mehmet.

"Do you understand all those radios?" I asked him. The United
States, which dropped Uygur broadcasts as part of its rapprochement
with China in 1979, had restarted two hours a day of Uygur programs
after the founding of Radio Free Asia in 1996.

"The ones in our Turkic languages, yes," Mehmet said, adding bitterly that they couldn't understand English broadcasts because there
were no proper English lessons at the Uygur-language schools, which
most Uygurs attended.

The radios were a small chink in the latterday Great Wall which China
has built to block the flow of information to the Uygurs. But it was only a
beginning. One of Mehmet's friends, Iman, a thin man with a moustache,
had the latest model of Ericsson mobile phone. I set its language to
Turkish and proudly showed it to him, but he couldn't read the Latin script
and showed no interest when I read out words that were the same in his
own language. A sense of literary confusion is understandable among the
Uygurs. China phased out the traditional Arabic script in 1962 in favor of
Latin letters, to wean the Uygurs off their old, Islamic identity. But when
Latin-script books started flowing in from Turkey, China moved the language to a unique, modified Arabic script in 1980. Two generations in a
row were thus cut off from their parents' written culture. Even then, books
are destroyed at the slightest sign of separatist dissent; in 2002, such
charges annihilated tomes with humble titles like *Ancient Uygur Literature*

and Ancient Uygur Craftsmanship and *A Brief History of the Huns.*

We squatted on our haunches by the side of the road, watching the more impatient Uygur donkey- and camel-cart drivers cajoling their antique contraptions through drifts of sand on a desert track alongside the blocked-up road. Mehmet pointed out the discrepancy with the motor vehicles used by Chinese. As we talked, I realized that he and his friends' lacked an ideological concept of opposition, Islamic or nationalist. All they had was raw anger.

"If we work for a month, we earn enough for a bicycle," said Mehmet, who said he'd given up his poorly paid state teaching job to go back to farming. "But if the Chinese work for a month, they get enough for a car."

"They've taken all our money—98% of the Uygurs are poor. They take our oil, our gold, our everything to China," chipped in the conductor of the bus, making a dismissive gesture over the Taklamakan desert.

"We can't say a word. If we do, just one word, it's straight to prison, and we get shot. So everyone shuts up," said Iman. "A friend of mine was sent to prison for five years. When he came back he'd gone mad."

Reports of mind-bending drug injections figure among Chinese abuses of Uygurs listed by human rights groups like Amnesty International. Death sentence rates and torture in Xinjiang are worse than the rest of China, said an in-depth report done by the group in 1999. Some cruelties are unique to the territory: wires are forced under nails, chilli powders stuffed into the nose or genital organs, and rough horse hairs threaded into penises. One prisoner told how paper was shoved up his anus by interrogators, who then lit it and made him run in the "'flying aeroplane" position, arms spread out and bent forward.

"We're like slaves. Slaves. Exactly like slaves," Iman muttered. Like all of them, he wanted to fight back by any means. "There will never be peace in Xinjiang."

The Chinese traffic police arrived. They efficiently cleared the crashed bus to one side. We clambered back aboard ours. As we edged past the accident scene, we craned our necks and saw that the bus had collided with a cart making its way home from the local market. A man and his headscarved wife lay dead on the roadway. Their cart was splintered into matchwood. Further on lay their donkey, his guts spilled out over the tarmac. All had been flattened by their horrible clash with the modern world, much as the Uygurs of Xinjiang felt bulldozed by the onrush of China. The big Chinese bus, however, also looked a write-off. My neighbors tut-tutted over the scene and invoked the name of God.

"What's more important to you? Your Turkish side, or your Muslim side?" I asked Mehmet as we pulled away. He thought for a moment.

"I am a Turk in language," he answered, "but a Muslim in my heart."

A longing for international strength and legitimacy lay behind the Uygur embrace of Islam. It gave them a perhaps misleading sense of equality in numbers, since there are nearly as many Muslims in the world as Chinese. In most houses I visited, people rigorously observed Islam's five daily prayers. In Uygur villages, mosques were usually the tallest and best-built buildings for miles, their street fronts decked out in fancy tile-work and a line of four or six slender minarets. At the weekly communal prayers in Kashgar, old gentlemen always wore the gorgeous garb of old Central Asia: loosely wrapped turbans, striped silken gowns and long soft leather boots. Uygur women mixed Muslim propriety and fashion. In villages, they walked with open faces, wearing a loose head-scarf, if they covered their heads at all. In town centers, middle-class women draped thick, brown woolen cloths over their heads to mask their faces from the view of men. But a conservative Arab, for instance, would not have recognized the rest of their dress as Islamic. Middle-class ladies wore well-cut jackets and calf-length skirts wrapped in dreamily pat-terned gauze. Some sported high-heeled, white patent-leather shoes. Fabric colors could be as daring as hot pink.

Walking in Kashgar's old town, I found a little bookshop and asked about writers on Uygur history. The owner had to blow the dust off his few old volumes. His fast-moving bestsellers turned out to be the Koran and teach-yourself Arabic books. Indeed, while my improvised Uygur-Turkish chitchat generated trust and warmth, I generally won more respect for speaking Arabic. Islam was a safer kind of dissent. It bene-fited from a minimum of toleration by the Chinese state, which banned almost every objective, secular Uygur expression of a different identity. But lack of education meant Uygur Islam often merged with supersti-tion. The prize possession of one Kashgar shopkeeper was a poster of natural "miracles" proving the truth of Islam. One detail showed a copse of trees in Germany, its trunks twisted together to form the Arabic spelling of *allah*, or God. The seeds in a cross-section of a watermelon appeared to write out the name of the prophet Mohammed. Similar miracles leaped from a cut turnip, a slice of tomato and a honeycomb populated by a particularly clever swarm of Turkish spelling bees.

The fashion could be purely social. When I asked the modern young Uygur woman teacher who showed me the way in Isa Alptekin's hometown why some of the young men bicycling past wore such thick black beards, she told me that "there are more and more of them like that. They just want us to stay home and have babies."

Islam was a vehicle for the Uygurs' political frustrations, too. Fundamentalist youths raked me with angry stares of hostility at a Kashgar neighborhood prayer house and I was told to get lost by an intolerant old watchman in a mosque in Urumqi. Sensing the threat, the Chinese have usually feared and sometimes hated Uygur Islam. During the Cultural Revolution, Red Guards destroyed mosques, cut the beards of imams and poisoned Muslim wells with pigs. Later, in the 1980s, China allowed more freedom for religious teaching. But the "open door" years got out of hand in 1989 when a Shanghai publisher put out a book called *Sex Habits*, which repeated common Chinese slanders that mosque domes represented breasts, minarets stood for penises, and that the annual pilgrimage to Mecca was a lascivious feast that included sex with camels. The authorities punished the publisher and closed several Muslim religious schools in the same year. It was unclear if the two actions were connected, but it marked the end of China's experiment in the liberalization of Islam.

The late 1980s demonstrations included marchers who shouted the name of Uygur leader Isa Alptekin, echoes of which had even reached me in Istanbul. After his death in 1995, however, his sons told me that his legacy of secular, non-violent nationalism came under threat. Radical Islamic Uygur youths became common both in Xinjiang and among the usually secular-minded Uygur exile communities in Central Asia. A few beat a path to the Taliban in Afghanistan. Some even fell prisoner to U.S. forces and languished in jail in Guantanamo Bay. After the Sept. 11 attacks on America, however, Alptekin's eldest son and political heir, Erkin, said he felt a shift back to the non-violent cause.

"I was telling them for years that while you might admire a suicide bomber, the outside world will see him a terrorist. Now they come and tell me, Erkin, you were right," he told me by telephone from his office in The Hague. "I don't take much notice of labels, though. In the 1950s, the Chinese called us the 'agents of the American paper tigers.' In the 60s, we were 'agents of Soviet hegemonists'. After the Iranian revolution in 1979, the Chinese turned us into 'fundamentalists.' In the 1980s they began blaming everything on my father, saying he was sending weapons hidden in Korans. In that time we became 'splittists.' Since September 11, we are 'terrorists.' But what the Chinese are really scared of is our Turkic identity, what Chinese newspapers call 'the poison coming from Turkey.'"

As in Western societies, religion and nationalism were inextricably entwined. Anne Philippe, a French reporter who visited Alptekin's republic in the late 1940s, described the Uygurs as Muslim fanatics. But Isa Alptekin, a pious Muslim, insisted to me that this was not so. For him, Islam was taken for granted, and didn't need to be part of the political agenda. Secular, nationalist Turkey had been the true beacon of his republic. There was little Islamic about the revolutionary edicts handed down by Alptekin and Masoud Sabri, an Istanbul-educated Turkic nationalist who took the title of president. They changed the name of the government's official gazette from *Xinjiang* to *East Turkestan*. They banned names for ethnic groups such as Uygurs, Kazakhs, Kyrgyz and Tatars. All became Turks, in official literature and in schools. Alptekin went to Turkey to buy books for the first Turkish-language library in East Turkestan. China bided its time, and the Russians bristled. Soviet Radio had railed against the East Turkestan regime, saying: "The center of pan-Turkism used to be Ankara. Now it is Urumqi."

Today's Central Asian despots now present Islam as the enemy as they busily build more narrowly nationalist identities for their states. The experiment may yet trip over their own injustice and corruption. But because they face competition from no single dominant interpretation of Islam, they have a margin for error. They can count on the politically secular proclivity of the Turkic peoples, as I learned from watching the competition for influence in their lands between secular Turkey and theocratic Iran.

17. AN EMPIRE OF THE MIND

TURKISH PRAGMATISM OUTFLANKS
IRANIAN THEOCRACY

My Dad is Sunni, Mum is Shia, a pearl am I!
Not Persian, not an Indian. A Turk am I!
In town, at prayer, drunk in wine-house gardens, it makes
No odds! In truth, what a smart fellow am I!
—Azerbaijani satirist MIRZA AL-EKBER SABIR, 1862-1911

THERE SHOULD HAVE BEEN NO CONTEST IN ONE OF THE NEW GREAT
Games for influence in Central Asia: that between Turkey and Iran.

Iran was far closer, its great landmass lying just to the south of
Central Asia's deserts and the bare, rolling buttresses of Turkmenistan's
long Kopet Mountain range. The big east Iranian city of Mashad was just
a half-day's drive from the Turkmen capital, Ashgabat. By contrast, the
industrial heartland of the Turkmen's ethnic cousins in Turkey was ten
times farther away.

Yet Iran lost. Its theocratic regime was not taken seriously even
among its fellow Persian-speakers in Tajikistan, to judge by the jokes
cracked by a Tajik official who had taken a course in diplomacy offered
by Tehran. There were many reasons for the failure. In Turkmenistan,
as in much of Central Asia, Turkey's pragmatism, business acumen and
U.S. support gave it the edge. Elsewhere, it was a problem that Iran was
naturally allied with Russia and Armenia, traditional enemies of the
Turks. An Islamic sectarian difference mattered, too. Turkey is pre-
dominantly Sunni Muslim, like most of Central Asia, while Iran is
defined by its Shia identity, which focuses its devotion on the family of
the prophet Mohammed and, since the 1979 Islamic revolution, its

insistence on a dominant political role for the priesthood. But Turkey's dominance was not entirely a victory for secularism, or for the Turkish government. It had much more to do with the initiative of ordinary Turks.

Arminius Vámbéry, who set out in the 1860s through the Ottoman Empire, Iran and Central Asia to trace the Turkic roots of his native language, described the essential difference a century and a half ago. "I accord to the Persian all the politeness of manners, and all the readiness and vivacity of wit, that are wanting in the Osmanli (Ottoman Turk); but in the latter, the absence of these qualities is more than compensated by an integrity and an honorable frankness not possessed by his rival," he wrote. "The Persian can boast a poetic organization and an ancient civilization. The superiority of the Osmanli [Turk] results from the attention he is paying to the languages of Europe and to the progress European Savans [thinkers] have made."

Iran's Islamic Republic often talks about its natural geographic role as a gateway to Central Asia and has opened up new trade and minor pipeline routes to the region. But the dead weight of its bureaucracy makes trans-Iranian shipments expensive and time-consuming. On the streets of Ashgabat, the Turkmen capital, Iranian commerce was first represented by cheap-and-cheerful goods of a holding company known as the Martyrs' Foundation, which ran factories in Iran confiscated from the deposed Shah and his family. But as the years went by, the Martyrs' market began to look forlorn. Cluttering up three floors, the stacks of childrens' clothes, toys, fridges and household goods were produced by factories starved of new technology for decades. Few wanted the glum black chadors or dark overcoats which Iranian women were condemned to wear. Instead, the one stand where Turkmen clustered sold cheap, bright red Iranian-made lipstick.

The Turks, on the other hand, never looked back from a first exercise in hand-me-down capitalism in 1992. Italy's Benetton fashion company gave a marketing license to their Turkish partners, the Turks appointed a 22-year-old ethnic Russian weight-lifter called Dimitri as store manager, and Dimitri hired Turkmen girls as shop-assistants. His attempt to dress them in tight, garish Benetton garb only lasted a month before they reverted to their flowing Turkmen gowns. But this small showcase was the harbinger of dozens of Turkish-built shops, hotels and factories that spread through the country. The vast, state-of-the-art Turkmenbashy textile and clothing complex outside Ashgabat was built, managed and partly owned by a Turk, who also became the deputy minister of industry. Another Turk became Turkmenbashy's ambassador to Washington for much of the 1990s.

Over at the Iranian embassy, ambassador Mehdi Miraboutalebi complained bitterly about these setbacks for his mission. Even the capital's one Persian restaurant served alcohol and was run by a chic Iranian gentleman who wore a tie—the symbol of Atatürk's revolution, Turkic-style secularism and the West, loathed by the Iranian revolutionaries in their pointedly collarless shirts. The ambassador blamed America for all Iran's difficulties in projecting its influence. Washington had planted a bunker of an embassy on Ashgabat's main boulevard and erected a wall of opposition to Turkmen-Iranian projects. He was pleased, however, with the fact that the first small independent gas pipeline out of Turkmenistan went to Iran.

"We hope others let our country have peaceful relations with neighboring countries. There are some 10,000 miles away [Americans] who are trying to profit from bloodshed," he said.

The U.S. Senate barred American companies from making significant investment in Iran, hobbling plans for bigger Turkmen oil or gas export pipelines that might have taken routes through that country. The Iranian ambassador was right that this was largely due to pro-Israeli lobbies in Washington that sought to isolate Iran, a theme he elaborated as we continued our conversation at a Turkmen independence day cocktail party for Ashgabat's diplomatic community. His solution was simple.

"You should kick the Jews out of your country," the ambassador said.

"How do you know that I might not be Jewish, when you say something like that?" I replied.

"Oh yes, I forgot. All the media in the West is owned and run by Jews."

Taken aback, I took an ostentatious gulp of wine and stalked off. But Miraboutalebi knew his enemy. I walked straight into the arms of Gideon Weinstock, a diminutive representative of Merhav, the small Israeli company which, thanks to its intimacy with the Turkmen president, handled a great deal of the Turkmenistan's early refinery and pipeline business—and also worked to block any initiatives by Iran.

In many ways, Turkey's overtly secular republic and Iran's theocratic one were mirror images of each other. Iran's regime demonized women who appeared without headscarves in public, while Turkey's system demonized women who tried to appear with their headscarves in state institutions like parliament or university. Weirdly, this official pressure has produced a situation where the Turkish population is rather pious and is constantly spending its private money to build mosques, whereas Iran's constant religious propaganda has rendered its once-pious population remarkably secular in private. ("How would you feel if you had to put up with Christmas every day?" an acquaintance in Tehran once asked me). Whereas few private mosques can be seen under construction in Iran, there are so many domes and minarets sprouting up in the Turkish urban and village landscape that Istanbul's mufti, or religious leader, was formally trying to stop them. While the Iranian state spent two decades failing to finish its main revolutionary prayerdrome complex in north Tehran, the Turkish state was sending money to build mosques in Central Asia. Indeed, as young people in independent "northern" Azerbaijan felt their way to a new piety after years of communist atheism, they could feel alienated by the fact that their "southern" Azeri kinsmen from Iran, subjected to years of Islamist propaganda, had developed an almost pro-communist hatred of religion.

In sectarian terms, Iran and Turkey are also two sides of the same coin. Iran's population is mostly Shia, but has a significant Sunni minority. Turkey, meanwhile, is majority Sunni, but has a minority of perhaps one fifth of the population which is "Alevi," a kind of folk cult with strong Shia elements. In ethnic terms, the paradox is more complicated. Turkey, while claiming a strong ethnic link to Azerbaijan, is actually home to only a few hundred thousand full ethnic Azeris—other Turks are close, but more like ethnic cousins. Yet few people realize that perhaps one quarter of Iran's population are ethnic Azeris. There are other Turkic speakers too, like Turkmens close to the border with Turkmenistan and the nomadic Qashqai tribe that roams as far south as

Shiraz. Indeed, if one takes into account the large Kurdish-speaking minority, perhaps only one half of the people of Iran speak Persian as their first language at home.

In a similar paradox, the courts of Turkic rulers—the Seljuks, the earlier Ottomans, the Central Asian Khans of Bokhara and Khiva, and even the Mogul dynasty of India—all used Persian as their official language, even as the ruler spoke Turkish with his immediate family. Like French in 19th century Europe, it was considered international, refined, and the premier medium of literature and poetry. It was also because Turkic rulers—or Turkic armies under Mongol command—have held sway in all or parts of Iran throughout most of the past several centuries: Mahmud of Ghazna, the Seljuks, the White- and Black-Sheep dynasties, the Timurids, the Safavids, the Turkmen raider Nadir Shah, and the Qajars. Turkic culture was mostly neglected until the Republic of Turkey appeared, with its self-conscious mission to raise the cultural development of the Turks. From this perspective, the Turkic speakers in Iran are in some ways as undeveloped as the pre-republican Turkish countryside. Trying to tune in to a group of Iranian Shia pilgrims one day in a hotel lift in Baghdad in 2002, it took me half a minute to realize that they were speaking rustic Azeri. Likewise, sitting down to negotiate in Turkish the purchase of a domed hat with an aged Qashqai felt merchant in Shiraz felt like talking to a child. Education and free access to information among such peoples will certainly broaden and deepen the importance of Turkish in the world, and in Iran. Already, with an eye on their advertisers, Istanbul satellite TV stations are taking respectful note of their Iranian Azeri audiences.

Indeed, as U.S. policymakers started looking once again for points of weakness to put pressure on Iran in the early 2000s, some focused on Iran's Azeri question, or, as Turkic nationalists put it, the problem of "south Azerbaijan." Iranian Azeri dissidents have appeared in Washington to build a case for greater national rights. But, whether from Shia solidarity, a common history or simply fearing the loss of their leading role in the Iranian economy, virtually no Iranian Azeris demand an independent state or union with the Republic of Azerbaijan. During the bloody Iran-Iraq war of 1980-88, none fought harder for the country than the Iranian Azeris. The loyalty to Iran was so strong that when I sat next to an Iranian Azeri engineering student on a plane to London from Istanbul, I simply could not persuade him of Turkey's relative progress — even though he had just spent 10 days being amazed at Istanbul, had a Turkish girlfriend and kept telling me how depressed he was by the backwardness of Iran. He didn't even admit he was an Azeri and could speak fluent Turkish until late in our conversation, as if it was a dirty secret.

"The Turks are just copying the West," he insisted.

"Yes, just like Japan and China used to. But they've just won the prize for producing the most energy efficient fridge in Europe!" I replied.

"Really?" he said. But it was too hard for him to overturn the deeply rooted anti-Turkish prejudice. He looked back down at his feet. "No, sorry, I can't help it. Iran can't learn anything from Turkey," he went on. "Only America can save us."

Still, Iranian Azeris feel the kindred spirit. They helped tear down the border fence between Iran and Azerbaijan's little exclave of Nakhichevan when the latter became the first part of the Soviet Union to declare independence in January 1990. When an Iranian Azerbaijani statelet declared autonomy in December 1945, it was certainly a creature of Soviet foreign policy. But it found ready Azeri collaborators before the experiment was crushed a year later by a reconstituted Iranian Imperial Army. Iranian Azeris feel legitimate grievances. Ruled by shah or mullah, Iran has pursued standard Middle Eastern policies against the minority: bans of the Azeri language in education and official contexts, jailing and execution of dissidents, changing of place names, and a refusal to allow Azeri broadcasts. As Iranian Azeri poet Mohammed Hussein Shahriyar put it in his poem "Azerbaijan":

> Your wealth, your strength, the whole world knows
> Made Iran prosper, set it free, O Azerbaijan!
> For Iran did your young warriors die. Only sorrows
> And pain did it gave you back, O Azerbaijan!

In fact, the history of Turkey and Iran is so interleaved that French orientalists focus one of their most important publications on the "Turco-Iranian World." Turkish and Iranian sparring can seem like a family feud.

Turkey's Alevi community are partly the legacy of Shia missionaries sent into Anatolia by the 16th century Safavid Shahs in order to win the population over from the Ottomans. The Alevis today are mostly staunch republicans—viewing secularism as their best guarantee against absorption by the Sunni Muslim majority—but in 2003 the newspaper *Cumhuriyet*, or the Republic, showed Turks' continued sensitivity. It reported an Iranian invitation to Alevi associations to visit Tehran under the front-page headline: "Mullahs Bid to Hook Alevis." On the other hand, in the early 20th century, it was Turkey's modernizing republican founder Kemal Atatürk who was influencing the Iran of Reza Shah. The Iranian dictator went even further than Atatürk, ordering his soldiers to strip veils off women in the street. His strongarm methods were one reason that the Iranian population rallied closer to the Shia clergy, who were then as independent from the state as the Turkish clergy is under their state's thumb.

I wanted to travel to Iranian Azerbaijan to take the measure of Turkic feeling in Tabriz, one of the country's great cities and economic centers. But, although I visited many other parts of Iran and lived in Tehran for a year, it proved hard to arrange a trip to Iranian Azerbaijan when I wanted it. Iran can be as self-consciously closed to foreigners as Turkey is open. I got close in the Hotel Tabriz, the main hostelry in Nakhichevan, the small Azerbaijani territory wedged between Armenia, Iran and Turkey, where I had occasion to feel most grateful to an Iranian Azeri.

It was late one night that I arrived in the hotel's dirty, downcast lobby in 1994, during the darkest days of Azerbaijan's adventure in independence. I waited for several minutes for a rumpled receptionist to emerge from a door behind the desk. He slowly wrote me out a pass for a room, but said that the floor lady would not be back with the key for a while. In a monosyllabic way, he indicated that the lift didn't work and that if I still wanted to be in possession of my moveable property in the morning, I should lock it into a caged-in cave under the stairs. I gripped my bags close as I felt my way forward and up the ill-lit stairs. On the first landing, a half-drunk group of Azerbaijani militiamen spilling out of a bar malevolently left me little space to pass.

At this moment of mutual appraisal, I was saved by the appearance on the landing beside me of a new and rather forbidding figure with a jet-black beard. He had the unshaven, deliberately unkempt posture of a post-revolutionary Iranian, but had an educated look in his eyes. He looked like somebody I could at least relate to, if not instantly trust.

"You need help?" he asked in Azeri, escorting me past the militiamen, who drifted away to lose themselves in a new toasts to each other.

"How do I get into a room here?" I asked in front of my door.

"It's a problem. Put your things in my room and we'll sort it out later."

My new friend's name was Mohammad, and our shared distaste for our surroundings soon drew us together. He knew a place for dinner that would be better than joining the squalid and threatening scene in the bar. It was a formerly grand restaurant used for weddings, and its walls were decorated with Soviet mosaics of *naïf* village girls and boys. Their wide-open eyes now stared down on empty metal tables. We had to make our way to the kitchen to ask a lone cook what he had to offer. We were not aware of a plague then ravaging Nakhichevan's cattle stock and settled for long, flat, Iranian-style kebabs, which we washed down with cans of Turkish beer. We talked politics. Armenian forces had recently overrun Azerbaijani defences in Nagorno Karabagh, and I assumed Iranian Azeris would be burning to aid their beleagured ethnic kin as much as the Turks of Turkey. But for Mohammed, Turkic solidarity wasn't a big deal.

"We've had a couple of student demonstrations. OK, I agree, an ethnic Azeri in Tabriz is an Azeri first, an Iranian second. But we don't want an independent state. What would we live off? We are very integrated in Iran," he said.

He was right. Even Iran's supreme leader was of Turkic stock. Ayatollah Ali Khamenei was from an Azeri family that had moved to the eastern city of Mashad, and spoke Azeri in meetings with the Azerbaijani president. Former Prime Minister Hossein Moussavi was an Azeri, as was perhaps half of the ruling Islamic revolutionary elite. The Tehran bazaar is dominated by Azeris, and many of the capital's grocers are Azeris too. Many are still shy of their ethnic identity, but it certainly counts. The workers who built the Intercontinental Hotel in Tehran in the 1970s were mostly from Azerbaijan, and many stayed on to become its staff. In 2002, I was standing by a televised soccer international in the lobby of the hotel—now called the Laleh, or Tulip—when one of the aging bellboys shouted with unusual joy as a member of the Iranian squad shot a goal. I asked the reason, and he wouldn't say. Finally he blushed and admitted it was because the scorer, like him, was "a Turk." The reason for diffidence is that Persians mock Azeris as rough and stupid "Turks," even though some Iranians realize Turkey has now far outstripped Iran in economic development. This was acknowledged in the choice of a Turkish-Austrian company to build Tehran's fine new Imam Khomeini airport and a 2004 decision by Tehran to licence Istanbul's Turkcell to set up Iran's first GSM mobile phone network. The reason for Iranian backwardness is not hard to find: after the first flight into Imam Khomeini airport, it was closed down by Revolutionary Guards on the grounds that foreigners were compromising Iranian security. Iran is seeing other, less welcome changes as Turks climb the social ladder. One of the bigger riots in Iran in the 1990s occurred when the ethnic Persians of Qazvin, the first major town east of Tehran, demonstrated against a perceived take-over of their town by Azeri immigrants.

Back in the Hotel Tabriz, I asked Mohammed what he really thought of the "northern Azeris." "Don't you feel you have a lot in common? Deep in your heart, wouldn't you prefer to be ruled by Baku, not Tehran?"

"If it came to unity, the Azeris of Azerbaijan should be careful about who would swallow who. Even if we reunited, we in Iran are double their number. These Azeris here in Azerbaijan have a low culture. They only drink, they have no concept of work, they expect everything on a plate," he said. "We still remember eight years of war with Iraq. We don't want to get involved in conflict again."

Mohammad sipped his beer, but the availability of alcohol didn't seem to be the reason he had taken a break from the Islamic Republic.

"Why do you come to a dump like this?" I asked.

"We don't need a visa to come here. I can't afford anything else, and wanted to see something different. Try being an Iranian and going anywhere abroad!" he replied.

A teenage militiaman lurched over to our table to scrounge a drink and scraps of conversation. He was drugged up to his glazed killer's eyeballs, and propped his Kalashnikov rifle up against the table with metallic clatter. It was time for Mohammad and I to leave. We crossed the dark, empty square, entered the tomb-like lobby of our hotel and mounted the black tunnel of the stairwell. By the light of a weak bulb, we retrieved my luggage and found the middle-aged floor lady. She showed me into my pit of a room, trained her enormous pointed bosom in my direction and brazenly propositioned me.

It was hard to imagine a more unappealing idea. The room in the Hotel Tabriz had no curtains, the sheets were filthy and nothing in the bathroom had worked for years. The only thing that was clean was a sleek, plump brown mouse nibbling at something by a table leg. At best such places had been artificial Soviet implants on the landscape. Their spirit was broken, and they would have to be rebuilt from new. And until independent Azerbaijan became an obviously better-run and prosperous place, the eyes of Iranian Azeris were likely to remain firmly fixed on Tehran, not Nakhichevan or Baku.

Turkey's predominance over Iran in the Caucasus and Central Asia didn't mean that Islamic revivalism was banished from the agenda. In fact, Turkish businessmen often finance schools in Central Asia founded by Turkey's modern Muslim sects, the most powerful of which is a movement run by a former Turkish cleric, Fethullah Gülen. His organization bankrolled satellite television channels, printed local language newspapers in many Turkic states and coordinated a network of 300 schools in over 50 countries around the world. In public, the Gülen message was of tolerance and pragmatism, and the schools were opened in non-Muslim, non-Turkic countries too. But the secular establishment that runs Turkey is intensely suspicious of him, with some reason. In Turkey, Gülen activists would lure Central Asian students into their dormitory houses with offers of fine accommodation, in return for which they would be expected to pray together and ultimately to join the group. Videos of Gülen preaching were required viewing, and his passionate flights of oratory were designed to reduce members of the audience to tears.

Education has long been a primary battleground in Turkic countries, and so far Iran has had only a small role to play. When Russia tightened its grip on Central Asia a century and a half ago, the first Turkic reaction was a growth in Islamic education, with students occasionally sent abroad to the great Arabic seminary of al-Azhar in Cairo. Then, partly thanks to the quick absorption of reformist ideas among the westerly Tatars, a new wave of modern reform in Turkic populations was started by "jadids," or renewers. Several of these had initially done full courses of study in the old-fashioned religious *madrasa* schools. But especially after 1905, many of them went on to further studies in the Ottoman capital Istanbul, where 19th-century pan-Islamist ideas were giving way to a mix of romantic pan-Turkic dreams and more realistic Turkic nationalist ideas. Most Central Asian intellectuals also read the newspaper *Tercüman*, published by Tatar intellectual Ismail Gaspıralı, which spread a message of nationalist rather than religious revival.

With their calls for an autonomous Turkistan within Russia, the *jadids* in some ways set the ideological stage for the new states that emerged in the 1990s. But the study of the *jadids* is still in its infancy. They were long the subject of vilification by the Soviet Union, and, from the Turkish side, ignorance and neglect. One great loss was a memoir dictated to a friend by leading *jadid* Osman Hoca, who founded new model schools, briefly became president of free Bokhara in 1920 and died in exile in Turkey; the work was thrown away by the scribe's daughters in Ankara, who understood nothing of their father's notes in Arabic script. We do know that the *jadids* tried to stir up the national spirit of Turkic Muslims in the Tsarist Empire, and that their main enemies were initially not the Russians, but Islamic conservatives. Pre-Soviet khanates would shut the *jadid* schools down, nervous that they could be nurturing rivals to their monopoly grip on power. Later, during the tumultuous period after the Russian revolution, an alliance of social conservatives and Islamist fundamentalists, sensing the threat to their faith, power and privileges, sided with the Russians against the *jadid* renewers. The reverse happened in modern Uzbekistan. President Karimov thought the Gülen schools such a threatening Islamic alternative that he closed them all down.

There is however a major problem for both Turkish and Iranian Muslim revivalists: young people of Soviet education are not necessarily attracted to Islam. When given freedom to do so, as they were in Azerbaijan, people were also interested in a wave of Christian missionaries that spread over the former Soviet Union. There was plenty of confusion, as I discovered when interviewing the president of Adjaria in Georgia, the little autonomous republic on the border of Turkey. When he said he was a Christian, I passed over the matter. Most Adjarians are Muslim, though not Turkic, and their faith was not my current concern. I wanted to know about Azerbaijani oil exports from Batumi, the rusting port he controlled until 2004.

"But I tell you, I am a Christian," the diminutive Aslan Abashidze insisted, taking my disinterest to be disbelief. "Yes, my grandfather was a Muslim. And my father was an atheist. But I am a Christian!"

Once again I pressed him about oil shipment volumes, but it only made the president more upset. He brought out the baptism photographs of his grandson. He sent for the Bishop of Adjaria, who, somewhat flustered, arrived a quarter of an hour later.

"Tell him," Abashidze said. "Tell him I am a baptized Christian!"

The bishop did his best to back his leader up, by which time, of course, there truly was disbelief on my face. So Abashidze dialed a number on the phone by his chair and barked a few orders. Twenty minutes later, a three-person presidential photographic team arrived with polaroid pictures just taken of Abashidze's bedroom. On the television was a statue, which he pointed to triumphantly, clearly believing the image to be of the Virgin Mary. It was a model of New York's Statue of Liberty. I was speechless. He gave up.

"We have to integrate with the Christian West," he said, a trace of resentful pleading in his voice.

Similarly, when I talked to young Azeri Muslim converts in Baku, it seemed they were as attracted not so much to Christian ideology but to the clean-cut confidence, the open culture and the wealth of the Western convert-seekers. Most of these were of Anglo-Saxon origin, worked as English teachers and looked passably like the denizens of the films people had seen of the rich West. In Baku, the main Muslim, Russian Orthodox and Jewish communities took the unusual step in 1996 of issuing a joint communique against the threat to their dominance. It bitterly noted the foreign missionaries' nice cars, their big meeting halls and their music. But Azerbaijan's official Shia Muslim chief, Sukrullah Pasazadeh, a rotund hold-over from Soviet times, seemed at a loss when I asked him what he was doing to rally his flock.

The newcomers were exploiting difficult economic circumstances, he said "in a state that is just learning to stand on its two feet. For 70 years, we only had this atheist propaganda. People are not ready for these new religions." He then lit up another Marlboro, and moved onto a more pleasant topic: a jolly recent visit to Istanbul.

Muslim fundamentalist missionaries did win a certain following, but it was tough going. In Riyadh, the Saudi capital, I met a Wahhabi missionary who briefly served in Baku before giving up and heading to the headier climes of Afghanistan. He recoiled at the memory of the difficulties he had faced trying to organize single-sex picnics to discuss the rigors of his faith, and told of his disgust at the way female neighbors hung about unveiled on his communal staircase. He said he'd converted one or two people, but was unsure if they'd stuck to it after his departure. Even so, all through this new Turkic region, there was a deep-seated longing for a place in life free from corruption and hypocrisy. One Azeri Muslim, Emin, a 22-year-old messenger, said he had even tried the Orthodox church, but found the tradition-bound religious services incomprehensible. Then he went to a bible class organized by the U.S.-based evangelicals of Greater Grace World Outreach, who, he said, explained religion "much better." His need was all for transparency and spiritual directness. He went on to convert his whole family.

Still, few could rival Turkey's moderate Gülen movement in breadth and depth of organization. In Turkmenistan alone, the Gülen group set up 13 schools and a university. Their curricula stressed national pride more than any overt religious agenda. Only an hour a week was spent on instruction on the "history of religions." But, like the colleges started by American Protestants in the Near East a century ago, teachers had every reason to hope that students would be attracted by their moral example. They were usually succesful. In the tiny, Turkic republic of Tuva on Russia's border with Mongolia, a Gülen schoolteacher married the president's daughter. In Turkmenistan, local elites crowded schools with applications for the few places available. Even Armenians enrolled their children.

I asked to visit the Gülen group's International Turkmen Turk University in Ashgabat, which had taken over and refurbished the abandoned wreck of an old Soviet institute. It was a pristinely kept, model educational institution. By 2000 it was attracting more than 700 students. Turkmens could buy something approaching a modern education for $15 dollars a month. Two-thirds of the 65 teaching staff were from Turkey. I was shown round by two Turks, Asim Kırıcı, a psychologist from Turkey who acted as the university counselor, and Murad, a businessman who was helping to finance the place.

"We're very conscious that our Turkish people originally migrated west from here, so it's like we're showing our loyalty to them after all these years," Kırıcı said.

As we toured neat Internet rooms, satellite television monitoring salons and language laboratories, it seemed as though local people were at last getting something tangibly good after the wrenching transition to independence. The boy students I met were busy, neat and keen. They seemed somewhat uptight and all wore ties—soon afterwards, however, the Turkmen leader decreed that Turkmen boy pupils should also put the white skullcaps worn by some traditional Muslims. Kırıcı the university counselor was defensive when I questioned him about religion.

"Our students are very close to their Islam," was all he would say.

On the way out, we stopped by the university notice board. There were photos of a recent "Feast of the Sacrifice," the biggest religious festival in the Muslim calender. Not all the Turkmens had been taking things too seriously, it seemed. In one picture, a Turkmen boy laughed as he playfully blew up the pink lungs of a sacrificed sheep like a party balloon.

Murad, the school's sponsor, struck a happy-go-lucky attitude, too. Islam for him was just one part of a busy, secular life. From the port of Mersin on the south coast of Turkey—close to the Toros Mountains, where many villages still proclaim a specifically Turkmen heritage—he had ended up in Turkmenistan by chance. Now he was importing containerloads of frozen chickens from the United States through Iran. He was prospering, had brought his family over, and gave me a tour round town in his big, wide American car.

He showed off the projects in which Turks from Turkey had taken a leading role—hotels, the airport, shops, cars and even the roads. In this backwater, Murad and his compatriots had added an unexpected footnote to the great westward Turkic migrations of a millennium ago. Or was it more than that? I asked him again why he gave money away to the school.

"We have no political agenda. It's just business," he maintained.

"But aren't you trying to build up some kind of new empire here?"

"If so, it's an empire of the mind. The university, the schools, they are to give the Turkmens a sense of national identity, of pride," he said contentedly. "These schools will help determine the fate of the world."

The Gülen movement was very much in harmony with another phenomenon in Turkey in the 1990s, the rise of a moderate Islamic movement, which took power in 2002 with the most stable parliamentary majority of any Turkish government for 15 years. Turkey, ahead of its eastern neighbors once again, had found a new compromise between church and state. The movement's eventual leader, Tayyip Erdoğan, had no lack of self-regard: he insisted that his party's mixture of faith, competence and separation of religion and politics was an example not just to Muslims but to the whole world. To explore the phenomenon, I made my way to Konya, a city deep in Anatolia and long a stronghold of Islamic resistance to the secularist agenda of the early republic.

18. RUMI'S LEGACY

THE TURKS ADOPT A
KINDER ALLAH

> *Be as you appear or appear as you are.*
> —JELALEDDIN RUMI, 1207-73

MY TOP-OF-THE-LINE MITSUBISHI BUS SPED ACROSS THE CENTRAL Anatolian highlands under the command of a uniformed *kaptan*. The driver's assistant, as serious as an in-flight attendant, moved up and down the cabin dispensing plastic cups of water and, as a restorative, splashes of pungent tobacco-leaf cologne. Our route followed long straight roads, sweeping smoothly over the wide, rolling, tree-less landscape that leads to the provincial city of Konya. The name derives from the ancient Roman Iconium, and its most notable monument is associated with the universal Muslim mystic Jelaleddin Rumi. But for Turkish secularists, and even some religious-minded Turks, the city has now above all become Turkey's "castle of Islam."

My fellow-passengers lapsed into the same state of extraordinarily placid inaction as people adopt on buses in Central Asia. Their features were a distinctive mix of what I think of as Turkish. But there is no single key to this ethnicity; only a minority had much hint of the high cheekbones and narrower eyes of the eastern steppes. Medieval Christian chroniclers believed that the Asiatic Turkic tribes who rode this way from the 10th to 13th centuries may have added just one person to every ten of the Byzantine-era population of Anatolia. As late as the 19th century, travelers remarked how peoples divided into the age-old provinces of Anatolia looked and behaved quite differently. Similarly,

the Turks combine an unusual number of religious identities. A new ety-
mological dictionary of the main 12,000 words in modern Turkish shows
that only 15-20% derive from Turkic roots, making it one of the most
hybrid languages in the world; however, most of this is passive vocabulary, and a typical Turkish newspaper article is two-thirds "Turkic." This
complexity has long vexed the Turks of Turkey, who are still debating
whether geography, race or religion should be the common denominator
of their official identity.

Şevket Süreyya Aydemir, an idealistic Turkish officer who served in
the Caucasus in the First World War, wrestled with the question of his
troops' identity as he rode east with the Ottoman army in 1914 on its ill-
fated quest to conquer a pan-Turkic empire. Aydemir wanted to educate
the illiterate Anatolian villagers who manned his machine-gun company.
One day, when their unit stood down for a rest from the front, he began
with some questions. Who was the sultan? Few knew that. The name of
the imperial capital? Even fewer answers. When Aydemir asked what
nation they belonged to, they gave different answers. So he asked them,
in Turkish, of course: "Are we not Turks?" Some of his men replied:
"*Estağfurullah,*" a self-effacing phrase from Arabic that means "God forbid!"

For the soldiers, the word *Türk* was associated with rustic nomad
schismatics. Only half of Aydemir's men, however, consciously thought
of themselves as part of traditional Sunni Islam. They were confused
about whether the prophet Mohammed was still alive, and about whether
or not the prophet might be Enver, the war minister and leader of the tri-
umvurate then in power. "I had thought our men were religious and fundamentalist, but they turned out to be plain ignorant," Aydemir wrote.
"Their identity papers said their religion was Islam, but underneath this
mass of people lived a whole series of contradictory religions, or dregs of
religions, sects, beliefs, and brotherhoods."

In the modern Turkish context, the city to which I was heading,
Konya, appeared the most sure of its Muslim identity. A demonstration
in favor of Islamic law here in 1980 provided one of the justifications for
the military coup of that year. Konya's veteran parliamentarian,
Necmettin Erbakan, rose to become Turkey's first Islamist prime minister in 1996, and was subsequently ousted after the generals' "soft coup"
of Feb. 28, 1997. Soon afterwards, an army-backed propaganda cam-

paign took aim at another threat to the secularist establishment: Islamist businessmen, based in places like Konya. The best known of these was Haşim Bayram, and I called for an appointment. He invited me to meet him at the headquarters of his company, Kombassan.

I waited in Bayram's spacious, open-plan office, surprised at its poorly fitted carpeting and cheap iron-and-laminate furniture. There wasn't a straight line in sight. Bayram himself bustled in late for our evening appointment. His style was disconcerting: he wore the crumpled jacket and baggy trousers of a conservative local shopkeeper, but made sure I knew that he had just flown in by helicopter. I wanted to know about his businesses, and how he had persuaded at least 30,000 people to invest in them. But it took more than an hour for him to get to such details. First he wanted to explain his ideas about the human spirit. To do that, he called for paper, a pair of scissors and some glue.

"There are three kinds of heads, you see. The small heads, the medium heads and the big heads. The big heads have the ideas," he said, shuffling appropriately sized pieces of paper around a low table. "You see, I'm one of the people with a big head."

He lectured me further about the day of judgement, lightwaves, the lifespan of the soul, sin and repentance, the transitory nature of life, evil, global values and the brotherhood of man. He told me about his poor beginnings as a shepherd boy. He spoke of his long studies through cold winters and his 18-hour days as head of a tutorial college. And then, finally, he came to his idea to wake the sleeping business tiger of Anatolia.

"I collected the top people of Konya—I knew them because their children were my pupils—and I said 'let's make a factory.' They remonstrated with me. One said: 'Hoca, nothing will come of this. Go to some rich people.' So I went to a merchant. He said: 'You are still a child. Who came from Anatolia and got rich? Don't take up space in my shop.' I went to pray in the mosque. I cried and I cried. I went back to the college, and a man in patched clothes and a flat cap came to me. He was a poor man, selling things from a barrow. He said: 'I heard you're making a factory. So I sold my home.' And he put the money on the table. The second was a woman who sold two small bracelets and a ring to raise money. Soon I had 50 people. In Anatolia and Europe, our people keep their money under the mattress, because we are against the concept of interest and banks. When their money is held individually, it can't do anything. When it comes together, we reach a critical mass."

Such story telling unlocked an impressive flow of money. In its first 10 years, Kombassan had collected $250 million, had founded 30 factories and businesses and was setting up 24 more. In theory, state agencies were watching its tax books and issuing of shares. In practice, every Turkish business keeps several sets of books, no Turk believes official figures, and Kombassan publishes none anyway. Investors handed their money over to Bayram in an act of faith and the promise of high payouts, again unpublished, but up to an annual 15-20%. Kombassan's annual report pictured the five members of the board, a vague, rapidly mounting graph and a curious mission statement: "We are determined to become a society ready to compete with the world, bearing our beliefs and principles to wider horizons, and standing by our national and moral values."

The double-talk of Turkey's political Islam is designed to be interpreted as fundamentalist or moderate to taste. For instance, the first two letters of the acronym of Turkey's main pro-Islamic business group, MÜSIAD, stand for *müstakil*, or independent, but every one subliminally understands them to stand for *müslüman*, a formulation that would break Turkish law. The ban against appeals to religious ideology means that nobody can be sure how Islamist any public group is. The Turks are not massively radical, however, and MÜSIAD remains medium-sized.

Where the law failed to help, the republican establishment tried all kinds of tricks to derail Kombassan. The company suffered asset freezes and repeated investigations. Kombassan was one of the 1,000 companies on an "Islamic capital" blacklist surreptitiously published by the army in an attempt to stampede them out of business.

I pressed Bayram about whether he considered his business Islamic. I expected Islamist marketing talk about how a pre-determined "profit-share" is different to "interest," which is banned in the Koran. He responded with a new concept: the Anatolian.

"Don't mix things up. The campaign against us is not religious. This is a war between Anatolian and *Istanbullu* capital," he said, lighting another cigarette. "Yes, there is radical political Islam. But then there are believers, like the Anatolians, who are just conservative people. Then there are the Istanbul people who have abandoned their culture—they are not Turks, they are not Europeans, they are not Americans. They're stuck in the middle."

A few fraudulent "Islamist" companies collapsed under the establishment's pressure, and Kombassan stumbled on occasion. Bayram might look fusty and crumpled, but the companies he had mobilized did not. The next morning, he ordered a car to drive me to the outskirts of town where Kombassan had set up an aluminum-frame window factory. Its manager, Ahmet Şan, had been 15 years in Germany, first at business school and then as an internal auditor at electronics giant Siemens. "Quality is profitability," said the slogans printed on sheets and hung from the white-painted walls.

"I had the ideal that I would learn Western technology and bring it back to my country to be useful. I've achieved that ideal," he said in his wood-paneled office at the top of a marble-lined staircase. "We even have military customers, you know."

Atatürk's generation of army officers and secularists had set out with the same idealism to educate the peasant Turkey of the republic's early decades. And, like the early republicans who introduced the Swiss civil code and Italian penal law, Şan kept speaking admiringly of Western models of civic behavior, not any Islamist principles from Mecca, Qom or Kabul.

"But surely," I asked, testing one of the slogans of the pro-Islamic politicians, "your reference point is Islam?"

"Not at all. Islam has its place in my private life. I'm a republican. The trouble is, our democracy is very weak. I want to have the democracy and secularism I found in Germany. When I fasted in Germany or prayed, I was respected."

Konya was certainly a self-respecting town. Rising over the fresh-built city center was an office block being constructed by Kombassan in reflective glass. Beside it were alcohol-free restaurants with Ottoman themes, and underneath it was one of Turkey's more luxurious commercial centers, another Anatolian business enterprise. Roaming up and down the aisles were nuclear families, much the same as elsewhere except for their more Islamic attire. Sales on credit were subject to a "financing charge," not interest. Most women, including female security guards with nightsticks, wore Muslim headscarves, but many young girls used make-up too. Boutiques sold the latest in fashionable Islamic clothing for women. The soft shopping muzak was interrupted for both sales announcements and the call to prayer. Few people, however, moved off to the mosque.

The 1997 army blacklist, the supermarket manager said, had the effect of boosting sales in Konya of products made by companies on it. But he reckoned a more lasting reason for his supermarket's success was cheaper prices than those in outlets run from Istanbul, with their unionized labor and expensive headquarters. Similarly, people appreciated local government by the pro-Islamic party on the grounds of competence as much as politics. They returned the party to Konya's municipality with about half of the popular vote each time.

Konya's mayor, Halil Ürün, agreed to see me in his new and well-appointed city hall. Ürün was soon telling me of how he had helped the Islamist businesses get going, while railing against the "centralizing, militarist tendency" in Ankara. To assert his Islamist credentials, he displayed beside his desk a shell-case from Chechnya's war of resistance against the Russian army. In reality, most of his foreign trips were to Europe. He took me out onto the balcony to show off his city. A newly installed electric tram made its sweep past his office. He looked as proud as a boy with a new train set. Indeed, I sometimes thought that the army's reaction to the Islamists' growing power was actually jealousy. "Feelings are welling up inside me . . . I'm going crazy," retired general Nevzat Bölügiray wrote to a newspaper in 2003, contemplating with a quivering pen the reformed, moderate Islamists who won a great victory in national elections in 2002.

From the mayor of Konya's office, concrete apartment blocks of uniform height marched up wide avenues stretching out to both sides. Unusually for Turkey, the municipality was enforcing building codes and sweeping streets clean. It looked less like a fundamentalist hideout than an ambitious city with civic pride and hunger for commercial success. The mayor pointed out an Ottoman-style water fountain by a pavement, one of 500 such sources of potable water he had connected with an all-new pipe system to a pristine spring in the mountains.

"Now, nobody will have to walk far for water to drink," he said. Since his citizens were still reluctant to drink tap water, it was a useful, if curious, improvement in their lives.

"It looks like a European town," I lied.

Actually, it looked more regimented than Europe—and duller. My remark pleased Ürün, however. He confided that during his last trip to Germany, he had been shocked to see a 60-year-old woman driving a taxi. But his attempt to make girl students take segregated buses to Konya University failed after two days. It simply wasn't practical. Similarly, Islamist pressure including bombings and window-smashings in the 1990s failed to close down secularist businesses in Konya. There were limits to how far the pragmatic Turks would go with the Islamist program. As Ürün himself said, even old radicals like him had to become more flexible. I raised another paradox of the squeaky-clean image of Konya's million people.

"Why is it that more *rakı* is sold here per person than most other places in Turkey?" I asked.

"Oh, it's nothing to be frightened of," he replied, and gave an enigmatic smile.

On my way out, I picked up some local business prospectuses at the municipal publications office. Conspicuous Islamic fervor had become a kind of marketing tool. One businessman predicted the imminent economic collapse of the West, the rise of more Anatolian tigers, the Turkish commercial conquest of the Turkic republics, and the ousting of European business from the Middle Eastern countries that were, after all, "our former provinces." Another business called Ittifak Holding had published a book of prayers to say when on the toilet, when looking in the mirror or when eating fruit. I decided to call on them.

I walked there past the new park Kombassan had built in the city center. It was a miniaturized panorama of famous Turkish sights. There were imitations of the eroded stone fairy chimneys from Capadoccia and a pond shaped like Cyprus, replete with the latest fashion in molded concrete rocks. It all seemed artificial. But the man who greeted me at Ittifak Holding's boxy concrete building looked like a real, hard-edged, West-rejecting Islamist. Seyyit Mehmet Boğa had a thick black beard and a striped polo shirt. Above his desk were verses from the Koran embroidered onto velvet. At a round meeting table he handed over a copy of his annual report. As I flicked through it politely, my eyes lighted on a paragraph. "We're happy to see that believers are rapidly getting organized. The dominant Westernizing forces are disintegrating and will soon give the way to the truth."

Boğa called for tea, and, stiffly at first, began to tell me about his company, which mainly operated in retailing and robotics software. Over the past 10 years, he had collected 20,000 investors. A 10th generation inhabitant of Konya, and a descendant of the prophet Mohammed, he said he and a group had decided in the mid-1980s to band together against the big Istanbul companies—mainly to get their share of commercial incentives paid by the state. Money had been the main prize in the battle, the fight over Islam secondary.

"Then are these companies the means to an Islamist order, or an end in themselves?" I asked.

"I just want to win God's satisfaction."

"You can't keep politics out of it, though."

"For sure. When I was a student in the 70s, we were very radical. It was right for those days. I thought it was very important to carry a gun. I still do. I don't believe in life without *jihad*."

Jihad, meaning holy struggle in Arabic, covers everything from studying hard for exams to outright war against the infidel. It was hard to pin down what Boğa was struggling for, but even if it was once radical, it now seemed to have little to do with the cataclysmic caliphate of an Osama bin Laden.

"Back then, we believed we had to start setting the world to rights with *jihad*. Now we believe it has to start with diplomacy. The road is guidance, dialogue and proselytism," he said. "The problem is bigotry, by which I mean people who believe in something without knowing why. And the biggest bigots are the secularists. Only education will save us."

The secularists also saw the Turks' salvation in education, and not that which Boğa had in mind. But, like them, he had compromised. He had gone beyond the old Islamist totalitarianism. He believed in variety and commercial competition. Life was less tough than it used to be, he said, his black eyes boring into mine, when people had trouble feeding their families in the hardscrabble villages of Anatolia.

"We used to think that forbidding a lot of things made you religious, made you harder. We had that sort of culture."

"So your view of God has changed?"

"His mercy has conquered His glory," said Boğa. "In the difficult lives we had, we couldn't tell the difference between resilience and toughness. We have changed."

The truth is that Turks have always had many competing visions of Islam. Modern times and the information age have dissipated the ignorance noted by the officer Aydemir. But under the superficial label that declares Turkey is "99% Muslim," diversity has become entrenched. Many beliefs are old survivals, sometimes attractive to modern Western tastes and sometimes tinged with superstition and intolerance.

I once met a shaman, a witchdoctor-priestess of the kind whose origins lie deep in Turkic history. She was a minor guest of honor at a gathering of the Turkic peoples of the world, held in a sports hall in the Turkish Black Sea port of Samsun. I had drunk tea with a Turkmen activist from Afghanistan, who was drumming up support for his cause in a soft-sided woolen cap. I had chatted with a Qashqai tribesman in a felt helmet who looked like he had come to life from a stone carving on the walls of the ancient Persian capital of Persepolis. He had said he had dressed himself and his sister up in their colorful costumes because no one paid him any attention when he wore a Western suit to the last Turkic get-together.

Then I saw Nadya Yuguseva arrive. She wore a splendid, tall, round hat of reddish fur. I complimented her on it, and she told me it was a traditional shaman artefact made from the tails of 12 foxes. I had imagined shamans as wizened old men, naked save for feathers and fetishes. But Yuguseva was a neatly presented, well-dressed woman. In her 40s, she appeared sensitive, and sensuous too. But there was something tremulous in her voice, as if she was a wild animal that could run off at the slightest hint of danger.

"Most of us are women. But we have a problematic history. In Soviet times, they called us charlatans," she said.

Up until a millennium ago, most Turkic peoples in Central Asia

followed such shamans, who guided them in worship of natural phe-
nomena like trees, the sky, and fire. As time went by, the Turkic peoples
experimented with several religions. Some became Jews, following the
decision of the kings of a 7th-11th century Khazar empire northeast of
the Black Sea. Some became Christians, like the early Mongols and
Uygurs or the present-day Gagauz of Romania. The Tuvans and other
small Turkic groups deep inside China became Buddhists. Most Turkic
people became Muslims, however. The conversion to Islam started in
the west, and slowly moved east. The more nomadic Kazakhs and
Kyrgyz kept up shamanic traditions until well into the 19th century.
The Turkic peoples of Siberia and the Russian far East, like Yuguseva's,
still do.

Yuguseva came from Altay, the forested Central Asian mountains at
the point where the borders of Russia, China and Mongolia meet. The
modern Turks count Altay as their legendary motherland. Indeed,
Yuguseva said her people considered themselves the purest of all Turkic
peoples, and the center of the world. Turkey's Turks are taught that the
first Turks were saved by a she-wolf that led them from danger in Altay;
Nadya said that her people had a similar legend. She claimed her
shamanism was the oldest religion in the world.

"Our spirit comes from the sky. We believe there are spirits in all
things, and that in every hundred people, there is only one who can
speak the language, who can become a shaman. It's transmitted in the
genes, that's why we have strict rules of marriage," she said. "I received
my shamanism from my uncle's side, although my uncle hid it, and so
did I. I didn't know until I was 25."

A chief engineer in a Soviet factory at the time, Yuguseva said that
her life changed one day that she suddenly found that she was paralyzed.
Doctors couldn't identify the disease. So she paid a secret trip to a
shaman to see if he could cure her. He did so. But he told her that she
was a latent shaman too, and that she would have to decide in six
months whether to become one. She tried to sidestep the vocation, but
paralysis struck her again. In the end she accepted her calling. She
would be called to sick people's houses, where she would sit for days on
end, waiting for the spirits to speak to her.

"I see people's insides like an X-ray film. But to cure people you have to talk to the soul. A woman has 40 souls; men have just one," Yuguseva said. "But when people laugh at shamanism, the soul just leaves."

Yuguseva said she could see traces of old shamanistic beliefs here in Turkey, in the Turks' respect for trees, fire and water. At that point a Turkish lady who was eavesdropping suddenly drove away the spirit of our conversation.

"Let's go to my house together tomorrow. Then you can tell all our fortunes!" said the woman.

She treated Yuguseva as if she was a mere adept at the traditional Turkish ladies' art of conjuring the future out of the thick smudge of grounds left in the bottom of a cup of Turkish coffee. Her tone agitated the highly-strung shaman, and she slipped away.

Shamanism does not theoretically exist in Turkey today, and the bureaucracy rejected the application of one man who tried to register himself officially as a shamanist. But some functions of the shamans of the ancient Central Asian Turks live on in the role of the *dede* in Turkey's Alevi minority, who are mostly descendants of tribes of Ottoman Turkic nomads. Alevis number about one quarter of the modern Turkish population, and, as their self-consciousness rises after centuries of oppression, they are more distinct than ever from mainstream Sunni Islam.

Their intense *sema* gatherings are becoming more public. Candles are lit by the *dede,* generally a mustachioed elder of the community, an *ozan* singer accompanies a song on his long-necked *saz* guitar, and men and women in colorful Anatolian costumes dance in a circle. On the walls above them gaze green-swathed head portraits of Ali, the prophet's cousin and son-in-law and the hero of the Shia. Ali is often flanked by an image of Atatürk, whose name is evoked with the same religious intensity as other members of the Shia pantheon; many Alevis believe Atatürk's secularism protects them from the Sunni majority. Books are appearing that begin to categorize Alevi doctrines, consisting in a belief in humankind, in love and in Ali, as well as in the supremacy of their own saints and native Turkic traditions over orthodox *sharia* religious law.

As the Alevis become more secure in their distinct identity, they are building places of worship, religious associations and launching their own political party. In this they are following the development of other religious groups and orders in Turkish society, often now officially blessed. Turkish President Demirel would visit the yearly gathering of the Bektashis, an Alevi order once favored by Ottoman elite troops known as the Janissaries, whose central Anatolian shrine preserves Janissary standards that include old Turco-Mongol symbols like animal tails. Sunni Muslims have several orders too, from fundamentalists to versions of Western Masonic lodges or Rotarian people of good works. The Nakhshibendis are the most widespread of these orders and follow a moral code based on the teachings of a medieval mystic from the Central Asian religious center of Bokhara. In the Turkic east, the order is deeply Islamist, but it is more liberal in the west and strongly associated with Turkey's progressive 1980s leader Turgut Özal.

Konya is the center of the *mevlevis,* the seven-century-old order of mystics also known as the whirling dervishes. They are remarkable as the only sect that was not officially closed down by Atatürk's republicans in 1925. Atatürk approved of the *mevlevi* approach to God as being "an expression of Turkish genius" that reclaimed Islam from what he saw as hide-bound, backward Arab tradition. With the black humor of the Turks, he teased nervous *mevlevis* during a 1931 visit that he had only not banned them in order to honor Rumi's lines: *"Locks bar all gates except Your own door / So lovers of the mysteries lose their way no more."*

Nevertheless, Atatürk confiscated their property along with that of all other sects. Even now, the ministry of culture allows one elite chapter of the *mevlevis* to rent back their dervish monastery in Istanbul only once a week to stage a ceremony as a "touristic attraction." But there is a renaissance underway. As the breathy music of the *ney* flute floats over the softly turning figures in the 18th century octagonal kiosk, the master of the lodge watches benignly over the dreamily rotating young people. The concrete materialism of modern Turkey slowly floats away. Since 2001, they have included both sexes in their ceremony, the men in white and women in colored skirts. These modern-day dervishes also engage in weekly intellectual debates. A more proletarian dervish chapter gathers in the poorer, more conservative suburb of Fatih, where worshippers turn their back on the whirlers and focus on communal prayer dominated by deep unison breathing. In Konya, however, the dervishes are employees of the state. They whirl for busloads of visitors in a spo hall, an event repeated for politicians from Ankara who visit at the December anniversary of the death in 1278 of their founder, *mevlana*, or our lord, Jelaleddin Rumi.

Turks love to visit Konya's restful stone-built *mevlevi* complex, built around Rumi's tomb. I sat in a shaded archway to watch a steady stream of families and devout visitors pass by. Many women stroked auspicious-looking outcrops of stone, wood or metal grill to soak up an aura of blessing. Rumi wrote his poetry in Persian—30,000 verses that defy any doctrinal framework, lyrical with metaphors from nature, cooking and sometimes sex—but the Turks have adopted him wholeheartedly. Indeed they cannot bring themselves to admit the possibility that this refugee from the 13th century Mongol invasions may not be one of them. Leaflets given out at the entrance present his hometown of Balkh in today's northern Afghanistan as a "center of Turkish culture." It was probably actually only ruled by a Turkic dynasty, but the leaflets claim one of the dynasty's members was Rumi's grandmother.

I found myself wrestling with a different detail from Rumi's life. His entranced outpourings were inspired by the disappearance of his soul-mate, a vagabond mystic called Shams-e Tabriz. A persistent legend has it that Rumi's followers had knifed him to death, hating the way he monopolized, distracted and debased their master, and Rumi's son supposedly buried Shams in a plastered-over tomb. It seemed an odd point of departure for a sect that prides itself on its open, peace-loving world view. But even modern Turks are not always tolerant. In a European-sponsored survey in 2003, 49% of more than 1,200 Turkish youths questioned said they would not want Jewish neighbors and 44% said they did not want to live next to Christians.

Much of the problem is ignorance, a persistent burden that is arguably one of the things Westerners understand least about a Muslim world that has suffered so much isolation, poverty and oppression. Typical of this was a conversation I had with my local ironworker in his basement workshop in Istanbul.

Şenol was an open-faced, friendly man with pale skin, a high, bald forehead, the prominent nose of his Black Sea coast hometown and a gray-streaked beard. He put little store by the skills or status of his craft, although he made hard-to-callibrate, heavy-duty scales. For him, Islam was the most important thing in his life. But his was a faith as curious as his radio, a battered machine held together with packaging tape on a shelf. This was tuned to a lugubrious all-day continuum of calls to prayer, sugary lectures on the moral benefits of Islam, and acted-out stories of traditions of the prophet Mohammed and great early Muslim rulers. All the actors spoke with electronic echo effects; Mohammed's fine bass reverberated like a wise Hollywood king in a great hall.

"Is Islam a personal thing for you or a communal thing?" I asked after we designed the ceiling hooks I wanted.

"Let me put it this way," Şenol replied, pausing before lighting his welding torch with a pop. "When the armies of Islam went to Iran they didn't want to shed blood any more than necessary. They just wanted the Persians to convert, or to pay the tax. That's all. The Iranian commander came over, and they told him: 'Islam will open up the world for you.' That's what Islam is for me. A whole world."

"Did the commander accept?" I asked, not really understanding.

"Yes. He joined the armies of Mohammed and fought against his own men. He became a martyr in that battle," he said.

I digested this blessing in silence as we did some heavy lifting with the metalwork. He was good at his job, with the Turkish talent for improvising his way round problems.

"Maybe what's unique about Islam in Turkey is the way that most people don't interfere with how other Muslims interpret it," I tried again. "I expect you and your father see Islam differently, but tolerate each other."

Şenol thought about that.

"Actually, my father and I have big arguments about Islam. He's really superficial about it," he said. "But we can interpret Islam for ourselves. Turks, Arabs, they all have a different approach, but the essence is one. Well, at least for the Sunni Muslims, it's one."

I had often bumped up against such intolerance, sincerely dressed up as tolerance. Despite its real diversity and general rule of communal peace, Turkish history is peppered with uprisings of its heterodox Alevi minority and Sunni suppression of them.

I changed the subject to the Arabic phrases he had chalked up onto the wall beside his tools. It was calligraphy for beginners, words like

"Allah" and well-worn formulae like "In the name of God, the most merciful, most loving-kind." Somewhat like those Christians who believe that Latin is the only language worthy of the Christian liturgy, Şenol, like most Muslims, believed that the essence of the Koran lay in the Arabic original, being the immutable and exact words of Allah as directly revealed to the prophet Mohammed.

"It's best for boys to learn the Koran when they are very young, before they know it's meaning," Şenol said. "When they get older, you see, they start looking around, seeing girls, they can't concentrate anymore."

If ignorance was better than experience, Şenol believed, prevention was also better than self-discipline. Mere commandments against sins like adultery were not enough. Women should wear the veil to nip male sexual ardor in the bud.

"You know," Şenol added, widening the gap between us still further. "In America, people don't have souls like us Muslims. They have djinns [spiteful spirits], who confuse them."

The conversation seemed doomed not to connect. I claimed that Muslim practice and his very words showed that there was flexibility in Islamic beliefs, but Şenol claimed nothing could dilute the rigid purity of Koranic commandments. I couldn't understand his unquestioning faith, but he could not comprehend my instinct that rational explanations must count for something. Sometimes he argued logically, but when he did, he started from a completely different set of assumptions.

As I left his workshop, Şenol caught my skeptical look. We were both slightly pained. Apart from the theological disconnect, we got on very well.

"There's proof of what I'm saying about America, you know," he said, handing me four excellently wrought pieces of ironwork. "They have Unidentified Flying Objects there. And UFOs are djinns."

Perhaps due to past difficulties in obtaining information to clear up such areas of theological debate, Turks often like their Islam to be associated with a living teacher or *hoca*. I understood why when I visited a sheikh of the Qadiri sect, Misbah Erkmenkul, who lived in a small wooden complex in a 19th century quarter of Istanbul. An electrical fault had sparked a fire in his wooden mosque two months before, burning it down and leaving an acrid smell that lingered in his home. Sheikh Erkmenkul was philosophical about it. He was 66 years old, short with a big round belly, merry dark eyes, a pink shirt, a gold tiepin and muscular dystrophy that he bore with benign fortitude. For him, Islam was not a religion of fear, proselytism and 1,400-year-old rules. It was to propagate happiness.

"*Keyyifler bol olsun,*" he said. "Let the pleasures be many."

I told him how strict an image Islam had in the West, and he laughed quietly. He strongly disapproved of some of the sects that surfaced as Turkey liberalized in the 1990s. These could be as bizarre as a small group known as the *Aczimendis*, which channeled its rebellions against the dry dictates of official secularism in showy bus-borne raids on Ankara. Resplendent in long hair, turbans and dark robes, its adherents usually briefly landed up in jail. Other sects believed in marrying religion to violence, and could have a terrible impact. One grisly faction calling itself Hezbollah, apparently connected only in name to other groups of that name in the Middle East, came to light in 2000. It had tortured and killed more than 60 people.

Sheikh Erkmenkul, always trying to reinforce the human link between people, believed that the *ezan*, the Muslim call to prayer, should be kept short, so as not to distract others wanting to go about their business.

"Do you allow yourself to drink alcohol, then?" I asked.

"Yes, if everyone else was drinking, and it would make other people feel uncomfortable if I didn't. I will never break the customs of the people I am with, as long as everyone is relaxed," he replied.

"But isn't that like being an unbeliever?"

"I don't fear anyone but God. I have respect for all religions. Jews and Christians join us for our ceremonies. People come drunk. They all get the same treatment. People have to get better themselves. I don't force them."

The message, like the silver-haired man himself, was seductively humane. The high wooden ceilings and gentle spaces of Sheikh Erkmenkul's house were different from the bare concrete walls that often housed the more bigoted Islamists. An ornate family tree traced his lineage back to 1617, when his ancestor had brought the Qadiri teachings from Baghdad to the capital of the Ottoman Empire. His forebears had passed on some basic rules for survival.

"I tell my son, on no account get into politics, like the Nakhshibandis, and never do business representing yourself as the *tekke* [dervish lodge]," he said. "Islam should live as Islam."

Sheikh Erkmenkul led his sect through their ritual in an upstairs room of his house. It was a far cry from the peasant followers of the Qadiri sect in the remoter reaches of Anatolia, who released themselves from earthly cares by winding themselves up into a trance, eating glass and piercing their cheeks with shish-kebab skewers. Sheikh Erkmenkul was part of a sophisticated, urban tradition. He often headed the ceremonies with his son, who wore jeans and a mobile telephone on his hip. The men kept up a rhythm of grunts, while the women participated quietly from a next-door room.

Sheikh Erkmenkul believed that Islam gave all rights to women, and that it was societies and rulers who had introduced oppression of them. When given a chance, he tried to talk women out of wearing the black all-enveloping chador. To brighten life up for himself, he kept a collection of colored gowns for the great days of the Muslim calender.

"I pity those women all covered up in the street," he said. "Just as it goes against society to be naked, so it does to be wrapped up in black."

In whatever way the Turks dress up Islam, however, some form of the religion has become an indivisible part of Turks' identity. The autobiography of one grand lady of the republic, Mina Urgan's *Memoirs of a Dinosaur*, tells of a life dedicated to communism and atheism. Before she died in 2000, she asked for a non-religious burial. Yet her daughter insisted that a funeral procession to a secular monument be followed by the usual Muslim last rites at a mosque. Atatürk's sister had done just the same for the founder of the secular republic. A rarely used verse in the Turkish national anthem by Mehmet Akif Ersoy illustrates even the republicans' ambivalent relationship with Islam when it comes to dealing with the Christian West:

The West may sheathe itself with steel;
Belief in God arms us. Fear not, great nation!
Our faith won't break beneath the heel
Of that toothless monster "civilization."

Similarly, most Turkish Islamists rarely stray far from a national consensus that no longer wants Islamic *sharia* law. Indeed, the closer they get to the consensus, the more successful they are. This was the reason that the Justice and Democracy Party, known by its Turkish acronym as the AK Party, was able to win 35% of the vote in 2002. Its leader, Tayyip Erdoğan, then 48, a tall, physically imposing former food wholesale executive and soccer player, certainly had a fundamentalist past and an authoritarian streak. As late as the early 1990s, he would state that his "reference was Islam," and that he based his political concepts on an "Islamic state." He would say that sovereignty resided in God and that "Islamic principles" should replace Kemalism, the republic's secular nation-state ideology. He hoped that alcohol drinkers would drown in their wine "as we march on with our yogurt drinks and our apple juice." He viewed the Western powers as a Christian gang set on hobbling the Muslim world. To win the national vote, however, he had to adopt the profile of a tolerant moderate. Secular Turks insisted that he was merely acting a part to gain power, using a Shia principle of "takiyyeh" to conceal his true intentions; indeed Erdoğan himself once said "we want to change the regime, and I'm ready to wear a priest's outfit to win this struggle to power."

When I visited him AK Party's ultra-modern headquarters before the election that finally gave him the prime ministership, he wearily but firmly repeated for the hundredth time that he had really changed his Islamist mindset.

"The old period is over, finished," he said. "We were anti-European. Now we're pro-European." As for mixing religion and politics, he was well-rehearsed: "Islam is a religion, democracy is a way of ruling. You can't compare the two. We just want to increase the happiness of the people." From the sofas around us skilled aides chipped in from time to time. He operated with a mix of talented young people, an edgy authoritarianism and old-fashioned political methods of raising money for the party from cooperative businesses. His children studied in the U.S., paid for by a group of business friends; he claimed his daughter went to university there because, unlike in Turkey, she could wear her headscarf. He appeared in public holding hands with his wife, a woman who withstood the curled lip of the secularist press and gave a brave lead to Muslim women who wanted to both cover their hair and be fashionably elegant.

There was good reason for Erdoğan to change. It wasn't just that advocating Islamic law was illegal. Even hinting at it would have made him unelectable. Furthermore, by the early 2000s, nobody could have imposed the 7th century Islamic laws of the Arabian peninsula on a country that was so modern and diverse. Even among pious Sunni Muslims, the fundamentalists are just one voice. Others include a popular religious columnist of a big-selling newspaper, who, on one typical day, devoted a whole page arguing that Islam needed no priesthood, that the religion needed renewal, that Muslims should never offend others and that the "most sacred law is humanism." In his own newspaper column elsewhere, the long-serving head of Turkey's 80,000 state-run mosques, Mehmet Nuri Yilmaz, argued that Islam should not be monotonous and should accept variety and change, quoting from Goethe and lines from Rumi like:

Take the road to rebirth, O hodja! Leave what's old.
On your journey you'll find dull earth will turn to gold

Indeed, in the early 2000s, Turkey's religious establishment quietly tried to lay the foundations of a broad-minded Turkish interpretation of Islam that could be distinguished from orthodox Sunni Arab and Shia Persian models. They held a conference in Bosnia and printed a modest booklet on the subject. Its existence was probably more surprising than its contents, but when I asked for it the religious affairs directorate's official bookshops never had it in stock. The international response from the Turkic world and non-Turkish Balkan Muslims was muted, partly due to differences between states and languages. But it was one more Turkic step towards the formalizing of Islamic diversity, aimed to formulate a more humanist, gentler, modern, "white" Islam.

When I visited party organizations in western Turkey, most activists who worked in Tayyip Erdoğan's party were young, enthusiastic and modern in outlook. Women could lead district organizations, working with and without Muslim headscarves. "For people like me, the association with something Islamic means honesty, good intentions and good morality," said party co-founder Ali Babacan, a bright 35-year-old textile wholesaler and graduate of a U.S. business school who went on to become minister of the economy. "Nobody wants to interfere in any-body's lifestyles. Banning things like alcohol never works anyway."

A rare, comprehensive poll in 1998 by Germany's Konrad Adenauer Foundation found young Turks moralistic, but secularized. About two thirds believed democracy and Westernization would prevail. Overtly religious values ranked fifth behind values of family, intellect, society, and the individual. Just 6% of Turkish youths regularly went to a mosque. Just two per cent said they belonged to an Islamic club or charity. Even so, one third believed there would be greater Islamic observance in social and political life in the future. Some 90% believed in God, and two-thirds fasted during the holy month of Ramadan.

Turkish society's quiet adoption of pluralistic religious values is one reason why few Turks were initially moved as Osama bin Laden tried to mobilize the Muslim world for a Holy War against the unbelievers. This contrasted with a greater sympathy felt by Arabs for the man and his goals, if not his methods. The crisis over bin Laden and Islam, most Turks felt, validated Atatürk's decision to separate church and state. They disapproved of terrorism and disliked the fact that bin Laden was an Arab, a race that many Turks view with deep prejudice. Still, in 2003, a Turkish group influenced by bin Laden launched suicide bombs in Istanbul against two synagogues, a London-based bank and the British Consulate General, killing 62 people. From my sitting-room window 200 yards away, I saw the nitrous yellow smoke and debris from the last blast barreling skyward. It also ripped through the small covered market street where I usually shop. I was shocked at the bombs' success in driving a wedge between my neighbors and me. While hating the fundamentalist bombers, most people I talked to busily trying to clean up their shattered workplaces angrily blamed the Christian West and its ally Israel for messing up the Middle East to the point where such bombings had become so common—and had reached them.

Turkey became increasingly uncomfortable with Israeli Prime Minister Ariel Sharon's tactics against the Palestinians. By mid-2004 Tayyip Erdoğan's government had put the political part of its relationship with Israel on ice, although the army ensured that Turkey remained the only Muslim country in a strategic military relationship with the Jewish state. Mr. Erdoğan said his reaction was as a "human," not Islamic, and, indeed, many Christians in Europe shared his feelings. Interestingly, too, the reaction of the Turkish opposition to the U.S. invasion of Iraq in 2003 showed that politics were as strong a force as any Islamic sentiment. It was secular groups on the far left who gloated most over the discomfort of the American superpower, not the Islamists. Erdoğan's pro-Islamic party sought to align itself to the United States and especially the European Union, while the "pro-Western" army and republican establishment sought to keep Washington and Brussels at arm's length.

In the Turks' rush for change, it is sometimes difficult to tell whether the Turkish secularist is really all progressive and the Muslim all reactionary. For instance, it is in the most conservative Turkish Muslim areas of Istanbul, the market streets along the Golden Horn, that the old Ottoman cohabitation with minorities like Jews, Armenians and Greeks is best preserved. And it was during the supposedly modernizing republic and preceding Young Turk eras that the ethnic cleansing of Anatolia's Armenian and Greek Christians took place. Ironies now abound in who wants what from the West. The Turkish army, which had launched the campaign for Westernization two centuries before, had by the turn of the 21st century become one of the Turkish institutions most staunchly resisting the liberalizing legal reforms required for integration with Europe. The Islamists, who only a generation before had condemned everything that came from the West, were looking to the European court of human rights in Strasbourg to defend themselves.

It is in the Netherlands that Turks' willingness to integrate with Europe faces one of its most telling tests. The Turkish community in Europe didn't have much of a chance in their main destination, Germany, where racism was long quietly ingrained in attitudes and nationality laws. (The situation in Germany was in fact rather similar to that in Turkey, where there is subtle discrimination against foreigners in business and in law courts.) Holland, however, was a country that had a far more open attitude to assimilating immigrants from all over the world, and a relentless ideology of integration. Even the nationalistic Muslim migrants from Turkey found it hard to resist.

19. EUROTURKS

A MUSLIM ISLAND IN
HOLLAND'S CHRISTIAN SEA

I carry two worlds within me
But neither one is whole
They're constantly bleeding
The border runs
Right through my tongue
—ZAFER ŞENOCAK, German Turk poet, b. 1961

SET BETWEEN PLACID CANALS AND A TIDY, LOW-INCOME HOUSING ESTATE
outside Amsterdam, the Zaandam mosque was a surprising new import
to the homogeneous landscape of Holland. With its Turkish-style dome
and minaret, the building didn't look Dutch. But it didn't look Turkish
either, with its carefully planned car park, a lawn stretching to the bank
of a waterway and a design that put all the emphasis on a façade that
turned out to be that of a community center.

The ambiguity continued inside. There was a Turkish teashop, but a
sign asked for Dutch-style payment in advance. The *imam* was appointed from Ankara, but the Dutch royal family made a point of turning up
for a special occasion. In a battle of wills between Turkish national pride
and the Netherlands' powerful instinct to integrate any new minority, the
Zaandam mosque represented a compromise over the country's 400,000
ethnic Turks, who make up about 3% of the population. The main priority in the *imam*'s latest talks with the local mayor, the mosque notice
board said, was the question of a zebra crossing.

I had bicycled up unannounced to visit the mosque on a Sunday
afternoon, and introduced myself to a group of Dutch Turks gathered by

their cars. They were happy to discuss their second homeland. But their confused reactions to it almost led to an argument after Ahmet, a bearded believer, admitted in front of the others that he rather liked his life in Holland.

"Why should I go back to Turkey? I'm not allowed to be a Muslim there. At least here we're allowed to learn about our religion," he maintained.

Muslims are often freer to pursue dissident religious interests in Christian Europe than in many Islamic countries. Muslim rulers have long known how easy it is for demagogues to use Islam to channel the frustrations of their populations. But such criticism of the Turkish motherland brought a sharp riposte from Selamet. He had a long, bony-nosed face and was wearing a lurid velveteen shell suit.

"Why are you going against the state that filled your belly?"

"But it's not my state. I'm living here in Holland."

The exchange went to and fro. Sinan, a bus driver, chipped in that back home in Turkey his excellent religious school had been closed down, ruling out the chance that his children could go and study there. On the other hand, he hated Holland's gray climate, its lack of sun and its bland-tasting vegetables. The others pointed out Turkey's own troubles, and Selamet subsided. He turned out to be the supercharged type of Turkish nationalist who was so virulently attached to his country that it could never meet the high standards he set for it. Like many Turkish immigrants in their late 30s and early 40s, he struggled with the paradox that he loved his country, but no longer wanted to return there.

"Everything bad is now coming from Turkey, corruption, mafia, drug dealing," he muttered, retreating into a sullen silence.

The one thing the group could agree on was that the Turks of Holland were better off than the Turks in Germany. One even criticized the German Turks' aggressiveness towards the Germans. They were sensitive to growing Dutch impatience with them, as shown by high votes for an anti-immigrant party in elections in 2002. Another said Turkey was wrong to send official Turkish *imams* as prayer leaders in most Dutch mosques, and they supported the Dutch state's counterattack: Dutch tests for *imams* and opening up a Muslim theological faculty to supply Dutch mosques with *imams* from within the Dutch-

Turkish community. The first graduates were due in 2006, and mosques are now obliged to hire from among them. Similarly, new and old immigrants who have failed to learn Dutch must now go to language classes. Most of the men were resigned to the idea their children would become Dutch citizens. This change in mentality was soon to be adopted by the pioneering leadership of the northern Dutch chapter of the most conservative Turkish-Islamic group in Europe, the *Milli Görüş*, or National Vision. By 2004, its leaders had switched to policies that, while still condemning assimilation, advocated a broader integration.

"Will you leave your children free to choose their religion?" I asked Ahmet.

"I want my daughter to wear a headscarf, for sure," Ahmet replied. "But what happens when she grows up is not my business. My responsibility ends at 18. If she wants to take the headscarf off, even marry a Christian, that's her affair."

Afterwards, I took their advice to cycle over to nearby Beverwijk to see "Europe's Biggest Covered Bazaar." If the Dutch mindset was laying seige to the Turks, the Turks were also influencing the fabric of Holland. In the fruit and vegetable hall, Turkish music blared from loudspeakers and tea was served in Turkish tulip-shaped glasses. Between themselves, the Dutch Turks called the Dutch currency the "lira," not the guilder or the euro. Turkish posters jostled with Dutch hot chocolate ads. Bagel-like *simits* were on sale, although they looked bloated compared to the dark-toasted, sesame-coated rings of Istanbul. A Dutch Turk sold counterfeit cellphone parts from a stall. At a newspaper and tobacco stand in the main hall, signs supported Turkish candidates in the latest Dutch parliamentary elections. Two Turkish women, from both main parties, won seats in the 150-seat legislature.

The owner of a grocery shop had crossed out the word *Maroc*, or Morrocco, on his shopsign. In its place he had scrawled *Türkiye*, the Turkish name for Turkey. As I passed, the grocer served a customer, a heavily built, kindly man with a bag of shopping in each hand. He carefully ordered six kilograms of tomatoes, specifying that they should be in two bags of three kilograms each. Seeing my quizzical expression, a smile spread across the grocer's face.

"Two wives!" he explained in a stage whisper.

The double husband smiled sheepishly when I asked how he managed to defy Dutch laws against bigamy. According to Islam, a man may take up to four wives at a time, and having more than one wife is still just socially acceptable in rural Turkey, even though it is theoretically illegal. He answered me on a different level, however.

"You have to be strong," he said. "And you have to have two hearts."

Having two cultures invested life with much extra meaning for Fidan Ekiz, a Dutch Turk born and educated in Rosenburg, a working-class community on the Rhine estuary west of Rotterdam. Her home, in a suburb of small houses and modest blocks of concrete flats, was superficially similar, she said, to that of her family's Dutch neighbors. But her parents had put up a framed Arabic medallion with the word for *Allah*, and a wall-hanging depicting Istanbul; she remembered how the air was heavy with the frying smell of Turkish cuisine, topped with a lemony scent of cologne used to refresh the hands of guests. In social development, Ekiz compared her Rosenburg micro-community of 200 ethnic Turks to what she had heard about the old-fashioned, unchanging Amishes of America.

Her father had come to the Netherlands in 1969. He had done a variety of welding jobs around the country, showing an opportunistic readiness to travel for work common among Turks in Europe but not often found among Europeans. Within three years, he brought his wife from Turkey to Holland, where she worked as a cleaner and a florist. But he was initially inflexible about what life could hold for his daughters, of whom Ekiz counted herself lucky to be the second.

"My elder sister pushed the way open for me. I still remember when she went to the municipality to get her Dutch passport. My father went crazy, he asked, 'Why did you do that? They're taking your nationality away. It's a plot. They want to make us Dutch,'" Ekiz recalled. "But when it was my turn, it became very normal to get a Dutch passport. Recently my father and mother got one too."

As they progressed through Dutch schools, Ekiz and her sister broke many of their society's old-fashioned Turkish taboos. Her sister had to use all her powers to persuade her father to let her join her class in summer camp, a first in the community, and fought against similar community resistance to become one of the first local Dutch Turks to take the bus to a better high school in a nearby town. By the time Ekiz won a place in journalism school, her parents were delighted at her achievement and willingly let her go. Marriage would be the next test. She thought she might get away with marrying a Dutchman. But as a Sunni Muslim, her family might not accept a son-in-law from Turkey's schismatic Alevi minority.

"Our parents agree with us children at home, but they are influenced by other people, especially the Turkish men. In the Turkish café they're all busy brainwashing my father. I hate them," Ekiz said. "Luckily my mother is strong, she knows what she wants. Nowadays my father has nothing to say."

Unlike such tight-knit socio-religious islands as America's Amishes, however, the Dutch Turks' solidarity is rooted in a shared motherland. Many in the second generation of Euro-Turks spend part of their time in Turkey, working in tourist resorts on the south coast, setting up businesses there that make use of bilingual skills or restaurants to match European standards to tastes in Turkey. Ekiz went to Istanbul as part of training for her chosen career of journalism, and later became the correspondent in Turkey for a group of Dutch newspapers. Her feelings were mixed about her experiences in a motherland that at first she barely knew.

"There are certain things that put you off, the poverty, the way some people are treated. I did a journalistic investigation into Turkish prisons, I thought that would make me want to go home to Holland. But I found that I didn't want to leave Istanbul. It's nice and crowded. I loved the color, the excitement, the sound of the *ezan* [call to prayer]."

Ekiz didn't look very religious, with her striking black hair and the tight clothes hugging her athletic body. But in Holland, she freely chose to read the Koran to herself at home on the holy nights of the year. As a child, she had had the Koran drummed into her during private Islamic classes. The *imam* would tell his young listeners to hold their hands near a fire, so they could know how hot it would be in hell.

"I become less religious being in Turkey. I sin so much. I am so afraid my plane home will crash because of that."

"But aren't you much freer in Holland?"

"In *Ramadan* in Holland, I would feel guilty if I didn't fast," she said. "But seeing people eat in Turkey, now I don't. Maybe I learned to be a part-time Muslim."

But Ekiz had not become a part-time Turk. It was more of a case of being a Turk with a double life.

"The Turks of Holland are different from the Turks of Turkey. In Turkey I meet lots of people who are leftists. In Holland most of the Turks I meet are right wing. Because they don't want to lose their identity, they are Turkish nationalist, conservative, it's suffocating. In fact, my parents are shocked every time they go to Turkey. Turkish society is more modern in Turkey than in Holland."

"Do you think you'll stay in Turkey?"

"I could never live without Holland, where I feel safe, where it's my home. I speak and write Dutch better than Turkish," Ekiz said. "But when I'm with Dutch people interested in my culture, I can get very excited about it. I'm very proud. So then, maybe I feel more Turkish."

Her time in Turkey had made her wonder for the first time about marrying a Turk, who would share and understand her culture.

"It's good that I have Turkey," she said. "I'd like to use it for my wild young years."

Not too wild, however. She had chosen a Dutch girl as her flatmate in Turkey, and whenever they had gone out for a drink, the Dutch girl went to sit at the bar. Ekiz sat demurely at a side table.

"It's like a social control I feel inside me. My Dutch friends think it's strange. But I don't think like them. I don't see things in black and white. Actually, I feel more sophisticated than them," she said. "People say it must be so hard to mix the two cultures. But it's not a problem at all. It makes you think all of the time. It's beautiful to be in the middle."

SECTION V

OIL AND WATER

*What attracts Westerners' interest in the lands
of the Turks, and what drives them apart*

20. HURRICANE HYDROCARBONS

THE CASPIAN OIL BOOM

Like fools, we'll surrender rich oil for cents
Our sweet Tengiz crude'll fuel Toyota and Benz
The cash will build up foreign states, not us,
As hope into sulphurous smoke combusts
—ORYNBAI ZHANAIDAROV, Russian-language
Kazakh poet, 1989

EVERY PORE OF THE WIND-BUFFETED AZERBAIJANI CAPITAL, BAKU, EXHALES the heavy, acrid scent of hydrocarbons. Crude oil tars the Caspian Sea coastline south of the city where rusty black 'nodding donkeys' lazily swing up and down amid a century-old forest of oil derricks. Natural gas leaks odorously from the foot-wide, low-pressure gas pipelines that snake disjointedly at head height around the city. Pungent vapors rise from oil slicks in the harbors. Semi-combusted fumes pour from the traffic and flares blaze high over metal oil processing jungles outside town. And everywhere, in the grand old turn-of-the-century mansions, in the shiny new office buildings, in the luxury car showrooms, in the flashy new Western boutiques, lingers the addictive and corrupting smell of oil money.

Further east in Central Asia, oil riches seem more theoretical, diluted by the under-populated vastness of the steppe, the distance from capitals to oil fields, the dominance of Soviet architecture in the cities and the gap between rulers and the ruled. But particularly in Azerbaijan, Turkmenistan and Kazakhstan, the region's easy oil money fuels an absolutist political culture. Governments can fund budgets and distribute patronage without any need to consult the people, a situation that corrodes legitimacy, breeds corruption, discourages free enterprise and undermines the national sense of purpose. By contrast, Turkey pumps a bare 7% of its energy needs, one reason why it has a more pluralistic political culture and the biggest and most successful mixed economy in the Middle East. The Kyrgyz Republic has only hydroelectric power, perhaps explaining why it is the Central Asian state with the most open system of government.

Oil is not just a black curse for domestic political health. Since Baku became the world's first oil-boom town in the late 19th century—the origin of the fortunes of Alfred Nobel, who endowed the famous prize, and of a branch of the Rothschild family—it has attracted foreign competition and intervention. The need for Azerbaijani oil hardened the determination of Soviet Russia to crush the fledgling independent republic of Azerbaijan of 1918-20. The Baku oil fields were a prime target of Hitler's catastrophic 1941 invasion of the Soviet Union. Even today, cheap access to Turkmen natural gas and control of Kazakh oil pipeline export routes are critical ingredients of Russian power. The lure of Caspian oil underpinned post-1991 U.S. interest in the region. In 2003, the U.S. government calculated that at least 17 billion barrels of oil in the Caspian basin had been proven to be extractable, and that 3-4% of the world's oil reserves lay buried there, about the same as in the North Sea or the Gulf of Mexico. The region is however under-explored, and the eventual total level of reserves is—just possibly—10 times as large. Kazakhstan has just over a half of the proven reserves, Azerbaijan just under a half; of the potential reserves, Kazakhstan has three times as much as Azerbaijan. In terms of natural gas, the Caspian region produced as much in 2001 as the Americas south of the Rio Grande, and will likely produce as much as the whole Middle East in 2010. Here, Turkmenistan is the big player, with the world's fifth biggest natural gas reserves. Hydrocarbons are not the region's only resource. Kazakhstan has huge deposits of uranium, iron and copper. Not surprisingly, Almaty's tree-lined boulevards are lined with the offices of future Nobels and Rothschilds, as well as oil majors, embassies, mining outfits, accountants, fixers and salesmen from all over the world.

The Kazakhstan International Oil and Gas Exhibition has become one of the main international parades of the year, with elaborate stands in a series of great halls taking the place of floats. The best stand usually goes to ChevronTexaco, lead developer of the nine-billion-barrel Tengiz field, and, with its partner British Gas, trying to find ways past an obstructive Russia to ship products from their big Karachaganak field in the north. Royal Dutch/Shell, Exxon Mobil and a family of other oil companies are drilling off Kazakhstan's Caspian Sea coast, where the Kashagan field is the biggest of them all. Immaculately dressed oil executives promise great achievements. Posters advertise miraculous technologies and pristine rigs that drill deep down and sideways into black fields of oil. Smaller stands peddle Danish satellite communications systems, oil service ships from Finland and German automated metal "pigs" for cleaning pipelines. Little of it is particularly Kazakh, except for the crowds who press in after the big shots move on to hospitality suites in the five-star hotels. They voraciously collect the key rings, plastic bags and pens that are the crumbs from the tables of these billion-dollar businesses.

But it is still unclear exactly what the people can expect from oil. In Azerbaijan, one-track-minded development means that oil accounted for 70% of the economy and 90% of export income in 2003. Other economic activity has withered away. In 1990, the country produced 239,000 tons of aluminum, 654 million cans of food and 151 million square meters of fabrics; in 1999, the figures fell to 76,000 tons, 49 million cans and virtually no fabric. In Kazakhstan, oil and minerals were responsible for 80% of export earnings, while 40% of the population lives in poverty. By 2003, the number of hospitals had fallen by a third since 1995 and only 11% of the population had land-line telephones. In a preface to a 2003 study warning that the "Caspian Oil Windfall" might not answer Turkic hopes for new prosperity, American economist Joseph Stiglitz summed up years of academic warnings about the black curse of oil: "It is sad but true that most natural resource-rich countries do not grow faster or perform in other ways better than those with few natural resources do."

The Caspian boom was blowing full force at the 1997 Kazakh oil exhibition, when, eyes glazed over from listening to dark-suited oil company 'government relations' men, I paused to sit at the stand of an obscure Canadian company. Its name fitted the times: Hurricane Hydrocarbons. Like Chevron's coup in snagging control of Kazakhstan's giant Tengiz field, Hurricane's story dated back to the pioneering late 1980s as the Soviet Union collapsed. In exchange for a piece of technology then needed by Kazakhstan's oil industry, a Western oilman acquired a license to invest in an oil concern called Kumkol. This was a youthful oil field that produced 50,000 barrels of oil per day, close to Kyzylorda, an old town on the Syr-Darya (Jaxartes) River, roughly in the middle of the country. The oilman sold his concession on to a group of Canadian-led investors. They in turn bought a controlling interest in the Kumkol oilfield for $120 million. In the United States, the equivalent oil reserves would have cost 10 times as much. The discount was partly because, as always in landlocked Central Asia, Kumkol was isolated from export outlets. And, as many early investors in Hurricane were to learn, the political and financial risk was great.

As everywhere in the former Soviet Union, the Canadians inherited a wide array of unfilled social and pension obligations left behind as rules and rubles withered away. They found they owned operations like a jewelry manufacturer, a premier Kazakh soccer team and a herd of 818 double-humped Bactrian camels. In short, they had taken over responsibility for the welfare of the whole town. Their burden was by no means unique in the Caspian. Azerbaijan long tried to sell an oilfield that was paired with responsibility for a local leper colony.

I learned all this quickly from a bright young American who had come to Kazakhstan for adventure and perhaps to make his fortune. As Sam Patten talked, it was hard not to be excited by the myriad dimensions of their project. He and his boss were keen to get their story out to the investor readers of *The Wall Street Journal*, and hoped to burnish their image with the Kazakhs as well. I wanted to write about a Central Asian oil company in action. I happily accepted an invitation out to the oilfield.

Hurricane Hydrocarbon's small charter plane filled up with two dozen oilmen, piles of duffel bags and gleaming aluminium packing cases. After an hour's flight over the nearly featureless steppe, we taxied to a halt in front of Kyzylorda airport's dilapidated terminal building. We drove into the town's gloomy, decaying island of look-alike Soviet concrete apartment blocks. Hurricane Hydrocarbons' headquarters had been given the only fresh coat of paint anywhere to be seen. Inside was a modern office, too. Western oilmen took the lead, but most employees were Kazakhs, still looking slightly self-conscious about the necessity of moving round an office with a name on their lapel.

"None of them even had a badge when we came a year ago," said the soft-spoken, red-haired Canadian who ran Hurricane's Kyzylorda operation, Keith McCrae. "There was no central payroll. Some people were being paid double. Some were being paid in rice. Some of the employees we had names for didn't exist at all."

With the intensity of missionaries, Hurricane was trying to win the local population over to Western ways. McCrae first showed me the oilfield company's old Soviet pioneer camp, left for dead by the collapse of the Soviet system and an evaporation of community spirit. Hurricane had turned the camp round, straightening totem poles, erecting wooden climbing frames, sprucing up dormitories and cleaning meeting halls.

"I've never heard of this being done anywhere else in the world," McCrae said. "But it's not pure charity. We need it to get cooperation. We'd be tossed out of the country if we just arrived and stuck at the oil patch."

Next stop was the 10,000-seat stadium of the Kyzylorda football team, recently renamed after the oil company. Manager Kasim Imanberdiyev's face was deeply creased with smiles. Two years before, the team had stopped playing as subsidies dried up from former backers like Soviet workers' unions. This had been a psychological disaster for a town where soccer games were the number one local event. Now, thanks to a $1 million annual subsidy from Hurricane, it had finished seventh out of 16 teams in the Kazakh first league in the last season.

"Without Hurricane, there would have been no team," he said. "Before Hurricane came, people were rather afraid. They said: 'The capitalists are coming, thinking only of themselves and profits.' Now the citizens are sort of grateful. People started to trust them. We fly the Kazakh and the Canadian flags when we play."

The *akim*, or governor, Berdibek Saparbayev, was grateful too. He was of the short-legged, muscular Turkic mould, with a compact, low center of gravity in his boxy, square-shouldered suit. A soccer player too, he liked to play center-forward. He felt good about himself, and about what Hurricane was doing. Small wonder. Under Canadian management, the oil company was now contributing half of the tax revenue of his whole *oblast*, or governorate, of 600,000 people. Cash was replacing barter, pensions had been paid, and the government was up to date on salaries. Down at the newly refurbished local bank, the oil company accounted for 95% of business and had inaugurated what was probably Central Asia's first electronic payroll. In the new climate, local investors were emerging to revive commercial life. A pasta and a flour-milling factory was being refurbished, and a Bulgarian company was finishing a hotel on the edge of town.

"A lot depends on Hurricane," said the *akim*. "The main point is that they calculate results from every cent invested. I believe that a good owner is an owner who calculates, who embraces everything."

McCrae sat in on my conversation. I had the feeling that the *akim* had been well embraced too. The U.S. State Department found that in the mid-1990s tens of millions of dollars of oil majors' money had ended up in the private accounts of the president, the state oil company chief and the prime minister of the period. Further down the scale, in places like Kyzylorda, this became new four-wheel drive cars and holidays abroad. That is why all multinationals bend over backwards in the Caspian region to sponsor art competitions, musical shows, and, here, pioneer camps. It was one of the only ways to bypass the grabbing hands of the politicians and to filter money—and a better image—down to the population at large. It also defused the old local employees' resentment of the well-heeled, efficient foreigners.

"I was pretty intimidated by the stony-faced people when I arrived. The start position was just give us the technology, we'll do it. I realized how much we had to do if we were not going to be tossed out," McCrae said as we dined on beef and beer, the only customers in a restaurant that had cropped up to cater to the oilmen. It was an island of cleanliness and keen, short-skirted waitresses.

The town was gradually pulling itself together. After lunch, McCrae led me round Hurricane's collective farm near Kyzylorda. When post-Soviet life had plunged to its nadir of poverty and disorganization in 1993-94, those running the company had sold off or eaten half of its flocks and herds. Now the farm's meat-packing shop was spick and span. Everyone sported brand new white uniforms as they stuffed sausage skins with cuts of horse, cow and camel. "I feel like a ballerina," said one hefty Kazakh lady. I felt as if I was in a Soviet propaganda film, but there was more. The company helped to refit the Kyzylorda hospital, spent $1 million on redoing the town's telephone exchange, and even sent humanitarian assistance to the people further down the Syr Darya River, whose livelihood had disappeared with the shrinking away of the Aral Sea. About the only thing Hurricane refused to do was to put the 50 government teachers at its farm school on the company payroll.

The oilfield itself lay in the desert 125 miles to the north. There was little traffic on the highway, which the unflagging Canadians were repaving with a road-building company they had inherited. As we left the Syr-Darya behind us, the grass-tufted steppe became more barren. But it was not lifeless. An enterprising local was returning from the desert with a truck piled with high-performance metal alloy debris from the jettisoned stages of Russian rockets, which blasted off not far away from the Soviet space complex at Baikonur. Elsewhere the landscape was home to the timeless yurts of the Kazakh sheep-, horse- and camel-herders, who were now also in the Canadians' pay, since the 2.3 million-acre company farm stretched most of the way along the road. A Hurricane collective farm truck stood by one yurt, helping a nomad shepherd move to fresh pastures with his wife, two children, a stove, bedding, a wooden cupboard and his own set of steel milk churns. "We're paid on time now," the shepherd said with a smile. "I hope the Canadians stay."

All these efforts—and gnarled workers at the oilfield who happily praised good meals, back salary payments and a restoration of discipline —did not protect Hurricane Hydrocarbons from a near-catastrophic collapse. The 1998 fall in the price of oil to about $10 a barrel was a blow to the whole economics of the project. Within a year, most of the worthy-looking, committed-talking foreigners I had met at Hurricane had switched to better jobs. After 18 months, the one-time stock market darling had become a sick penny share seeking bankruptcy protection. Instead of receiving stock price-lifting visits of investment analysts and journalists, it became the target of destructive vulture funds. Kyzylorda's soccer team slumped back down the league. The situation was hard enough to explain to sophisticated investors. To a people emerging from 70 years of communism, it was a brutal dashing of hopes. Ultimately, Hurricane saved itself with an opaque merger with its main customer and former nemesis, a south Kazakhstan refinery. The interests of those high in the government were doubtless embraced. It changed its name, its shares rocketed up by a multiple of 100 and China's national petroleum company snapped it up in 2005. Many of its original workers and investors, however, were left by the wayside. And relations remained tense with the Kazakh government, whose attitude was always to renegotiate contracts and impose taxes on any company that began to show good profits.

Disharmonies of a more cultural sort were already surfacing at a grand dinner held during my visit in a colorful Soviet-era yurt in the dairy farm yard. Toasts of vodka led down paths as well worn as the yurt itself.

As the host, Keith McCrae toasted the "coming together of cultures to form a stronger team, that can go forward with greater success." On my left side, an enthusiastic 29-year-old Canadian agricultural econo- mist talked about "working himself out of a job." On my right sat the wrinkled chief herdsman of the farm, who paid little attention to the new generation of foreigners' rhetoric but resolutely downed the vodka. A young girl in "Kazakh" fancy dress struck up a plaintive Kazakh tune, accompanied by a practiced keyboardist on an electric organ.

"For the first time, the people feel as if they are morally decent . . . they trust in you and will go out of their way to help you," the chief of the collective farm declared as he toasted his new Canadian overlords.

The Kazakh had exactly the same high cheek-boned face as a chauffeur I had employed for a year in Istanbul, a man from part of north-central Anatolia where many of the Turkic tribes from Central Asia settled a mil- lennium ago. He had the same shiftiness in his eyes, a look born, in the case of my ex-driver, of a resolute and often-stated conviction that nothing was worth doing honestly if it could be done illegally. Indeed, a dissident oilman whispered to me later that the collective farm truck somehow never arrived at the oil field with the same load of supplies as it set out with.

The canny McCrae, meanwhile, was ready with a thrust of the knife that I had not expected. When the main delicacy of the feast appeared, a roasted sheep's head, he took over to perfection the role of the Kazakh toastmaster. His blade dug into the animal's skull as he looked at me, the prize guest and captive journalist of the evening.

"Here is the eye, that you may see," he announced to the assembled company, holding up the sheep's eyeball.

There was no escape: I bit into it. I dreaded juicy eye fluids, but, when my teeth closed on it, I was surprised by a dry, floury taste. Pressing his advantage, McCrae wielded his knife again.

"And here is the ear," he continued, "so that you may listen."

The sheep's ear was fatty and slippery. Cut off close to the head, it had interwoven folds of a certain anatomical interest. It was like biting into a thick, over-cooked sheet of unsalted pasta.

Next to me, the Canadian agricultural economist's chin dropped as he was noiselessly sick down the front of his checkered shirt.

21. WHITE GOLD

A LUST FOR COTTON
STRANGLES THE ARAL SEA

> *When the salts rose, the frogs disappeared.*
> *Then the storks left. The old nests you can see*
> *on the minarets are the only mementoes we*
> *have of them now.*
>
> —Tour guide in Bokhara

FROM THE AIR, CANALS LEADING AWAY FROM THE AMU DARYA, OR OXUS
River, glistened through the haze like fat silver ribbons woven through
the dun grid of cultivated land. For more than half a century now, they
have drained off the lifeblood of Central Asia to irrigate fields of cotton,
the cash crop so loved by the region's rulers. But irrigating the steppe is
like substance abuse—the more water the farms use, the more they
need, because the weight of the water brings up ground salts deposited
in the prehistorical era when the whole of Central Asia was a great sea.
Beside the canals, the sun glared back from mirror-like sheets of water
where collective farm managers had flooded fields to wash these salts
and agricultural chemicals out of the soil. Other canals, the collector
channels, drew the used water off into vast dead lakes in the desert
known as sinks. From here the water slowly evaporated, leaving acrid
bowls of salt and dust behind.

The lack of water is not new in Central Asia. The gradual drying up
of the steppe is one reason given by historians for the great westward
movement of the Turkic peoples. It could date back to pasture failures
when the skies darkened after an enormous explosion of Krakatoa, the
Indonesian volcano, in 535 AD. But the modern calamity is a creeping

daily tragedy for the inhabitants of Karakalpakstan, an autonomous republic of Uzbekistan. About 1.4 million people live here south of the Aral
Sea, evenly divided between Uzbeks, Kazakhs and a Turkic people close
to the Kazakhs, the indigenous Karakalpaks. What made their growing
water shortage harder to bear was that stemmed mostly from bad planning, wastage and government greed.

Karakalpakstan once lived from the fish, ferry routes and a softer climate fostered by the Aral Sea. In the past four decades, however, the former fourth-largest inland body of water in the world has shrunk to half
its surface area and one-third of its volume. Soviet and independent
Uzbekistan's addiction to revenues from the cotton crop is not the only
demand on the Aral's tributary waters. Kazakh farmers drain water from
another river flowing to the Aral Sea, the Syr Darya. Turkmenistan
siphons Amu Darya river water into the Karakum canal. Further upstream,
Tajikistan has a hungry cotton habit to feed as well. The Soviet Union
dug a total of 20,000 miles of canals, raised 45 dams and laid out 80
reservoirs to service its cotton agro-business. Little able to influence
their fate, the Karakalpaks take refuge in a dry sense of humor.

"As you can see, our fish comes pre-salted," joked Ghulam, my host
in Karakalpakstan, serving yet more food at a welcoming feast.

As if to defy the region's problems, Ghulam had crowded his table
with tins of German beer, quart-sized plastic bottles of Coca-Cola, bowls
of apple sauce, plates of salami, egg-plant canapés, steaming meat
dumplings, bowls of soup and spring onions as thin as straws. He tore up
rounds of thick bread into piles and we began to eat. It wasn't just the
fish that seemed salted. The tomatoes were misshapen and a little brack-
ish. Even the locally distilled *arak*, the local kind of vodka, seemed to
have a tang.

"When I'm in Tashkent, you know, I find the water insipid. And
when I wash my face, I find that it's still covered with soap. Here, at
least, everything comes off with the water," Ghulam went on with a
smile. "In fact, when they bring me food in Tashkent, I spend my whole
time shaking salt onto it."

More and more food arrived as he spoke. Central Asian feasts are a
serious business. Rural Turkic peoples don't go for the Western idea of
three regular meals a day, and I once journeyed with a Turkmen who

wolfed down one big meal every three days. A century ago, a feast could involve actually eating a whole horse. Travelers relate that it was a point of honor not to rise until all was gone. The trick was to let one's trousers out as one went along.

Ghulam laughed when I protested at his lavish hospitality at a time of drought.

"This is the lightest meal you can give to a guest here," he said, as a woman of his family brought us men another great oval dish, this time stacked with grilled meats.

Ghulam was in charge of a local investment office, the kind of place where, aside from passing diplomats and journalists, he had entertained many of more than 200 expert missions to the Aral Sea. The Aral Sea crisis has attracted a fine array of thirsty and competing bureaucrats, United Nations agencies, World Bank teams, ecological organizations and groups with opaque acronyms like ICSDSTEC (the Inter-state Commission for Socio-Economic Development and Scientific, Technical and Ecological Cooperation). The experts wrote reports that spoke of of Urgent Human Needs and Immediate Impact Projects. But Ghulam complained that only one in twenty of delegations passing through did anything of significance. They couldn't share his need to save the land where his ancestors' bones were buried.

"People here say this is our country, we were born here, we have to live here, and make it fit for our children. But it's hard. You have to be organized," Ghulam said.

His practiced tour of Karakalpakstan's struggle to survive started in the government offices on the dust-blown main square of Nukus, the chief city of Karakalpakstan. The region's senior trade official, Kutlumurat Sultamurat, received me in front of a cupboard in which samples of everything his territory had to sell fitted onto six chipboard shelves. A length of fibrous root turned out to be a main export: liquorice. The republic sold 1,000 tons of the stuff a year, at $500 a ton, doubtless mere pennies compared to the profits made from liquorice sweets in distant lands. Rolls of loose cotton bandaging might have found a market a century ago. And, of course, there was salt, packaged in plastic by a Turkish company. I asked Sultamurat what the outlook was, and his face turned gloomy.

"The Amu Darya is down to its worst flow ever," he said. "The rice harvest is extremely bad and we have bad feelings about the cotton. Everyone is just trying to keep things going as they are. The only thing that's getting better is the drinking water. But that's just because the field drainage system is not working properly, and we can't afford to put fertilizer in the fields."

"What can you do?" I asked.

"Do you think anyone would be interested in our new project? We want to make paper out of rice husks, stalks and cotton plants."

"Doesn't that use up a lot of water too?" I asked.

"That's holding back the plan, yes. We'd need chemicals from Russia, too. But we're drowning in kaolin!" he said, bravely persuasive.

"I suppose you could cut back on cotton production . . ." I said.

"For that, you'd have to ask the man in Tashkent!" he replied, smiling widely for the first time and showing his magnificent set of gold teeth.

Cotton is no joke in Uzbekistan, the world's fifth biggest producer. Cotton has been cultivated here since antiquity. It makes up two-thirds of the country's gross output and employs 40% of the population. Uzbeks pick four million tons of raw cotton a year, which translates to about 1.25 million tons of ginned fiber for textiles. Four-fifths of that is sold abroad for about $1.5 billion, netting between a third and a half of Uzbekistan's foreign currency income every year. Indeed, Uzbek cotton exports are usually second only to those of the United States. The Uzbek product however trades at a discount to world norms because it has not yet overcome a reputation for shipping gritty, short-fiber, poor quality cotton.

Cheating on the cotton crop—not to mention on the environment —goes back a long way. Even before the Tsarist Russian Empire made vassals of the khans of Bokhara a century ago, an Italian merchant complained that the Bokhariot merchants mixed seeds and old cotton into the bales. In the mid-1980s, the Soviet Union found Uzbekistan's communist barons guilty of faking harvest figures and over-billing Moscow to the tune of billions of rubles (then nominally equal to dollars). President Karimov now stoutly defends his predecessors, saying that the scandal was a Russian plot against patriotic Uzbeks. His independent republic renamed Tashkent's old Lenin Boulevard after Sharaf

Rashidov, the Uzbek communist leader disgraced by the scandal. He posthumously exonerated the minister of cotton production, who was executed in 1986.

As we passed through a gray wasteland outside Nukus, I asked Ghulam to stop so that we could speak to a farmer standing in a field, staring at his scraggy cotton bushes. Many of the bolls had not opened, and did not look like they would. Beneath his faded velvet cap, the farmer looked shrunken and prematurely aged.

"I lease two hectares from the collective," he explained. "I planted it all with cotton, with my family, all by hand. But we only got the first water from the Lenin canal in July, too little and too late. I think I'll be lucky to get four tons of cotton."

"Don't you ever think of going to live somewhere else?" I asked.

"If we knew somewhere better to go, we would. But I don't. We're 12 people in my house, I have to support them," he said.

The farmer lifted his head to take a look at me, screwing the eyes up on his weather-beaten face against the sun. He made me feel soft and spoiled, and he read my thoughts.

"People here have seen worse times, you know, like after World War II. We went through a period when we had nothing, you could buy nothing, even if you had money. And then, of course, millions of people died in the 1930s."

We were silent for a while.

"Isn't there anything else you could do with the land?" I asked at last.

"I think it would support 15 cows. That would pay more. But the collective wouldn't rent me the land if I didn't grow cotton. And if I planted some melons or corn, they wouldn't give me water," he said.

In a modern form of feudal share cropping, the collective took half the cotton crop in return for supplying the cottonseed, a lord-of-the-manor role in the government's foreign currency supply chain. The other half had to be sold to the government at artificially low prices, a rule backed up by minefields on the border, laid partly to deter the smuggling out of any cotton. As I walked back to my comfortable car, I saw someone watering cattle knee-deep in the poisonous-looking sludge of a drainage ditch. The herdsman shrugged off my apalled questions. "They adapt," he said.

Uzbekistan's drive to fulfil the cotton export plan means that some fields have not properly rotated crops for decades, forcing some of the heaviest fertilizer use anywhere in the world. The chairman of the Karakalpak parliament, Timur Kamalov, a Soviet-era water engineer, seized his desk with both his powerful hands and roared at me after I challenged him with the idea that cotton was damaging his people.

"I cannot agree that cotton is a monoculture, or that it damages the environment. Every state has the right to do what is best for the country. We used to have a problem with floods. Now it's sandstorms. So what?" he said. But with an air of quiet satisfaction, he gave a backhanded answer to my question: "Now you too must fear our salts. The winds are carrying them your way."

Returning to his script, he pointed out that over the centuries, the Amu Darya has often carved itself new courses through the sandy steppe. His namesake Tamerlane had even diverted the whole river to conquer the stubborn resistance of a medieval city near Nukus.

"What about global warming, then? Where will you get your water in the future?" I asked. I told him of a journey I had made to a mountain-top gold mine in the Kyrgyz Republic, Central Asia's great reservoir of frozen water, where dirty lines in the snow showed how the glaciers are steadily melting away.

"You get accustomed to such environmental conditions. You survive," he said. "There is no such thing as a dying region. We don't despair. My people are patient."

World Bank reports on Karakalpakstan list all that Karakalpaks have to be patient about. Only five per cent of the population has piped water inside their houses, and even then the water runs a mere two hours a day. Just one-third of population can afford soap and children only wash three times a month, usually at public baths. Two-thirds of Karakalpak families believe that their worst problem is lack of food, on which they have to spend 90% of their income, but which, like the cotton farmer, they are not allowed to grow. A half to three-quarters of water used on farms is wasted. More than half the irrigated land is already saline, and even more could be unusable in a few decades as bedrock salts leach up from below. The city of Tashkent itself uses three or four times as much water per head of population than Western cities because of profligacy and leaky taps.

There is enough water to go round. But nobody has the willpower or resources to change water usage and the rock-bottom pricing that encourages waste. Russian officials perpetuate the exploitative mentality at regional conferences where they talk of selling water—and increasing their influence—by diverting part of the River Ob in Siberia to Central Asia. The existing water suppliers, Tajikistan and the Kyrgyz Republic, are too weak to change usage patterns, even though storing water in dams for their wasteful neighbors for use in summer means that their own citizens lack power in winter. The water consumers, Uzbekistan, Kazakhstan and Turkmenistan, have made clear they will not pay for water or change their ways—and at least one of them has conducted military exercises to simulate the seizing of dams.

In Karakalpakstan, most people seem to have given up on saving the Aral Sea and put their faith in folk legends that it has shrunk and grown back before. Five centuries ago, Prince Babur wrote that during the summer months the waters of the Amu Darya would not even reach Bokhara, let alone Karakalpakstan. There is a slim chance that they may be right to hope. Nobody yet knows why the level of the even bigger Caspian Sea next door rose two meters from 1978 to 1994, and then started falling again.

Indomitable toughness is the only way to explain how Karakalpaks deal with the problems they face, often on a diet of little more than bread and tea. For decades river silt has carried to them the residue of Central Asia's over-use of fertilizers, pesticides, defoliants and industrial discharges of heavy metals. Few know what more dangers may be inherited from the Soviet testing of biological weapons on an island in the Aral Sea, which became a peninsula as the sea shrank. Karakalpakstan suffers an infant mortality rate double the Central Asian average, and some of its highest rates of anemia, cancer and hepatitis.

The air even tasted of salt as we drove past drifting herds of camels one day into to the semi-desert outskirts of Nukus. Ghulam wanted to show me a first attempt to diversify the Karakalpak economy. The textile factory had opened three years before to add value to Karakalpakstan's cotton, but it looked aged before its time. Desert winds had already sandblasted the buildings, stripping off the paint in Uzbekistan's national colors of white, turquoise and gold.

The Turkish-built complex was one of the first Western factories in Central Asia, and had been plagued with difficulties. Little versed in modern transactions, 33 Karakalpak collective farms agreed in 1992 to barter the factory from Turkey for 11,500 tons of cotton. As a result of rising cotton prices, they'd ended up paying double the cash value of the equipment. The second-hand machinery from Turkey was Italian in origin, but was installed with only a one-year maintenance contract. When the Turks left, the Karakalpaks were on their own.

"We couldn't cope. Spare parts and maintenance are a constant problem. We had to send someone all the way to Italy to try to find the original manufacturer," the manager, Bakhtiar Setimbekov, said in his wood-paneled retreat.

The Italians had been pitiless, and had charged the Karakalpaks $5,000 for a copy of the operating manual.

In a storage hall at the entrance to the main factory building, thick bales of raw cotton stood waiting to be processed. Back-breaking labor had gone into preparing the fields, to grow the difficult, disease-prone bushes, to pick each boll of cotton, but even now these six-foot-cubed bales were only worth a couple of hundred dollars each. Not earmarked for export, this cotton had the shortest of fibers, and was full of seeds and grit. Several machines in the lines of spindly equipment waiting to receive the bales stood in various stages of dismantlement. Overcome by impurities or waiting for spare parts, only six of the 10 lines of thread-spinning units were clattering through their work.

In a long, half-empty warehouse next door, unhealthy-looking seamstresses were making t-shirts and tracksuits out of the factory's production of primitive, slightly rough cloth. They suffered from bronchial and skin diseases, their forewoman told me. But these ailments were endemic to Karakalpakstan and few were allowed to miss work because of them.

Still, the Karakalpaks have not given up. Deeper into the scrub-tufted desert, an annual day out of horseback games was in progress. A gaggle of cars clustered around a small stadium, and cheery faces watched 50 young people on horseback milling around a sandy oval racetrack. They galloped after each other and mimicked cavalry attacks. In one game, a girl would appear from the left, galloping after a boy; if she caught him, she was entitled to a kiss. All were dressed up in the fanciful garb of Soviet-era oriental fables, the women in pointy hats and filmy gauzes of pink and purple, the men in Mongol helmets, wielding opera-set swords and shields. The girls charged with thin, eery war cries, the men with a howl worthy of their conquering forebears. I felt a surge of excitement as I mingled among them. For on their high-cheekboned faces and in their rough and practiced handling of the panting horses wheeled the wild and untamed spirit of a Turco-Mongol horde.

The odds were stacked against the Karakalpaks' struggle. Back in Nukus for a last evening in the state guest house, even the outsize balls of the billiards table were all but impossible to hit into the narrow pockets. The only other guests of the government invited me to join them at their table for dinner. One was Oral Ataniyazova, a diminutive former Soviet academic who was the principal activist for public health in Karakalpakstan. Her people accepted hardship as their lot, Ataniyazova argued, because it was all they had ever known.

"This is not a high-level crisis, like the radiation from Chernobyl. It's a chronic exposure to low doses of chronic pollutants. As a biological subject, we can survive," Ataniyazova told me over another salty meal. "People are very tough. They don't know what a normal life is, otherwise they could not cope with the stress. We are not in an ecological, but an economic extreme."

Heading out towards what was left of the Aral Sea with Ghulam the next morning, it became clear how even Nukus was living through the modern-day equivalent of one of Tamerlane's river-diverting sieges. The Amu Darya stood stagnant and 100 feet wide, mocking the 1,000-yard-wide riverbed. Cars clanked across it on a short metal pontoon. A grand project for a new concrete bridge stood half-built alongside us, abandoned and stuck in the sand. On the crest of a dirt bank on the other side, young boys and wiry old women sold some of the last fruit of the waterway. The long, thick-scaled pike-perch were wrapped up in old padded Central Asian *khalat* coats to protect them against the broiling sun.

We drove for two hours over flat scrub desert until we reached the outskirts of Muynak, the closest inhabited point to the disappearing sea. We came to a halt on a hillock by Muynak's jagged concrete memorial to its dead in the Second World War, and looked out over the old shoreline. Until the 1960s Muynak had been relatively prosperous, a green fishing port. Now, the seabed was empty, sparsely self-seeded with a patchy blanket of tamarisk, wormwood and camel thorn. A mile out, a small boat lay rusting among the bushes. The water had disappeared far over the horizon, its edge more than 50 miles away, and was still receding.

The local prefect, Otirmurat Kalmuratov, was clearly used to the phenomenon of the dumbstruck visitor. He oversaw a paltry economy dependent on foreign aid and the last gasps of its broken old workhouse of a fish cannery. Outside, desert winds were whipping up the old seabed, veiling the modest buildings of the town with a silken, blinding mist of salty dust.

"What we are doing is learning to live without the Aral Sea," Kalmuratov said. "We'll never get it back."

The groundwater in Muynak is three times as salty as even the salt-tolerant people of Nukus can drink. The town's strategy of damming up what river water it gets—one-tenth to one-fiftieth of the previous flow, according to whom one believed—keeps a paltry flow of fish to the cannery. More fish were brought in by refrigerated train from Turkmenistan's Caspian coast. Still, the factory was working at 10% of its capacity. Greasy plates of pike-perch dominated a rudimentary feast laid on by the cannery. They looked about as appetizing as the jars of pickled fish in Muynak museum. They are all that is now left of the Aral Sea's many vanished species, displayed on shelves among the ropes, anchors and other paraphenalia salvaged from the town's long-dead port.

"The type of people who are left here, you would have to put an automatic gun to their head and they wouldn't leave. It's their land," the prefect said, dabbing at his diseased eyes with a handkerchief. "As governor of this district, I tell you the people are optimistic."

Actually, the ecological upheaval had persuaded half of Muynak's 28,000 people to leave; the town takes more than the average Karakalpakstan toughness to survive.

Tea was with one of the cannery's pensioners, Disen Varbustinov. All six of this hardy ethnic Kazakh's children had joined the exodus from Muynak. But Varbustinov and his wife, a former member of Karakalpakstan's Soviet-era parliament, were determined not to leave.

They had even seized an opportunity as the sea retreated, building a comfortable new home with eight rambling rooms where waves once crashed onto the beach and fishermen drew up their boats. A metal canoe round the back of the house lay ready for fishing expeditions in the few canals with enough water left to float it. In front, Varbustinov showed off his invention of a rice de-husker, made out of a big can, some knives and an old electric motor.

"In the old days, I could hear the fish splashing in the water as I lay outside to sleep at night," he said. "But we can't just cry about it and give up."

On his plot of land, he was growing vegetables and grapes in a gray soil that looked like pure sand.

"I mix the sand with fertilizer. But you have to do the proportions carefully," he said, showing a cracked tomato suffering from a fertilizer overdose. "You can just about grow a marrow, if you look after it."

For months afterwards, I couldn't look contemplate a body of open water with any sense of certainty, imagining the seabed underneath, wondering whether this sea too might not suddenly disappear. When I next saw the Amu Darya again, it was still a broad river, far upstream from the Aral Sea at one of the ancient crossing points to Turkmenistan near Bokhara. It seemed placid enough, but as I drove deeper into Turkmenistan, I was to be constantly reminded of the parched lands I had left behind me. We kept criss-crossing the Karakum canal, which was silently draining yet more water from the Amu Darya River. The government admits 28% of the water is immediately wasted, leaching through the cracks in the canal's concrete bed; scientists say the loss is closer to 60%. Over-irrigation in its use brings up ground salts that stains the farmland like dirty snow. For all that, the canal is of course a lifeline for the Turkmens, who reject any alternative plans for the water. They even talk of vast new irrigation projects and a great new lake.

The Turkmen leader did not create the problem, and nor could he solve it without cooperation from other Central Asian leaders. But they barely talked to each other. They all feared sharing, knowing that it would undermine their absolute and unearned monopoly on power. This failure to pool common interests for the greater good was what brought Central Asia under the Soviet yoke for most of the 20th century. Water will not be the only problem for the 21st century. Energy pipelines are constantly used by one leader as a lever against another. Once barely noticed Soviet borders have become chokepoints. And traveling the road across three Caspian states from Bokhara to Baku showed how long any real improvement is likely to take, thanks to a morass of petty corruption that holds back the whole Turkic world.

22. SILK ROAD SHAKE-DOWNS

CORRUPTION AS A WAY OF LIFE

> *None compare to us as liars*
> *We curse behind our sweetest nod.*
> *We rob our land to heart's desire*
> *Free of fear, or fear of God.*
> *My freedom was my death-knell*
> *Our fate decreed this disconnect*
> *The rope that saved me from the well*
> *Is now the noose around my neck.*
>
> —From *Slave Market*, by
> Azeri poet BEXTIYAR VAHABZADE, 1996

IN A WAY, THE IMAGES CONJURED UP BY THE NAME SILK ROAD ARE A romantic deception. Way back in the second century BC, Chinese chronicles do mention a price of 40 bolts of silk for every "blood-sweating, heavenly horse" bought from Central Asia's Ferghana Valley. The Romans, too, may have exchanged gold for Chinese silk, but probably did it by sea. But overland east-west trade and travel rarely prospered through the lands that came to be dominated by Turkic peoples. Distances were too great, slave-snatching brigands too prevalent and rival khanates waged too much war against each other. Silk was well-known outside China in the early Sassanian and Byzantine empires, and the most valuable purple silk could only be made from crushed shellfish of the eastern Mediterranean. Camel caravans did carry merchandise along the interconnecting trade routes of Central Asia and Turkey, but itineraries tended to be a regular shuttle between ports, inland cities and oasis towns. The name Silk Road itself was dreamed up by German geographer Baron Ferdinand von Richtofen in the late 19th century, and gradually grew into an orientalist vision of camels plodding ever-westwards for thousands of miles laden down with Chinese silks.

The geographical idea of the Silk Road nonetheless does describe something that is now flickering to life. The end of the Soviet Union has seen an uptick of east-west trade, and some of the many interwoven trade routes of Central Asia are exceedingly old, from the mountain roads snaking above the Turkish port of Trabzon to Afghanistan's Khyber Pass to the legendary Jade Gate in the Great Wall of China. Lavish U.S. and European backing has burnished and connected these historical trade routes as a new Silk Road, a useful ideological tool to promote with an "East-West Transportation Corridor" that is opening up Central Asian markets and oil wells to foreign capital. One new rail line now stretches eastward from Kazakhstan to China, another westward from Turkmenistan to northeastern Iran. Central Asian airports are shaking off their Soviet decrepitude with connections around the compass. New energy pipelines run, or are planned, in many directions. Millions of tons of Caspian oil began to be shipped each year across the Caucasus, avoiding both Iran and Russia—by barge across the Caspian Sea, by pipeline to a rail terminal, and then by rail car to the Black Sea port of Batum. Western companies have plans for a fiber-optic cable to Shanghai from Germany's Frankfurt-am-Main. But even as a new Silk Road, it's as well to remember that it has never been a single highway, and that there isn't anything silken about it.

In fact, if Central Asian states really hope for prosperity through trade, they first have to beat the self-defeating, pocket-filling mismanagement of Turkmenistan, the self-rightously corrupt bureaucracy of Uzbekistan, the arrogant kleptocracy of Kazakhstan or the demands for money that have become the dominant mentality throughout Azerbaijan. They have collectively prevented the new Silk Road from acting as a through-route for trade; it almost only serves to supply local Central Asian markets. Standing in angry frustration at some border points sometimes made me feel the states barely deserved to be called proper countries, and underminde any idea that the Turkic world could one day band together meaningfully against shared rivals like Russia, Iran and China.

Perhaps Uzbekistan's intentions had been good when it built the Alat border post with Turkmenistan in the mid-1990s. The grandiose design even included a ceramic wall portrait of a Bactrian camel, the ship of the Central Asian desert. Like everyone else, Turkic leaders loved the Silk Road mythology, and no Central Asian capital was complete without its Silk Road Boulevard. In Uzbekistan, one of the only local Internet servers even went by the name of silk.com. But the reality was that within a few years cracks and gap-toothed holes had opened up in the blue tiles covering the artificial domes of the Alat border post roof. In a white-tiled restaurant in the basement, factory-sized kitchen equipment dwarfed a few pots of the only food on offer: thick, heavy bread and a bowl of broth and meat on a splintery bone. A ruffianly crowd of customs officers and smugglers conspired at the plastic tables. Between grunted conversations, they watched a grainy pop music show on a Soviet-era television set, kept alive by a chicken's thighbone jammed into the control console.

The Uzbek authorities had pasted so many long lists of closely printed regulations around the customs hall that they looked like wallpaper. All of them were signed in Soviet style by "Islam Karimov, President." They ranged from bans on "materials that could damage the state" to a mysterious injunction that I vowed to honor: "no clichés." Expensive X-ray equipment and metal turnstyles lay disused. Officials waited in ambush with questions about financial transactions in Uzbekistan. A white-coated medic watched for dangerous foreign diseases, apparently carried by banknotes. The Turkish truck drivers, to-ing and fro-ing with their documents, laughed at my irritation.

"You got off lightly. That bit would have cost me $10. The customs officers here are thieves. Keep your hand on your wallet!" trilled Bilal, who hailed from the far-away Turkish city of Konya.

When 19th century adventurer Arminius Vámbéry visited the badlands here, indeed, rapacity was a public and positive virtue. In one group of Turkmen yurts, he chanced to witness the return of a raiding party. First everyone listened to the tale of the chief raider, whose excitement was mixed with outrage that his Persian victims should dare to resist being plundered. Then the family went to ogle the spoil. Elder women greedily grabbed stolen cooking utensils. Children jumped about, trying on clothes. Nearby squatted a captured teenage Persian girl, crying and stained with her mother's blood. One of the Turkmen, it turned out, had chopped the woman's head off because she had been unable to keep pace with his horse. Vámbéry had trouble maintaining the studied look of indifference that was the most challenging part of his Turkic disguise: "Here was all triumph and merriment; not far from it a picture of the deepest grief and misery. And yet no one is struck by the contrast; everyone thinks it very natural that the Turkoman should enrich himself with robbery and pillage."

Times change, and the pillaging at places like modern Alat mean that commercial traffic is just a trickle of a few dozen vehicles each day. Bilal the Turkish truck driver grumbled that he had to spend up to $1,000 on under-the-table expenses to get his 20-ton cargo of biscuits from one end of the new Silk Road to the other. I knew what he meant. In the Caucasus, greedy traffic cops jumped out like highwaymen at every intersection, and neglect meant deep ruts of mud or flocks of sheep had forced my car completely off the road. For businessmen, the railways are little better. Kazakhstan talks airily of sponsoring the construction of a $5 billion high-speed rail connection to cut the China-Europe transport time in half—but the route involves the same, foot-dragging suspects, Turkmenistan, Iran and Turkey. To send a container by rail from the Chinese port city of Shanghai through Central Asia to Hamburg in Germany still costs double and takes twice as long as transporting it by sea. Cheaper, easier sea routes were the main reason, after all, that there wasn't really any old Silk Road.

Oppression and corruption dogged my journeys, but there was another side of the coin: sweet moments of selfless human goodness, romance and adventure. Whatever the rivalry between Iranians, Turks, Russians and Americans, many of the various players entertained themselves in the restaurant where I spent an evening in the Turkmen capital before resuming my westward journey to the Caspian Sea. Out-of-the-way Ashgabat can sometimes boast a certain international buzz. Shots of vodka smoothed over any roughness in the electric guitar riffs of a loud and energetic band that whipped up Russian, Iranian and Turkish hits. A lonely Finnish businessmen asked women from every table out onto the dance-floor. Turkmen officials emerged from private rooms with primped-up Russian wives. Turkish engineers from the building sites around the city entertained each other with lavish feasts. Tanked-up salesmen from Iran's Caspian Sea province of Mazandaran, escaping from the dead hand of Islamic revolutionary morality, wantonly danced away the burdens of their lives.

The next morning, a man I had hired from among the long-distance taxi-drivers collected outside Ashgabat's main bus station picked me up for the day's long drive. Tajmurat was a fit, broad-shouldered fellow with trustworthy eyes. His body filled a whole side of the little car, the best-kept Zhiguli I had seen. Over the air vents he had added a local touch, brass covers tastefully pierced in the curving paisley patterns of Turkmen bridal jewelry. Our first stop was on the edge of town to pick up supplies from his family's spacious, whitewashed concrete bungalow in a walled-in acre of land. As we left, his mother flung a bowlful of water after the car, sending out a wide arc of spray. The gesture is common from one end of the Turkic world to the other, signifying a wish for a safe journey and a safe return.

We then stopped by the market that forms every Sunday on the edge of the desert stretching to the north of Ashgabat. I passed by on each visit to Turkmenistan as a welcome antidote to Ashgabat's sterile grid of streets, where the Turkmen could appear anaesthetized by their long Soviet sleep. I would lose myself for hours among the camels, the ankle-deep dust, the mingling of nationalities, the bantering, the bargaining, the calls of Turkmen names like "Given-by-God," "White-Mohammed" or "Faith-has-come." Among the displays of the jewelry sellers were pointed Mongol-style helmets that Turkmen girls wear for their weddings, a throwback to the days when the princely courts of Genghis Khan and his descendants made up Central Asia's ruling class. There were also little bells that Turkmen mothers sewed onto their children's clothes to prevent them getting lost in the sands. Like its blood brother, the great Uygur Turk market in Kashgar, five hundred miles to the east in China, it conjured up the energy and magic of millennia of trade and travel.

I tore myself away and headed to the jumble of cars parked amid the straggling walls and waist-high drifts of sand at the edge of the market.

There I found Tajmurat—delighted to have found two good new tires—and we drove off to the main east-west highway. This followed a genuinely old route for invaders and such caravan trade as there was; if anything was the old Silk Road, this was it. All the way from Kazakhstan to the Caspian, mountains rise to the south, their snow-capped peaks protecting Turkic domains against first China, then Afghanistan and the Indian subcontinent, and finally Iran. Northwards stretch hundreds of miles of steppe or desert, for centuries an effective barrier against Russia. In between the mountain and the desert, all along the way, the Turkic peoples have made their home for the past thousand years. The smooth foothills are still dotted with flocks of sheep, tended to by shepherds on horseback.

From time to time among the naked rock of mountains and the flat dry, shrub-covered desert, we drove by straggling concrete villages in which the Soviet Union had settled the Turkmen tribes. Women in sweeping gowns and loosely tied, flowery headscarves moved serenely about their work. Camels rested in pens near many homes. Others roamed free, starting up with their loping canter when surprised by our passing. Then we left even those scarce habitations behind as we headed through sandier desert on the last 200-mile stretch to the Caspian. I settled in for the hot, uncomfortable ride. Then, in the midst of a vast, barren expanse, the car's engine suddenly died. We coasted to a halt.

Tajmurat twisted the ignition key. As the starter motor chattered valiantly, his expression turned from puzzlement to disbelief. The cylinders would not fire. We stepped out of the little world of the Zhiguli into the wilderness all round. An hour of dismantling later, we narrowed the problem down to the distributor cap. Inside the small turntable of the distributor was lodged a tiny fuse or condenser. The bakelite plastic was charred and smelled burnt.

"I've got a spare one in the boot," Tajmurat declared.

Ten minutes of burrowing proved him wrong. The afternoon was wearing on, and the landscape had not a single feature of human habitation. He started to flag down the cars and trucks that passed us every five or ten minutes. Most stopped, and their occupants made good-natured offers to help. The ritual was unchanging. The "mechanic" aboard each of these ships of the desert would wander knowingly over to our open bonnet.

"Try the ignition," he would wisely say.

Heads would bend over the frustratingly simple engine block. Out would come the screwdriver, off would come the distributor cap, and once the whole distributor assembly.

"Ah, you see, that's your problem there," they would pronounce with profound satisfaction, pointing at the fuse housing, and wander back to their vehicles.

Pleasant as they were, I was glad of Tajmurat's presence. In times past, Vámbéry said a Turkmen's protection was the key to survival here. "A nomad may be cruel, fierce, perfidious, but never inhospitable," he said. Tajmurat certainly felt unable to turn away any of the well-wishers who kept stopping unasked to visit their screwdrivers upon our engine. Up to three car-loads at a time pored over it. Most innovative were two Russians wearing only vests and underpants. They tried to replace the fuse by hacking a sliver of aluminum out of a can tossed out on the road-side. Most generous were a pair of Turkmen farmers in a pick-up truck, who left us the gift of a big plastic cola bottle filled with prickly, semi-fermented camel's milk.

Night would soon fall. I suggested that Tajmurat set off and buy the part from the nearest town, 60 miles away. We tried one last substitute for the fuse, a rusty nail. It didn't work. He hesitated: it was a weekend, and I, a near stranger under his protection, was to be left in command of his most valuable possession. But there was no other way but to trust each other. We waved goodbye. The sun slowly set, leaving the horizon luminous with purples and reds. The traffic thinned to one or two vehicles an hour. A desert cold descended.

I ventured into the scrub by the roadside to forage for brushwood. I was cautious. It was near here that a scorpion had stung Vámbéry on the toe. The poison had sent a stream of fire coursing up and down the right side of his body; he had wanted to beat himself to death, but survived after his companions tied him to a tree. I collected my fuel safely, and a bonfire of crackling dry sticks sent flames roaring up high.

My spirits restored, I took a more philosophical view of the obstacles that the new Silk Road threw up. Even the absurdly inadequate main road bridge across the Amu Darya, a clumsy Soviet-era metal pontoon, could be viewed in a romantic light. Each 30-foot floating barge took on a heaving life of its own as convoys of trucks bumped over it. Ahead of them danced a man, judging axle-weights, watching the balance of the pontoons and gesticulating to each driver. He kept the trucks at a precise distance between each other, so that the pontoon-ends would be at an equal height as their wheels crossed. He was for all the world like an old *kervanbashi*, or head of a caravan, coaxing a line of camels across a tricky quicksand. I savored the memory, gazing up from my patch of desert at the brightest and most immaculately detailed carpet of stars I had ever seen. I reassured myself that my delay was but a moment compared to the eons of wasted time that suffocate most initiative in the populations of the Turkic world.

Vehicles had long stopped passing, and a dull ache of worry at my situation was growing. As midnight approached, a pair of headlights appeared on the horizon. A few minutes later they turned into an approaching truck, which, seeing my car by the roadside, slowed down. I felt uncomfortably exposed. The cab door opened, and out jumped Tajmurat, to his and my intense pleasure.

"I had to throw myself in front of this truck to get aboard. Nobody wanted to give me a lift," he said apologetically.

"Don't worry. Did you find the part?"

"Yes, look."

The inch-long piece of white plastic and metal was crude but lovely to our eyes. Our practiced fingers pried open the distributor cap, inserted the fuse and tightened the screws.

"Go for it, Tajmurat!"

The engine turned once or twice and faded away. The battery had given up. I got out and pushed: no luck. Again I threw my weight behind the car, hard and long, panting and running in the darkness. Nothing. A third time, a fourth time. Tajmurat joined me, pushing from the driver's side door. Finally on the fifth, the engine coughed and started. Delighted, we cheered, jumped in, sat down, closed the doors and shook hands. But the car would not go faster than a few miles an hour, bucking painfully on three of its four cylinders, an unwelcome throwback to camelback riding.

"The timing!" I said. "That Russian changed the timing, remember?"

Back in the blackness under the bonnet, we tried to work it out. A dim memory stirred. I seized the distributor and gave it a twist. The engine ran slightly better. Long days of student life playing truant from Persian grammar and tinkering with my Triumph Spitfire engine suddenly did not seem misspent. Tajmurat gave the distributor a wrench. Perfect! We zoomed off into the desert night, toasting our success in camel's milk. The Zhiguli flew like a magic carpet. Without the adversity, success would never have tasted so sweet.

At last, just before dawn, the glow of our destination appeared on the horizon. We pulled up in front of the main hotel of the Caspian Sea port of Turkmenbashy. I was on my way to Azerbaijan, on the western shore of the Caspian. When I went down to the docks early in the morning, luck seemed to be on my side. A substantial, new-looking rail ferry was in port. The clerks at the shipping office thought it might sail in the afternoon. I should keep coming back every a few hours to check, they advised, not quite looking me in the eye.

In the lobby of the hotel, a man approached me. He was one of the traders from the Indian subcontinent who competed with the Turks of Turkey at the lower end of the market for labor and sales of cheap goods. He spoke English, and we exchanged pleasantries about how we had bribed the receptionist for access to a room.

"What are you doing here?" I asked.

"I'm a professional con-man," he announced, as if, in Turkmenbashy, there was no point in standing on ceremony.

He misinterpreted the surprise in my eyes.

"Only proper cons," he hastened to add. "I only con big companies that can afford it."

His name was Omar, and he came from Pakistan. He too was waiting for the ferry, and there was no escaping from him. Omar soon launched into a list of the big-name banks that he had cheated using a variety of tricks, lies and travelers' checks.

"I've reported hundreds of missing bags to airline companies to pick up the compensation, hundreds and hundreds," he said.

"Why are you telling me this?" I asked.

"I'll never see you again. It doesn't matter," Omar said airily. "I'm getting my revenge. You bloody people colonized us for two hundred years. You owe me, not the other way round."

Irrepressibly, he revealed the descending layers of his dishonesty. He was utterly untrustworthy. He even cheated in an unspoken competition we had over how little we had paid in assorted bribes for services. He winced at the memory of how much he had had to pay to stay in a Moscow hotel in order to meet the son of a Turkmen leader—he hinted it was Turkmenbashy himself—in order to become the middle-man in the construction of a new cement factory. That, he said, was the latest big "con" into which he was investing his ill-gotten gains.

"He got me in to see his father. It's that easy. I like things on the table. So when I got into to see the chief, I said: 'Look, I'm paying your son this much, so I expect this deal to go through for my friends,'" Omar said. "The bribes are just five per cent—four per cent for your son, and a one per cent cut for me."

He shook his head disbelievingly at the memory of one of the government ministers who had tried to block the deal.

"I told him to take the bribe. He said he couldn't. I told him to do it for his children. He just looked at me and said he was brought up with communist ideals and would die with them."

It was an odd irony that in Central Asia, "communist" had come to mean "too morally pure." I sympathized with the communist. The fat of Omar's belly spilled over his trousers, his shirt buttons were randomly undone and his short shirttails hung out over his flabby bottom in the style of an English schoolboy.

"How does anybody believe you, dressed as you are?" I asked.

"I'm only like this because I don't want to be robbed," he replied.

He pulled a thick wad of bills from his trouser pocket and gave me a glimpse of green, low-denomination dollars. He also had two enormous suitcases, which made him look like a dealer in Pakistani fake leather jackets, a class of trader for whom he reserved a special scorn.

"If you've got so much money, how come you want to take this awful ferry?"

"I'm economizing. You've no idea how much money all these presents and plane tickets for people are costing."

Even if Omar wove a web of lies, they were a true reflection of the way things got done in Central Asia and the Caucasus. Western airlines stopped flying to Baku when they became fed up with being fleeced. Cigarette factories struggled in Uzbekistan's constantly shifting tax climate. Even a straight-laced U.S. company like ExxonMobil one day found one of its executives under investigation after he admitted pocketing a $2 million kickback from a bribe.

Finding a berth on the Trans-Caspian ferry put to rest any doubts I might have had about how things were being organized. Here, "privatization" had taken on a meaning not recognizable to the International Monetary Fund. "Privateering" would be a better way to describe the way the crew had seized control of the Azerbaijan-owned ship and was plundering its passengers.

Government authority ended with the name of a professor brother of Azerbaijani President Haidar Aliyev, crudely hand-painted at the bow. The only pretence of state revenue collection was a cheap official ferry ticket, but the clerks at the ticket office rarely bothered to go through the motions of selling them. When I finally found a ticket-window open, I was deemed ineligible, as a foreigner, for any ticket at all. For the other resigned-looking passengers, the fragile piece of brown paper was just an opening bid in the new Central Asian game. They sat listlessly behind the customs shed, watching their piles of cheap suitcases and rope-tied bundles, waiting for the next move.

It was a full thirty-six hours later that a bossy voice rang out through the tinny loudspeakers: prepare to board. For once, it wasn't a false alarm. Everyone rushed to form a scrum around a small gap in the wire fence, then, one by one, they dragged their bales of baggage towards a wooden shack between the railway tracks. Here officers of the Turkmen state were harvesting the benefits of passport and customs procedures. I soon gave up hope that I would make it through the 20-person deep crowd. Omar lurked nearby, watching my movements, his hand round his bankroll deep in his pocket. A kindly Russian who had taken me to the port suggested I move away from the crowd and contact one of the go-betweens standing expectantly near the customs shed.

I went up to the bars of a locked-up gate and signaled to a tall, thin Turkmen on the other side of the fence whose uniform looked as though it gave him influence.

"Can you get me on board?"

"Maybe."

"I'll pay."

"How much?"

"Fifty dollars for the cabin, twenty for your trouble."

The official disappeared into the customs shed.

"OK. It'll be 120 dollars. The captain will take 50. But I take 70."

I was lucky and relatively rich. Most of the other passengers were poor, and seethed with anger at having to wait days for the humiliation of being ripped off at every turn. Protests and sometimes tears of impotent frustration flowed as crewmen extracted tolls both at the bottom and at the top of gangway. Chambermaids auctioned off their allotment of cabins to passengers collecting on the decks. My "official" divided up my dollars all the way along the dock and into the ship. The lion's share went to the purser, who accompanied me obsequiously to a cabin. He even carried my luggage. I had clearly paid far too much, although I didn't believe Omar's gleeful story later that he had only paid $30.

It was with relief that I settled down later to celebrate in a privatized restaurant offering macaroni and mince laced with splinters of bone. I took dessert in a privatized kiosk that stocked indestructible Dutch chocolate cakes. I washed it all down with Bulgarian beer, served in decapitated cola cans with razor-sharp rims. For further entertainment, a crewman had even privatized the forward upper deck lounge and installed a television to play a pornographic video. His only would-be customer, however, was Omar, and the Pakistani was too cheap to spare the few Azerbaijani manats the crewman wanted. I was treated without payment to sensurround sex that banged and grunted through my thin cabin wall as we began the long wait for the ship to get under way.

At that early stage, knots of people, relieved to be on board at last, had broken out impromptu picnics and shared them happily. Then the hours of waiting lengthened. The decks and corridors of the ferry gradually became as full and began to smell as foul as a refugee transport. Everybody missed the old certainties of the Soviet Union; all compared the misery and expense of this ferry with stories of flying to Moscow for a handful of roubles. The atmosphere soured. Groups of unshaven men lost themselves in vodka oblivion, argued and gambled hopelessly at cards.

"When money comes in the door, faith leaves through the window," intoned a bearded and lambskin-hatted Azeri cleric with whom I spent a half-hour pacing the afterdeck.

Finally, 13 hours later, the ship's engines started, and we cast off from Central Asia. The Turkmen coastline slipped away. The captain had invited me up to the bridge—my cabin was next to his and there was no charge for taking me into his island of professionalism on board—and I watched the port of Turkmenbashy fade into a smudge of green in the embrace of barren mountains. We passed a final headland, tipped by what might once have been a lighthouse but was now a junkyard of old Soviet navigation equipment stagnating under three feet of water. The Caspian Sea opened before us. An uneasy swell passed by at what seemed a walking pace. Once or twice Caspian seals cut through its filmy, oil-rainbowed surface, floating effortlessly by like lazy snorkellers.

After navigating through the dangerous shallows of the port approaches, Captain Towfiq, who had decided I was his entertainment for the voyage, took me down to his cabin. He had a friendly, round face, his neatly pressed khaki uniform draped over a firm, mountainous belly that kept the deteriorating world all around him at bay. Punctuated by his sporadic interest in a soccer match on television, he explained that his rail ferry had been built in Yugoslavia in the mid-1980s, but that Azerbaijan's Caspian Sea fleet had suffered much since then.

"We sent the best boats to the Baltic Sea to earn hard currency. Five of our eight ships are out of order anyway. Spare parts are a bit hard to get from Yugoslavia these days," he said, trying to fix the fading, grainy TV picture with a knife and a length of wire.

Fourteen hours later, we made fast against the dockside in Baku. Pandemonium, pushing and shoving broke loose once again. All the pressure-cooked torture of the passengers was now bottled up at a single gangway down which the Azeri customs authorities were allowing people off at a rate of one a minute.

"Hey, go easy!" shouted one Azeri at me as one of several scuffles broke out. We were jam-packed in a corridor as we waited to start down to the quayside 10 meters below. "We're not in Turkmenistan now!"

That seemed unfair on the Turkmens, a few of whom I could pick out by their calm faces in the crowd. Disorder and corruption were the warp and weft of Azerbaijan. On one trip to Baku, I was hit up for money by the first person I met, a policeman doubling as an airport porter, and was importuned by the last man I saw as I left, the baggage handler on the tarmac under the plane. He used the telling Azeri word for tip: *hörmet*, or "a sign of respect." At the port in Baku, self-respect disintegrated with Caucasian speed. Some passengers began climbing off the ship onto a flying gantry. Crew members tying up the ship had to duck and take cover as shapeless bundles of baggage came whistling past their ears to thump onto the dock below.

"Animals," a crewman swore as he fought past us, abandoning the passengers to their anarchy and self-imposed, pointless discomfort.

"What a nation of idiots we are," shouted another man in furious despair.

The inefficiency bred by corruption seemed to suit many of the Turkic ruling classes, along with their necessary partners, an unfree media, and big private enterprises run by rulers' relatives. It drew a make-work veil of confusion behind which they could operate as they liked. The Turks even have an old saying for it: "wolves like misty weather." The absence of a respectable legal framework is one reason non-oil foreign investment in Turkic states is relatively low.

For instance, two companies that rushed ill-advisedly into Turkey during the 1990s mobile phone boom, Motorola and Nokia, ended up filing a racketeering suit against their former partner for what they said was the theft of $3.0 billion. The case forced the U.S. Embassy to warn American companies against investing in Turkey, even as Washington encouraged the International Monetary Fund to give yet more loans to keep the budget of their regional ally afloat. Motorola's erstwhile partner, meanwhile, blithely went on to found a political party that won 7% of the vote in the 2002 parliamentary elections on a virulently populist, anti-IMF, anti-Western platform. He only narrowly missed a parliamentary seat and its accompanying immunity from prosecution, since parties must win 10% of the national vote to enter the assembly. Eventually he fell foul of the Turkish state's strong instinct for self-preservation. In 2003-04, a new government confiscated the alleged fraudster's family bank and 200 other businesses. But when I asked ordinary Turks why they wanted to vote for someone accused of larceny, many replied with satisfaction that they admired him because he gouged the cash out of rich America. It was like the Turkish newspapers, which trumpeted the securing of IMF loans with headlines that made it sound as if a military expedition had won a great victory and was marching home with cartloads of booty.

The social context of corruption was driven home when I started doing some minor improvements to my house in Istanbul, such as weather-proofing my balcony. Municipal regulations made this all but impossible in theory, but that went for almost any development in the city. During the first stage, my foreign identity allowed me to sweet-talk away the men who came round with sledgehammers to break it down. My only outlay was the gift of a book about the Ottoman Emire to a local official who was an amateur historian. At that moment, however, I forfeited my right to complain about any of the other rule-breaking going on all round me. Then, for a basement conversion a few years later, like the oilmen in Central Asia now facing trial in New York for paying commissions, I was busy and allowed my contractor to take care of everything. The bribes were brazenly typed into his bills; I felt lucky not to have to pay tax on them too. But once launched down this slippery slope, the greed of the officials turned out to be bottomless. Punishment came quickly, in the form of an underground stream, which would probably have been detected in any Western legal framework of surveys and permissions. It forced me to give up my plan at a substantial loss, and the basement joined the hundreds of abandoned and half-finished buildings, factories and projects that litter the Turkic landscape.

Corruption was not the only way Turkic elites co-opted their active population and protected themselves from answerability. To handle those who publicly question the system, they have long employed brute force, leading to widespread violations of human rights. Like corruption, police brutality delegitmizes governments and brings tension with Western interlocutors. The bad behavior of Turkic states has even persuaded the boards of international companies to vote down deals with them. The most advanced and open of the group is Turkey, and thus it is the state that feels most vulnerable to criticism on this score. But when I met a Turkish police chief seeking to improve his force's image by applying for international quality certification for his police station, I learned that not all of the old has made way for the new.

23. MIDNIGHT ESPRESSO

THE TURKIC PROBLEM
WITH HUMAN RIGHTS

> *We love being tyrants, from childhood, it's said*
> *Discord flows from our land, from its rockiest bed*
> *We tax our own kin, and we leave them for dead*
> *Habits like this can't be beat from our head*
> —Azeri satirist MIRZA AL-AKBAR SABIR, 1862-1911

IN THE HERALDIC COAT OF ARMS OF THE OTTOMAN EMPIRE, THE SCALES of the law hang only a hair's breadth from a pistol's trigger guard. Early Ottoman sultans, like some medieval European states, even defined the use of beating and torture by law. The modern Turks' attitude to law-enforcement, despite their Westernizing achievements, is not that distant from their Ottoman forbears. Likewise, the Turkic republics mix the tough traditions of Central Asian khans with methods of Soviet totalitarianism. Even the friendly "Switzerland of Central Asia," the Kyrgyz Republic, faced international criticism for violations of rights to freedom of expression and organization. Uzbekistan executed more than 50 people in 1999 on what often seemed flimsy charges; in 2003, it had 6,500 political prisoners and a U.N. condemnation for the use of "systematic torture." Behind the placid façades of Kazakhstan and Turkmenistan, security forces dealt brutally with both opposition movements and dissident media. Half of Azerbaijan's neglected prisoners had tuberculosis. In Turkey, the main human rights group documented nearly 600 cases of torture in 1999 in which nine people died; noting significant improvements in 2004, Human Rights Watch said it was still receiving some reports of beatings, torture and mock executions. Westerners have long reacted with distaste. Venetian Ambassador Gianbattista Donato reported in 1684: "The Ottomans are the only ruling house in the world able to establish a permanent order based on fear."

But the Turks of Turkey, at least, have tired of their reputation as one of the major human rights abusers of the world. It was embarrassing for a candidate member of the European Union and put off foreign investors. So the Turkish police started cleaning up their act. In the southwestern market town of Aydın, police chief A. Tekin Akın wanted to go further. He applied for, and later received, an ISO 9000 certification for one of his police stations. The award is usually desired by factories and businesses to prove that their work procedures measure up to an international quality standard. Indeed, the Aydın police force was being sponsored in its effort by a major local jeans exporter, among other Western-minded businesses.

I called Police Chief Akın to ask for an interview, and he readily agreed. First, however, I looked into the record of the Aydın force. It turned out that only a few years before, a prisoner had been tortured to death in that same police station. I went to see the lawyer for the dead prisoner's family, Gül Kireçkaya. She worked in a warren of law offices near the courthouse of the regional center of Izmir. Dark-skinned and intense, a fine sense of irony saved her from seeming like one of the smoldering Turkish activists who are as inflexible as the security forces they confront.

"Quality awards won't make any difference," Kireçkaya told me straight away. "If someone gets taken in to a police station station, they get beaten. If you're on terror charges, and for as long as you don't confess, you'll be tortured. And by that I mean electricity, sexual abuse, whatever. This country is like that."

"Aren't the police in Aydın making at least an effort to do better?" I asked.

"There's two-facedness in everything in Turkey. Just because we open the biggest, most modern bus stations in the world doesn't mean we solved the traffic problem," she said.

Indeed, senseless traffic accidents in Turkey killed twice as many people every day than died under torture each year. It was rare that the families of either category of victim saw any justice.

But torture corroded the national psyche. Slack investigative methods meant that the police mostly collected evidence from confessions,
and force was the easiest tool to acquire them. Kireçkaya described the
police as a hierarchical, right-wing tribe that saw it as its duty to find and
punish criminals and to crush left-wing activists as enemies of the state.
The other side were often no angels either. Hard-core defendants intimidated witnesses or bribed low-paid judges. Likewise, convicts could buy
anything they wanted in jail, or send gunman accomplices round to
threaten the prison warders at home. Indeed, whichever gang is
strongest in prison tends to dominate the Turkish street, rather than vice
versa. In 1998, a notorious Turkish mafioso was discovered pulling so
many strings in the abortive privatization of a state bank that the Turkish
prime minister of the day was forced to resign. That mobster was not
even in prison in Turkey, but in far-away France.

The lawyer's stories kept coming, as bitter as her Black Sea coast tea
and as hard to digest as her hospitable offering of fried pastry rolls filled
with mashed potato. She told me that her client who died in Aydın jail,
Baki Erdoğan, had been 28 when he was picked up in a police raid
against a group called *Dev Sol*, the Revolutionary Left. Court documents
showed Baki had been kept alive at first so that he could conduct the
police to left-wing safe houses. Eleven days later, the authorities called
his father to a hospital morgue to identify his son's dead and battered
body.

"They say the bruises were from where he hit the bars himself; we
say he was beaten. They say his scars were on his shoulders, and were
from carrying a back-pack; we say the scars were in the armpit and
between the toes, and were consistent with electrical torture. And so it
goes on," Gül said.

"What sort of person was Baki Erdoğan?" I asked.

"A professional revolutionary type."

I felt wary. I remembered how the Revolutionary Left killed people
in the early 1990s, including foreigners. My friends would find their
company offices had been cased by "revolutionary types" and police
found their names on captured death lists. For a while even I had felt
obliged to hide my car, and had felt wary stepping out of my house in
Istanbul.

"What did he do?" I asked.

"He organized hunger strikes, put up posters, discussed the revolution, whatever," the lawyer said. "But they had no right to torture him to death."

The family sued the Aydın police officers involved. After some years, they were sentenced for the killing, an outcome that is becoming less uncommon in Turkey. The judge's sentencing was ambivalent, however. "The constitution and international agreements outlaw torture. This rarely happens in our country. We have laws to deal with it," he read into the record. "But we are happy that [Erdoğan's] confessions led to the discovery of safe houses and bomb fuses."

As the judge handed down his judgement in April 1998, Kireçkaya remembered how mayhem had broken out in the Aydın courtroom. Plainclothes and uniformed policemen surged forward to beat up the lawyers, relatives and supporters of the dead man's family.

"We thought we were going to be killed. We tried to hide behind the judge's bench, but he said: 'Get down, this is my place,'" she recalled. "One of our supporters was the daughter of another judge, and they really beat her. They even punched the prosecutor and swore at him."

Kireçkaya believed it was the embarassment of national television coverage of this court-room fracas that had spurred the Aydın police chief to apply for his quality certification. The police officers involved were still in their jobs after being sentenced for the torture murder. As the case went to appeal, they were even promoted.

The Security Headquarters in Aydın was a typical late 20th century piece of Turkish official architecture, a concrete block with a blank face of narrow rectangular windows. But this police station was freshly painted in shades of the new pan-Turkish police color, royal blue. I walked in to be challenged by a display of police power in the cramped entrance hall: a wall-to-wall poster featuring men and women officers posing on powerful motor bikes, beside cars, in light armored vehicles and around a helicopter. All of them were armed to the teeth. No wonder the Turkish army had recently stopped issuing the police with heavy weapons. Along the top, thick-printed letters spelled out the message: "We are the Guarantors of Human Rights and Democracy."

As the gravelly voice of balladeer Leonard Cohen crooned incongruously through the station's loudspeaker system, ultra-polite police ushered me upstairs to the office of the chief. Instead of the usual barebones metal desks and straggling plants, the suite was paneled in wood. Tropical fish swam in a tank. Niches were filled with certificates from training courses in America sponsored by the U.S. State Department, memorial shields declaiming gratitude from local associations and even a declaration that Chief Akın had been declared an honorary mayor-president of Baton Rouge, Louisiana. Old typewriters stood on display, as did mementos like the handcuffs of yesteryear. On a ledge behind his desk miniature flagpoles marched up a wooden pyramid, each of them representing a Turkic state, an increasingly popular decoration in better-off Turkish public offices. Pictures of past chiefs paraded along the upper wall. They were bald, military, intellectual, or bureaucratic according to the fashion of the time, including, during the Second World War, a rather menacing fellow with a toothbrush moustache.

The newest incumbent soon stormed in. Chief Akın was clean-shaven, pale-skinned and short, and a trim blue jersey concealed some of his bull-like bulk as he settled behind his desk. His gray-blue eyes locked onto mine. If I looked away while he was talking, he would stop and demand that I look into them again. I wondered if this was an interrogation technique. But we were still getting to know each other.

"Something to drink?" Akın asked, hitting an intercom button and holding it open.

"A coffee, perhaps?"

"Bring me a cappuccino," he barked.

"You have cappuccino?" I asked in surprise.

"Yes, cappuccino. We've got rid of the tea man. It makes work go faster," he said.

In any other police station or public office there would have been a *çay ocağı*, a small space under the stairs in which a functionary lorded it over a steaming array of polished brass or steel. From it he would dispense tea to all and sundry on a non-spill tray suspended on metal rods from a ring. A plastic machine now stood on each floor of the building, dispensing a selection of watery, undrinkable liquids. Akın was right that Turks do linger over their tea, with which every visitor to an office is greeted. But this piece of modernity was worse than no reform at all, the kind of bad copy of the West that gives Westernization a bad name.

"We're not the Orient here any more, you know. We are not the Iranian or Iraqi police. We're modern, the same as American police," he said.

He picked up my fax asking him about his quality revolution. Before I could get a word in, it triggered a new round of short, rapid-fire sentences.

"We want to be like private sector businesses. We're a bridge between old and new . . . we are white-collar workers now," he began.

My eyes slipped down to his uniform shirt. It was blue.

"Look at me, please," he ordered. "We are the state, you see. We have put on a neck-tie."

The tie is an important visual symbol of Atatürk's modernization, just as the red rimless fez had been for Ottoman Turkish reformers when it replaced the turban a century before. There was no discussion with Akın as he hit his stride. He wanted the police to be more efficient. He wanted to prevent crime, not just solve it. He wanted to break the vicious circle of bureaucracy. He wanted to conduct brainstorming sessions. He wanted to collect clues, not just confessions. He thought that the crawling pace of the legal system was the reason why so many Turks resorted to instant justice outside it. He produced books he had authored: *Police Policy*, and *The Dictionary of Total Quality*. No more, he vowed in an internal document, should Turkish mothers frighten their young ones with the old saying: "Eat up your food or the policeman will take it."

I was impressed. Akın's idea that the police were there to serve was revolutionary in a country where the police think they are the law, not only the enforcers of it. The worst drivers in Turkey are the traffic police, callously disobeying the most basic rules about U-turns and one-way streets. The police "should not think that the sentences of the judges are not applicable to them," one of Akın's documents said. Even a basic knowledge of first aid among policemen would save hundreds of lives from the annual slaughter of traffic accidents, he noted.

"It's education, education, education," he said forcefully, beating on his desk.

I summoned up my courage.

"What about political investigations? Is there room for improvement there?"

Akın's tone sharpened. He reminded me that he was an old *terörcü*, or one-who-deals-with-terrorism. Opponents of the state, he reminded me, were enemies who had stepped beyond the bounds of normal society. Yes, he had promoted the men who were sentenced for torturing Baki Erdoğan to death, and would stick by them as long as there was any chance of appeal. The media had turned them into "sacrificial lambs," he said. When I prompted him about the dead suspect, he began to anger.

"He was one of the terrorists trying to destroy the state. They are anarchistic. They are clinically certifiable cases. They are unloved by their families," he raged. "And I don't know if you've noticed, but all the terrorist girls are ugly."

Reform, Akın made clear, was efficiency and packaging. Only politeness prevented him from throwing questions about treatment of Turkey's ethnic minorities back in Westerners' faces.

"We don't go and scratch their wounds, do we? I saw the blacks sitting on the streets in America. They are second-class citizens, no question about it. But I don't go up and say to people, 'O, Great White Race, where are the Red Indians?'"

Disgruntled, he took off around his office, ending up for reassurance at a big wooden map of his province on the wall opposite his desk. With a flick of a switch, he lit up bulbs to mark every police station. Cutout models of squad cars had been pasted onto the roads between them. He pushed a button, and the board gave a police siren's wail. He smiled proudly. Drivers of real Turkish police cars now have the population so well cowed that they can clear people from their path just with the electronic snap and crackle that comes from pressing the microphone button of their car's loudhailer.

Akın's morale restored, we headed out to see his quality revolution at work. His era as chief was notable for the construction of a new police clubhouse, resplendent in bright white paint, chandeliers, a weights room and even a sauna. When we entered a lecture theater, 60 police officers shuffled up to attention. They looked deeply uncomfortable. The motorcycle patrolmen were still in their leathers.

"Merhaba!" barked Akın, standing to attention himself for the time-less greeting ceremony of Turkish uniformed life.

"Sağol!" shot back the reply, an antique 'be healthy' of thanks that can be heard all the way into the heart of Central Asia.

"We rehabilitate them here," the chief whispered in English as we slipped into seats facing them. "I'm washing their brains."

A senior woman officer continued with her lecture about how the future police of Aydın province should be.

"We mustn't look at the people with prejudice, but look at how we can serve them. The people want it this way," she said. "With the press and visual media everywhere, the people now see what the police do."

The audience listened to the briefer stony faced. Turkish police usu-ally suppress rowdy demonstrations with gratuitous and widely televised beatings and kickings of protestors.

"What do you do about corruption, then?" I asked Akın as he moved me on again.

"I make them feel ashamed. I tell them, what will your children say when you lose your job—Daddy is a thief?" Akın said.

The most systematically corrupt part of the force is the traffic police, and, perhaps to break the chain, Akın had appointed a woman as his provincial traffic chief. She was in her 40s. Women are now everywhere in the Turkish force, and are a major influence for change: the men have smartened up, and the hard edge of the police has softened. But even as traffic chief, she still served the tea.

"What did you think of the film *Midnight Express*?" I asked Akın.

The chief was taken aback. He'd never seen the 1979 Alan Parker film, a fictionalized story featuring relentlessly brutal treatment of an American drug runner in a Turkish jail. But he knew of its reputation, which, building on old prejudices, has truly blackened the name of the Turks for a whole generation of Westerners.

"We've turned over the page. There's a new generation now," he said. "We have no complexes about Midnight Express, we know we aren't like that. We want evidence now, not falaka [the bastinado to the feet]."

"Would you allow me to visit the cells in the anti-terrorism unit, then?"

Akın flinched. It was as if I had asked to see the sewage connection.

Instead, he took me to see the model precinct soon to win its quality award, known as the Victory police station. It was painted a pastel shade of blue that the chief said he thought was most inviting. "Welcome to your home" said a sign over the entrance.

"It's so people don't feel frightened when they come here," Akın said.

A pretty woman officer in the entranceway—an Akın touch repeated throughout the province—invited us in past a waiting area marked out by wicker screens and potplants from the low-ceilinged, concrete corridors all around. In the front office, a long list of rules about police questioning was pinned to the wall, in print too small to read easily. Pinned to the wall next to it was a doll-sized lawyer's gown. It was meant to indicate that a suspect's advocate should sit on a note-taking chair beneath, but it looked as sinister as a voodoo fetish.

I was not surprised to meet a Kurdish activist later that day who said he had been struck in the face by a policeman in that same Victory station a few weeks before. But Akın was right. Something had changed. The Kurd said he was was only hit once, even though he had freely insulted his interrogators; the police had accepted his refusal to sign a fake confession; and it was he who three times refused a police offer for anti-torture medical exams.

The straight-backed young chief of Victory station, Serkan Ömercioğlu, symbolized a new spirit in the force. Unlike the uneducated mass of police officers of the past, he had not only finished secondary school, as required by new regulations, but he had been to a police academy. Like Akın, his father had been a cop, but he believed his career would be different.

"There are a lot of new ways of getting information. We learned that we mustn't look at people as automatically guilty," he said, pretending to like his watery cappuccino. "We had human rights lessons two hours a week from the very beginning. It gets into you after four years."

The Turkic states of the east are only beginning to move down the road taken by Turkey. Citizens have few rights to protect themselves from their despotic rulers and self-serving security services. Perhaps the worst of the group is the Central Asian state of Uzbekistan. But this did little to put off the U.S. government in its search for regional allies. During the Cold War, the U.S. overlooked Turkey's human rights violations as the peccadilloes of an important ally. Similarly, half-hearted American remonstrations against Uzbek regime's oppressive methods in the past have been swept aside by the need for its help in the U.S. "war on terrorism" after Sept. 11, 2001. In this struggle, Uzbekistan has happily found itself a key forward base.

The Twenty-First Century is Ours

*Freed as their borders opened after the end of the Cold War,
the Turks feel their way forward to a better future*

24. STEP-SONS OF TAMERLANE

THE GRIM DETERMINATION OF UZBEKISTAN

The anger of an Afghan is nothing compared to the pity of an Uzbek.

—Central Asian proverb

SILVER MIG WARPLANES ROARED LOW OVERHEAD. SECONDS LATER, PUFFS of smoke billowed from the bare, rolling foothills of the great Ala-Too massif to the south. The explosions sent a shiver of satisfaction through the ranks of Russian, American, Central Asian, Turkish and other military delegates watching from a reviewing stand. In a shallow valley of agricultural fields before us, units of soldiers shifted uncomfortably. Here on the border between Kazakhstan and Uzbekistan, I had come to witness the start of Central Asia's first U.S.-led joint military exercise. Six years after the break-up of the Soviet Union, America was planting its feet in the middle of what had once been the Soviets' jealously guarded back yard. It was America's show of commitment to the emerging Turkic world. Four years later, America reaped its reward. Uzbekistan and the Kyrgyz Republic quickly offered forward bases for U.S. operations against the Taliban and Osama bin Laden in Afghanistan.

As the first mock strike ended, small, dark dots appeared on the horizon. They slowly resolved into a lumbering line of American transport planes droning in at a steady 1,200 feet. They had flown 19 hours with 500 troops of the U.S. 82nd Airborne Division, a non-stop journey one-third of the way around the world. It was the longest-distance airborne exercise in U.S. military history. As the big green aircraft came abreast of the stand, the first bundles of jeeps and supplies popped out. Within minutes, the Central Asian sky was filled with a mile-long curtain of parachutes, floating slowly down onto patches of cornstalks, beans and strawberries.

I ran forward to talk to the men. They were tired, monosyllabic, and non-plussed that their first contact was with an English-speaking reporter with a pen and notebook. I attached myself to a "reconnaissance party" wading through the fields to meet their "friendly partners" on the ground. The need for such exercises quickly became clear. There was no joint language between the Central Asians and their new friends from America. Indeed, even though all sides were trying to use standard North Atlantic Treaty Organization commands, NATO and former Soviet troops had different map-reading techniques and conflicting ways of giving orders. Translators from Central Asian ministries, mostly middle-aged ethnic Russian ladies, had been bundled up for the day in battle fatigues to help out. They crouched incongruously with American and Central Asian officers among the cabbage patches and tomato fields. Sign language turned out to be the easiest common medium.

The uniformed spin doctors in the media tent later declared that the 1997 war game of reinforcing Central Asia "against dissident elements" had worked well. Centrazbat, the new, NATO-backed unit that mixed troops from Kazakhstan, Uzbekistan and the Kyrgyz Republic, was born. But only U.S. money and willpower kept them together. The Kazakh and Uzbek units kept themselves in barracks on each side of their national boundary, 40 minutes apart by road and two hours apart by time zone. But, in a foretaste of future cooperation the U.S. would enjoy in Afghanistan, the exercise included waves of parachute jumps by troops arriving separately from Russia and Turkey, the other rivals for the heart of Central Asia.

"I rolled over on my parachute and looked up to see a couple of (Russian-made) MiGs. I thought, it really is a different world," said U.S. Marine Corps Gen. John J. Sheehan, the tall chief of the U.S. Atlantic Command and the first parachutist to jump. "The message, I guess, is that there is no nation on the face of the earth that we cannot get to."

American troops were soon indulging in deaf-and-dumb chitchat with their new Turkic buddies and handing over filter cigarettes and chewing gum. Among the officers waiting near the review stand was a handsome representative of the Russian defense ministry, Commander Alexander Mikhailov. Once the deputy captain of a nuclear submarine, he refused to rise and attack my provocative questions about his feelings.

"The world *has* changed. I took part in the preparation of the exercise, and I got a positive impression," he said. "We are no longer enemies. Nobody dictated any conditions to us. Their opinion is the same as our opinion: we need to cooperate."

Still, Russians often had to bite their lip. In the early 1990s, the United States accommodated Russia in Central Asia. Afterwards, as in this exercise, Moscow had to accommodate Washington. According to the American ambassador on the reviewing stand, Stanley Escudero, American interests lay in what he called the "second largest hydrocarbon reserves on the planet." Of course, the U.S. still wanted to "help these nations toward free markets and democratic processes." Not surprisingly, "we also want American companies to be able to invest profitably'" Finally, and perhaps most ambitiously, he noted a desire to 'see that cooperation will make them bigger than the sum of their parts . . . to enable Central Asia to form a reliable buffer between Russia and whoever lies to the south.'

For some in the United States, the heart of that buffer against states like the Islamist regime in Iran should be Uzbekistan. With 24 million people, Uzbekistan is the most populous state in Central Asia, and one of the more homogenous, with Uzbeks making up more than 70% of the population. The country is the only doubly-landlocked state in the world, that is, one whose imports and exports must cross the territory of two states to reach the sea. But it is also the only Central Asian country with borders to all four of the others, as well as Afghanistan. "Uzbekistan is the anchor store in the Central Asian mall," says a late-1990s report for the U.S. military's Strategic Studies Institute. Uzbekistan is however constantly wrestling with its instinct to be Central Asia's imperialist, an attitude that threatens to drive its neighbors into other alliances. It is the only Central Asian state that has developed a cohesive military, numbering 60-70,000 men. It has published a defensive military doctrine, but reserves the right to intervene regionally for "stability." It does not hesitate to do so.

Tashkent threw its weight on the ex-communist, secularist side in the civil war in neighboring Tajikistan, ordering aerial attacks, sending arms and otherwise supporting armed insurgents. It argued against Turkmenistan's rights to draw more water off the Amu Darya, or Oxus River. It cut gas supplies to impoverished Kazakh cities like Shymkent when they failed to make payments required by the new borders and capitalist accounting. Its security men seized dissidents from Bishkek, the capital of the hapless Kyrgyz Republic.

When I returned from the exercises to my dreary hotel in Tashkent, the Uzbek capital and the biggest metropolis in Central Asia, the lobby was suddenly full of American soldiers. Some were in shorts, carrying big plastic bottles of water like tourists and wearing tee shirts adorned with Gothic skulls or legends like "Headhunters." Others wore sharp-pressed fatigues, kept their hair short, bristling and warlike, like the officer I sat talking to on one of the wide sofas by the elevators.

"What do you think the Russians make of all this?" I asked the major, pointing out the scene after he had given me a lengthy speech about NATO's partnership with Uzbekistan.

The Russians had already moved their bases out of Uzbekistan, a situation unique in Central Asia. Only Azerbaijan, in the Caucasus, had achieved the same.

"The Russians can get used to it, or get out," he replied with a humorless smile.

Uzbekistan's President Islam Karimov had great ambitions for his post-Soviet regime, and tried to rally his people behind it as the balance of strategic power shifted in Central Asia's new "Great Game." He adopted a new symbol of national grandeur: Tamerlane, the awe-inspiring Turco-Mongol conqueror who lived from about 1336 to 1405. His name derives from his Persian nickname, *Timur-e Leng,* or Timur the Lame. In Uzbekistan he is known as *Amir Timur,* or Prince Timur. As merciless as his distant Mongol forebears, he built towers of skulls from the massacred population of any city unwise enough to stand in the way of his goal of reuniting the Asian empire of Genghis Khan. The capital of his short-lived empire was in Samarkand, on the territory of today's Uzbekistan.

From here he conquered Iran, the Tatars of the Golden Horde as far as Moscow in Russia, the early Ottoman Turks as far as Izmir on the west coast of Anatolia, and the peoples of northern India as far as New Delhi. He died while marching on China.

Uzbek school textbooks printed Timur's wise sayings in place of those of Lenin. Uzbek television praised his empire-building achievements. His exploits became the subject of one of independent Uzbekistan's first epic films. President Karimov allowed that "not all of what Tamerlane did can be lauded," but his cruel reputation was downplayed. Indeed, guides lecturing schoolchildren gathered around the long jade cenotaph that covers his grave in Samarkand left it out altogether. His statue rose over a central square in Tashkent, a horseback monument to replace previous statues on the same spot of Karl Marx, Joseph Stalin, and the Russian conqueror of Central Asia, General Kaufmann. On its plinth a new inscription reads "Strength in Justice," a motto attributed to Tamerlane. Karimov liked to quote Tamerlane as saying, "Freedom is There Where Law Prevails." Karimov's idea was that if totalitarian rule was based on a written code, it could be classified as a democracy. The laws were merciless, in theory and practice. Timur would have understood.

Even Karimov's official hagiography concedes he is "a competent but rather uncomfortable person," preferring "tough but justified reality to populism." Born to a poor family in Samarkand in 1938, he went to a school where he and most other boys walked barefoot. Becoming a mechanical engineer, he rose through the state planning department to lead the republic's communist party just before independence, a position he converted to the presidency through rigged polls in 1991, 1995 and 2000. Autocratic and nervy, he was given to furious public outbursts. In one speech to parliament, he said of Islamic fundamentalists: "Such people must be shot in the head. If necessary, I'll shoot them myself."

Uzbek law arrived on the blade of a bulldozer as I was walking near the Tashkent bazaar, where the back streets of 19th century mud-brick houses recalled the lovely old Turkic quarters of towns in Xinjiang. Just as in China, they were being leveled to the ground. People said it was to make way for a lucrative new building project of the mayor's, as well as to eliminate some difficult-to-police neighborhoods. As in Xinjiang, compensation had been offered in the form of land or smaller new homes in apartment buildings. Some men coated in demolition dust were picking through the debris.

"I liked my old house, but what can we do about it? The demolition was done according to the law," said Abdusamad, pulling out old beams to build his new abode.

"We're angry. But we can't say anything," muttered Bakhtiyar, stacking salvaged bricks, his expression a mix of bitterness and resignation.

They had been given little time to clear out. The remains of their previous life lay scattered around the courtyard: a well, white shelves from their stucco-walled reception room, porcelain basins, a bread oven and a big metal cauldron in which Uzbeks make meat-and-rice *plov* to celebrate feasts and high days with families and friends. Abdusamad said the house had been in his family for a century.

"We won't have an oven like this where we're going, there'll be no courtyard," he said. "If we talk to you, we'll be taken away, like our local *imam* (prayer leader). We're scared. You have to live a quiet life."

Central Asian oppression also troubled Arminius Vámbéry, the Hungarian adventurer. But he voiced understanding when he arrived at the ethnically Uzbek court of the sallow-faced, sinister Khan of Khiva, a once important city state whose mudbrick walls and narrow streets survive abandoned in the dry and distant deserts of Uzbekistan. "In a country where pillage and murder, anarchy and lawlessness are the rule, and not the exception," he wrote, "a sovereign has to maintain his authority by inspiring his subjects with the utmost dread and almost superstitious terror for his person; never with affection."

Karimov's new "democracy" went on show every year on occasions like independence day, or the newly coined official celebrations around *Navruz*, from Nowruz, meaning "new day" in Persian. Marking the first day of spring on March 21, or the New Year of the solar calendar, this is an old Iranian festival shared by the eastern Turks and other peoples like the Kurds. President Karimov now decks Tashkent out in flags to greet *Navruz* with an official intensity once reserved only for the Bolshevik revolution.

A florid invitation from the Foreign Ministry allowed me access to a stage set up in the town center beside the new parliament. Its flat, blue-ribbed dome recalled the tomb of Tamerlane, but it was topped with a flagpole like the spike on a Prussian helmet. Sheer gilded walls of reflective glass glinted behind colonnades, an architectural reminder that the Uzbek government makes no pretence of transparency. Spot on time, ministers, bureaucrats and the stern-faced leaders of collective farms took the seats of honor in their stiff Sunday best suits and pork-pie hats. Amid 50-foot-high inflatable tulips and fake bouquets of blossom, the celebrations started with a speech by President Karimov. He spoke in Uzbek, but I was astonished as familiar clichés rolled through loud and clear. As part of the new Uzbek identity, Karimov had simply copied the vocabulary of Turkey's politics—word for word.

"Navruz is a symbol of hope, our traditions and customs . . . national pride . . . independence . . . peace . . . stability in our country . . . respected citizens . . . dear brothers . . ."

Behind him, a huge, open-mouthed yellow plastic fish gasped for air on the far side of the stage. As Karimov finished, a parade of actors crossed the stage dressed as cartoon animals, including a man wearing a Central Asian padded *khalat* coat and, extraordinarily for a Muslim country, another wearing the head of a pig. In the background floated an inflatable statue of a stern Prince Timur, flanked by trees and a pink-and-yellow inflatable gorilla.

Dancers acted out a festival of the seasons. Summer arrived as a massive white boll of cotton, from which a girl leapt like a party stripper. She was followed by a copy of the entertainments of the old Central Asia: a trumpeter on stilts, a child acrobat tumbling in mock combat with an alter-ego doll and a skit on the accident-prone figures of Middle Eastern fun, Nasruddin Hodja and his donkey. The present was illustrated by a satire on the cellphones that are the badges of the Uzbek elite, and a woman in futuristic plastic clothing, lip-synching in front of a hard-rock band.

The collective farmers around me remained impassive. "The national character of the Tatar," the traveler Vámbéry noted, "is chiefly marked by seriousness and firmness; to dance, jump, or show high spirits, is in his eyes only worthy of women and children. I have never seen an Uzbek person of good manners indulge in immoderate laughter."

Karimov was smiling happily enough as he took his leave, glad-handing the front row of dignitaries. Somehow his appearance did not fit his position, however. He had none of the well-tailored smoothness of Kazakhstan's President Nazarbayev, the open-eyed charm of the Kyrgyz Republic's Akayev, the opulent egotism of Turkmenistan's Niyazov, or the canny confidence of Azerbaijan's Aliyev. But Karimov had the most stubborn determination of any of his Turkic colleagues to build a strong nation.

Turkey was one model. Karimov had wept and kissed the airport tarmac on first arriving in Ankara after the declaration of Uzbek independence, and once declared that "the road to Europe lies through Turkey." He changed the Uzbek alphabet from Russian-style Cyrillic to Turkish-style Latin in 1993. Visiting a television and refrigerator factory in the Turkish city of Eskişehir, he said: "Uzbekistan and Turkey are not only joined by culture, language and history, but by their future. As I went round this factory, I saw that some people's faces resembled those of the Uzbek people. I was jealous because they had come west before us. Nothing can separate these two countries."

Karimov later distanced himself from Turkey, considering it a political rival. He accused it of subversion, criticized its big-brother airs and started flirting with more autocratic "models" from southeast Asia.

A proper dictatorship, however, depends on a full treasury. Uzbekistan's draconian efforts to direct cash into the state coffers strangled the country's shallow efforts to move to a free market economy. While the Internet and globalization conquered the world, Uzbekistan outlawed the concept of petty cash. All business had to be transacted through banks, but documentation bogged down the smallest transfer. Quotas on the amount of foreign exchange that could be sent out of Uzbekistan were imposed out of the blue, and the mechanics of making such transfers were kept secret. "Our most important duty," read a banner hanging outside an Uzbek bank, "is to make our currency strong as other respected currencies in the world." But there were sometimes 16 different exchange rates for the unloved Uzbek *som*.

Such circumstances forced traders to develop complicated systems of barter, but even that barely worked. An international consulting company slipped a copy of a report under my hotel door, in which it told the Uzbek government that it faced a "bureaucratic nightmare." The company complained of "incompetent or obstructionist employees" standing in the way of its efforts merely to register for business, at the end of which a senior official had asked for a fat bribe.

The Uzbek government hated its poor image, but, just like Turkey, often refused to listen to outside advice on how to put it straight. It took out an advertisement in London's *Financial Times* boasting about who was doing business in the country. It did not inform most of those whose logos were reproduced, in a few instances photocopied from representatives' visiting cards. President Karimov flew to Europe to address a group of investors, but the show of credit at his side was primitive: a stack of Uzbek gold. He labeled Uzbekistan's go-it-alone development "our path" or "the Uzbek model." He spoke of the dangers of pulling down the old house before the new one was built and "avoiding pseudo-revolutionary leaps."

Karimov had reason to be cautious. At one point in the early days of independence, stocks of flour to make bread had plunged to two days of reserves. He was not entirely unsuccessful, either. His Soviet-style controls and relentless efforts to keep the old system going resulted in Uzbekistan enjoying the least drastic economic downturn in the former Soviet Union, and the earliest return to some growth. Pensions and salaries were small but usually paid on time. Planes left on schedule. Alongside a few new buildings in the capital, like a reflective-glass skyscraper for the National Bank, more old ones were refurbished. As often as not, rusty old Soviet equipment and streetcars were maintained well enough to keep doing their jobs. The fountains played smoothly on the vast expanse of Independence Square, formerly Lenin Square, and metro trains disgorged hundreds of people into sumptuous subway stations every few minutes. Oil production tripled to make the country self-sufficient in energy. The quality of cotton exports slowly improved. Foreign debt was held to a few billion dollars. And despite the difficult conditions, some foreign investors did open factories to make products for regional markets, including cars, shoes, milk, furniture and macaroni.

But Uzbek officials found it hard to tell these stories to people as uncontrollable as foreign writers. Some realized how much better a freer Uzbekistan could have done, and many feared that saying the wrong thing would destroy their career. One of the few who dared to talk was a deputy chairman of the Central Bank, Jamshid Kuchkarov. Just 32 years old, a sense of purpose burned in his ebony-black eyes.

"In Uzbekistan, we say we have to measure seven times, then cut once," he said. "I don't want my children to work as peasants or at supermarket-checkout counters. I want them to produce cars and consumer goods."

But in rural parts of Uzbekistan, where people went hungry in order to grow cotton for the benefit of state foreign currency revenues, the dogmatic insistence on state control looked like a policy of enforced poverty. Some believed that it was a deliberate tactic to deprive the people of the energy to rebel. While Uzbek officials may have manipulated nationalism to motivate their people, some clearly believed in it as well. They wanted to be masters of their own country, and Central Asia. Such thoughts fired up high-flyers like Rostam Azimov, then chairman of the National Bank.

"This is Uzbekistan," he said, pointing to a painting as we passed down a corridor in his bank headquarters.

Firm brush strokes depicted a stolid giant crouching on the ground, his muscular arms wrapped around legs as thick as Central Asian minarets.

"We're gathering energy, concentrating our thoughts, waiting for the day. We're getting ready to rise up," Azimov explained.

To underline his ambition, Azimov laid on a dinner for me at a show house in a new compound on the outskirts of Tashkent. He called the two dozen houses his "cottages," but the compound of luxury villas looked as if it had been built for the nouveau riche on the outskirts of Istanbul. Indeed, a Turkish contractor had done the work. One by one other guests arrived, but, although everything was ready and waiting, it was considered impolite to enter the house before the boss made his appearance. We waited uneasily outside in the ill-lit, half-finished compound street, wondering at the concrete stands for future tennis courts. President Karimov liked tennis, so the social life of the political elite necessarily revolved around it; five centuries before, Central Asian courts also followed their princes' leads to find relaxation in polo, wrestling, archery contests and even, according to Prince Babur, leapfrog. At last Azimov drove slowly up in a small, old-fashioned

Zhigouli. It was a regal display of humility, Azimov's politically correct reply to the high-rolling arrogance of other Central Asian magnates.

After dinner, Azimov led the way up for cognac on a wide first floor balcony to survey the martial rows of villas around us. The buildings were being kept empty for another of Azimov's dreams.

"This place is only for bankers, for the future financial community. I want to make Tashkent the financial center of Central Asia," he said.

Given the lack of a modern banking system and the way President Karimov had hobbled the economy, the idea sounded far-fetched. Indeed, as time went by, Azimov was forced to open up to more general tenants. Azimov gradually rose in Uzbekistan's authoritarian system, becoming senior deputy to Karimov in the cabinet in 2005 and fighting hard against the Uzbek establishment to improve its battered relations with institutions like the International Monetary Fund. But Uzbekistan has continued to develop according to the stern precepts of its regime, just as early republican Turkey insisted on its right to develop at its own pace. As in Turkey, its stubborn self-reliance and narrow-minded government have delayed its development. Again like Turkey, it may well help create a coherent new Turkic nation, although scars will be left by Karimov's widescale and often vicious oppression of the Muslim-minded countryside. A Soviet legacy of urban planning, literacy and education may even give it advantages over Turkey in some areas. That's because Turkey, as in the more backward parts of the Turkic east, is a country where people still in their 30s can have lived the whole transition from a medieval to a modern lifestyle.

25. TO THE CITY

THE SECOND TURKISH CONQUEST
OF CONSTANTINOPLE

My lovely tree!
When your sap dries up
We too, by the grace of God,
Will have moved on to another neighborhood
—ORHAN VELI KANIK, Turkish poet,1914-50

ISTANBUL—ONCE CONSTANTINOPLE—WAS CAPTURED BY THE TURKS under Sultan Mehmet the Conqueror in 1453. In the second half of the 20th century, a new wave of invaders laid siege to the city. The rural new-comers' encampment of badly built concrete buildings surrounds the city from 40 miles out. Not all that is new is unattractive as the city digests the ex-villagers and Istanbul's urban culture is reborn. The first suspension bridge built over the Bosporus in 1974 is graceful and superb. Behind it rise the mirrored glass towers of Istanbul's financial district, spreading along the crest of the hill on the other side. Built mostly in the 1990s, the buildings express the power, wealth and confidence of the new Turks. The pleasing, unplanned harmony of the skyscrapers is a worthy counterpoint to the beauty of the very different skyline of old Istanbul at the southern entrance of the waterway. There a smooth, low mass of buildings and bazaars is studded with the leaded domes and soaring stone minarets of imperial Ottoman mosques.

When the Republic of Turkey was founded in the 1920s, town dwellers made up less than 20% of the country's population; by the end of the century the proportion had risen to 70%. Most inhabitants of Istanbul are thus not born in the city. Yet the city, where I lived in for nearly two decades, has kept its power to put those who move there under its spell.

Istanbul's geographical position made it the capital of three empires—the Eastern Roman, the Byzantine and the Ottoman—for most of the past two millennia. The 20th century isolation caused by Turkey's early autarchism and the Cold War freeze of normal regional trade was exceptional. Today's open borders mean that Istanbul's geographical centrality is focusing prosperity on its inhabitants once again. Historically, much of that advantage comes from Istanbul's place on the Bosporus, the northernmost section of the Turkish straits that divide Asia from Europe. The Soviet and NATO warships that were once a regular sight have all but disappeared, and their place has been taken by oil tankers and commercial shipping. This natural waterway felt like the fulcrum of all my Turkic journeys, which I would wake up to see from my bedroom window each time I returned from my travels. The Turks themselves first crossed the straits on plundering raids into the Balkans and Europe in the mid-1300s. For a long time, I wanted to conquer the strait myself by swimming across, but was intimidated by its unceasing traffic of skiffs, trawlers, ferries, freighters, speedboats and supertankers. My chance came one summer's day, when the international shipping lane briefly closed for the annual cross-Bosporus swimming race.

Joining a throng of athletic young Turkish men and women, I stripped down to my bathing trunks on a wooden pontoon tied up to a ferry stop on the Asian side of the Bosporus. The race was from Kanlıca to Ortaköy, a few miles to the south on the European side. A Dutch and an American companion joined me for the attempted crossing. The self-confident swimmers boisterously plying themselves with grease accepted our presence without comment; when I first came to Istanbul in the 1980s, by contrast, most Turks would have reacted to strangers with fussed surprise. I dared to hope we could have our clothes taken across behind us with the club boat. But we did not have the regulation orange bathing cap and identification number.

"Are you registered?" an organizer demanded to know, catching me as I tucked our bags under a bench on his wooden ship.

"We'd like to swim along. We're foreign writers, you see."

In the past, such a pompous introduction, especially when delivered in Turkish, was sure to elicit a hospitable "come on in," be it when I arrived late begging for a press pass to a popular soccer match or when I asked for a last-minute seat on a Turkish Airlines flight. Well-connected Turks had their own version of this, a haughty "Do You Know Who I Am?" But Turkey is more sophisticated now. Turks run the growing risk of being told that no, he or she is not recognizably important. Foreigners are certainly not the exotic rarity they once were.

"Get out of here!" the race official bellowed. "What do you think this is, your father's farm?"

Shamefaced, we stepped off the boat, and lingered in the crowd on the pontoon. Perhaps, we thought, the confusion would allow us to slip into the water. But the organizer was no fool, and this was his swimming club's big day. Seeing us once again dabbing ourselves with grease, he called the police. The officer, one of the new, better-educated ones, found it hard to take the task of evicting us seriously. But in the end we had to drape our clothes back over our sticky skins, move to a waterside café and watch the excitement with disappointed frustration. The strait emptied of ferries and cargo ships. Navy commandos sped to and fro in black inflatable dinghies to make sure that, as at all Turkish public events, nobody got the impression that pleasure was possible without strict supervision. A starting gun fired. A salmon run of orange-hatted swimmers splashed into the water and churned off towards Europe. The race organizers' small ship steamed officiously behind them. I felt as though I had failed in my meagre effort to echo the achievements the Mogol Prince Babur, who swam the Ganges and other rivers of his empire, or Lord Byron, who swam over the Hellespont, the southern end of the Turkish straits near Troy. We would have to take a taxi through bumper-to-bumper traffic over a bridge, quite a contrast to the summery, open horizons of the Bosporus.

Except, I noticed, for a wooden skiff, which bobbed up and down in an inlet beside the ferry stop. I wandered over. It belonged to a thickset fisherman, Captain Ahmet, who joined me from a tea-house. As we debated a price for a ride over, I realized that we could swim alongside the boat. Ahmet gruffly granted his assent to this idea. Our spirits rose and we clambered aboard. Ahmet cranked his 10 horsepower diesel engine into life, and we pock-pocked out into the channel. Seen from sea level, our enterprise looked daunting. The Bosporus is more than half-a-mile wide at Kanlıca. But there was no turning back, and, one by one, we leapt into the water. It felt clean. One reason was a decade of efforts by Istanbul's municipality to clean up the environment. There was also the steady southerly current, which sweeps away filth that is still pumped into the waterway, the refuse that collects along the shore-line and the blooms of jellyfish. This moving surface layer is fed from rivers that empty into the Black Sea. This fresh water barely mingles with the Black Sea's salty, sulphurous depths and flows out through the Bosporus. It tasted almost like lake water. Underneath is another current, deeper and slower, which carries salt water into the Black Sea. It was a metaphor for the Turks themselves, perhaps, who keep heading toward the prosperity of the West but find their hearts constantly tugging them back east.

The top current picked us up and swept us along. I flipped over onto my back to appreciate the magnificence of the mile-wide span of the northern suspension bridge over the Bosporus, sailing 200 feet overhead. The early republic spurned its Ottoman past; but this bridge built in 1988 had been named after Mehmet the Conqueror. We were soon nearly across, but the water was so balmy that we decided to float on south past the wooded hills and expensive wooden villas on the waterfront known as *yalıs*. We bobbed past the round towers of the castle at Rumelihisar, built by the 21-year-old Sultan Mehmet and his generals as part of their naval blockade of the last Byzantine emperor in Constantinople. I could even see one of the great bronze cannons he used in the victorious siege of 1453, lying unmarked at the base of one of the fortress walls.

The surface stream bore us and the diligent Captain Ahmet on past the district of Bebek and the rich people's yachts anchored in its calm bay. Then a voice boomed through the sunny morning peace. I looked over my shoulder. A Turkish coastguard cutter was bearing down on us.

"Where are you going?" an officer shouted through a metallic loud-speaker.

We were obviously swimming down the Bosporus, so I ignored him. It was as hateful as the Turkish policemen who bark orders through scratchy megaphones mounted on their battered dog-shark squad cars. Another broadside rolled over the water.

"Are you with the race?"

I paused to turn round. The ship was close. I treaded water and yelled a placatory offering.

"We're swimming to Ortaköy, my commander."

On the bridge, white-uniformed officers discussed what to do. They soon worked out that we didn't have the right orange caps. We had been discovered defying authority, and there was only one possible outcome.

"Swim to the shore!" the voice ordered. "It's for your own safety!"

"Of course, my captain," I shouted back, turned back round and kept swimming straight on.

Striking for the shore at that point did not seem sensible. Currents race in front of Bebek. We were half way across the mouth of the wide bay and a sudden tongue of cold water surged up to lick my legs.

The voice commanded our little lifeboat to approach the cutter. So much attention to our safety could put us in serious danger. Treading water again, I tried to work out our fate from Captain Ahmet's body language. The grizzled fisherman had adopted a common and often effective posture that might be rendered as: "I bow my head in deference to your rank and authority, O Powerful One, so that you may now release us without anybody losing face as a result of this awkward and unnecessary complication of your own making." But the coastguard captain had a shiny new ship and would not be defied. The loudspeakers boomed back into life.

"Start moving to shore immediately!"

The cutter's bow bore down on us, forcing us into the bay. Cold whorls of water churned up from the deep. Ahmet followed loyally close as we approached Akıntıburnu, or Current Point, where a ridge of land pushes in to form the narrowest point of the Bosporus, 700 yards wide. The waters flowing south from the Black Sea can pick up speed with the prevailing northerly wind to resemble a rip tide running at over 10 miles an hour. The coast road loomed intimidatingly close several feet above us, its concrete edge chipped and buckled by frequent collisions when ships misjudge the turn. There was nowhere to land, a situation made more complicated by boats and cruisers tied up to the pavement dock. The coastguard was now steaming away self-importantly, its duty done. Close to the stern of the 1001 Nights, a wooden galleon-cum-bar, a backwash started pulling one of my companions faster than she could swim. We tried to strike out for Ahmet's little skiff, but the currents were giving him trouble too. It was an alarming moment. Luckily, Ahmet was skilled and nosed in to save us. We clambered aboard, and Ahmet conducted us safely to the Arnavutköy ferry landing. We dried and dressed in the sun, triumphant.

I lived for many years in Arnavutköy, an old Bosporus village amalgamated into but not crushed by Istanbul's urban sprawl. The last of my three homes there was a wooden house with 12-foot high doors where electricity bills would arrive in the ponderous name of Podromos Patunyan, its former Christian owner. Arnavutköy was mainly built by Greeks, the heirs of the Byzantines who dominated Istanbul's business and cultural life long after the Turkish conquest. Even the name Istanbul is either a Turkish corruption of Constantinople or the Greek *eis ton polis*, "to the city." The ethnic Greeks lasted until the 1960s, when Turkish harassment and the attractions of Greece encouraged most to leave. One of the 3,000 or so left was my opposite neighbor, an old Greek lady who would sit in her window and conversationally shout across the alley steps about the good old days.

In the minorities' place had come waves of Turkish, Kurdish and other migrants from the Anatolian countryside, who by the turn of the 21st century had overwhelmed the city's social fabric. In Arnavutköy, whose inhabitants once decked out their wooden houses with elaborate furniture and hung their carved windows with fancy lace curtains, the new migrants sat on the floor to eat from a cloth spread over the carpet and stacked their bedding nomad-style against the corniced walls. The villagers settled *"like smoke in the deepest hollows"* of Istanbul, wrote the English poet and Arnavutköy resident John Ash, and on the staircase landings *"Their shoes/sit at doorways as if begging for admission."* Most moved to Arnavutköy in the 1960s from poor hamlets in the mountains south of the Black Sea, then a 24-hour bus ride away. The new arrivals were too poor to wreck the old houses and build concrete substitutes, or to defy the zoning laws watched over with corrupt inefficiency by the authorities. As a result, many of the 19th-century wooden houses survived. A new Turkish bourgeoisie gradually moved in alongside the villagers. They rebuilt the old houses with wooden exteriors. Musty old general grocers and the cavernous darkness of the Armenian coffee grinder's place gave way to more smartly painted shops, restaurants and boutiques. Even more impressive was the transformation of some of the migrants themselves.

A typical journey was that of Hayriye and her husband Şerafet. They were born in mountain villages 400 miles east of Istanbul, without electricity, cars or even radios. Yet by their late 30s, despite many hardships along the way, they had achieved the lifestyle of a modest nuclear family similar to that in parts of southern Europe.

The childhood of Hayriye abruptly ended when her sick mother was taken away on a lumbering wooden cart pulled by a pair of oxen.

"It was meningitis, people said. I never saw her again," she told me in the symbol of her later success, a neat new Arnavutköy apartment. "Later a telegram—there was no telephone—came to the headman's house saying she was dead. Much later, my brother went looking for her grave. He found it in a paupers' lot. Someone else had already been buried on top of her."

When her mother died, her youngest brother was three months old. Just five years old herself, the task of looking after him and the household devolved onto her. The housework included walking miles to the forest and climbing high in trees to break off dead branches for firewood. Paralysis struck her grandfather, and her grandmother went blind. Then her father remarried at the age of 40 to a girl of 18.

"My stepmother was nice enough, but had no experience of running a house. I kept having to do everything," Hayriye remembered. The woman was sick, too, with a kind of epilepsy. "She became completely unmanageable when the djinns [evil spirits] took control of her. She had to be held down by several people sitting on top of her."

Nobody thought of taking her to hospital.

"They would go to the *hoca* (the religious man of the village) and he would say some things and blow prayers over her."

By the age of seven, Hayriye looked after a household of a dozen people. In summer she would have to walk twice a day up to the *yayla*, or high pasture, to take care of and milk a buffalo, two cows and 40 sheep. There was cheese to make, butter to be churned and dough to be kneaded. Hayriye never grew more than 5 feet high, but became immensely strong, able to lug a 110-lb. bag of fertilizer. Her experiences explain why Turkish advertisers still avoid rural images when promoting their products. They fear it may remind too many people of the back-breaking burdens of their past.

"I had an internal clock, a kind of fear, that woke me up before the morning call to prayer, even if the real clock didn't. One night in winter I was at the village oven to bake our bread and the family forgot I was still outside. Nobody heard me shouting or hammering on the door. By the time my grandfather realized my bed was empty, I had collapsed and had long icicles on my dress," she said.

A first radio arrived in the village in 1973, brought back by her father after the month of every year that he spent far away in Thrace, earning cash by scything hay. Hayriye's aunts, puzzled by the voices coming from a box, struggled to understand how people could be squeezed inside. Hayriye was meanwhile progressing through the village primary school, despite being one of 70 children crowded into two classes.

"I studied hard. But I still had to look after the family. I had to come back in school breaks, to do the washing, and all the other jobs. My father threatened to take me out of school if I couldn't do the work," she said. "My father may have been poor, but in a way men like him lived like sultans. There was a huge distance between us."

The hard culture of Anatolian villages meant it was also considered undignified for a father to display appreciation of his daughter, let alone any affection. It was taboo for men to caress or take any children publicly into their arms. Perhaps as a reaction, the newly rich classes in Istanbul today have veered to quite the other end of the scale. They pamper and spoil their children, bribing and threatening teachers to give them an easy ride through school and university.

Urbanization has revolutionized the once strict and patriarchal Turkish way of life in other ways. A survey by Germany's Konrad Adenauer Foundation—a rare, independent view of Turkish youth published in 1998—found that 70% want to choose their own spouses, most want marriage in their mid-20s, that 90% of women and 77% of men will practice birth control, and that more than 57% want two children or less.

Only 15% still object to getting to know their spouse before marriage, although 61% disapprove of pre-marital sex.

Such choices did not exist for Hayriye's generation. At the age of 13, Hayriye's father engaged her to Şerafet, her third cousin, whom she had never met. The high bride price of 10,000 liras (worth $400 at the time) that Şerafet's family had to pay her father for her was such a talking point that her schoolyard nickname became "Ten Thousand Hayriye." She was married the next year. She was lucky, and not just because Şerafet gave her a better life than some of her relatives. Shortly afterwards, her brother eloped with a girl in the village. To appease the girl's family, Hayriye's sister was married off to the girl's mentally disturbed brother and was thus condemned to a life of poverty and unhappiness.

Şerafet's family was better off than Hayriye's, since his father had worked for seven years in a Ford automobile plant in Germany. Hayriye initially thought marriage would be a liberation from her domestic drudgery. But as the newest *gelin*, or bride, in the house of her in-laws, she had merely exchanged one slavery for another. Once again, she was required to do most of the housekeeping. This included washing the clothes of up to 30 people—by hand.

For eight years the couple stayed in Şerafet's family house. Giving birth to a child would have released her from her bondage, but she was unable to conceive. Aunts induced her to eat herbal fertility preparations or taunted her. "Trees without leaves are cut down," they would say. They bound her eyes and covered her body with leeches in another failed effort to make her pregnant, causing Hayriye to fall ill from blood loss. Şerafet left to work for a year on a Libyan construction site, earning $20,000, but was obliged to hand the money over to his father. Eventually his father gave him a small sum to take Hayriye to a doctor in Istanbul. When they got off the bus in an outlying suburb, Şerafet found that the money had disappeared. All they had left was a heavy roll of bedding, and miles to walk to the address of a distant relative. But whatever happened, they did not want to go back.

"In the end, he got a job in a factory that made batteries for tractors. That was a good job, but he got lead poisoning. He was in a kind of coma for 45 days, in hospital. To visit him I used to jump on and off the trains without paying. We had no money at all," Hayriye told me.

In the Dickensian atmosphere of Istanbul's industrial hinterland, Şerafet was fortunate that the battery manufacturer paid his hospital bills and that he recovered most of his faculties. But he couldn't return to the factory. He took an entry-level Istanbul job, as a janitor, which is what brought them to the first building where I lived in Arnavutköy. They lived in a room next to the boiler, feeding it with the soft brown lignite coal that enveloped all Turkish cities with mind-numbing smog before the use of natural gas became widespread in the 1990s. In winter, their room filled with foul fumes and fine dust. For five years the building's owner gave Hayriye no money even though her new servitude meant she cleaned both his town apartment and summer house every week.

Their turning-point came when Şerafet found a salaried job as a clerk in a small holding company. The security made it possible for them to buy their own one-bedroom apartment in Arnavutköy. Soon carpets lay on the floor, big sofas lined the walls, and a display cabinet filled with knick-knacks and a large television. Hayriye bought shiny new shoes and impressive headscarves for going on family visits, the main component of their social life. But there remained a heart-burning problem: they couldn't have children.

Children are an issue of prime political importance within a traditional Turkish extended family, allowing a couple to declare some independence. Adoption isn't an option, triggering taboos about blood lines and inheritance. Bringing up the child of a relative is one solution, but binds a couple still further to the extended family. And until a couple succeeds in having a child, they continue to be considered as a cash machine for the others. In times of trouble, this extended family works as a social security safety net, but at others it is a cage. Hayriye and Şerafet had to contribute to an uncle's second car when they had none, and put up relatives who came to stay for as long as the visitors pleased.

"Hugh *bey*, you're so lucky," Hayriye would say. "When my relatives come to visit me, the first thing they expect is for us to take them all out shopping. When people come to visit you, at least they bring their own clothes."

But much has changed. Members of Hayriye's extended family increasingly have their own budgets and their own problems. The oldest male father-figure, once the supreme arbiter of financial decisions, has less influence now that the family has spread all over Istanbul. Just a few elderly relatives are left in their distant home villages. No longer does a weekly bus arrive in Arnavutköy from the Black Sea mountains, disgorging sacks of agricultural produce and taking back cargos like cast-off city clothes. Hayriye and Şerafet find themselves with a bit more independence every year. And, after 20 years of trying, three miscarriages and brushes with ruinously expensive malpractice in fertility clinics, Hayriye became pregnant in 2001. She gave birth to healthy twins, a boy and a girl.

Hayriye thus obtained at last the honored status of a mother, and is determined to educate her children into a more Western social mindset. With respectability came confidence, and she began to wear trousers and less tightly wound headscarves in public. But there is a restlessness in the Turkish spirit, perhaps a relic of centuries of migrations. Even though Hayriye and Şerafet had traveled far to their new lives in Istanbul, they would have seized any chance to move on to join relatives living and working in Europe. And as I was to discover in Germany, Europe was itself not the farthest reach of the Turks' opportunistic ambition.

26. ALL CHANGE AT ESSEN

NOW GERMANY IS NOT ENOUGH

From far-flung villages, via Istanbul
German customs checked them through
Like purchased goods.
Suck them in and chuck them out, the Germans thought.
But those peasants were too crafty to be bought.

—*Selaminaleyküm*, by German Turk rappers ISLAMIC FORCE

THE SEARCH FOR PLUNDER OR FRESH PASTURES HAS LONG POWERED THE Turkic peoples' migrations and raids. For the Huns, whom the Turks proudly claim as early Turkic peoples, the attraction was the remains of the Roman Empire in Europe. The early medieval Mamluks and the Seljuks found sustenance in the Arab Middle East. For the Mongol-led armies of Genghis Khan and his Turkic allies, it meant the conquest of both the Middle East and China, as it did for Tamerlane. Under the Ottomans, the Turks conquered the Balkans and twice threatened Vienna. From the 1960s onward, the Republic of Turkey eagerly supplied the manpower to fuel German's economic miacle. After the fall of the Berlin wall, defying the prejudices against them, entrepreneurial German Turks spread through the former eastern Germany, setting up bars, snack-stands and other businesses in small provincial towns.

Even in the center of gravity of Turkish settlement in Germany, the west of the country, most people had a nomadic eye for greener fields elsewhere. To visit them I rode a succession of grimy old slow trains and slick two-story expresses into the Ruhr, Germany's aging industrial heartland. The Turks left nobody unmoved, not even a Tajik refugee from Afghanistan, who drove the taxi that took me from the railway station in Essen. His fellow Turkish taxi drivers, he complained, were too rough.

They talked too loudly into their cellphones while driving. They smoked in front of customers in their taxis. They had no culture at all. They were barbarians, in short. The well-spring of anti-Turk feeling took me straight back to his Tajik cousins in Samarkand. Central Asia was just an eye-blink away.

There was nothing uncouth, however, about the German Turks I had come to meet in a once-derelict area of Essen's brick-built factories. My destination was a former armaments plant bought by the city's Institute for Turkish Studies. Once inside, I found myself in a bright, well-designed workplace that would have done any European think-tank proud. Faruk Şen, founder and director of the institute, was a political operator as smooth as the dark cashmere roll-neck under his well-cut jacket. From his desk, like everyone who is anyone in the Turkish élite, he kept half an eye on Turkey's private TV news channels. In recent weeks, news from the motherland had been good. Turkey's Turks were obeying the latest prescriptions of the International Monetary Fund. Germany had made it easier for Turks to acquire German nationality. Turkey's application to be a candidate for membership of the European Union had been accepted, in principle at least. Now the prime minister was on the screen announcing the nationalization of five irresponsible, shaky private Turkish banks.

"They're getting their act together at last!" the 51-year-old Şen exclaimed.

Şen already had his act together. Every time I asked a question, he answered it with a publication. Soon an unlucky minion was despatched to photocopy every newspaper article he had written for the past six months. I tried to deflect the flood by asking what had drawn him to Germany in the first place.

"My father was a fanatical Germanophile," he said. "He'd never been to Germany, but believed that everything that Germany did was perfect. He enrolled me in the German high school in Istanbul, then I came here to university. The Germans always used to put us Turks in technical schools. But thanks to a pen-pal, whose house I stayed in, I got to study management. I've been in Germany ever since."

If anybody symbolized a stable future of the German Turks, anchored and integrated in Europe, Şen should have been it. He was married to a German, too.

"So you consider your family settled here now?"

"Not at all, not at all! I feel like a vagabond," he protested. "The Turkish community has expanded as far as it can in Germany. The way is blocked. I advise the kids that they should either go into international institutions or to America. I'm telling my daughter: go to Harvard, go to Yale! America is the country of the future."

"So the Turks are only here in Europe temporarily?" I asked.

"The Turks are always ready to go on further. I'm not saying they weigh everything in their heads. It's bravery, or perhaps foolhardiness. They'll try new things out, take a risk. And as often as not, they succeed," Şen replied.

Despite devoting considerable effort to secure benefits from whatever government they lived under, Şen maintained that Turks did not really believe that any state will look after them. I had to agree. From a Turkmen-run barber shop in northern Iraq to a little *döner* kebab joint in a hut by the site of Dresden's Frauenkirche, Turkic people would often ask me, sometimes immediately, for information or help to find better jobs elsewhere. This restlessness was not always directed westwards. Two million of the Turks who worked in Europe went back to Turkey when Turkey's outlook improved. A million Azeris went to work in Russia. The Kyrgyz headed to Siberia. Thousands of Uygurs had headed to the richer towns of eastern China.

"Most of our people have one foot here, and one foot in Turkey. Even for me, it's cheaper to fly from Essen to Istanbul than to Munich," Şen said. "I advise people to have a critical loyalty to Germany, but a critical solidarity with Turkey."

The resistance to assimilation among German Turks was especially strong in the two-thirds of the community who were from conservative and rural backgrounds. Neither Şen, nor anybody else in his institute, believed that they would become truly German any time soon. Far from settling into a European Christian milieu, the institute's researchers reckoned that one in five of the Turks in Germany was actively trying to convert Christians to Islam, an act that they believe will cleanse their sins and open their way to heaven in the afterlife.

For decades, both the German and Turkish states told ethnic Turks that they were only in Europe temporarily, so it was not surprising that few took much initial notice of their surroundings. Four decades after their first arrival, the situation has changed, and 80% of Turks now view their departure from Turkey as permanent. A spate of racist and neo-Nazi German attacks on them in the early 1990s frightened few away. But the community's reaction has been to turn in on itself even more. It makes no attempt at self-criticism, to ask whether its closed ways may not have fuelled German ignorance and resentment. Its large numbers make it self-sufficient for most social purposes and it has begun to attract other Turkic immigrants into its orbit, like the Azeris. Turks rarely marry Germans. Brides are still sent from Anatolia, as are the official mosque preachers. Few people watch German television, preferring the babble of Turkish shows beamed up to satellites from Istanbul. And a paradox of Germany's free society is that the Turks can and do organize exclusively for themselves in ways not possible back home.

The German Turks are modernizing nevertheless. Yunus Ulusoy, a 37-year-old economics graduate and one of Şen's researchers, was a conservative Muslim in his attitudes. Yet he wore elegantly matched suits and ties and a designer watch. He kept his documents immaculately organized on bookshelves behind him. A lawyer-size briefcase waited for his commute home. He stayed to the point in a conversation and kept an eye on his watch. He finished his Turkish telephone conversations with the German slang farewell, *tschüss*.

Ulusoy's father had been one of the first Turks to come to Germany, arriving in 1963 from Turkey's Black Sea coast to work as a miner in the Ruhrland coalfields. Ulusoy joined him at the age of nine in 1974. He was one of the first Turks to enroll and graduate from an Essen high school.

"It has been terrible for me. When I had been at school in Turkey, we were taught that 'a Turk is worth the whole world.' We left classes proudly singing the national anthem. We really thought we were something. Then I found myself in a school where the fact that I was Turkish didn't just mean that I was a nothing, it meant that I was dirty scum. They used to beat me up," Ulusoy said. "I had three choices. I could fight back, but I was alone. Or I could withdraw into myself. Or

I could prove that I was as good as they are. And that's what I did. The first year, the teachers sometimes sent back my work crossed out with a note that they couldn't even mark it. The next year I came top of my class."

The very contrast between Turkish and German attitudes brought Ulusoy a new national consciousness. He rebelled at the way his German textbook only mentioned Turkey in passing. A bare half-page summed up Ottoman history and its end as the "sick man of Europe." The Republic of Turkey was dismissed in a couple of sentences. Back in his schooldays, little information about Turkey was available in German bookshops either.

"People thought Turkey was all about camels and oriental lifestyles. You could write a whole book of the German jokes about us," Ulusoy said. "What really upset me was when someone would first say he thought the Turkish language was a kind of Arabic, and then start giving me lectures about Turkish domestic politics."

Whereas loneliness had forced Ulusoy to make German friends, now 20-30 Turks graduated each year from his old school. The community had taken on a life of its own, and had become nationalist. He was shocked that no Muslim from another country, let alone Germans, joined the new generation of young students for an *iftar*, or banquet to break the daylight-hours fast practised by Muslims during the holy month of Ramadan.

At the same time, he felt his community was growing apart from society in Turkey. German Turks have got used to German orderliness. They find it hard to deal with the Istanbul traffic, complain of lawlessness in Turkey and have lost the knack of bargaining over purchases. They are more individualistic than Turks at home, and have even developed a slightly different language. Attitudes to a strange European like me coming up and speaking Turkish are different too: in Turkey, it triggers a welcoming smile, in Germany, a frown of suspicion. Despite the satellite television link, German Turks resist the dynamic of social change back home, including, ironically, the more freewheeling European lifestyle developing in higher strata of society in Turkey.

"Living here, you look at things differently. I just wouldn't be able to kiss the hand of a prime minister in Turkey any more. I now think of politicians as public servants. I could kiss the hand of a religious teacher, I suppose, but only if I really respected him," Ulusoy said.

He had developed a consciousness that was post-republican and almost neo-Ottoman. He had met and married a girl from Bosnia, once a province of the Ottoman Empire. He liked the inherited similarities of their customs. He also loved the way that his father could understand some of the old Ottoman words his wife used. He could not, since he had been educated in the *öz türkçe*, or pure Turkish, of the Republic of Turkey. He felt proud of a Turkic past as well.

"I don't have a Central Asian ethnic identity. It's more subconscious. It's like an accumulation of social experience and history," he said.

Similarly, Turkish-owned businesses in Germany have developed a distinct identity alongside their immigrant drive to succeed. Ulusoy introduced me to 39-year-old Karadeniz Karadeniz, doubly named after the Black Sea. His yogurt-making business in the suburbs of Essen was just one of the 61,300 businesses set up by the Turkish community in Germany by the end of 2003. The number had tripled since 1985, even though the community's numbers went up by only a half. Indeed, Turks are the biggest single group of foreign entrepreneurs in Germany, and continued their successful growth even during Germany's economic doldrums after 2000, challenging a complacent German prejudice that Turks are lazy exploiters of state welfare. One-third of them have retail shops, a quarter sell prepared food, and four per cent are in construction or manufacturing. By 2003, they employed more than 310,000 people, quadruple the 1985 figure, and did business worth more than $29 billion. Not counting the contribution of the majority who work in German concerns, German Turkish enterprises produced the equivalent of one sixth of the whole Turkish economy, or the output of the German car maker Audi.

I found Karadeniz in an old brick warehouse, newly painted white and with proud flagpoles for the company's blue-and-white logo out front. Upstairs, past a model cow, the executive suite was done in the same good taste as the Turkish Institute. Karadeniz himself was a compact, lightly built man with dark, short curly hair and ambition burning in his black eyes. His grandfather had taught him the principles of trade in a small electric appliance shop on Turkey's Black Sea coast. He came to Germany in 1980, and he gradually worked his way up through jobs and night school. Now, after just five years with his own company in Essen, he employed 300 people. Like many German Turks, he found it hard to get bank financing, so he built the business up with his own capital. He stocked restaurants and sandwich bars in Germany, the Netherlands, France and Belgium. He was selling 200 tons of yogurt a month, not counting truckloads of sealed cups of *ayran* yogurt drink. He was branching out into electrical goods and *gazöz*, a sweet lemon soda popular in Turkey.

"It's doing very well. We'll sell a million bottles next year. I've had Pepsi here to talk about getting involved, and Coca-Cola's interested. I'm turning them away. I want to remain independent," he said.

Even though he was relying on a staff drawn almost entirely from his community, and sold mainly to Turkish outlets, he refused to be associated with an ethnic label. He banished overt signs of Turkishness in his office, and refused to enter business premises nationalistically decked out with Turkish flags. Instead, he kept jumping up to discuss the 'non-straight lines' of the paintings in his wall calendar of modern Viennese art. He wanted to make his yogurt pots more ecological. He hammered on about rain forests, his opposition to the sale of German Leopard tanks to Turkey, the changing color of the Taj Mahal, Turkey's ill-fated drive to install outmoded nuclear power stations and the death of fish in his beloved Black Sea.

"You sound like a German member of the Green Party."

"I'm a Turkish Green. When I think of those concrete buildings on the Black Sea coast, my hair stands on end!"

"So is that your dream, to go back and fix up Turkey?"

"I don't want to be seen as just a Turk. My dream is more universal than that," he said. "I don't want to be rich. I want to be powerful. My company will one day be very strong. Then they will listen."

Making my way back to downtown Essen, I took sanctuary in another German-Turk enterprise from the cold wind that swept over the bleak inner city landscape of malls, tarmac and concrete. *Ünalan's Döner Kebab* was a small eatery that symbolized a Euro-Turkish fusion. The bread was too thick and fluffy to be Anatolian, the spicy smells too strong to be European. There was the thick barrel of marinated lamb meat revolving on its spit, typical of all post-Ottoman countries, but the long *döner* knife was being wielded by a waitress, an unthinkable trespass on male prerogatives in Turkey. Another sacrilege was committed when she spooned a dollop of *cacık*, a yoghurt, cucumber and garlic sauce on the sandwich. That's something only added to the dish in Greece and Israel. At the same time, a satellite connection piped in radio music from a studio in Istanbul.

"Any chance, do you think," asked the young German Turk munching on his *döner kebab* next to me, "of getting me a good job in England?"

When they weren't getting their start with small restaurants, the Turkic peoples often found a niche in grocery shops. These could be found throughout the Asian and European continents. Turkish-speaking Iranians dominate the bazaars of Tehran. Ex-Soviet Azeris fan out over the Russian federation with their fruit and vegetables. Every few street corners in Berlin, the awning of a German Turk-owned "Istanbul Market" shields a half-pavement full of produce from the rain. When I followed the trail of Turkic migrants across the Atlantic Ocean to where they are at last finding a foothold in north America, therefore, it came as only a small surprise to find that New York's small chain of Amish Markets had recently been bought by a Turk.

27. FOREVER YOUNG TURKS

A NEW HORIZON IN AMERICA

*We are from the same root, we are a large family. If
we make no mistakes, the 21st century will be ours.*
—Turkish President TURGUT ÖZAL, 1992

THE WEATHER WAS UNKIND TO NEW YORK'S FIRST TURKISH DAY MARCH OF
the new millennium. A steady shower of thick raindrops fell into the
canyon of gloomy skyscrapers flanking Madison Avenue. The Turks of
the New World bunched under storefront canopies or waited patiently
under their umbrellas in a thin line behind the blue wooden police barriers. They readied small red Turkish flags and video cameras, shy but
excited. To the north, closer to Central Park, rent-a-floats stood parked
in side streets. Knots of people attended the empty, forlorn juggernauts,
decked out in red and white plastic flower petals. They refused to let
their enthusiasm be dampened by the rain that was lightly and steadily
soaking them through.

I greeted a group of girls by one float, interrupting their chatter in
Turkish and English. The thick black hair of the Kurdish-Iranian border
region poured over the shoulders of one dark-skinned beauty. Another
enjoyed tall, blond Slavic good looks. The third had the high cheekbones
and flatter face of Central Asia. They were dressed in extraordinary, long
dresses that I told them I had not seen anywhere before.

"It's the first time we wear them," giggled one.

"One of our ladies made them specially," another proudly said.

"They're Ottoman," stated a third.

Well, perhaps, if Ottomans had accessed a Sears catalogue, had con-
sulted a Celtic peasant style guide and had swapped their women's veils

for garlands of flowers. In similarly eclectic fashion, Turkish-Americans are constructing yet another synthesis in the kaleidoscope of Turkic identities. Some are from an élite whose education brings them easy access to the wealth of America. Others are working their way up from the bottom. One of the latter was a man with thick, graying hair, whom the girls pointed out as the chief of their neighborhood community center, a "Turkish Hearth." I introduced myself. He broke step from his organizing hurry.

"My name's Gary," he said.

"Gary? Aren't you Turkish?"

"Oh, yes. I mean, my name is Gürkan, I just use Gary here in America."

Gürkan had arrived in New York at the age of 28 and had started work as a mechanic. Two decades later he had bought his own gas station, a profitable line of business several Turks have chosen. Gürkan was well settled, yet he had not strayed far from his home roots. He had married a Turk and sent his two daughters to be taught Turkish customs and language at classes held on the second floor of the Turkish consulate-general.

"So you'd like your girls to marry Turkish boys?" I asked.

The 'Ottoman' girls had already told me they would try to wed Turks if they could.

"I wish!" Gürkan joked, raising a pair of clenched fists in a joking gesture of powerlessness.

We were all thoroughly cold and wet by the time the powerfully built men of the New York Police Department allowed the parade to commence. The vanguard was a rather self-conscious group numbering few more than 100 people. The red organizers' sashes, rosettes and see-through plastic ponchos were very American. The faces and formal dress of the parade's leaders were not. Most sported thick black moustaches and the square-cut 1940s suit beloved of the Turkish and Turkic bureaucracies, with dark ties knotted tightly on their white collars.

The Turks of Turkey dominated the group, since few other modern Turkic peoples have yet settled in the New World. There was the Turkish ambassador from Washington, the consul-general in New York, and a few parliamentarians from Ankara. But there were also envoys from

Turkic states. The most striking figure strode at the fore, a small man in a black lambswool *kalpak* hat. He had an intense expression and a thin, long moustache of the nationalist type. He was Mustafa Cemiloğlu, the legendary leader of the Crimean Tatars. He won fame in the 1980s as one of the first Soviet dissidents to exploit *glasnost*'s openness to draw attention to the suffering of his community, murderously deported from their homeland by Stalin in 1944. Close by walked Azerbaijan's nationalist pioneer, Abulfez Elchibey.

This international Turkic dimension had simply not been there a decade before. Then the only Turkish "state" outside Turkey was the Turkish Republic of North Cyprus, the statelet that was set up in 1983 to legitimize the Turkish military occupation of the northern third of the island in 1974. Now about half of the original north Cypriot population has chosen life in the West over international isolation, abandoning their place on the island to poorer immigrants from Turkey. This strength in the diaspora made the flag of the administration of tiny north Cyprus, which is recognized as a state by no country other than Turkey, best established among the marchers in America.

A party of 20 people followed a sign announcing the New Jersey branch of the Azerbaijan Society of America. The Turks of the Balkans, too, had a large marching group, as did the Crimean Tatars. Then there was a curious float paid for by the Turkestanian-American Association— representing those coming from Turkmenistan, Uzbekistan, Kazakhstan, the Kyrgyz Republic and even Tajikistan, according to the float's signboards. Enthusiasts from the Istanbul-based group of an eccentric pan-Turkic activist, Turan Yazgan, marched past with impressive discipline and brandished all the flags of the Turkic pantheon. In honor of the Uygurs of China, they even bore the blue-and-white star and crescent of what nationalists call East Turkestan.

The most spirited groups were congregations attached to local Turkish-American mosques. Names like "Mosque of the Conqueror" recalled the great Istanbul edifices of the Ottoman Empire. But there was no sign of religious fundamentalism and unveiled young girls often led the way. Several Turkish newspapers had sponsored floats. None was modest. *Hürriyet*'s float represented the arrogance of Turkey's big-brother view of its role in the Turkic universe, with a banner that trumpeted "The Leading Turkish Newspaper in the World." The main feature of the float was a great globe girdled with a thick illuminated belt that spelled out the newspaper's masthead motto, a memorial to Turkish complexes about race, self-esteem and foreign threats: "Turkey for the Turks."

The marchers did indeed seem hung up about something. The rain had kept many young Turkish-American families at home. Nobody seemed to be enjoying themselves much, except for the happily grooving African-Americans hired for the day from the New York #1 Marching Band. The event was about pride and duty, not fun and games. Two straight-faced marchers led a group with the enigmatic sign "Forever Young Turks." Another group paraded behind a portrait of Turkish republican founder Kemal Atatürk as if it was the image of a deity. Organizers rushed about making sure that everyone kept in line. The first moment spectators really enjoyed was an opportunity to cheer the giant rain-soaked flag of the Istanbul soccer team Galatasaray, which had three days before won a European cup for the first time in Turkish history. Turkish newspapers on sale that day had trumpeted Galatasaray's success as a "Conquest of Europe," explicitly presented as an omen that the Turks would not be held back forever by their 17th century failure to force the gates of Vienna.

The soccer victory led the news in a copy of *Zaman North America*, pushed into my hand by a young man who rushed past my spot on the police barriers. *Zaman*, or Time, is the organ of the progressive-Islamic Fethullah Gülen movement and the first Turkish newspaper to publish a special U.S. edition in north America. Worthy and unsensational, *Zaman* is also the only newspaper to print local Turkic language editions all over the Turkic world, some 15 editions in all. The *fethullahçıs* are determined to prove that some higher moral purpose links the Turkic peoples, and their efforts had been a familiar companion on my journeys from east to west. In New York, these pioneers had just proudly and symbolically located their office in the Empire State Building.

At last, as the floats turned off Madison Avenue, some real excitement broke out. Two dozen young Turkish-Americans had collected on the street corner and were screaming insults across the street. They rhythmically punched the air. Their hands made the sign of the

Gray Wolf—the snout formed by the thumb and middle fingers, the ears by the pricked-up index and pinkie—a Turkic legend press-ganged into service by Turkey's nationalists.

"What's going on?" I asked one chubby, breathless youth.

"They always spoil it for us!" he shouted back.

His face was flushed with delight. He filled his lungs again and joined his friends in a lusty stream of invective.

"You bunch of faggots, get down where you belong!" they all yelled in boisterous unison.

The object of their attentions turned out to be a group of 20-30 protestors fifty yards away, well-defended by policemen and barriers. I had to walk round the block to get closer. The anti-Turks were having a grand time too. Some were wrapped in blue-and-white Greek flags, others in Kurdish flags and someone had a marching banner in yellow that seemed to be connected to the Armenians. "Admit to genocide" read one placard. "Long Live the PKK" said another, referring to Kurdish separatist guerrillas. My favorite bore only a bare, simple and surly interjection: "Low Life Mongols." They were trying to crown their protest by burning a Turkish flag. From time to time a flame and a straggling cheer would rise from their knot of people, but no smoke. The Turkish flag's day was saved by the rain.

In Istanbul, I had prepared myself for the Turkish community in the United States by lunching at the top of one of the city's gleaming new business towers with Koray Arıkan, one of the deputy chiefs of the Turkey branch of the former Chase Manhattan Bank. The branch symbolized one American view of Turkey's regional role, at least in commerical terms, as a kind of neo-Ottoman Empire. Its U.S.-educated boss, from Turkey's small Jewish minority, used Istanbul as a base to run Chase's business from Russia to Israel, and Almaty to Bucharest. The staff in the Istanbul branch was largely Turkish, too. Arıkan himself had gone to college in the United States and had risen to a Washington, D.C. job turning third-world debt into protected rain forests. But like a surprising number of Turks who go to the United States for higher education, he had in the end wanted to return home, at least for a while. In doing so he was answering a mixed call of patriotism, family and the fact that Turkey itself can now offer opportunities to the well-educated as tempting as those in America.

Arıkan had told me of a small community of his Turkish American friends in New Jersey, clever scientists working in the laboratories of technology companies. Call Tanju Çataltepe, Arıkan said, and he will help you understand the dilemmas of being a Turkish-American.

So it was that one evening I threw myself into a bull-rush of commuters to catch the 5.27 from New York's Penn Station. The train pulled out of Manhattan and headed down the North Jersey coastline. The initial industrial wastelands were as repellent as any in the world, but the temptations of American life soon came: wide Atlantic estuaries, pleasure ports and dormitory suburbs with their numbered parking lots and neat, prosperous houses set among the trees. After an hour, the train halted at the small town of Red Bank, New Jersey. I alighted by the tracks, and a red Toyota Camry turned into the forecourt. Its driver was clearly Turkish. Çataltepe may have been living an American dream, but he had kept his countrymen's distinctively spare, ascetic frame, wheat-colored skin, black hair and moustache.

As we settled into his comfortable house, I embarked on the time-honored Turkish ritual of asking exactly where a new acquaintance hails from.

"Sivas," he replied, naming a conservative central Anatolian city.

"The town itself?"

"Actually, a small town called Zara, you probably don't know it . . ."

Çataltepe's wistful tone prompted his wife Zehra to dive into the conversation. Her eyes rolled up to the ceiling.

"These men! Anybody would think Zara is paradise on earth!" she teased her husband with a smile. "I guess the reason why you guys like your home town so much is that none of you have to live there!"

She had the fuller figure of an Anatolian mother and wore a Muslim headscarf, but her eyes were bright, blue and a little rebellious. She relished America's religious freedom and described discrimination against her Islamic and female identity in Turkey. Little tempted her to head home.

"They spend their whole time talking about the Kızılırmak (river)," she said to me. "When we got there, it was just a miserable creek."

Her husband's pride was hurt.

"I suppose Zara is the sort of place people go through on the bus without noticing," he said ruefully.

Two powerful computers lurked on a desk at the end of a sitting room lined with shelves full of Islamic reference books, philosophy in Turkish translation and computer programming. After coming to the United States for his college education, Çataltepe had become an electrical engineer at AT&T. He met his wife via e-mail. Zehra now worked at home for a small company that aimed to pump data ever faster through the Internet.

It soon became clear that even for such privileged Turks, who could hold their own anywhere in the world, assimilation into mainstream America was limited at best. For a start, their circle of friends was largely Turkish, drawn from about 120 Turkish-Americans working in Red Bank's high technology businesses. Their principal circle consisted of his brother's family and several others from the community who lived a five-minute drive from their home. As they juggled their one-year-old son Ali between them, Zehra threw a dinner together. The dishes had taken on American volumes, but the savory yogurt and fried *börek* pies came from the heart of Turkic cuisine.

Çataltepe spent much of his spare time running a website about his distant home town. A picture of Zara's *yaylas*, or summer pastures, showed a back of beyond with the ruined stone foundations of a house and a few cattle grazing on the thin spring grass. Another shot caught the serene beauty of the great rippling hills of Central Anatolia, their dun flanks speckled with shrub oaks and scrub bushes.

"You'd be surprised how active the website is," said Çataltepe defensively. "There are now two Internet cafes in Zara."

His website's interests ranged further than Zara, of course, reflecting a surprisingly humorous, Muslim perspective on a secular-dominated world, discussions about Turkey—in conversation with American Turks like Çataltepe, "the government" is always Turkey's, not that of his adopted United States—and stories about Turkish-Americans.

For some contributors to Çataltepe's webzine, however, Turkish-ness was not enough to sustain their new Americanized identity. As with the Uygurs in their Chinese ocean, sometimes only the deep tradi-

tions of Islam could support their need to maintain a sense of distinct
pride and culture. Ayşe Gül Yeşilyurt, for instance, commented with
comic ease about her determination to wear the Muslim headscarf
and raise a child as a Muslim in North America. She remembered the
moment when someone asked her if she was a nun, even though she
was eight months pregnant. "I should admit I find being
different "cool," rewarding and challenging," she wrote. She told of her
struggles against a child culture so embedded with the seductive
Christian glitter of Halloween, Christmas and Easter that Muslim parents give into it because "they-are-just-kids." In Internet discussions,
she tried to reach out to fellow Muslims, telling them how to be different without feeling isolated. She suggested that her readers should
make Muslim holidays seem more attractively American by imitating
the festive hanging of balloons. In all her advice on how to present a
positive image of Muslims, she never mentioned her Turkish identity.
She seemed to be fighting an uphill battle, but there were moments of
victory for her Muslim point of view. "It brought me tears of joy," she
wrote, "to overhear my son telling his little friend they could not play
gods in the Hercules movie, because (her son) insisted, 'there is only
one God!'"

A ring on the doorbell announced the arrival of Çataltepe's younger
brother Tayfun and his wife Zeynep. The two brothers had stuck together as they both moved to America, rose through universities and took up
work with the same employer. Their wives had even given birth at about
the same time. A clannish Turkish chatter filled the house. I took my
leave. While the headscarfed Zehra asked me to drink a cup of tea for
her by the Bosporus, the more secular Zeynep asked me to toast her with
a beer in the crowded pavement restaurants of Istanbul's Flower
Passage.

It wasn't just in secular social customs that Tayfun was more relaxed.
As we headed to Red Bank station, he revealed that he and his brother
had an Internet start-up of their own, too, with a partner in Turkey. This
ambition matched a duty he felt to go back. After all, most Turkish-
Americans are still first-generation immigrants, who have been drilled in
the need for proud service to the Turkish nation.

"I think it's important, it's the people you grew up with. It's also partly that you want to put a bit back," Tayfun said. "After all, we don't want to work for AT&T forever."

A week after the Turkish Day parade, its organizer sat behind his desk in a cramped one-room office suite next to Grand Central Station. The weather may have been unkind to Egemen Bağış, owner of a Turkish-English translation bureau and President of the Federation of Turkish-American Associations, but the Turkish media was not. Crowd estimates for a parade that attracted at most 5,000 people ranged from "10,000" in moderately Islamist *Türkiye*, to "tens of thousands" in the nationalistic *Hürriyet* to "45,000" in the populist *Sabah*. Their images made it look as if Atatürk's portrait and delirious throngs waving Turkish and American flags had filled not just Madison Avenue, but also New York, and, by extension, America. The Turks had conquered and Egemen Bağış could hold his head high. He was no fool, however. He may have had a grand title, but he knew the limitations of his community.

"Not one line in *The New York Times*," he said with quiet regret, "or any other of the papers here."

Appearances can be deceptive. Egemen had recently spent six days in and out of the company of President Bill Clinton as an official translator during the latter's November 1999 trip to Turkey. His was the voice that translated Clinton's speech to Turkey's parliament when the American president had stirred the Turks with thanks for "half a century of friendship, mutual respect and parternership." Clinton had articulated a glowing view of Turkey's leading regional role in the new century, "defining itself as a strong, secular, modern nation, proud of its traditions, fully part of Europe." He spoke of Turkey as a bridge between Islam and Christianity, between East and West, between closed and open societies.

Just one paragraph of President Clinton's seven-page speech referred to the Turkic states of the former Soviet Union. Clinton talked of Turkey's help as "a leader, reaching out in particular to nations that share ties of language, culture and identity." U.S. policy-makers no longer hoped, as some did in the early 1990s, that Turkey's unusual mix of influences over its eastern neighbors could act as an explicitly political guiding force. Despite upsets over Turkish attitudes to the U.S. war in

Iraq in 2003, President Bush went back to the Cold War view of Turkey as a strategic military ally. It was valued for its role in the American "war on terror", for its new skills as a supplier of international peace-keepers, as one gateway to the Middle East and as a stepping stone to the new-found U.S. strategic interest in Central Asia.

Turkish-Americans, however, numbered just 500,000 people, according to Egemen; 136,498 according to the 2000 U.S. census, one-third of them in New York state and New Jersey. Turks have not traditionally headed to America for work or play. As opposed, say, to persecuted Armenians or dispossessed Greeks, Turks have had little reason to seek a place of refuge in the mainly Christian New World. Indeed, in the past 150 years, Anatolia has been the place of sanctuary for Muslims and Turks in the way that America was in preceding centuries for poor or persecuted European Christians. Without a pressing reason to go, money and distance have also been barriers. New York is a 10-hour flight from Istanbul, and direct connections only date from the 1990s. Only a few talented Turks have yet made their mark, like Ahmet Ertegün, founder of Atlantic Records. Perhaps it should be no surprise that a recent CBS television series called *Turks* was about an Irish-American family. The future may be different, even if college placement specialists complain that children of the Turkish élite are reluctant to tear themselves away from Istanbul's vibrant social scene. Some 5,000 young Turks now make their way to the U.S. every year to study, more than from any country in western Europe.

Egemen said that thanks to their late start, the Turks could claim to be the fastest growing ethnic group in the United States, with numbers rising by 15% a year. He counted 42 groups in his Federation of Turkish Associations, and said more were joining every year. The Turks were getting richer and more powerful, he said, symbolized in 2000 by the razzmatazz surrounding the first listing of a Turkish mobile phone company on the New York Stock Exchange.

"The aim of our parade is to show the strength of the Turkish-Americans to our enemies and our numbers to the politicians, to show that we have doctors and engineers," said Egemen. "I put the African band in the parade in to remind my children and others that we are also Turkish-*Americans*. Nowadays we are almost as American as we are Turkish."

"Almost" was an overstatement. The poster on the wall beside his desk proclaimed *"Our Strength is in Unity."* It referred to solidarity among Turks in America, not any allegiance to America's cross-cultural mix. Originally from the town of Siirt in eastern Turkey, where his father had been mayor, Egemen returned to do his military service in Turkey and planned to persuade his infant son to do so too when the time came. It was the only way for a man to maintain his Turkish citizenship and full property rights. Even though Egemen's family was originally Arabic speaking, like many in Siirt, his embrace of Turkishness was not untypical for Muslim minorities in the republic. In 2002, he was grinding through a week of translating for Turkish anti-terrorism explosive experts in Baton Rouge, "bored out of my mind," he later told me, when he got a call from a friend close to Tayyip Erdoğan, the leader of Turkey's AK Party. Erdoğan wanted him in Turkey the very next day, to discuss giving him a place on AK Party's parliamentary electoral list. Egemen called his wife for an okay, and they light-footedly gave up their American life. He was duly elected to parliament from Istanbul and found his way into Erdoğan's inner circle. He offered Erdoğan a rare familiarity with the American system, and also a handle on Siirt, Erdoğan's wife's home town and Erdoğan's eventual constituency.

I remembered that even when I first met him in 2000, Egemen had been ambivalent about his future in America.

"Will your son be American or Turkish, do you think?" I had asked before I left his New York office.

"I want my son to grow up here. But I'm teaching him Turkish at home," he said. "For Italian-Americans, eating spaghetti once a week is enough. It will not be like that for the Turks. In 100 years from now they'll still be proud Turkish-Americans."

EPILOGUE

If the Sky above does not collapse, if the earth below does not give way, O Turk people, who can destroy your state and institutions?
—Orkhon inscription in today's Mongolia, c. 730 AD

IN THE YEARS AFTER I MET ISA ALPTEKIN IN HIS ISTANBUL FLAT IN 1988, I witnessed remarkable changes in the Turkic world. Political links sprung up where there had been none, a new commercial region became well-established, a community of more pragmatic Muslims felt a growing solidarity and intellectuals explored a new cultural and linguistic space. Despite its energy, youth and strategic possibilities, however, the Turkic world does not yet add up to the sum of its many parts. It is like the legend of the old Silk Road, whose many paths link the Turkic peoples between Asia and Europe, but which has never been one clear-cut highway.

The dwindling band of pan-Turkic nationalists are still a long way from their dream of a Turkic bloc "from the Great Wall of China to the Adriatic Sea." Efforts by intellectuals, leaders and diplomats have failed to build a Turkic League, let alone a pan-Turkic union, a unified alphabet, or even regular meetings that everyone attends. Different goals motivated the many leaders whom I met, not least the need to stay on top of their particular regimes. Some dreamed of greater Turkic brotherhood—notably Isa Alptekin on behalf of the Uygurs in China, Abulfez Elchibey in Azerbaijan, Turgut Özal in Turkey, Rauf Denktash in Cyprus and even small players like Sadık Ahmet, the late Turkish community leader in Greece. But in the end, all communities and countries followed in the footsteps of Turkey's republican founder Kemal Atatürk and gave priority to their local national development.

This fact depressed the Turkish professor who described himself as the world's last remaining pan-Turkist. Turan Yazgan had blazed a pioneering path as the Soviet Union broke apart. His charity, housed around the stone courtyard of an old Ottoman school in Istanbul, busily organized schools and conferences to promote Turkic consciousness. It was typical that on one far-flung journey, I met a leader of the Chuvash from central Russia who said that it was only a visit from Yazgan in the early 1990s that made his people realize that they had any Turkic connection at all.

Yet Yazgan was not optimistic about the future of the Turkic peoples. Where I saw a resurrection of Turkic identities in Central Asia, he felt that the division into smaller nationalisms represented dwindling and assimilation, especially of the smaller Turkic communities in the Russian federation. The Turks hate themselves, he said with a trace of bitterness, and the Russians need no longer fear a united Turkic front. But Yazgan also maintained that the Turks do have a unique, non-European character. Indeed, despite the acceptance of Turkey as a candidate member of the European Union in 1999, and many signs of Turkish cultural, economic and sporting convergence with Western norms, one survey showed that just 39% of young Turks believe that they will in the end achieve full political partnership with Europe.

"Turks and Europeans just haven't done the same things in their national lives," said Yazgan, a stocky Anatolian who had pegged out the Turkish national symbol over his office door, the skin of a gray wolf.

To my mind it is this sense of distinction from their non-Turkic neighbors that is bringing Turkic nations closer. They are, after all, still only finding their feet. In Turkey, five generations have now been taught from books that stress the common origin and destiny of the Turkic peoples. But the country only began to take on an international role in the early 1990s; the biggest Turkish conglomerate, Koç Holding, staked out its plan to become a Eurasian trading giant only in 2001. It was rapidly highly successful. Central Asia is only beginning to reconstruct its identity after 70 years of Soviet rule wiped out its educated classes and banned all public hint of a larger Turkic and Muslim identity. In

Europe, the Turks are winning the battle for equal rights, but still struggle with their own sense of inferiority. They still face some prejudices, too. On the border with Greece, the first thing a Turkish traveller sees is a customs house whose wall is decorated with a much-magnified reproduction of a Byzantine picture of Constantinople—with the Turks still outside the city's fortifications.

Since most Turkic peoples are Muslims—although there are marginal communities of Buddhists, Christians and Shamanists—Islamic ideologies and terrorists have been posited as a potential threat to pro-Western stability, especially in oil-rich Central Asia and Turkey. Certainly, young people have been attracted to militant Islam in the unusually oppressive atmosphere of Uzbekistan. But I found that the pragmatic mainstream Turkic interpretations of Islam make an Islamist takeover look unlikely. In fact, it is rather the Turkic peoples' relatively successful mix of Islam and secular government that is becoming appealing to the Iranian and Arab worlds. Turkey, which blazed the trail by declaring a secular republic in 1923, still leads the way in trying to forge a more appealing balance between Islam and modernity. Turkish religious thinkers are developing humanist new interpretations of the Koran and Turkish women are pushing hardest to join the lines of male worshippers in mosques.

In this respect, the United States is right to argue that the largely secular Turks can be a model for the more modern, democratic Muslim world that Washington fitfully tries to foster. A sense that the Turks are no longer turning their backs on Islam—represented by the arrival in power of the pro-Islamic AK Party in 2002, whose leaders, unlike their predecessors, actively court their Middle Eastern counterparts—has helped raise Arab and Iranian interest in Turkey and its example of commercial success and compatibility with the West. The trouble for those who would spread a Turkish model, however, is that the Turks are a special case, since they are largely free of political disputes with America. As non-Arabs, they do not feel the same level of anger with Washington over its support for Israel against the Palestinians, or the same level of opposition to the U.S. occupation of Iraq. Unlike Iran, they have not experienced a blood feud like that caused by the Islamic revolutionary takeover of the U.S. Embassy in Tehran in 1979. Indeed, the Turks' very alliance with the U.S. tends to undermine its acceptability as a role model for the others in the Muslim world.

However secular the Turkic style of government is judged, Islam and nationalism are inextricably entwined at the heart of any Turkic identity. Europeans once recognized this with the expression for becoming a Muslim, "turning Turk." The Turkic states with the strongest Islamic movements—Uzbekistan and Turkey—are also those with the strongest sense of national identity. In the political struggle for Uzbekistan, both propagandists for the nationalist state and also underground Islamist dissidents deployed the concept of struggling for something in *Turkestan,* or land of the Turks, as a hot-button word to legitimize their cause.

It's worth noting that whether communist, nationalist or Islamist, ideology has always come second to sheer military power in the Turkic world. History shows that lands populated by Turkic peoples have achieved political union only under all-conquering dynasties like the Seljuks or the Ottomans, or under individual conquerors like Genghis Khan and Tamerlane. Of these, arguably only Genghis Khan, a Mongol, ruled over the entire range of the Turco-Mongol peoples of his time. Joseph Stalin, a strongman of obscure ethnic descent from Georgia, ruled over more Turkic speakers than Turkey has ever done. When the United States stepped forward as a new military power in Central Asia, local Turkic regimes, true to form, have lined up behind it rather than alongside each other. Similarly, when U.S. credibility stumbled over the Iraq war, Turkic regimes began adjusting their strategic balance toward powers like China, Europe and Russia.

Thanks to their relatively secular and opportunistic outlook, the Turks have shown themselves to be more open to Western ideas than other major Islamic peoples. This is another reason why Turkic states have not hesitated to join the United States as allies against Islamist extremism. U.S. troops did encounter some hostility in Turkey, but it was nothing compared to what they faced in the Arab world. In fact, an American military and economic presence in the region has made Turkic states feel more secure in their secular identity. By 2004, over a thousand American soldiers were stationed in Uzbekistan at Khanabad, a desert staging post on the Afghan border, while another 2,000 US. and allied troops were based at the main airport of the Kyrgyz Republic. Even isolated, ostensibly neutral Turkmenistan opened air corridors to U.S. warplanes. Azerbaijan is being considered for a way-station role. Moreover, the major air base at Incirlik in southern Turkey played an indispensable logistical role in both the Afghanistan war and U.S. air attacks on Iraq throughout the 1990s. Turkish unhappiness over the 2003 Iraq war limited its use in that conflict to non-combat logistical support, but it remains open for future use.

The Turks view themselves as natural soldiers, and see military cooperation with the United States as a legitimate means of securing economic and political advantage. Just as Turkey sent troops to fight in Korea in the 1950s to win its place in NATO, Uzbekistan's agreement to host U.S. bases for the war in Afghanistan in 2001 was its way of winning a greater acceptance. A medieval Turkic chieftain would have felt quite at home conducting Turkey's negotiations with Washington on proper compensation for leading the international peacekeeping mission in Afghanistan in 2002, or, until the Turkish parliament blocked the deal, in trying to squeeze maximum advantage for a possible mobilization to join U.S. forces in Iraq in 2003. In northern Afghanistan, ethnic Uzbek leader Rashid Dostum keeps up the tradition at a lower end of the scale, holding court as a modern-day warlord available for occasional hire.

As the heir to the 19th century Great Game between the British Empire and Russia for dominion over Central Asia, the United States seems bound to remain engaged for decades to secure oil interests and to control terrorism. The U.S. is already having the same debates as Britain once did about Central Asia's real value. One U.S. academic report, believing the benefits of Central Asian oil to be exaggerated, dismissed involvement there as a "Mediocre Game." Others view the 1990s Caspian oil rush as a passing fashion, now displaced by Siberia or west Africa. Just as Britain's Foreign Office once opposed the "forward school," which wanted to intervene in Central Asia in order to protect British India from Russia, there are diplomats in the U.S. State Department who believe that American interests would be better served by leaving the volatile, Muslim region within a Russian sphere of influence. Russia, after initially challenging the U.S. and Turkic nationalist movements and governments, is turning out to be more of a partner than a competitor. Indeed, there are even Russians who believe they are well rid of their expensive, Soviet-era obligations to the region.

This U.S.-declared interest in Central Asia's strategic value—enshrined in an unusual moment of policy-making clarity in 1995—has already resulted in a small, independent new source of energy. Work is nearly complete on a first big non-Russian, non-Iranian main oil export pipeline from the Caspian basin, stretching from near Baku in Azerbaijan, through Georgia and across eastern Turkey to the Mediterranean oil terminal of Ceyhan. It is due to open in 2005, followed by a big Azerbaijani gas pipeline along the same route a year or two later. As the U.S. wished, none of the Caspian states have joined the main oil cartel, the Organization of Petroleum Exporting Countries, and most other export routes have by-passed Iran's Islamic Republic. Caspian oil production rose to 1.5 million barrels a day in 2003, adding to the international oil market about as much as Canada or Mexico supplied to the U.S. in that year. Oil production is expected to reach three million barrels a day by 2010.

The United States may be setting the pace in the Turkic world, but it seems unlikely there will be a return to the old situation of one great power having exclusive control of Central Asia. At the same time, Turkish politicians and Turkic dictators, like the Turkic khans of the past, have proved more likely to attack each other for short-term personal gain than to unite against outsiders wanting to dominate them. "The governments of these countries approach nearer to a state of nature than can easily be conveyed. Self-interest is the basis of every action, and to this is sacrificed every consideration of equity," a Major Archer of Britain's Indian Empire wrote to a colleague from today's Turkmenistan in 1835. "In some (khanates), everything depends on the personal character and talents of the ruler; in others, on the qualities of the chief minister."

I saw such stubborn qualities on display when observing the irregular meetings of the leaders of today's six independent Turkic-majority states—Turkey, Azerbaijan, Turkmenistan, Uzbekistan, Kazakhstan and the Kyrgyz Republic. The chiefs of Kazakhstan and Uzbekistan always vie to be seen as the leading power in Central Asia. Turkmenistan and Azerbaijan squabble so intensely that they failed to agree on a project of joint importance, a U.S.-backed Trans-Caspian Gas Pipeline. Uzbekistan's President Karimov felt vitally threatened by the idea that Turkey should have any contact with exiled nationalist opposition leaders, and flip-flopped between truculent rejection of Turkey and servile courtship. But, as in the 22-nation Arab League, such frictions showed that the actions of one member of the Turkic family could intimately affect the other. One of my most poignant memories is of standing next to Erkin, the son of Isa Alptekin, the late leader of China's Uygur Turks, on the margins of the first Turkic summit in 1992 in Ankara. Turkish President Özal had just outlined a vision of Turkic secretariats, regional cooperation and great joint projects for the future. "You wait, we'll be here in 10 years time," Erkin had said with an excited light in his eyes.

Such Turkic unity of purpose was a political improbability, and the Uygurs may have to wait decades for anything like freedom in China. Yet at the government level, there are subtle signs of convergence. Ankara has granted Turkic leaders prize plots of land on its Mediterranean coastline for use as summer palaces, and some of them have taken to holidaying there. At one moment of medical crisis, the late President Aliyev of Azerbaijan chose treatment in the military hospital in Ankara, although as his condition worsened he did switch to the U.S. In early 2000, Aliyev arrived in Ankara to tell Turkish leaders that he had been nominated by his fellow Turkic presidents to give the message that they liked Turkish President Demirel and wanted the Turkish parliament to extend his term of office. For other reasons, the Turkish parliament balked at this idea. But such exchanges would be unthinkable between states that did not feel themselves to be kin.

There is also a steady drumbeat of Turkic conferences and contacts between this long-scattered family of peoples, most of which attract little outside attention. Turkish Airlines has pioneered new links not just with all the main Turkic capitals but such historic Turkic locales as Kazan in Tataristan and Simferopol in the Crimea. Turkish internship programs meant that by the turn of the new century I was meeting speakers of Turkish not just among Turkic presidential delegations but on border points, in ministries and on the streets of Turkic cities. Turkic officials are also laying long-term groundwork for lower trade and legal barriers between Turkey and the Turkic states. It is still far from the copy of the European Union aimed at by the Turkey's President Özal. But that organization, it should be remembered, took decades to reach its current closeness.

Until the 1990s, Turkey spent practically nothing on Turkic research. It feared the Soviet Union and acted as though it despised its eastern neighbors. It was only during a burst of post-1991 Turkic enthusiasm under Turgut Özal that an attempt was made to remedy this situation. One step was to set up an Institute of Turkic Studies in Istanbul's state-run Marmara University, headed by Nadir Devlet, the son of Tatar dissidents who fled the Bolshevik revolution. But it was squashed uncomfortably into a campus apartment and its small flow of cash dwindled after Özal's death in 1993. Turkey's distracted, turbulent state budgets have made even less money available since then. When I visited Nadir, his spare office chair was missing an arm and kept tipping me backwards. Once proud projects like a first common Turkic dictionary and a first encyclopaedia of Turkic literature had stalled.

Despite Turkey's nationalist ideology, top Turkish universities run most of their programs in English. This paradox, like the use of Persian in old Turkic courts, reflects an age-old Turkic lack of faith in their own formal culture. Timur Kocaoğlu, head of Turkic studies at Koç University and the son of a nationalist revolutionary from Bokhara, had to close down his course in Uzbek because so few students could see commercial or cultural advantage in it. Far higher quality research on the region is coming from the wealthy institutions of the United States.

The westward-looking Turkish élite is ill-informed and uninterested in the Turkic east. While U.S. President Bush put pressure on China to free Uygur leader Rebiya Kadeer, and she was an official guest in nine European countries afer her 2005 release, no Turkish institution contacted her for nearly a year. Still, she gamely told her first Turkish interviewer that "all East Turkestani Turks nurture a holy love for Turkey."

Nevertheless, the Turkish-Turkic relationship is broadening. Several

U.S. multinationals now use offices in Istanbul, or their Turkish affiliates there, as their regional base. From nothing in 1990, Turkish companies did build up a substantial presence in contracting and services in the Turkic world, and Turks constituted the biggest foreign business community in most Turkic capitals. But direct exports to the five main Turkic republics were just 1.9% of the Turkish total in 2003. Direct exports to the five Turkic republics were just 1.9% of all Turkish exports in 2003, but this figure looks low partly because of the relative size of the Turkish economy. In Azerbaijan, for instance, Turkey was usually the second biggest single supplier of goods and services. Turkish workers and businessmen dominate foreign construction, hotel-keeping, shop, textile and restaurant businesses in Turkic countries, 12,000 of them in Turkmenistan alone, where they have created a new bourgeoisie. Turkish companies are leading sub-contractors building oil pipelines in Kazakhstan or working the Kumtor gold mine amid the glaciers of the mountaintops of the Kyrgyz Republic. Turks may not have much political influence in Central Asia and the Balkans, but weightier things will surely follow the arrival of the Turkish chocolate and soap I saw for sale all the way from the Albanian coast of the Adriatic Sea and, if not on the Great Wall of China, at least on the border of China and Kazakhstan.

Even if the late Turkish leader Turgut Özal went too far in predicting that the 21st century would belong to the Turks, it is hard to imagine that they can experience much worse than the catastrophes meted out to them in the 20th century. The newer Turkic states are still at the beginning of the nation-building process, and, like Turkey, they have a young population endowed with an opportunistic genius, a hunger for success and frustrated national ambition. I was struck by Uzbek officials' passion to succeed, however misguided their methods. Oil-rich Kazakhstan is on a firmly upward path, with a banking system that has even overtaken Russia. Azerbaijan's capital, Baku, now has the vibrant feel of a world city. And while walking through a park near Istanbul one day, I was astonished by a fit young Turk who burst into the open from an overgrown sidepath and lustily shouted out Atatürk"s slogan: "How Happy Is He Who Says He Is a Turk!" It is hard to imagine a young Briton or Egyptian doing anything similar. This national energy helps explain why Turks are now winning international prizes in soccer, film, literature and music in a way inconceivable a decade ago.

Still, few people know quite what to think of the Turks themselves. The expression "young Turk" has passed into the English language in approval of a daring, rebellious decisiveness in the Turkish character. But many of their neighbors fear and hate them. Arab Muslim traditions ascribe to the prophet Mohammed dire predictions of flat-faced raiders riding out of the East as horsemen of the apocalypse, apparently a reference to Turks and Mongols. Europe had moments of admiring "Turcomania," but mainly latched onto a vision of the Turk as an ambitious, hungry and wantonly destructive enemy with a hostile religion. As early as the 14th century, English poet Geoffrey Chaucer has his knight take on the "hethen in Turkye." The Shorter Oxford English dictionary defines the word Turk as "a cruel, savage, rigorous or tyrannical man." In Central Asia, Persian-speaking Tajiks can still insist that their Uzbek neighbors are barbarian "Turks." In the Caucasus, Armenians use the word Turk to focus hatred on their Azerbaijani enemies. Yugoslav Serbs use the word Turk to denigrate Bosnian Moslims and Kosovar Albanians alike, even though the two are ethnically distinct. In Holland and Germany, the word Turk denotes any immigrant worker, and it packs a whole range of negative meanings: cruel, rough, dictatorial, lazy, ugly, jealous and dangerous.

Such prejudices are created by fears. My own misplaced wariness of the Turks prompted me to make phone calls to friends based in Turkey before I felt comfortable bringing my family with me on my first permanent posting in Istanbul in 1987; I have myself become used to e-mails from acquaintances asking vaguely if it is 'safe' to visit. The Turkish reputation for fierceness, arising not just from great conquests but from well-documented atrocities, such as the massacres of Armenians between 1890-1921, fails to do justice to the complexity of Turkish history.

It is not just that the Turks preserved the great Byzantine monuments of Constantinople and built states and empires. They can also lay claim to a share of victimhood. As the Ottoman empire shrank, many Turks and Muslims were uprooted from their homes. In the Soviet

Union, communism quickly betrayed its early promise of advancement for minority Turkic peoples. More than 40% of the Kazakhs died in Joseph Stalin's 1930s purges and famines. Nearly half of the 200,000 Tatars of Crimea died in the first two years of a forced exile from their homeland in 1944. This was not the beginning of their suffering—Tsarist Russian policies had already reduced their numbers from 500,000 a century before—nor was it the end. Recent attempts by Crimean Tartars to return from Central Asian exile to their homes, now part of Ukraine, have met resistance, discrimination and the bulldozing of the makeshift dwellings in which some of the 250,000 Tatar returnees are forced to live. In Bulgaria, I witnessed the results of the communist government's mistreatment of its Turkic minority. In the Caucasus, I saw the refugee columns of some of the 800,000 Azeris forced out of their homes by Armenians during the war over Nagorno Karabagh.

There is also, of course, no simple Turkic stereotype. On my journeys, I found broad similarities between Turkic peoples on issues of religion, politics and leadership, but also great contrasts between Turkic societies and circumstances. Some live as primordial mountain nomads in round felt tents, others as multinational business leaders. Their homelands range from the poverty of remote Siberian regions of Russia to the cosmopolitan delights of Istanbul.

Turkic peoples shared more physical traits than I had expected in such a widely scattered group. That was even true for the 3,000-year-old stone figures that dot the pine-clad mountain valleys of Altay, the aboriginal Central Asian homeland of the Turks where the borders of Russia, China and Mongolia meet. I stood before one such sculpture, a warrior with a round face, high cheekbones, big eyes, and a handsome moustache. With a cup in one hand, a sword in the other and a dagger in his belt, he stared defiantly out at the world. The look on his face reminded me exactly of a photograph I'd come across in a Turkish right-wing political instruction manual that showed an activist demonstrating "The Expression of Toughness."

Foreign observers have generalized about other Turkish characteristics. French academician René Grousset's classic 1930s account of Central Asian Turkic empires speaks lyrically of "stunted, stocky bodies" forged into a sinewy invincibility by the rigors of the steppe.

Arminius Vámbéry, the 19th century Hungarian explorer of the Turkic world, admired the Turks' adaptability and pragmatism. "Full of superstition, and a blind fatalist, [the Turk] can easily support the constant dread of danger. Dirt, poverty and privations, he is accustomed to, even at home. No wonder then that he sits content in clothes which have not been changed for months, and with a crust of dirt on his face," he wrote from the wastes of what is now Turkmenistan. "At evening prayers, in which the whole company took part, this peace of mind struck me most forcefully. They thanked God for the benefits they enjoyed."

More intangibly, I became convinced that a certain genius informs and binds together Turkic peoples from Kashgar to Cologne. Turks maintain they can identify each other abroad by an appraising glint in the eye, a look that seeks both opportunity and human contact. Even rivals like the Iraqi Kurds concede that, unlike the more wily Iranians, at least the Turks are open and frank. In 1718, Lady Mary Wortley Montagu, wife of an English ambassador and unabashed Turcophile, asserted that "'tis very rare that any Turk will assert a solemn falsehood." Everywhere in the Turkic world, business works through personal trust, not legalistic contracts. A Turkish cola-bottling executive once told me happily that he and his new-found Turkic cousins in Central Asia even tried to cheat each other in the same way. Kai Kaus, an Iranian sultan who resided on the southern shore of the Caspian Sea in the eleventh century, offered a jaundiced view that is held—even by many Turks—to this day. "Without any doubt, what is fine in the Turks is present in a superlative degree, but so also is what is ugly in them. Their faults in general are that they are blunt-witted, ignorant, boastful, turbulent, discontented and without a sense of justice. Their merit is that they are brave, free from pretense, open in enmity, and zealous in any task allotted to them."

I gradually built up my own, unscientific composite of frequent Turkic qualities. Among them I would count an engaging bluntness, loyalty to the family, fearlessness and a rash love of risk. To these, I would add an inordinate respect for elders, an aversion to planning, a tough resistance to pain, a refusal to apologize or recognize faults, a love-hate relationship with leaders, and an in-born animus to take charge. Many Turks prefer the audio-visual to the written word.

Hospitality towards strangers is mixed with a quick readiness to exploit. Ignorant pride can often give way to bombastic, insecure assertions of superiority. A constant struggle in many Turkic hearts pits a love of authoritarian rule against a belief that the pleasures and profits in life are to be gained from bypassing the law in the manner of the heroic, mustachioed brigand. Turkic peoples, I found, share an inferiority complex about their language and culture. Alongside modern concoctions like "a Turk is worth the whole world," their folk proverbs are full of self-deprecating jibes such as "a Turk only thinks when he flees or he shits" or "the mind of a Turk: always wise after the event."

My journeys through two dozen countries still pale beside the efforts of one indomitable Turk from Turkey, the photographer Arif Asçı. He decided he would lead a camel caravan through the lands of the Turks from Xian in China across Central Asia to Turkey. It took him and his three companions 15 months to cover the 7,500 miles, which, to my mind, proved just how unlikely it was that there was ever much end-to-end land trade between China and the West; even Asçı called the account of his adventures 'The Last Caravan on the Silk Road.' Not long afterwards we sat having lunch and swapping discoveries at a pavement table in old Beyoğlu, a 19th century district of Istanbul abandoned by its former non-Muslim inhabitants but which is now undergoing rapid gentrification by newly appreciative Turkish owners. Asçı, taking a break from restoring his formerly Jewish-owned apartment nearby, was still angry at the way Turks lack credibility in the eyes of Western institutions.

"We went to see National Geographic for sponsorship. They said it just wasn't possible to go such a long way with camels," he said.

Moving in the 15-mile stages of ancient times, and eventually sponsored by a Turkish ceramics manufacturer, Asçı did not have an easy time. Neither did his beloved camels. They fled, terrified, from horn-honking truck drivers. He had to make them shoes against the hot summer tarmac and then to prevent them from freezing in three-foot-deep snow as they battled over the mountains of the Hindu Kush. Four camels died along the way. But the expedition made it to Turkey, exhausted, triumphant and happy that they would never have to endure the smell of camel spit again.

"Only a group of crazy Turks could have done it," said Asçı, who walked almost all of the way, despite a bad limp from a bout of polio in his youth. I was touched that he clearly now counted his American team member as a Turk.

I told him I had just come from Ottomania, a nearby shop cashing in on rich Turks' new-found enthusiasm for historical European prints of the glory days of the old Ottoman Empire. The owner had voiced his theory that the secret of the Turks' genius was precisely their lack of a grand culture. According to him, centuries of uneducated women had preserved an essential Turkish toughness. The Turks just took things from here and there, he reckoned, and, like crab weed, once they got into a place, nobody could get them out.

Asçı laughed heartily.

"While walking with my caravan I kept thinking about what we Turks are, looking for the 'red line,' like the storyline in a soap opera," he said. "Whether in Iran, or China, I marveled at the homogeneity of the faces of the Turkic speakers. I would think, maybe it's a blood thing. But Uygurs can't be the same as us, they're too far away. Then I would think, maybe it's Islam. But we're Sunni, and the Azeris are Shia. I can't work it out. Let's eat. *Afiyet olsun* [bon appetit]!"

We tucked into our meal. A summer soup of mint, yogurt and cracked wheat came alongside fried pastry rolls of mince and walnut. The ingredients, if not the style, could have been from anywhere in Central Asia. The same was true of our next course of *mantı*, a dish of meat wrapped in pasta like ravioli. A few *mantı* are big enough to fill a bowl in the Turkic east, but they become almost pea-sized by the time the dish is eaten in Turkic homes in the Balkans.

"Maybe the food really is the red line. Here we are in Istanbul, surrounded by fish and olive oil from the Greeks, but we keep making ourselves nomad food," he said.

Indeed, the sophisticated and much-loved Turkish family picnic has traveled with the Turks to Europe, with its charcoal brazier, roast meat and rope-and-blanket swings for the children. It is now copied by Germans in the parks of Berlin. Asçı and I agreed that the "red line" of the Turkic world was more food, baby swings and crazy looking projects than any Turkic race. We finished up. Arif tapped his pocket for a cigarette, but couldn't find a packet. Politely but imperiously, he requested, and received, a cigarette from the waiter.

"Maybe that's the essence of Turkishness," he said.

"What's that?"

"*Otlamak*," Asçı replied.

In Istanbul slang, the verb now translates as "'to cadge."

But its origin lies deep in the nomad history of the Turkic peoples, meaning the perennial search for fresh pastures on which to graze.

APPENDIX A

NOTE ON TURKIC LANGUAGES
AND ALPHABETS

For the love of you, my mother tongue
I wore out the years of my life, the months, the days
Just for you, my language
I lost the sight of my right eye
Only you I did not lose
O symbol of my existence

—ABDULATIF BENDEROGLU, Iraqi Turkmen poet

THE MEANING AND PROPER USAGE OF THE WORDS "TURK," "TURKISH," and "Turkic," are fluid and often confusing. A Cypriot Turk calls himself a Turk, an Iraqi Turk says he is a Turkmen, and an Azerbaijani Turk thinks of himself as an Azeri. Yet they speak similar dialects of the same language, and they all probably come from the same branch of the Turkic family tree.

For clarity's sake, and although this goes against a much broader old usage, I have tried to use the words Turk and Turkish to refer only to the people, customs and language of modern Turkey. "Turkic" denotes the broader ethnic group and the Altaic languages. Politically, since the collapse of the Soviet Union, there are six independent states that can be described as Turkic—Azerbaijan, Kazakhstan, the Kyrgyz Republic, Turkey, Turkmenistan and Uzbekistan—all of whose main ethnic groups and main official languages are distinct. The self-styled Turkish Republic of North Cyprus declared itself independent in 1983 but is only recognized by Turkey. To the north, the Tatars of Russia's federal republic of Tataristan are moving to a kind of quasi-independence. In the east, the Uygurs theoretically have autonomy, although in reality any national aspirations are being crushed and their land assimilated by China.

The academic names of Turkic language groups overlap as confusingly as that of the history of their peoples. Debate also continues as to how close Finnish and Hungarian are to Altaic, and the relevance of strong grammatical similarities with Japanese and Korean. There are four branches in the main Altaic family: the southwestern or "Oğuz" group, comprising the Turks, Azeris and Turkmens; the southeastern or "Karluk" group which includes the Uzbeks and the Uygurs; to the northwest, the "Kipchak" group of Tatars, Kazakhs, Kyrgyz and Karakalpaks; and in the northeast, a fourth small group of Siberian Turkic languages like Yakut. Within each group, mutual intelligibility is reasonably high, but between groups it is much less so. Unlike the Arabs, who have the Koran, or the Persians, with their great body of poetry, the Turkic peoples have no great literature or indigenous religious work to bind their languages together. Nevertheless, even though they are spanning the outer boundaries of the Altaic family, Japanese diplomats and Istanbul bazaar boys learn each other's languages unusually quickly.

Turkic alphabets, meanwhile, have long reflecting the turbulent political and geographic fate of the Turkic peoples. Just as they inhabit the faultlines between China, Russia, the Mediterranean and the Islamic world, so their alphabets have flip-flopped between the four scripts of those regions.

The first written Turkish comes from the the 8th century AD Orkhon inscriptions in Mongolia, in which the Göktürk people used a runic alphabet derived from runes that spread from northern Europe. This literary Turkic became common to all of Central Asia. After Turks began to convert to Islam in large numbers in the 9th century, Arabic script gradually supplanted it. From the 15th century on, the spoken Turkish of the Ottomans in the west drifted away from the eastern Turkish of their cousins in Central Asia. Still, the great eastern Turkish poet Nevai, whose language is usually called Chagatay, himself always called it Turkish. As late as 1883, when Ismail Gaspıralı, a Tatar journalist, launched a first pan-Turkic newspaper *Tercüman*, Turkic intellectuals from the Balkans to Siberia could mostly read and understand its Ottoman-Tatar texts in Arabic script. *Tercüman*, or the Translator, voiced a pious hope for the Turkic world in its motto: "Unity in Language, Thought and Work."

There followed a century of disasters for the Turkic peoples. The advance of the Russian and Chinese empires made physical communication between the various Turkic groups difficult. The communists in Moscow and later Beijing imposed their own ideologies and drove them further apart. For a brief historical moment, Turkic intellectuals fought back at the First Congress of Turcology in 1926. Meeting in the expropriated palace of an oil baron in Baku, Turkic men of letters decided by 101 votes to 7 to create a Western-looking, unified Latin alphabet applicable for all. This recognized at last that the Arabic script's stress on consonants did not suit Turkic languages' stress on vowels and vowel harmony. (The Mogul Prince Babur had tried to rationalize the Arabic script used by pre-modern Turkish, but had failed due to resistance from his Islamic clergy.) In 1926, the new Latin script was adopted for all Turkic speakers in the young Soviet Union. Few now remember that Kemal Atatürk was following this lead when he ordered Turkey to adopt a similar alphabet in 1928.

Stalin, however, had been watching suspiciously over the debates in Baku. He probably only agreed to the joint shift to Latin script to harness the energy of the intellectual, secular modernizers of the Turkic world against the Islamic clerics who were virulently opposed to communism. A decade later, he cynically dumped the Soviet Turkic Latin alphabet into what he hoped would be the dustbin of history. He forced his Turkic domains to adopt the Cyrillic of the Slavic world. Not only that, but he insisted that all dialects be written down differently. Four letters in the first Cyrillic alphabet for Azeri did not even represent sounds in that language. The Uzbek alphabet was modeled on a rough proletarian dialect. Soon afterwards, Stalin purged the intellectuals, too, devastating the educated Turkic memory. Of the 27-man Azeri delegation to the First Congress of Turcology, for instance, only one died a natural death.

Turkic scholars who remained began to weed out anomalies in their Cyrillic alphabets after Stalin's death. At the same time, up until 1990, Soviet-era exiles from Central Asia tried to create an intellectual unity by publishing most of their tracts in a joint eastern Turkic written language known as the "Middle Language." But it was only after the collapse of the Soviet Union in 1991 that real new initiatives could be taken. In 1992, Turkey's Turkish Language Foundation convened a new congress to which it invited many academics from the Turkic world. In the pervasive euphoria of the time, all agreed on a joint 34-letter Latin alphabet. This academic initiative had some influence, but was no master plan, and had no political backing. In the following years, Azerbaijan, Turkmenistan, Uzbekistan and eventually the Russian federal republic of Tataristan chose to return to Latin. But these were individual decisions and each has adopted a slightly different alphabet.

So it is that often closely related Turkic languages are now written down in no less than 21 versions of the Latin, Cyrillic and Arabic scripts. Some are bizarre. The free-spending leader of Turkmenistan initially made letters out of signs for the U.S. dollar, the British pound sterling and Japanese yen. In a literary reflection of his shift away from the West, he later changed these for east European-style diacritical marks. Uzbekistan started with Turkish-style ç and ş, but when relations with Turkey soured, it moved to English-style *ch* and *sh*. Some religious minded intellectuals of Kazakhstan and the Kyrgyz Republic talked of going back to the old Arabic script, but their people have been too long assimilated into the Russian cultural orbit for the idea to take root. Azerbaijan, meanwhile, arguably the most culturally independent-minded ex-Soviet Turkic state, is now stammering through 11th major and minor change to its alphabet in a century. A presidential decree orderered a new attempt at full Latinization in 2000.

It's a serious problem. A Turkish friend who owned a soap factory in a Turkmen town on the Amu Darya had a raw materials shipment stopped by his American bank because the name of the town, Chardzhou, was unrecognizable on the documentation after having changed alphabet three times. Some common American usages, derived from Russian orthography, also stick in Turkic throats. The most jangling imposition of Cyrillic—which has no hard "h"—is the substitution of "g" for "h" in Turkic names. The late Azerbaijani President Haidar Aliyev's name is not pronounced Gaidar.

Ironically, too, Atatürk's drive to cleanse Arabic and Persian words from modern Turkish, and substituting words from eastern Turkic roots, made Turkey a linguistic island that perplexes other Turkic speakers now that free exchanges are possible. It is the reason why dialects of the old western Turkish still spoken in Azerbaijan, western Iran, northern Iraq, north Cyprus and the Balkans all sound similar, and different to Turkey's Turkish. Still, the Turks' slick new broadcasting on two dozen glitzy satellite channels from Istanbul is a strong new influence on the Turkic family of languages. The other force at work is the growing confidence of languages like Azeri, Uzbek, Kazakh, and Turkmen now that state power is behind them.

As with the adoption of similar Latin alphabets, this is bringing convergence between the various Turkic languages. Mutual comprehension is rising. There is some political resentment of Turkey as a would-be big brother, but modern Turkish is proving attractive as the most modern, developed Turkic language. It boasts a vibrant commercial market and a long-established television, radio and film-making culture. Scholars are only beginning to take note of the phenomenon. There has, as Dutch linguist and sociologist Abram de Swaan pointed out, been exceptionally high "language retention" among the Turks, "even under intense and enduring political repression." As he put it in major lecture in Istanbul in 2002: "Turkish constitutes the hub of an emerging language constellation. Until the 1990s, it was probably the most invisible, or inaudible, world language on earth. However, ten years later, Turkish is unmistakeably making its comeback as a world language."

APPENDIX B

A TURKIC FAMILY TREE

Huns (c. 200 BC–500 AD) Göktürk empire (511–744 AD

├─ Uygur empire (western Mongolia 744–840 AD
│ └─ Karakhanids (Kashgar c. 950–1130 AD
│ ┌ - - ->└─ Modern Uygurs (Xinjiang from c. 1920)

├─ Oğuz tribes (start westward from Mongolia in 9th century)
│ Seljuks (11th–14th centuries)
│ ├─ Turks of Ottoman Empire (c. 1290–1922 AD)
│ │ ├─ Turks of Turkey
│ │ ├─ Balkan Turks
│ │ ├─ Turkmen of Iraq and Syria
│ │ └─ Cypriot Turks
│ ├─ Azeris in Azerbaijian, Iran, Georgia, Turkey
│ └─ Turkmen of Turkmenistan, Iran, Afghanistan

├─ Golden Horde and White Horde (13th–16th centuries)
│ ├─ Tatars in Russia
│ ├─ Crimean Tatars
│ ├<- - - - Uzbeks (emerge in c. 1400 AD)
│ ├─ Kazakhs (emerge in 16th–17th centuries)
│ ├─ Karakalpaks (emerge in the 16th century)
│ └─ Modern Kyrgyz

└─ Ancient Kygyz (from Siberia, rule western Mongolia 840–920 AD)
   ├─ Tuvans
   └─ Altay clans

The Turkic peoples are notoriously hard to classify. The foregoing illustration is not scientific, aiming at simplicity to show the broad connections between nations mentioned in this book. Turkic peoples are believed to descend from Huns and perhaps other Central Asian groups, and emerged under the umbrella of the Gök Turk Federation in the Orkhun River valley in western Mongolia between 551–744 AD. Thereafter they mixed with both the Mongols, who supplied a ruling class for many medieval Turkic peoples, and with the original Indo-European populations of Central Asia that they conquered. The Mongols are ethnically distinct but have mingled much with Turkic groups over the centuries, especially influencing the Kyrgyz. The use of some names for both ancient and contemporary nations, notably the Uygurs and the Kyrgyz, do not necessarily mean that they are strongly or directly descended from the same body of people. Politics also confuses classification: most Turkic states grouped federations of clans, giving numerically unrepresentative historic weight to the ruling clan, like the Seljuks; other Turkic clans were large but formed weak or no states, like the Karluks or the Qipchaks, and have therefore languished in obscurity.

ACKNOWLEDGMENTS

Many hands have helped me along the long and often arduous roads I have followed in these journeys. First of all I owe much to Jessica, my wife, frequent traveling companion and never-failing first editor. She and my loyal daughters Vanessa and Amanda have not only forgiven the many absences and holidays devoted to this alternative labor of love, but also lent me the deeply appreciated support I needed to complete this volume.

Many of the people to whom an author would normally express his gratitude appear as themselves in the narratives of this book; to them, many thanks. Only in the chapters about Xinjiang have names been changed; the Chinese authorities have severely punished Uygurs who step out of line, and many of those I spoke to didn't know that they were speaking to a writer. Other helpers eased my passage through the Caspian states. In Kazakhstan, Steve and Nurilda LeVine were open-hearted hosts. In the Kyrgyz Republic, I remain indebted to John Kazakoff and Camaco, who took me into the glaciers to see the highest gold mine in the northern hemisphere. Uzbekistan would not have been the same without the help of Ronald Kennedie, or the hospitality of Elif Kaban, Chris Bowers and Monica Whitlock at the BBC House in Tashkent. In Turkmenistan, I was honored to be shown over the great ruined city of Merv by archaeologist Prof. Dr. Georgina Herrmann. The early days in Azerbaijan would have been far more difficult without the warm help of Jihangir and Kamala Husseinov, and far less fun without the inimitable hospitality and headstrong leadership of Thomas and Hicran Goltz. In Greece, I learned much from a weekend spent with the late leader of the Thracian Turks, Sadık Ahmet. I would also like to thank Turkish Airlines, whose ever-flexible representatives rescued me more than once and whose pioneering passenger jets I was so often delighted to see arrive to take me home safely from the rough tarmac aprons of Central Asia.

Countless people have shaped my opinions of the Turkic world and expedited my travels over the past 15 years. I hope that I have forgotten none who were generous with their time and wisdom, but the list must include Afshin Abtahi, Arkhat Abzhanov, Şahin Alpay, Reza Deghati, Dr. John Gurney, Fiona Hill, Fehmi Koru, Tim Macintosh-Smith, Baqer Moin, Sevan Nişanyan, Soli Özel, Gail Pirkis, Nicole Pope, Padgett Powell, Jonathan Randal, Patrick Robertson, Murad Tadzhibayev, Hans Theunissen, Ferai Tunç, Sidney Wade and Mary-Ann Whitten. The sturdy companionship of my photographer brother Patrick Pope saw me safely through dangerous moments in Caucasus wars and lonely Turkmen deserts. I owe special thanks for gifts of books, offprints and a reading of my manuscript to Timur Kocaoğlu, one of Turkey's leading scholars of early-20th-century Central Asia. Any mistakes, of course, remain my own.

Throughout the years of writing, editing and smoothing, I am profoundly grateful for the love, support and proof-reading patience of my parents, Maurice and Johanna Pope. Beyond his hospitality in Azerbaijan, Azer Sultanov helped me often with his unique and encyclopaedic knowledge of Azerbaijani history and poetry. My agent Diana Finch was patient in times of trouble. Cengiz Hançer and Laura le Cornu gave morale-raising guidance. I owe a particular debt to John Ash for keeping me on the straight and narrow as regards the true nature of the old Silk Road.

The first inspiration and push for me to write a book about Central Asia, however, came from the old masters of the Great Game, Peter and Kath Hopkirk. On a memorable evening on a narrow palace balcony overlooking the Bosporus, the late and much-missed American foreign correspondent William Montalbano gave me the confidence to go ahead and collect these tales. The project formally became a book over dinner in New York with Steve Hubbell, who was the editor of its early chapters. Later encouragement came from Lawrence Malley of the University of Arkansas Press. Finally, I was thrilled that Peter Mayer, Tracy Carns, and David Mulrooney at Overlook took this volume over the finishing line.

No government, foundation, company or other institution made any financial contribution to this work. I am however most grateful to my talented editors at *The Wall Street Journal*, especially John Bussey, Mike Williams and Bill Spindle. This book would have been impossible without their sustained interest in reports from the Caucasus and Central Asia, and their forebearance in granting me four months of unpaid leave to start work on this book.

Last but not least, I must count out one more blessing from my youngest daughter Ella Scarlett. Without the happy season of fathering leave that accompanied her birth, this book would never have been finished. As the Turkish birthday greeting goes: *"iyi ki doğdun,"* how fine it is that you were born.

INDEX

PICTURE CREDITS

1: Photo © Hugh Pope
2: Photo ©Jessica Lutz
3: Drawing, Tokapı Palace
4: Photo © Jessica Lutz
5: Photo © Hugh Pope
6: Photo © Jessica Lutz
7: Photo © Hugh Pope
8: Drawing, Tokapi Palace
9: Photo © Hugh Pope
10: Photo © Hugh Pope
11: Photo © Hugh Pope
12: Photo © Hugh Pope
13: Photo © Hugh Pope
14: Photo © Hugh Pope
15: Photo © Hugh Pope
16: Photo © Hugh Pope
17: Photo © Hugh Pope
18: Photo © Jessica Lutz
19: Photo © George Simpson
20: Photo © Hugh Pope
21: Photo © Hugh Pope
22: Photo © Hugh Pope
23: Photo © Hugh Pope
24: Photo © Hugh Pope
25: Photo © Hugh Pope
26: Photo, courtesy of Uzbekistan Presidential Press Office
27: Photo, courtesy of Turkmenpress
28: Photo © Anıtkabir Derneği
29: Photo © Hugh Pope
30: Photo © Thomas Goltz
31: Photo © Hugh Pope
32: Photo © Hugh Pope
33: Photo © Turkish Prime Minister's Office
34: Photo © Hugh Pope

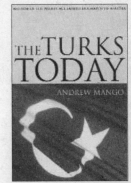
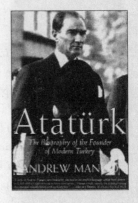